JESUS AND THE FORGIVENESS OF SINS

The Gospels record that Jesus purported to forgive sins. What significance would such a claim have had for his contemporaries and what would the implications have been for his identity as a first-century popular prophet? Tobias Hägerland answers these questions and more as he investigates the forgiveness of sins in the mission of the historical Jesus. The Gospels are interpreted within the context of first-century Judaism as part of a broader reconstruction of Jesus' career as a healer and prophet, and rhetorical criticism is introduced as a tool for explaining how the Gospel tradition about Jesus and forgiveness developed. Hägerland combines detailed exegesis and rigorous methodology with a holistic view of the historical Jesus, evaluating recent scholarship about first-century Jewish prophets, and utilizing previously neglected textual evidence to present a thorough investigation of the theology of forgiveness in early Judaism and primitive Christianity.

TOBIAS HÄGERLAND is a teacher of New Testament exegesis, theology and hermeneutics at Lund University, Sweden. He has published articles in journals such as the *Journal for the Study of the New Testament*, *New Testament Studies* and *The Catholic Biblical Quarterly*.

SOCIETY FOR NEW TESTAMENT STUDIES

MONOGRAPH SERIES

General Editor: John M. Court

150

JESUS AND THE FORGIVENESS OF SINS

SOCIETY FOR NEW TESTAMENT STUDIES

MONOGRAPH SERIES

Recent titles in the series

Jesus and the Forgiveness of Sins

An Aspect of His Prophetic Mission

TOBIAS HÄGERLAND

CAMBRIDGE UNIVERSITY PRESS
Cambridge, New York, Melbourne, Madrid, Cape Town,
Singapore, São Paulo, Delhi, Tokyo, Mexico City

Cambridge University Press
The Edinburgh Building, Cambridge CB2 8RU, UK

Published in the United States of America by Cambridge University Press, New York

www.cambridge.org
Information on this title: www.cambridge.org/9781107008366

First published 2012

Printed in the United Kingdom at the University Press, Cambridge

A catalogue record for this publication is available from the British Library

ISBN 978-1-107-00836-6 Hardback

CONTENTS

vii

TABLES

ACKNOWLEDGEMENTS

This monograph is a revised version of my dissertation, presented and defended at the University of Gothenburg in 2009. Professor Samuel Byrskog supervised the project in a competent and encouraging manner, for which I am immensely grateful, and he remains a treasured mentor and friend. I would also like to thank Professor Birger Olsson, who provided the opposition at the public defence of the thesis, Professor Thomas Kazen, who read the manuscript in its penultimate version, Professor Staffan Olofsson and Rev. Lennart Thörn, both of whom enthusiastically supported the project, and Professor Birger Gerhardsson, who graciously shared some of his inestimable scholarly experience with me after my transferral to Lund University. Last but not least in this array of scholars, my friend Dr Gunnar Samuelsson has merited a special word of thanks.

Also deserving to be thanked for their support are Mr Fredrik Hjort, Mrs Gunnel and Mr Per-Martin Hjort, and Mrs Inger and Mr Stig Hägerland. I dedicate this monograph to Hanna, my wife. To her, and to my children, Agnes, Elin and Linus, I prefer to say not 'Thank you', but 'I love you'.

ABBREVIATIONS

Books, series and journals

AASFDHL	Annales academiae scientiarum fennicae: Dissertationes humanarum litterarum
AB	Anchor Bible
ABRL	Anchor Bible Reference Library
AGJU	Arbeiten zur Geschichte des antiken Judentums und des Urchristentums
AnBib	Analecta biblica
ASNU	Acta seminarii neotestamentici upsaliensis
ATD	Das Alte Testament deutsch
AusBR	*Australian Biblical Review*
AYBRL	Anchor Yale Bible Reference Library
AzT	Arbeiten zur Theologie
BAC	Biblioteca de Autores Cristianos
BBR	*Bulletin of Biblical Research*
BDAG	Danker et al., *A Greek–English Lexicon*, 3rd edn
BDR	Blass et al., *Grammatik des neutestamentlichen Griechisch*
BET	Beiträge zur biblischen Exegese und Theologie
BETL	Bibliotheca ephemeridum theologicarum lovaniensium
Bib	*Biblica*
BIS	Biblical Interpretation Series
BTB	*Biblical Theology Bulletin*
BZ	*Biblische Zeitschrift*
BZNW	Beihefte zur Zeitschrift für die neutestamentliche Wissenschaft und die Kunde der älteren Kirche
CBET	Contributions to Biblical Exegesis and Theology
CBNTS	Coniectanea biblica: New Testament Series
CBOTS	Coniectanea biblica: Old Testament Series
CBQ	*The Catholic Biblical Quarterly*

CC	Corpus christianorum
CSCO	Corpus scriptorum christianorum orientalium
CSCOSS	Corpus scriptorum christianorum orientalium: Scriptores syri
DJD	Discoveries in the Judaean Desert
DSD	*Dead Sea Discoveries*
EC	*Early Christianity*
EHPR	Études d'histoire et de philosophies religieuses
EKKNT	Evangelisch-katholischer Kommentar zum Neuen Testament
ETL	*Ephemerides theologicae lovanienses*
EvT	*Evangelische Theologie*
FilNeot	*Filología Neotestamentaria*
FRLANT	Forschungen zur Religion und Literatur des Alten und Neues Testaments
FS	Festschrift
FzAT	Forschungen zum Alten Testament
FzB	Forschung zur Bibel
GCS	Die griechischen christlichen Schriftsteller
GFA	*Göttinger Forum für Altertumswissenschaft*
HBS	Herders biblische Studien
HBT	*Horizons in Biblical Theology*
HTKNT	Herders theologischer Kommentar zum Neuen Testament
ICC	International Critical Commentary
IEJ	*Israel Exploration Journal*
Int	*Interpretation*
Jastrow	*A Dictionary of the Targumim*
JBL	*Journal of Biblical Literature*
JBT	Jahrbuch für biblische Theologie
JJS	*Journal of Jewish Studies*
JR	*Journal of Religion*
JSHJ	*Journal for the Study of the Historical Jesus*
JSJ	*Journal for the Study of Judaism in the Persian, Hellenistic and Roman Period*
JSJSup	Supplements to the Journal for the Study of Judaism
JSNT	*Journal for the Study of the New Testament*
JSNTS	Journal for the Study of the New Testament Supplement Series

JSOTS	Journal for the Study of the Old Testament Supplement Series
JSP	*Journal for the Study of the Pseudepigrapha*
JTS	*Journal of Theological Studies*
KEK	Kritisch-exegetischer Kommentar über das Neue Testament
KfA	Kommentar zu frühchristlichen Apologeten
LCL	Loeb Classical Library
LNTS	Library of New Testament Studies
LSJ	Liddell, et al., *A Greek–English Lexicon*
LXX	Septuagint
MT	Masoretic Text
MThZ	*Münchener theologische Zeitschrift*
MTS	Marburger theologische Studien
NA27	Nestle et al. (eds.), *Novum Testamentum Graece*, 27th edn
NCB	New Century Bible
NF	Neue Folge
NGSt	New Gospel Studies
NICNT	New International Commentary on the New Testament
NIGTC	New International Greek Testament Commentary
NovT	*Novum Testamentum*
NovTSup	Novum Testamentum Supplements
NRT	*Nouvelle revue théologique*
NS	New Series
NT	New Testament
NTA	Neutestamentliche Abhandlungen
NTOA	Novum testamentum et orbis antiquus
NTS	*New Testament Studies*
NTTS	New Testament Tools and Studies
OT	Old Testament
OTP	Charlesworth (ed.), *The Old Testament Pseudepigrapha*
PEGLMBS	*Proceedings Eastern Great Lakes and Midwest Biblical Societies*
PVTG	Pseudepigrapha Veteris Testamenti graece
QD	Questiones disputatae
RB	*Revue biblique*
RBL	*Review of Biblical Literature*
RevExp	*Review and Expositor*
RevQ	*Revue de Qumran*

RSR	*Recherches de science religieuse*
SBF	Studium Biblicum Franciscanum
SBLDS	Society of Biblical Literature Dissertation Series
SBLECL	Society of Biblical Literature Early Christianity and Its Literature
SBLEJL	Society of Biblical Literature Early Judaism and Its Literature
SBLSCS	Society of Biblical Literature Septuagint and Cognate Studies
SBLSP	*Society of Biblical Literature Seminar Papers*
SBLTT	Society of Biblical Literature Texts and Translations
SBLWGRW	Society of Biblical Literature Writings from the Greco-Roman World
SBS	Stuttgarter Bibelstudien
SC	Sources chrétiennes
SCBO	Scriptorum classicorum bibliotheca oxoniensis
SEÅ	*Svensk exegetisk årsbok*
SJOT	*Scandinavian Journal of the Old Testament*
SNTSMS	Society for New Testament Studies Monograph Series
SNTU	*Studien zum Neuen Testament und seiner Umwelt*
SNTU B	Studien zum Neuen Testament und seiner Umwelt B
SSS	Semitic Study Series
ST	*Studia theologica*
STDJ	Studies on the Texts of the Desert of Judah
SUNT	Studien zur Umwelt des Neuen Testaments
SVTP	Studia in Veteris Testamenti pseudepigrapha
SzNT	Studien zum Neuen Testament
TANZ	Texte und Arbeiten zum neutestamentlichen Zeitalter
TBei	*Theologische Beiträge*
TENT	Texts and Editions for New Testament Study
ThRev	*Theologische Revue*
TSAJ	Texts and Studies in Ancient Judaism
TTK	*Tidsskrift for teologi og kirke*
TWNT	Kittel and Friedrich (eds.), *Theologisches Wörterbuch zum Neuen Testament*
UTB	Uni-Taschenbücher
VCSup	Vigiliae christianae Supplements
VT	*Vetus Testamentum*
VTSup	Vetus Testamentum Supplements
WBC	Word Biblical Commentary

WMANT	Wissenschaftliche Monographien zum Alten und Neuen Testament
WUNT	Wissenschaftliche Untersuchungen zum Neuen Testament
ZNW	*Zeitschrift für die neutestamentliche Wissenschaft und die Kunde der älteren Kirche*
ZTK	*Zeitschrift für Theologie und Kirche*

Ancient texts

1 Cl	*1 Clement*
2 Cl	*2 Clement*
1 En	*1 Enoch*
2 En	*2 Enoch*
2 ApocJas	*2 Apocalypse of James*
2 Esd	2 Esdras (Vulgate *IV Ezra*)
3 Bar	*3 Baruch*
Adv. Pelag.	*Adversus Pelagianos* (*Against the Pelagians*)
Ant	*Antiquitates Judaicae* (*Jewish Antiquities*)
ApJas	*Apocryphon of James*
ApocMos	*Apocalypse of Moses* (Greek *Life of Adam and Eve*)
ApocrEzek	*Apocryphon of Ezekiel*
ApolArist	*Apology of Aristides*
AssMos	*Assumption of Moses* (*Testament of Moses*)
Barn	*Barnabas*
Bell	*Bellum Judaicum* (*Jewish War*)
bHag	Babylonian Talmud tractate *Hagiga*
bMoedQat	Babylonian Talmud tractate *Moed Qatan*
bNed	Babylonian Talmud tractate *Nedarim*
bSanh	Babylonian Talmud tractate *Sanhedrin*
CD	Cairo Damascus (Damascus Document)
ConfLing	*De confusione linguarum* (*On the Confusion of Tongues*)
Const. ap.	*Constitutiones apostolicae* (*Apostolic Constitutions*)
Did	*Didache*
Didasc. ap.	*Didascalia apostolorum*
Diogn	*Diognetus*
Eccl. T.	*Commentary on Ecclesiastes* (*Tura Papyrus*)
Ecclus	Ecclesiasticus (Sirach, Ben Sira)

EgerG	*Egerton Gospel*
Ep.	*Epistula (Letter)*
Ep. ad Cyprianum	*Epistula ad Cyprianum (To Cyprian)*
EpArist	*Epistula Aristeae (Letter of Aristeas)*
GosEb	*Gospel of the Ebionites*
GosHeb	*Gospel of the Hebrews*
GPet	*Gospel of Peter*
GThom	*Gospel of Thomas*
Herm Man	*Shepherd of Hermas, Mandates*
Herm Sim	*Shepherd of Hermas, Similitudes*
Herm Vis	*Shepherd of Hermas, Visions*
Hist. Eccl.	*Historia Ecclesiastica (Church History)*
Ign *Eph*	Ignatius, *To the Ephesians*
Ign *Magn*	Ignatius, *To the Magnesians*
Ign *Phld*	Ignatius, *To the Philadelphians*
Ign *Pol*	Ignatius, *To Polycarp*
Ign *Smyrn*	Ignatius, *To the Smyrnaeans*
Ign *Trall*	Ignatius, *To the Trallians*
JosAsen	*Joseph and Aseneth*
Jub	*Jubilees*
LAB	*Liber antiquitatum biblicarum (Biblical Antiquities)*
Mos	*On the Life of Moses*
MutNom	*De mutatione nominum (On the Change of Names)*
mYoma	Mishnah tractate *Yoma*
NHC	Nag Hammadi Codex
Oxy840G	*Oxyrhynchus 840 Gospel*
ParJer	*Paraleipomena Jeremiou (4 Baruch)*
Philops.	*Philopseudes*
PKöln	Papyrus Köln (Cologne Papyrus)
Pol *Phil*	Polycarp, *To the Philippians*
POxy	Papyrus Oxyrhynchus
PraemPoen	*De praemiis et poenis (On Rewards and Punishments)*
PraepEv	*Praeparatio Evangelica (Preparation for the Gospel)*
Prog.	*Progymnasmata*
PSI	Papiro della Società Italiana
PsSol	*Psalm of Solomon*

QuaestExod	*Quaestiones et solutiones in Exodum* (*Questions and Answers on Exodus*)
Ref.	*Refutatio omnium haeresium* (*Refutation of All Heresies*)
SibOr	*Sibylline Oracles*
Strom.	*Stromateis*
TAbr	*Testament of Abraham*
TBenj	*Testament of Benjamin*
TGad	*Testament of Gad*
TgIsa	*Targum* Isaiah
TgNeof	*Targum Neofiti*
TgOnq	*Targum Onqelos*
TgPsJon	*Targum Pseudo-Jonathan*
TJob	*Testament of Job*
TJud	*Testament of Judah*
TLevi	*Testament of Levi*
TReub	*Testament of Reuben*
TZeb	*Testament of Zebulun*
V.A.	*Vita Apollonii* (*Life of Apollonius*)
VitProph	*Vitae Prophetarum* (*Lives of the Prophets*)

1

INTRODUCTION

Two Gospel episodes portray Jesus of Nazareth as someone who forgives sins. All three synoptic Gospels relate how Jesus once told a paralyzed man in Capernaum that his sins were forgiven (Mark 2.5 par.). This occasion instigated a controversy, which culminated in Jesus' declaration that the Son of Man has authority to forgive sins on earth (Mark 2.10 par.). In addition, Luke's Gospel includes an episode in which Jesus tells a sinful woman that her sins are forgiven (Luke 7.47–8), which made the onlookers wonder who he might be, since he even forgives sins (7.49).

It is the aim of the present study to enquire how Jesus related forgiveness and its proclamation to his own person and mission. I will attempt to answer, within the necessary limits set by the nature of historical reconstruction generally and of Jesus research specifically, the following basic questions: is it plausible that the historical Jesus did claim to forgive sins in some manner that resembles the way in which this is narrated in the Gospels? If so, in what sense did he purport to forgive sins? What, if anything, does this tell us about who Jesus claimed to be and how he was perceived by his contemporaries?

Previous studies and the present study

Relatively few monographs and articles have addressed these questions specifically, no doubt because, as just mentioned, this theme occurs only sparingly in the Gospels themselves and is not usually perceived as lying at the centre of Jesus' mission and message.[1] On the other hand, many scholarly portraits of the historical Jesus have touched briefly on the topic. To collect all these scattered comments and to list the view of each Jesus scholar on this question would transcend the limits of the

---

[1] See J. D. G. Dunn, *Jesus Remembered*, Christianity in the Making 1 (Grand Rapids, MI: Eerdmans, 2003), p. 788.

study undertaken here; instead, the following review will be kept brief, concentrating on the major contributions.

Since discussion of the topic has taken many different paths and has occasionally even moved in conflicting directions, a chronological presentation would be difficult to grasp. I will therefore group the contributions into three categories: first of all, those who have denied all historical value in the Gospels' portrayals of how Jesus forgives sins; secondly, those who have affirmed the historicity of these portrayals more or less *in toto*; and, thirdly, those who have argued a middle position, having found both a historical core and later theological developments in the Gospel depictions. While acknowledging the progress already made in the study of Jesus and forgiveness since the mid-nineteenth century, this review will also point out some of the shortcomings of earlier contributions that warrant renewed investigation of the topic.

Negative proposals

Bruno Bauer, William Wrede and Rudolf Bultmann

Bruno Bauer (1841–2) presented the first serious challenge to the historicity of Mark 2.1–12. Bauer thought that the episode contained a number of features that could not plausibly have taken place; for example, breaking up a roof of a house full of people would have been a far too dangerous activity.[2] Moreover, Jesus' knowledge of the thoughts of the scribes, which serves to introduce the topic of forgiveness, is a historical impossibility, and the offence taken by the scribes has been created by Mark for literary purposes. The forgiveness sayings (Mark 2.5, 10), Bauer argued, had originated as an expression of the belief of the primitive Church that Christ had a timeless authority to forgive sins. The community then created the surrounding episode about the paralytic as a miraculous demonstration of this authority.[3] In other words, Bauer thought that the Gospels had historicized what was from the beginning a theological conviction.

According to William Wrede's influential work on the messianic secret (1901), the Markan portrayal of the Son of Man, who forgives sins and who is lord of the Sabbath, reflects faith in Jesus as the Messiah – an

---

[2] B. Bauer, *Kritik der evangelischen Geschichte*, 2nd edn (Leipzig: Wigand, 1846), pp. 91–2. Earlier D. F. Strauss, *Das Leben Jesu, kritisch bearbeitet*, 4th edn, 2 vols. (Tübingen: Ossiander, 1840), vol. II, pp. 81–4, had used this to argue for the priority of Matthew's version.

[3] Bauer, *Kritik der evangelischen Geschichte*, pp. 91–3.

identity which Jesus did not claim for himself.[4] Three years later (1904), Wrede became the first proponent of the form-critical division of Mark 2.1–12 into a healing episode (2.1–5a, 11–12) and a controversy passage crafted by the primitive Church to express its christology (2.5b–10).[5] Wrede's solution differed from that of Bauer, since he did not take the theological concerns of the inserted passage to invalidate the entire historicity of the pericope, but his assessment of the forgiveness theme in the episode was as clear as Bauer's: this notion did not stem from the historical Jesus.

Rudolf Bultmann's consistent form-critical approach (1921) both confirmed Wrede's division of the Markan episode into two distinct parts and lent support to the view that Jesus himself had not claimed to forgive sins. The forgiveness sayings did pass Bultmann's first criterion of historicity, as they did not betray any Hellenistic influence, but were declared inauthentic by his second criterion, since they seemed to serve the interests of the primitive Church too well.[6] For Bultmann, the concern of the community was in this case not christological, but ecclesiological. Mark 2.5b–10 had been inserted not to express belief in the divine authority of Jesus, but to legitimize the community's own practice of forgiving sins.[7] To this he added another observation, originally made by Heinrich Weinel, which seemed to confirm the negative verdict: corresponding forgiveness sayings were absent from the rest of the tradition, with the exception of Luke 7.48, which Bultmann argued had been secondarily derived from Mark.[8] Bultmann's conclusion is dependent on the methodological principle that the criteria of discontinuity and multiple attestation may also be applied negatively in order to refute the historicity of Gospel material.

Peter Fiedler

In *Jesus und die Sünder* (1976), Peter Fiedler offered the first extensive treatment of the present topic within the framework of a broader

---

[4] D. W. Wrede, *Das Messiasgeheimnis in den Evangelien: Zugleich ein Beitrag zum Verständnis des Markusevangelium* (Göttingen: Vandenhoeck & Ruprecht, 1901), p. 222.

[5] W. Wrede, 'Zur Heilung des Gelähmten (Mc 2,1ff.)', *ZNW* 5 (1904), 354–8.

[6] R. Bultmann, *Jesus*, 3rd edn (Tübingen: Mohr Siebeck, 1964), p. 13, spells out his criteria briefly.

[7] R. Bultmann, *Die Geschichte der synoptischen Tradition*, 10th edn (Göttingen: Vandenhoeck & Ruprecht, 1995), pp. 12–14.

[8] H. Weinel, *Biblische Theologie des Neuen Testaments: Die Religion Jesu und des Urchristentums*, 2nd edn (Tübingen: Mohr Siebeck, 1913), pp. 45, 220–2; Bultmann, *Die Geschichte der synoptischen Tradition*, p. 13.

discussion of Jesus' attitude towards sinners. His investigation of the OT and early Jewish background discards the opinion that Israelite priests were recognized as having authority to forgive sins. Such authority was the prerogative of God. The forgiveness saying of Mark 2.10 and the public reaction of Luke 7.49 cannot, however, be taken to say anything less than that Jesus, as the Son of Man, did assume such authority for himself.[9]

According to Fiedler, the forgiveness episodes are unhistorical. Like Bultmann, he points out that the theme is sparsely, indeed singularly, attested, for Luke 7.48–9 is a redactional addition, which has been modelled on the Markan passage. Had Jesus actually offered forgiveness in this way, the notion should have left more and clearer imprints in the tradition. More probably, then, the primitive Church desired to secure a 'christologoumenon' in the life of the earthly Jesus. The occurrence of the self-designation 'Son of Man', which might not have been in use prior to the resurrection, points in the same direction.[10] In seeing christology, rather than ecclesiology, as the bottom line of the unhistorical forgiveness sayings, Fiedler sides with Bauer and Wrede.

Another objection to the historicity of these sayings is the causal connection between sin and illness presupposed by Mark. According to Fiedler, the notion of a link between sin and illness contradicts Jesus' stance as recalled in John 9.2 and Luke 13.1–5, and therefore cannot reflect an opinion taken by the historical Jesus.[11]

Fiedler's most decisive argument involves a discussion of the criteria of discontinuity and coherence. The lack of parallels in early Judaism, far from affirming the historicity of the saying in Mark 2.10, rather disproves it. Such a sacrilegious claim is incomprehensible in an early Jewish context and, accordingly, it cannot be ascribed to Jesus.[12] It is clear that Fiedler has moved the debate over Jesus and forgiveness into a mode of thinking that is now commonly associated with 'the third quest'.

Twenty years later (1996), Fiedler returned to the topic in an article on sin and forgiveness in the gospel tradition. Here he defends his earlier thesis, clarifying especially the argument pertaining to Mark's unrealistic portrayal of the scribes in the light of what is known about

---

[9] P. Fiedler, *Jesus und die Sünder*, BET 3 (Frankfurt: Peter Lang, 1976), pp. 104, 111.

[10] *Ibid.*, pp. 106–8, 111, 115–16. Fiedler appears to have received the impetus for speaking of a 'christologoumenon' from the more cautious suggestion of a possible 'theologoumenon' made in J. Michl, 'Sündenvergebung in Christus nach dem Glaube der frühen Kirche', *MThZ* 24 (1973), 25–35 (30–1).

[11] Fiedler, *Jesus und die Sünder*, p. 108.

[12] *Ibid.*, pp. 97–8, 112, 115, 275–6, 329 n. 376.

first-century Judaism: the historical scribes would not have heard the divine passive 'your sins are forgiven' as a claim to any independent authority, and the charge of blasphemy does not comply with Mishnaic stipulations.[13] Fiedler's most recent treatment of the topic (2004) brings his argument further up to date by taking into account the fragmentary *Prayer of Nabonidus* (4Q242).[14] Here Fiedler once more defends and elucidates a position that has remained unaltered for three decades: that the historical Jesus did not forgive sins.

Affirmative proposals

Responses to Bauer, Wrede and Bultmann

Bauer's attack on the historicity of Mark 2.1–12 remained largely unnoticed throughout the second half of the nineteenth century. Some scholars attempted to evade the disturbingly high christological implications of Mark 2.10 by suggesting that, retranslated into Aramaic, the expression 'Son of Man' was originally nothing more than a generic term for human beings.[15] Others, seeing that Jesus himself had not been immune to the mythical and apocalyptic thinking of his day, found it quite plausible that it was Jesus, and not the Church, who had formulated expressions of an elevated christology such as Mark 2.10. In this context Wilhelm Bousset (1892) argued that Jesus had proleptically claimed some of the privileges of the Son of Man that he was later going to become, one of which was the authority to forgive sins.[16]

Wrede's and Bultmann's arguments against the possibility that forgiveness sayings might have come from the historical Jesus were also questioned. Paul Wernle (1916) made an effort to turn the criterion

[13] P. Fiedler, 'Sünde und Sündenvergebung in der Jesustradition', in H. Frankemölle (ed.), *Sünde und Erlösung im Neuen Testament*, QD 161 (Freiburg: Herder, 1996), pp. 76–91 (pp. 86–7).

[14] P. Fiedler, 'Gottes Vergebungsbereitschaft und Heilswille', in L. Schenke et al. (eds.), *Jesus von Nazaret – Spuren und Konturen* (Stuttgart: Kohlhammer, 2004), pp. 164–92 (pp. 164–5).

[15] A. Meyer, *Jesu Muttersprache: Das galiläische Aramäisch in seiner Bedeutung für die Erklärung der Reden Jesu und der Evangelien überhaupt* (Freiburg/Leipzig: Mohr Siebeck, 1896), p. 94; H. Lietzmann, *Der Menschensohn: Ein Beitrag zur neutestamentlichen Theologie* (Freiburg/Leipzig: Mohr Siebeck, 1896), pp. 81–5.

[16] W. Bousset, *Jesu Predigt in ihrem Gegensatz zum Judentum: Ein religionsgeschichtlicher Vergleich* (Göttingen: Vandenhoeck & Ruprecht, 1892), pp. 110–11. Cf. the author's subsequent reconsideration of Mark 2.10 as a secondary addition in W. Bousset, *Kyrios Christos: Geschichte des Christusglaubens von den Anfängen des Christentums bis Irenaeus*, 2nd edn (Göttingen: Vandenhoeck & Ruprecht, 1921), p. 40.

of multiple attestation on its head, by arguing that the low frequency of sayings that imply Jesus' oneness with God – such as Mark 2.10 – should count as an indication that they are genuine.[17] Later on, Vincent Taylor (1953) accepted the form-critical division of Mark 2.1–12, but saw no reason to conclude that 2.5b–10 was unhistorical. The inserted pronouncement story was, according to Taylor, a historical account that had been merged with the surrounding healing episode in order to serve the urgent interests of the primitive community.[18] Against Wrede's general view of Jesus' ministry as non-messianic, British scholarship tended to claim that there was no trace of any pre-messianic stage in the gospel tradition, and that the amalgamation of the titles Messiah, Suffering Servant and Son of Man cannot be derived from primitive Christianity. As a follower of this scholarly tradition, C. H. Dodd (1970) argued that through offering the forgiveness of sins, Jesus both hinted at his messianic identity and ignited a controversy that was possibly called to mind during his trial.[19]

Geza Vermes

Jesus had been labelled a 'charismatic' already in 1934 by Rudolf Otto, whose idiosyncratic work placed the identity of Jesus as the Son of Man within the currents flowing from the Enochic Book of Parables. Otto had also suggested that the conjunction of healing and forgiveness in Mark 2.1–12 was typical of a charismatic person and historically plausible.[20] But it was Geza Vermes' scholarly work that definitely placed the conception of Jesus as charismatic figure firmly within the realities of first-century Galilean Judaism.

In *Jesus the Jew* (1973), Vermes pointed out that several of the christological titles found in the synoptic Gospels could be explained and properly understood in the context of charismatic Judaism.[21] One such title is 'Son of Man', which, according to Vermes, was a circumlocution for the speaker ('I') in first-century Aramaic.[22] Only in the gospel tradition was

---

[17] P. Wernle, *Jesus*, 2nd edn (Tübingen: Mohr Siebeck, 1916), pp. 317–19, 331–4.

[18] V. Taylor, *The Gospel according to St. Mark* (London: Macmillan, 1953), pp. 191–2.

[19] C. H. Dodd, *The Founder of Christianity* (New York: Collier, 1970), pp. 158–9.

[20] R. Otto, *Reich Gottes und Menschensohn: Ein religionsgeschichtlicher Versuch* (Munich: C. H. Beck, 1934), pp. 134–5.

[21] G. Vermes, *Jesus the Jew: A Historian's Reading of the Gospels*, 2nd edn (London: SCM, 1983).

[22] G. Vermes, 'Appendix E: The Use of בר נשא/בר נש in Jewish Aramaic', in M. Black (ed.), *An Aramaic Approach to the Gospels and Acts*, 3rd edn (Oxford: Clarendon, 1967), pp. 310–30.

this idiomatic expression – now coloured by and reinterpreted through allusion to 'the one like a son of man' in Daniel 7 – understood christologically. Consequently, whenever a 'Son of Man' saying exhibits no traces of influence from Daniel, it can be held to stem from Jesus.[23] In Vermes' opinion, this is indeed the case with Mark 2.10. Vermes juxtaposes the *Prayer of Nabonidus* with Mark 2.1–12: in the fragmentary episode from Qumran, exorcism, healing, and forgiveness appear to be closely interrelated. Vermes thinks that, in the same way as the unnamed Jew of the fragment, Jesus equated healing with forgiving, so that the claim to the authority to forgive sins was merely an assertion of his ability to heal the paralytic. The scribes were not accustomed to this kind of language and took it as Jesus infringing God's own prerogative.[24]

Twenty years later, in *The Religion of Jesus the Jew* (1993), Vermes approaches Mark 2.1–12 somewhat differently. He now makes a distinction between the bestowal of forgiveness and the declaration that sins have been forgiven. He focuses on the passive voice of Mark 2.5, which indicates that Jesus thought that God was the agent of forgiveness.[25] While Vermes did not hesitate to equate healing with forgiveness in his earlier work, in his more recent writings he draws a sharper line between the two. His conclusion that Mark 2.1–12 is historically plausible, however, remains unchanged.

Otfried Hofius, Otto Betz and Volker Hampel

Since the 1980s a group of Tübingen-based scholars have paid attention to the topic of the forgiveness of sins in relation to Jesus' self-understanding. This 'Tübingen School' defends the historical accuracy of the forgiveness sayings and assigns a messianic consciousness to the historical Jesus.

Otfried Hofius' articles on the forgiveness sayings in Mark provide several observations that have a bearing on the historical question. In his first article (1983), Hofius examines the allegation that Jewish priests pronounced absolution in a ritual context. He concludes that there is no evidence that this was ever the case.[26] In a second study (1994), Hofius

---

[23] Vermes, *Jesus the Jew*, pp. 177–86.

[24] *Ibid.*, pp. 67–9, 180.

[25] G. Vermes, *The Religion of Jesus the Jew* (Minneapolis: Fortress, 1993), p. 192. See also G. Vermes, *The Changing Faces of Jesus* (London: Allen Lane, 2000), p. 268; G. Vermes, *The Authentic Gospel of Jesus* (London: Allen Lane, 2003), pp. 40–2.

[26] O. Hofius, 'Vergebungszuspruch und Vollmachtsfrage: Mk 2,1–12 und das Problem priesterlicher Absolution im antiken Judentum', in H.-G. Geyer et al. (eds.), *'Wenn nicht jetzt, wann dann?'*, FS H.-J. Kraus (Neukirchen-Vluyn: Neukirchener, 1983), pp. 115–27.

seeks to demonstrate that the saying at Mark 2.5b cannot be construed as a mere proclamation of forgiveness, but must be taken as a formula that purports to effect forgiveness in itself. Both the literary context and parallel expressions in Aramaic literature indicate that the implied agent of forgiveness is Jesus. Mark thus portrays Jesus as doing what only God could do, and Jesus does so as being God, present on earth. For Hofius, this would also be what the historical Jesus laid claim to.[27] In his most recent article on the topic, Hofius (2000) argues against Klaus Koch's proposal that the Messiah of *Targum Jonathan* to Isa 52.13–53.12 is portrayed as someone who forgives sins.[28]

Otto Betz (1984) finds the key to unlock Mark 2.1–12 in Psalm 103, 'Jesus' favourite psalm', where forgiveness and healing are paralleled as divine works (Ps 103.3). Wrede's form-critical division of the Markan passage destroys a corresponding parallelism in Jesus' act of forgiving and healing the paralytic, and the unity and historicity of the episode should be maintained.[29] A pupil of Betz, Volker Hampel also argues for the integrity and authenticity of Mark 2.1–12 in his monograph on the historical Jesus as the Son of Man (1990). According to Hampel, the theme of forgiveness cannot have been introduced by the Church, for primitive Christianity did not connect forgiveness and healing. Moreover, one cannot find a suitable *Sitz im Leben* for this passage. Bultmann's idea that Christians thus legitimized their own claims to authority is not convincing to Hampel, since forgiveness was thought to be possible only by virtue of Christ's expiatory death and resurrection. Neither could the passage have resulted from a wish to apply the characteristics of the risen Lord to the earthly Jesus. Had that been the case, the designation given to Jesus would have been 'Son of God' or 'Christ', but not 'Son of Man', Hampel argues. He concludes that, in his capacity as the Son of Man, destined to be the Messiah, Jesus laid claim to God's own authority and expressed an understanding of himself as God's representative on earth.[30]

[27] O. Hofius, 'Jesu Zuspruch der Sündenvergebung: Exegetische Erwägungen zu Mk 2,5b', in I. Baldermann et al. (eds.), *Sünde und Gericht*, JBT 9 (Neukirchen-Vluyn: Neukirchener, 1994), pp. 125–43.

[28] O. Hofius, 'Kennt der Targum zu Jes 53 einen sündenvergebenden Messias?', in O. Hofius, *Neutestamentliche Studien*, WUNT 132 (Tübingen: Mohr Siebeck, 2000), pp. 70–107.

[29] O. Betz, 'Jesu Lieblingspsalm: Die Bedeutung von Psalm 103 für das Werk Jesu', *TBei* 15 (1984), 253–69.

[30] V. Hampel, *Menschensohn und historischer Jesus: Ein Rätselwort als Schlüssel zum messianischen Selbstverständnis Jesu* (Neukirchen-Vluyn: Neukirchener, 1990), pp. 189–99.

Chong-Hyon Sung

The most extensive project so far that sets out to provide an answer to the question of whether Jesus forgave sins is Chong-Hyon Sung's *Vergebung der Sünden* (1993), an edited version of a doctoral thesis written under the auspices of Peter Stuhlmacher and Betz.[31] Sung has divided his book into three parts. The first part deals with the concept of forgiveness in the OT, while the second extends the investigation into intertestamental and rabbinic literature. Finally, the third part is devoted to Jesus' activity of forgiving sins according to the synoptic Gospels.

To establish Jesus' view on forgiveness, Sung not only explores those texts that have Jesus voicing explicit claims to the authority to forgive, but also – like Joachim Jeremias and others before him – provides evidence of Jesus' attitude towards sinners on a broader scale: Jesus' dining with sinners, his parables, the Lord's Prayer and so on. In addition, Sung pays attention to the sayings of Jesus that express an intention to suffer and to die in order to bring forgiveness. Sung concludes that the concept of forgiveness was central to Jesus' entire mission, that Jesus thought of himself as dying for the sins of people, and that the historical Jesus did forgive sins during his ministry.

Mediating proposals

Martin Dibelius, William Manson and August Strobel

While scholars such as Betz and Hampel completely reject the excision of Mark 2.5b–10 from 2.1–12, others have argued that the form-critical division of this pericope should be modified. The first to argue in favour of such a mediating proposal appears to have been Martin Dibelius (1919). Doubting Bultmann's hypothesized *Sitz im Leben* for the Markan episode, Dibelius suggested instead that the controversy in Mark 2.6–10 had grown out of the original forgiveness saying (2.5) in the context of primitive Christian preaching.[32] In effect, while Dibelius would not apply the term 'rhetoric' to the preaching of the primitive Church, he was the first

---

[31] C.-H. Sung, *Vergebung der Sünden: Jesu Praxis der Sündenvergebung nach den Synoptikern und ihre Voraussetzungen im Alten Testament und frühen Judentum*, WUNT 2:57 (Tübingen: Mohr Siebeck, 1993).

[32] M. Dibelius, *Die Formgeschichte des Evangeliums*, 1st edn (Tübingen: Mohr Siebeck, 1919), pp. 34–5. Dibelius' critique of Bultmann was introduced in the 2nd edn (Tübingen: Mohr Siebeck, 1933), pp. 63–6.

to claim that the narration of a controversy over forgiveness developed out of a brief saying of the historical Jesus, with an intent to persuade.

William Manson added two arguments in support of Dibelius' ana-lysis (1943). Against the contention of Weinel and Bultmann that the rest of tradition was silent on Jesus' ministry of forgiveness, Manson claimed that the theme was implicitly present in the sayings that allow for the inclusion of tax collectors and harlots in the kingdom. Also, he argued that the forgiveness saying in 2.5b must also have been part of the original episode, or else the introduction of the forgiveness theme into a miracle story would be inexplicable. Hence, while regarding 2.10 as representing primitive Christian preaching, Manson insisted on the historicity of the saying in 2.5, which he held to be indicative of Jesus' messianic authority.[33]

August Strobel's study on sin and confession in Judaism and the NT (1968) includes a pondering of the theme of forgiveness as part of the ministry of the historical Jesus. While he agrees with Dibelius and Manson on the partition of Mark 2.1–12, Strobel differs from the vast majority of interpreters by regarding Luke 7.44–50 as a separate, pre-Lukan tradition, coherent with Mark 2.5 and confirming the historicity of Jesus' proclamation of forgiveness. While the primitive Church reinter-preted this proclamation as a declaration of forgiveness by Jesus' own authority, the historical Jesus intended to offer God's mercy and forgive-ness, which he expressed by the divine passive.[34]

Hans-Josef Klauck

An article by Hans-Josef Klauck (1981) deals with the issue of forgiveness in Mark 2.1–12 par. from a number of perspectives. Klauck's treatment of the Jewish background includes a discussion of both *Targum Jonathan* and the *Prayer of Nabonidus*, neither of which Klauck views as evidence for human mediation of forgiveness in early Judaism. Like Manson, when it comes to the historical question, Klauck argues that Jesus' posi-tive attitude towards sinners is multiply attested, and the saying in Mark 2.5 agrees well with this broader outlook on the part of Jesus. By con-trast, the 'Son of Man' saying in 2.10 betrays post-resurrection theology and probably originated in the community. Klauck follows the tradition

---

[33] W. Manson, *Jesus the Messiah: The Synoptic Tradition of the Revelation of God in Christ, with Special Reference to Form-Criticism* (London: Hodder and Stoughton, 1943), pp. 40–2, 116.

[34] A. Strobel, *Erkenntnis und Bekenntnis der Sünde in neutestamentlicher Zeit*, AzT 1 37 (Stuttgart: Calwer, 1968), pp. 56–62.

of Bultmann and views the controversy dialogue in 2.6–10 as crafted in defence of the forms of forgiveness practised in the primitive Church; this polemic, he thinks, was directed against Jewish Christian claims that God alone could forgive sins.[35] As 2.5 indicates that the agent of forgiveness is God alone, it exhibits some differences compared to the Christian interests evidenced by 2.10. 'Cum grano salis', Klauck is willing to invoke the criterion of discontinuity to affirm the historicity of 2.5.[36]

John Dominic Crossan

Only with some hesitation can John Dominic Crossan's treatment of the topic in his work on the historical Jesus (1991) be assigned to the category of mediating proposals.[37] Crossan takes Mark 2.1–12 and John 5.1–9a, 14 to be parallel episodes, formed around a common core with a basic claim to historicity.

Crossan argues that the historical Jesus did heal a paralytic. Like Vermes, Crossan alleges that the healings performed by Jesus were tantamount to an implicit declaration of forgiveness or of sinlessness. In the putative source that underlies the two pericopes in Mark and John, the themes of forgiveness and divine power were emphasized. Finally, the redactors of Mark and John developed the episode in different directions. While preserving the traditional conjunction of sin and sickness incongruent with Johannine theology, John did not elaborate this theme further, but turned the episode into a controversy over the Sabbath that results in the accusation that Jesus had placed himself on a par with God (John 5.1–18). By contrast, Mark made the forgiveness theme explicit and developed a controversy over this issue.[38] To sum up, Crossan appears to hold that the forgiveness of sins was an implicit aspect of the ministry of the historical Jesus, but that it was primitive Christianity which made the theme explicit and which saw christological ramifications therein.

Ingo Broer

Ingo Broer's article of 1992 begins by discussing the various form-critical proposals to break up Mark 2.1–12 and reaching the preliminary

---

[35] H.-J. Klauck, 'Die Frage der Sündenvergebung in der Perikope von der Heilung des Gelähmten (Mk 2,1–12 parr)', *BZ* NS 25 (1981), 223–48 (241–4).

[36] *Ibid.*, 241.

[37] J. D. Crossan, *The Historical Jesus: The Life of a Mediterranean Jewish Peasant* (HarperSanFrancisco, 1991), pp. 323–5.

[38] *Ibid.*, pp. 324–5.

conclusion that the historical problem cannot be solved on purely literary grounds. Broer then examines the Jewish material in order to decide
whether it is plausible that Jesus could have envisaged God's granting
forgiveness in a non-cultic setting. He suggests that it is indeed plausible, and that Jesus' practice of offering forgiveness (in effect preaching
God's forgiveness, as implied by the divine passive in Mark 2.5) should
not have been too controversial within the Judaism of his day.[39] By contrast, the saying in 2.10 is more likely to have originated in the primitive
Church than with the historical Jesus. Only after this does Broer feel
confident to acknowledge that the division of 2.1–12 into primary and
secondary material is justified.[40] The novel aspect of Broer's article is
primarily methodological: it reverses the practice of forming historical
judgement on the basis of hypothetical form- and source-critical analyses, which has been commonplace since the beginning of the twentieth
century, and gives precedence instead to the more specific criteria for
historicity.

The purpose of the present study

As the foregoing survey has shown, the study of forgiveness in the ministry of the historical Jesus has exhibited some steady progress, ever
since the case was opened by Bauer more than a century and a half ago.
Since Wrede, there has been awareness of the uncertainties concerning
the integrity of the primary episode (Mark 2.1–12); today, this question
must be addressed by anyone who ventures to assess the historicity of
the narration. Broer's recent contribution may be a sign of further development, since it acknowledges the hypothetical nature of all form- or
source-critical reconstructions and of the vulnerability implied in any
attempt to base historical conclusions on these reconstructions. Fiedler's
and Sung's investigations of Israelite and early Jewish conceptions of sin
and forgiveness have helped to fill out the picture, as have the discoveries
at Qumran. There has also been an increasing awareness, at least since
Vermes, that, if their historicity is to be affirmed, Jesus' forgiveness sayings must be interpreted within the parameters of first-century Judaism.
At the same time, these sayings are usually read in the context of what
historical Jesus research is competent to say about Jesus' attitude to sin
and sinners in general.

---

[39] I. Broer, 'Jesus und das Gesetz – Anmerkungen zur Geschichte des Problems und zur
Frage der Sündenvergebung durch den historischen Jesus', in I. Broer (ed.), *Jesus und das
jüdische Gesetz* (Stuttgart: Kohlhammer, 1992), pp. 61–104 (pp. 72–100).
[40] *Ibid.*, pp. 98–9.

Yet there remain obscurities and unresolved questions that call for a renewed, full-scale consideration of the topic. The remainder of this section will present the major questions and indicate briefly how the present study intends to come to terms with them.

First of all, the results of discussion of method in historical Jesus research during recent decades have not been fully and consciously applied to the topic of Jesus and forgiveness. Sung's study is especially deficient on methodology and therefore does not provide a satisfactory answer to the question it raises.[41] The criteria for historicity, which are in a constant process of development and refinement, have not been systematically utilized to assess the historicity of the forgiveness sayings. This is not to say that all previous studies have been methodologically flawed, or that criteria have never been appealed to before. Still, the fact that the same criterion may be invoked by different scholars, but may result in diametrically opposed conclusions, shows that some clarification is needed. The present study aims to contribute to this task.

Secondly, while several of the contributors to the debate build their case partly on the alleged primitive Christian attitude to forgiveness and its relationship to christology, these Christian notions have not yet been satisfactorily investigated. For example, beginning with Bauer, scholars have argued that the authority of the Son of Man to forgive sins in Mark 2.10 was derived from the primitive Christian conviction that the risen Christ was authorized to forgive sins. The evidence for such a conviction will be scrutinized here in an investigation that claims to take into account all Christian writings up to 135 CE.

Thirdly, scholarship has tended to concur with the scribal protest in Mark 2.7, thinking that the forgiveness sayings are practically unique in their early Jewish context. Recent studies, especially the one by Broer, have put this axiom into question. In order to establish a fuller picture of the human mediation of forgiveness, a renewed investigation of early Jewish literature, focusing more on first-century interpretation of the Bible than on the original meaning of the OT itself, will be needed.

Fourthly, earlier proposals to the effect that the forgiveness sayings in the Gospels are the products of development and reinterpretation have not presented a convincing explanatory model for how this development occurred. It is not satisfactory to hypothesize that unknown Christians interpolated and elaborated the tradition which they had received, unless it is also shown how this activity took place.

---

[41] See the reviews by P. Fiedler, Review of Sung, *Vergebung der Sünden*, ThRev 91 (1995), 386–8; B. Chilton, Review of Sung, *Vergebung der Sünden*, *RBL* 26 June 2000 (www.bookreviews.org/pdf/2562_1799.pdf).

Fifthly, almost all previous contributors who have argued for some historicity in the forgiveness sayings have attempted to pinpoint the self-understanding or self-claim expressed by Jesus in these sayings. Here the proposals vary widely. A sample of older and more recent contributions is enough to show that the sayings have been taken as evidence for Jesus being a claimant to divine authority;[42] a Messianic claimant;[43] a Son-of-Man-to-be;[44] Israel's eschatological high priest;[45] a usurper of priestly prerogatives;[46] Elijah *redivivus*;[47] a prophet;[48] a charismatic;[49] a proto-psychotherapist;[50] a medium possessed by the spirit of God;[51] an exorcist-healer;[52] a preacher of God's forgiveness;[53] a critic of cultic religion;[54] a critic of oppressive institutions;[55] a superhuman;[56] a human being of pure and noble mind;[57] a humble human being;[58] and a madman.[59] The present

---

[42] P. Stuhlmacher, *Biblische Theologie des Neuen Testaments*, 2nd edn, 2 vols. (Göttingen: Vandenhoeck & Ruprecht, 1997), vol. I, pp. 82, 120.

[43] M. Hengel and A. M. Schwemer, *Jesus und das Judentum*, Geschichte des frühen Christentums 1 (Tübingen: Mohr Siebeck, 2007), pp. 465–6.

[44] A. Schweitzer, *Geschichte der Leben-Jesu-Forschung*, 9th edn (Tübingen: Mohr Siebeck, 1984), p. 425.

[45] C. H. T. Fletcher-Louis, 'Jesus as the High Priestly Messiah: Part 2', *JSHJ* 5 (2007), 57–79 (71–4).

[46] E. P. Sanders, *Jesus and Judaism* (London: SCM, 1985), pp. 273–4, 301.

[47] U. Kellermann, 'Wer kann Sünden vergeben außer Elia?', in P. Mommer et al. (eds.), *Gottes Recht als Lebensraum*, FS H. J. Boecker (Neukirchen-Vluyn: Neukirchener, 1993), pp. 165–77.

[48] T. Keim, *Geschichte Jesu von Nazara: In ihrer Verkettung mit dem Gesammtleben seines Volkes: Frei untersucht und ausführlich erzählt*, 3 vols. (Zürich: Orell, Füssli und Comp, 1867–72), vol. II, pp. 175–6.

[49] Otto, *Reich Gottes und Menschensohn*, pp. 134–5.

[50] D. Capps, *Jesus the Village Psychiatrist* (Louisville, KY: Westminster John Knox, 2008), pp. 49–50.

[51] S. L. Davies, *Jesus the Healer: Possession, Trance, and the Origins of Christianity* (London: SCM, 1995), pp. 73–6, 97–8.

[52] G. Lüdemann, *Jesus after 2000 Years: What He Really Said and Did*, transl. J. Bowden (London: SCM, 2000), pp. 15–16.

[53] G. Theissen and A. Merz, *Der historische Jesus: Ein Lehrbuch*, 3rd edn (Göttingen: Vandenhoeck & Ruprecht, 2001), pp. 459–60.

[54] J. Weiss, *Die Predigt Jesu vom Reiche Gottes*, 2nd edn (Göttingen: Vandenhoeck & Ruprecht, 1900), pp. 206–8.

[55] R. A. Horsley, *Jesus and the Spiral of Violence: Popular Jewish Resistance in Roman Palestine* (Minneapolis: Fortress, 1993), pp. 181–4.

[56] E. Renan, *Histoire des origines du Christianisme*, vol. I: *Vie de Jésus* (Berlin: Springer, 1863), pp. 169–81.

[57] K. H. G. Venturini, *Natürliche Geschichte des grossen Propheten von Nazareth*, 2nd edn (Bethlehem, 1806), pp. 129–33.

[58] D. Schenkel, *Das Charakterbild Jesu: Ein biblischer Versuch*, 3rd edn (Wiesbaden: C. W. Kreidel, 1864), pp. 55–7.

[59] E. Rasmussen, *Jesus: En sammenlignende Studie* (Copenhagen: Nordiske Forfatteres Forlag, 1905).

study will proceed from the assumption that the implications of the forgiveness sayings can only be determined by a comparison with analogies in early Judaism.

Sixthly, it is desirable that an analytical approach, which involves detailed exegesis of the evidence, form- and source-critical considerations and the application of criteria to individual components of the tradition, should be combined with a synthetic approach, wherein the outcome of this detailed study is integrated with an overall perception of the identity and mission of the historical Jesus. Many previous studies have failed to do this, although there are exceptions (most notably Fiedler). Here I will endeavour to complement the largely analytical method, which focuses rather narrowly on a few episodes from the Gospels and which dominates the investigation, with a broader outlook on the career of Jesus as a healer and a prophet as I apply the so-called criterion of coherence to the primary material.

Sources and method

The nature and relationships of the sources

With the exception of Flavius Josephus' one or two brief mentions of Jesus, the entire corpus of primary sources of knowledge about the historical Jesus derives from primitive Christian writers. The lack of significant evidence from a perspective neutral or less sympathetic to Jesus, which could be used to countercheck the testimony of those who hailed Jesus as the risen Lord, necessitates the careful identification of criteria for sifting the sources. Later in this chapter, I will return to the question of criteria, but first of all the sources themselves will be briefly presented.

The genuine letters of Paul contain some basic information about Jesus and appeal to some sayings of the Lord, but none of this material pertains directly to the question of whether Jesus forgave sins. By contrast, in view of the possibility that the Letter of James may allude to a synoptic tradition connecting Jesus with forgiveness, it is noteworthy that there are now a good number of scholars who see in this letter an early Palestinian composition, which possibly even stems from James himself.[60] Currently there is also an interest in points of contact between this

---

[60] L. T. Johnson, *The Letter of James: A New Translation with Introduction and Commentary*, AB 37A (New York: Doubleday, 1995), pp. 108–21; R. Bauckham, *James: Wisdom of James, Disciple of Jesus the Sage* (London/New York: Routledge, 1999), pp. 11–25; S. Byrskog, *Story as History – History as Story: The Gospel Tradition in the Context of Ancient Oral History*, WUNT 123 (Tübingen: Mohr Siebeck, 2000), pp. 167–71.

letter and the synoptic-sayings material, to which it apparently alludes. Most would agree that the author did not employ any of the extant Gospels as a source of Jesus sayings, but whether or not he represents an entirely independent stream of tradition remains a disputed matter.[61] If indeed there is some connection between this letter and the teaching of the historical James, this makes the Letter of James an important witness to the historical Jesus. Unfortunately, the author never quotes Jesus explicitly, not even when he offers the most striking parallel to a synoptic saying (Jas 5.12 = Matt 5.34–7). Other allusions to sayings of Jesus can only be detected if we are already familiar with the sayings from other sources. This fact reduces the value of James as a source.

As in most historical Jesus research, the synoptic Gospels will be the primary sources on which the investigation is based. Mark's priority over Matthew and Luke is, on reasonable grounds, accepted by a large majority of scholars.[62] Throughout this study I will also presuppose the existence of Q,[63] adopting the convenient practice of referring to Q by chapter and verse in Luke (e.g. Q 6.20b indicates Luke 6.20b = Matt 5.3). Matthew and Luke constitute independent sources only in cases where the material cannot be derived from Mark or Q; even in these instances, one must be careful to distinguish redaction from tradition. My use of the designations M and L for the special material in Matthew and Luke, respectively, does not imply that I view this material as necessarily having been drawn from two specific documents, although the arguments for an actual L-source may be stronger than in the case of M.[64]

The use of John and *Thomas* for historical reconstruction is complicated by the unresolved questions concerning the relationship of these Gospels to the synoptics. Some of the narrative material in John may represent traditions independent of the synoptic Gospels.[65] At times, the

[61] See P. J. Hartin, *James and the Q Sayings of Jesus*, JSNTS 47 (Sheffield: JSOT Press, 1991), pp. 173–92; W. H. Wachob and L. T. Johnson, 'The Sayings of Jesus in the Letter of James', in B. Chilton and C. A. Evans (eds.), *Authenticating the Words of Jesus*, NTTS 28:1 (Leiden: Brill, 1999), pp. 43–50 (p. 438).

[62] See P. M. Head, *Christology and the Synoptic Problem: An Argument for Markan Priority*, SNTSMS 94 (Cambridge University Press, 1997); M. Goodacre, *The Case against Q: Studies in Markan Priority and the Synoptic Problem* (Harrisburg, PA: Trinity, 2002), pp. 19–45.

[63] See D. R. Catchpole, *The Quest for Q* (Edinburgh: T & T Clark, 1993); D. Burkett, *Rethinking the Gospel Sources*, vol. II: *The Unity and Plurality of Q*, SBLECL 1 (Atlanta: Society of Biblical Literature, 2009).

[64] K. Paffenroth, *The Story of Jesus according to L*, JSNTS 147 (Sheffield Academic Press, 1997).

[65] J. D. G. Dunn, 'John and the Oral Gospel Tradition', in H. Wansbrough (ed.), *Jesus and the Oral Gospel Tradition*, JSNTS 64 (Sheffield: JSOT Press, 1991), pp. 351–79.

Johannine traditions may even be historically more accurate than the synoptic ones.[66] As far as *Thomas* is concerned, not only the Coptic version recovered at Nag Hammadi but even the earlier Greek fragments from Oxyrhynchus appear to contain a text that partially reflects synoptic redaction.[67] On some occasions, however, there are indications that *Thomas* reflects an earlier form of sayings than the synoptic Gospels.[68] Accordingly, we cannot dismiss either John or *Thomas* entirely as sources of knowledge about the historical Jesus, but the strong theological tendencies of both writings must constantly be taken into account.

The remaining primitive Christian writings that purport to give information about the earthly Jesus can, generally speaking, contribute to historical Jesus research only to a very limited extent.[69] Some of these writings are fragmentarily preserved (*Oxyrhynchus 1224 Gospel*; *Egerton Gospel*); others offer very scant information about Jesus (Hebrews); still others may be dependent on the sources already mentioned (*Didache*); and to some of them, two or all three of these limitations are pertinent (*Gospel of Peter*; *Oxyrhynchus 840 Gospel*; some of the Apostolic Fathers). This is not to say that they are necessarily without value – only that they must be used with much caution, and that no argument should be overly dependent on any of them.

Criteria for evaluating the sources

The choice of criteria for authenticity

To distinguish between authentic and inauthentic elements in the sources is one of the prime objectives of all historical Jesus research. In principle, this process of evaluation can take either of two methodological points of departure. The first alternative is to set out from a plausible general picture of the historical Jesus and then to examine what sense individual traditions make within this picture. Such a method is advocated by N. T. Wright, Dale Allison and others.[70] The second alternative is to begin with

---

[66] P. N. Anderson, *The Fourth Gospel and the Quest for Jesus: Modern Foundations Reconsidered*, LNTS 321 (New York: T & T Clark, 2006), pp. 154–73.

[67] C. Tuckett, 'Thomas and the Synoptics', *NovT* 30 (1988), 132–57.

[68] S. J. Patterson, *The Gospel of Thomas and Jesus* (Sonoma, CA : Polebridge, 1993), pp. 18–73; Theissen and Merz, *Der historische Jesus*, 53.

[69] J. H. Charlesworth and C. A. Evans, 'Jesus in the Agrapha and Apocryphal Gospels', in B. Chilton and C. A. Evans (eds.), *Studying the Historical Jesus: Evaluations of the State of Current Research*, NTTS 19 (Leiden: Brill, 1994), pp. 479–533.

[70] N. T. Wright, *Christian Origins and the Question of God*, vol. I: *The New Testament and the People of God* (London: SPCK, 1992) and vol. II: *Jesus and the Victory of*

the analysis and authentication of singular components of the tradition, and then to reconstruct the historical Jesus from those components that have passed the criteria for authenticity. This procedure was dominant in twentieth-century scholarship, and it comes to its fullest expression in John Meier's yet unfinished *magnum opus*.[71] While both approaches can be regarded as legitimate and helpful, the latter method appears to be the more promising for the purposes of the present study, the scope of which is a limited aspect of Jesus' mission. This study will not, therefore, begin from an overall hypothesis of the historical Jesus, but from the specific items in the source material that speak of Jesus and forgiveness. These items will be scrutinized by traditional exegetical procedures and by the application of the criteria for authenticity, which will be laid out below, in order to determine to what extent they provide 'data' for the reconstruction of the historical Jesus. Towards the end of the study, these 'data' will be seen in relation to broader reconstructions of Jesus. Hopefully, this procedure will not only take seriously the criticism of an all too isolated criteria-oriented approach, but also illustrate the nature of fruitful scholarship in this area, namely the constant interplay between broad-ranging studies of Jesus and more narrowly focused investigations.

A recent study has suggested a reformulation of the criteria for authenticity conventionally employed in historical Jesus research. In their detailed treatment of the methodological question, Gerd Theissen and Dagmar Winter do not abolish these criteria, but revise them and integrate them into a unifying 'criterion of historical plausibility'.[72] Taking their point of departure in the criticism of the criterion of dissimilarity, which in their view overemphasizes the distinctiveness of Jesus, they outline the criterion of historical plausibility as consisting of two pairs of subcriteria: contextual plausibility and plausibility of effects. In effect, the latter comprises variants of the traditional criteria of dissimilarity (labelled Opposition to Traditional Bias and applied only to discontinuity with Christianity) and multiple attestation (labelled Coherence of Sources and subdivided into three types). Contextual plausibility consists

God (London: SPCK, 1997); D. C. Allison, *Jesus of Nazareth: Millenarian Prophet* (Minneapolis: Fortress, 1998).

[71] J. P. Meier, *A Marginal Jew: Rethinking the Historical Jesus*, A[Y]BRL, 4 vols. (New York: Doubleday, 1991–2001; New Haven/London: Yale University Press, 2009).

[72] G. Theissen and D. Winter, *Die Kriterienfrage in der Jesusforschung: Vom Differenzkriterium zum Plausibilitätskriterium*, NTOA 34 (Göttingen: Vandenhoeck & Ruprecht, 1997), pp. 175–232; see Theissen and Merz, *Der historische Jesus*, pp. 117–20. The English terminology has been adopted from the English translation: G. Theissen and D. Winter, *The Quest for the Plausible Jesus: The Question of Criteria*, transl. M. E. Boring (London: Westminster John Knox, 2002).

of Contextual Appropriateness (features that correspond to Jesus' first-century Jewish context) and Contextual Distinctiveness (features distinctive of Jesus within the historical context).[73] Items in the gospel tradition that meet both these pairs of subcriteria are plausibly derived from the historical Jesus. Yet Theissen and Winter also point out that the process of assessing the historicity of individual items is more complex than is sometimes recognized: historical Jesus research is not simply about dividing the tradition into 'authentic' and 'inauthentic' components, but should also provide historically credible explanations for the origin of the extant tradition.[74] In other words, when the derivation of a component from the historical Jesus is dismissed, it is necessary to argue in favour of some other and more likely derivation.

The critique of Theissen and Winter has been largely positive. Some reviewers have sensed, however, that their proposed criterion of historical plausibility is too blunt to be really useful. This applies primarily to the concept of contextual plausibility, which appears to be broad enough to accommodate, not only traditions derived from the historical Jesus, but also items that may have originated from primitive Christians familiar with first-century Galilee.[75] Tom Holmén observes that while Theissen and Winter are not entirely clear on the relationship between the two pairs of subcriteria, contextual plausibility cannot demonstrate by itself the historicity of an item that has not previously passed the test of plausibility of effects. Holmén designates this as the 'nexus' between the two pairs of subcriteria, which means that the test of contextual plausibility is subordinate to, and dependent on, the test of plausibility of effects. The traditional criteria of dissimilarity to Christianity and multiple attestation are therefore still decisive in the procedure of assessment.[76]

As a matter of fact, some notion of dissimilarity between Jesus and primitive Christianity seems to be integral to all historical Jesus research, or else the distinction between the 'historical Jesus' on the one hand and the 'Jesus of faith' or 'Jesus of the Gospels' on the other would be rendered meaningless. This is not to say that the presence of dissimilarities should be allowed to eclipse the arguably dominant flow of

---

[73] Theissen and Winter, *Die Kriterienfrage in der Jesusforschung*, pp. 176–91.

[74] *Ibid.*, pp. 208–9. A similar request had already been made by M. D. Hooker, 'Christology and Methodology', *NTS* 17 (1970–1), 480–8 (486–7).

[75] C. A. Evans, Review of Theissen and Winter, *Die Kriterienfrage in der Jesusforschung*, *JBL* 118 (1999), 551–3 (552); D. C. Allison, Review of Theissen and Winter, *The Quest for the Plausible Jesus*, *Int* 58 (2004), 88.

[76] T. Holmén, Review of Theissen and Winter, *The Quest for the Plausible Jesus*, *JTS* 55 (2004), 216–28.

continuity between the historical Jesus and primitive Christianity; not even Käsemann's classic formulation of the criterion of double dissimilarity suggested a complete lack of continuity.[77] On the other hand, Käsemann did suggest that the points of dissimilarity deserve more attention than the points of similarity. From the viewpoint of scientific historiography, this is an entirely gratuitous position, and one of the most valuable merits of Theissen and Winter's investigation is to have demonstrated the theological bias underlying it. A sound response to their study is, therefore, not to do away with dissimilarity as an authenticating criterion, but to assign it to a more modest and appropriate place alongside the other criteria.[78]

Since there is no essential disagreement between the method employed by most contemporary scholars who work with the criteria and the fundamental insights of Theissen and Winter's study, one might, according to Holmén, profit from the latter while keeping the traditional terminology of the criteria for historicity. The present study will follow this approach. While the conventional terminology will be retained, efforts will be made both to place the traditions derived from Jesus within a plausible historical context and to provide an explanation for the accretion of secondary elements.

A hierarchy of criteria

The set of criteria to be presented here draws on recent development in the criteriological approach to the authentication of material ascribed to Jesus.[79] Dennis Polkow's review of the criteria constituted a step forward in methodology, since it both fused nominally but not substantially different variants into a few major criteria and organized these into a hierarchical catalogue.[80] This approach will be taken even further here. Both Polkow's theoretically valid, although not always practicable, 'preliminary criteria' (which discount redaction and tradition respectively), and his 'secondary criteria' (which cannot, by themselves, verify the historicity of an item) will be excluded from consideration. Only what Polkow would term 'primary criteria' will be listed here (Table 1). The list is

---

[77] E. Käsemann, 'Das Problem des historischen Jesus', *ZTK* 51 (1954), 125–53 (144).

[78] Holmén, Review of Theissen and Winter, *The Quest for the Plausible Jesus*, 225–6.

[79] See T. Holmén, 'Authenticity Criteria', in C. A. Evans (ed.), *Encyclopedia of the Historical Jesus* (London: Routledge, 2008), pp. 43–54, and the literature cited therein.

[80] D. Polkow, 'Method and Criteria for Historical Jesus Research', *SBLSP* 26 (1987), 336–56.

Table 1 *A hierarchy of the criteria for authenticity*

	Positive criteria		Negative criteria
Independent first order	Embarrassment	Multiple attestation	Implausibility
Independent second order	Discontinuity		
Dependent	Coherence		Incoherence

prompted by the observation that the primary criteria are not all equal in autonomy and potential.

Positive criteria can be employed to establish that an item derives from the historical Jesus; negative criteria are used to determine that it does not. With the exception of the criteria of coherence and incoherence, a positive criterion cannot be reversed into a negative or vice versa. Each of the criteria functions on its own when applied to a specific item; put differently, it suffices that an item meets one of the criteria for that item to be regarded as (un)historical. A distinction is made, however, between dependent criteria, where judgement is reliant on a previously ascertained record of historical sayings, actions or events, and independent criteria, which can be applied separately from such an inventory. A further distinction is made between independent criteria of the first and second orders respectively, where the latter category comprises criteria – in reality, only the criterion of discontinuity – founded on argumentation from silence, while the criteria of the former category are based on reasoning from positive evidence. This will be clarified further below.

The hierarchical ordering of criteria expresses a conviction that they do not all establish historicity or the lack thereof with the same degree of certainty. Three criteria – embarrassment, multiple attestation and implausibility – are the most secure tools for assessing individual items of the tradition. A middle position is taken by the criterion of discontinuity, while the criteria of coherence and incoherence are the least reliable. It should be noted that it is their general trustworthiness that merits their inclusion among the criteria to be employed here.

Positive criteria

Embarrassment. Although the criteria of embarrassment and discontinuity are often taken together as one criterion of dissimilarity, there is reason to follow Meier in keeping them apart. While the criterion of discontinuity is, as we shall see, essentially an argument from silence, the criterion of embarrassment takes into account positive evidence of primitive Christian beliefs and is therefore a stronger criterion. Drawing on Meier, it can be articulated in the following way: Those 'actions or sayings of Jesus that would have embarrassed or created difficulty for the early Church' should be attributed to the historical Jesus.[81] The underlying logic is that Christians would not have invented traditions that they themselves found embarrassing.

A number of caveats should be mentioned. Firstly, only in a few cases does the embarrassment about gospel traditions manifest itself unambiguously in the sources. Secondly, from the fact that items authenticated by this criterion have an unusually strong claim to historicity, it is not permissible to conclude that these items are necessarily the most important for the reconstruction of Jesus' person and ministry. Thirdly, as stated above, this criterion cannot be reversed into a negative one. If an item seems to fit Christian interests by elevating Jesus, no verdict on its historicity can be made on these grounds.

Multiple attestation. According to this criterion, items are likely to be historical if attested in two or more sources, between which there is no literary dependence.[82] A variant of the criterion asserts that themes attested in different forms (e.g. parable and apophthegm) are to be judged historical.[83] By appreciating those motifs which evidently made a major impact on various quarters of primitive Christianity, and which therefore are likely to come from the historical Jesus, this criterion is a welcome balancing factor vis-à-vis the criteria of embarrassment and discontinuity.

While apparently the most widely accepted criterion for historicity, the criterion of multiple attestation is far from uncontroversial. First of all, its practical use is necessarily influenced by preliminary judgements about the relationships between the sources; for example, synoptic hypotheses determine whether or not the Q material can be treated as a source of its own. Secondly, all that this criterion can actually prove is that multiply attested items predate the literary sources in which they

---

[81] Meier, *A Marginal Jew*, vol. I, p. 168. See the earlier work by O. Schmiedel, *Die Hauptprobleme der Leben-Jesu-Forschung*, 2nd edn (Tübingen: Mohr Siebeck, 1906), pp. 46–8.

[82] F. C. Burkitt, *The Gospel History and Its Transmission*, 3rd edn (Edinburgh: T & T Clark, 1911), pp. 147–68.

[83] C. H. Dodd, *History and the Gospel* (London: Nisbeth, 1938), pp. 91–103.

are now found.[84] Thirdly, the common bias of all extant sources – with the possible exception of Josephus – was also shared by the transmitters of gospel traditions. Multiple attestation is, therefore, not tantamount to agreement between very different perspectives. Fourthly, it is almost impossible to imagine two entirely separate chains of transmission that have both led from the historical event to the fixation of tradition in literary documents.[85] It is nevertheless likely that a tradition which has spread early and widely enough to be included in two or more sources will represent the earliest available memories of Jesus, rather than originate from some primitive Christians, whose names we do not know in spite of the enormous influence they are assumed to have exerted.

Caution is required especially when attestation in different forms is used as a criterion. For example, the attestation of Jesus' healings both in sayings and in narrative material can only demonstrate the historicity of his career as a healer in general, not that of specific healings or sayings. Appeal to attestation in multiple forms to establish historicity more narrowly than in general themes is really tantamount to an appeal to the criterion of coherence, which is also a valid criterion, although a weaker one.

Finally, the criterion of multiple attestation must not be reversed into a negative criterion. In other words, the historicity of an item cannot be rejected simply on the ground that it is singularly attested.

Discontinuity. In this study, the criterion of discontinuity is taken to mean that items that cannot be derived from primitive Christianity – thereby exhibiting an amount of discontinuity between the historical Jesus and Christianity – are likely to be derived from Jesus himself. Together with the criterion of embarrassment, it thus broadly corresponds to what has frequently been called the criterion of dissimilarity. In recent years, an intense discussion of this criterion has resulted in its modification, restriction and a more appropriate location among the criteria for historicity.

Firstly, the formerly pervasive notion of *double* dissimilarity is being abandoned in current historical Jesus research. This form of the criterion presupposed that what can be derived neither from the Judaism of Jesus' day nor from primitive Christianity must come from Jesus.[86] However, as Holmén has convincingly argued, whether an item agrees

---

[84] E. Eve, 'Meier, Miracle and Multiple Attestation', *JSHJ* 3 (2005), 23–45 (29–42).

[85] Theissen and Winter, *Die Kriterienfrage in der Jesusforschung*, pp. 246–7.

[86] See, e.g., N. Perrin, *Rediscovering the Teaching of Jesus* (London: SCM, 1967), pp. 39–43. For further references, see Theissen and Winter, *Die Kriterienfrage in der Jesusforschung*, pp. 270–316.

or disagrees with conceptions known to have existed elsewhere in first-century Judaism is irrelevant for determining its derivation from Jesus. On the one hand, if an item is dissimilar to Christian interests but still preserved within the tradition, it has a claim to derivation from the historical Jesus, regardless of its resemblance to, or difference from, other early Jewish notions. On the other hand, if an item stands in tension with first-century Judaism but not with primitive Christianity, it could be derived from Christianity just as well as from the historical Jesus.[87] As a consequence, only discontinuity between gospel tradition and the emphases of primitive Christianity will here be taken as an indication of historicity.

Secondly, the tentative nature of all conclusions made with the help of this criterion should be kept in mind. It is essentially an argument from silence: since something is not known to have been the concern of Christians, it must have originated elsewhere. But we do not know about all the concerns of all primitive Christians.[88] An improved knowledge of primitive Christianity could alter the picture and invalidate the use of the criterion of discontinuity for the affirmation of the historicity of specific items. This preliminary character of the criterion of discontinuity makes it weaker than the criterion of embarrassment.

Thirdly, as Robert Stein has pointed out, in establishing the entity of 'early Christian theology' for the purpose of detecting discontinuity between the historical Jesus and Christianity, all material attributed to Jesus and not demonstrably secondary should be excluded. This is necessary in order to avoid a form of circular reasoning, according to which frequent attestation of an item in the Gospels would per se eliminate the possibility of discontinuity.[89] When such a route is taken, the result is a fundamental conflict between the criterion of multiple attestation and that of discontinuity.[90]

---

[87] T. Holmén, 'Doubts about Double Dissimilarity: Restructuring the Main Criterion of Jesus-of-History Research', in Chilton and Evans (eds.), *Authenticating the Words of Jesus*, pp. 47–80. Holmén builds on insights from B. F. Meyer, *The Aims of Jesus* (London: SCM, 1979), p. 86. The objections made to Holmén's argument by H. W. Shin, *Textual Criticism and the Synoptic Problem in Historical Jesus Research: The Search for Valid Criteria*, CBET 36 (Leuven: Peeters, 2004), p. 172, and Meier, *A Marginal Jew*, vol. IV, p. 174 n. 125, are invalid.

[88] Hooker, 'Christology and Methodology', 482.

[89] R. H. Stein, 'The "Criteria" for Authenticity' in R. T. France and D. Wenham (eds.) *Gospel Perspectives: Studies of History and Tradition in the Four Gospels*, vol. I (Sheffield: JSOT Press, 1980), pp. 225–63 (p. 245). For a more recent and fuller treatment, see T. Holmén, 'Knowing about Q and Knowing about Jesus: Mutually Exclusive Undertakings?' in A. Lindemann (ed.), *The Sayings Source Q and the Historical Jesus*, BETL 158 (Leuven: Peeters, 2001), pp. 497–514.

[90] Cf. Meier, *A Marginal Jew*, vol. IV, p. 174 n. 125.

Fourthly, one must refrain from reversing this criterion into a negative criterion of continuity or similarity. That an item is similar to Christian beliefs, or even appears to fit them perfectly well, does not rule out the possibility that it originated with the historical Jesus, and a reconstruction of Jesus made up exclusively of elements that differ from primitive Christianity would, as many scholars have pointed out, be seriously distorted.

Coherence. The criterion of coherence applies when an item positively coheres with other material already judged to be historical by the application of some other criterion. It is therefore a 'dependent criterion'. The criterion shares two problematic aspects with its negative counterpart (incoherence), namely, that these criteria seem to work on the basis of two presuppositions: firstly, that the historical Jesus always acted and spoke coherently, and secondly, that it is possible to agree on what would be perceived as coherent and incoherent behaviour in first-century Galilee or Judea. These two objections are usually raised against the criterion of incoherence and they will therefore be dealt with below, but they are equally applicable to the criterion of coherence. In addition, the criterion of coherence is subject to another point of criticism. If, as was obviously the case, primitive Christians elaborated on items that do stem from the historical Jesus, and even attributed their own creations secondarily to Jesus, one would expect that they imitated the historical Jesus tradition with regard to both form and content. In other words, such secondary material would frequently – though not necessarily always – be fully coherent with historical items and thus, by the criterion of coherence, be erroneously judged historical.[91] There seems to be no way of eliminating this risk. Coherence is therefore a comparatively weak indicator of historicity, which ought to be cautiously applied.

The requirement that items should cohere *positively* with other historical material is important, since it restricts the criterion from being applied too broadly and vaguely. A positively coherent item exhibits some distinctive trait(s) in common with the previously authenticated material.[92] Thus, Mark 2.17 is judged historical because it coheres in its distinct theme of 'Jesus consorting with sinners' with Q 7.34, the historicity of which can be argued by the criterion of embarrassment. It is the lack of such positive and distinctive coherence that motivates the dismissal of the proposed criterion of 'historical coherence', 'historical

[91] H. K. Nielsen, 'Kriterien zur Bestimmung authentischer Jesusworte', *SNTU* 4 (1979), 5–26 (13–14).
[92] Holmén, 'Authenticity Criteria', p. 50.

intelligibility' or 'rejection and execution' from the criteria employed in the present study. While it is permissible to demand that each overall portrayal of the historical Jesus should account for his violent death, it is inadvisable to turn this general principle into a criterion among others to be applied to specific items.[93] To do so could easily result in the mistaken assessment that all polemical sayings and conflict episodes are rooted in the life of Jesus simply by virtue of their general 'coherence' with the theme of rejection.[94]

As already mentioned, the criterion of coherence can be reversed into a negative criterion of incoherence. In view of the above, this is not to say that every item can be placed in one or other of these categories.[95] That something is not positively coherent does not make it incoherent; and, conversely, that something is not incoherent does not make it coherent.

Negative criteria

Implausibility. Being the only independent negative criterion, the criterion of implausibility assesses as unhistorical features which contradict known facts about the conditions of first-century Palestine. Such contradiction arises whenever an item appears to presuppose circumstances that were extant only in another geographical locale or in a period subsequent to Jesus' death. It would also apply when characters are depicted as acting or speaking in a way that is inconceivable on the grounds of our knowledge of the historical conditions.[96]

An objection to this criterion is that our knowledge of first-century Palestine is incomplete and may be subject to revision.[97] For example, the discovery of the Qumran writings has altered the scholarly attitude about what is plausible within Palestinian Judaism at the turn of the era on a number of points, and the clear-cut division between Palestinian and Hellenistic conditions that Bultmann presupposed can no longer be taken for granted.

Several attempts have been made to reverse this criterion into a positive one. A criterion of plausibility would affirm the historicity of those

---

[93] See Meier, *A Marginal Jew*, vol. I, pp. 177, 194–5 n. 66.

[94] For an example of this, see Shin, *Textual Criticism*, pp. 301–4.

[95] Holmén, 'Authenticity Criteria', p. 52.

[96] M. E. Boring, 'The Historical-Critical Method's "Criteria of Authenticity": The Beatitudes in Q and Thomas as a Test Case', *Semeia* 44 (1988), 9–44 (15–16).

[97] H. Schürmann, 'Kritische Jesuserkenntnis. Zur kritischen Handhabung des "Unähnlichkeitskriteriums"', in H. Schürmann, *Jesus: Gestalt und Geheimnis*, ed. by K. Scholtissek (Paderborn: Bonifatius, 1994), pp. 420–34 (p. 427).

items which fit known conditions of first-century Palestine. The positive criteria of Aramaic language,[98] Greek language[99] and Palestinian environment[100] are all variants of the criterion of plausibility. While plausibility is a general condition to be met in all historical research, it cannot function as a criterion by which to authenticate individual components of the tradition. Not only Jesus but also the earliest transmitters and elaborators of the tradition were familiar with Palestinian conditions and would in most cases have expanded the tradition with items that are realistic within that setting.[101]

Incoherence. This negative counterpart of the criterion of coherence applies when an item conflicts with other material already authenticated by positive criteria. As mentioned above, the criterion of incoherence faces two main objections.

Firstly, inconsistency is a general characteristic of human beings. Jack Sanders has even made a case for viewing inconsistency and randomness as strategies purposefully adopted by Jesus in his capacity as founder and leader of a new religious movement. Unpredictability increases charismatic authority, and scholars who look for a coherent Jesus look in vain.[102] These points are valid to some extent, but may serve above all to emphasize the distinction between the 'real Jesus' and the 'historical Jesus'.[103] While the former certainly was on occasion inconsistent in what he did and said, the latter will always be smoothed out into a coherent whole. If we do not presuppose that the historical Jesus should by and large be coherent, our method will dissolve; for a genuinely incoherent historical Jesus can accommodate every component of the tradition and every scholarly proposal.

Secondly, the criterion presupposes both the possibility of some scholarly consensus about what constitutes incoherence and the intersection of this consensus with first-century Jewish thinking. A prime example of

---

[98] J. Jeremias, *Neutestamentliche Theologie: Erster Teil: Die Verkündigung Jesu* (Gütersloh: Mohn, 1971), pp. 14–45.

[99] S. E. Porter, *The Criteria for Authenticity in Historical-Jesus Research: Previous Discussion and New Proposals*, JSNTS 191 (Sheffield Academic Press, 2000), pp. 126–64; S. E. Porter, 'Luke 17.11–19 and the Criteria for Authenticity Revisited', *JSHJ* 1 (2003), 201–24; S. E. Porter, 'The Criterion of Greek Language and Its Context: A Further Response', *JSHJ* 4 (2006), 69–74.

[100] Stein, 'The "Criteria" for Authenticity', pp. 236–8.

[101] Meier, *A Marginal Jew*, vol. I, pp. 178–80.

[102] J. T. Sanders, 'The Criterion of Coherence and the Randomness of Charisma: Poring through Some Aporias in the Jesus Tradition', *NTS* 44 (1998), 1–25. For a critical appraisal, see B. Holmberg, 'Karisma som sociologisk förklaringsmodell i tolkningen av Jesus', *SEÅ* 67 (2002), 61–77 (72–3).

[103] See Meier, *A Marginal Jew*, vol. I, pp. 21–40.

disagreement among scholars concerning incoherence is the question of whether or not the conceptions of God's kingdom as present and future are mutually exclusive. Some have found them to be in outright opposition to each other and they have argued accordingly that both cannot be derived from the historical Jesus. Others point to Paul as evidence that at least some first-century Jews could subscribe to two temporal dimensions of the kingdom simultaneously without sensing any inconsistency.

The difficulties pertaining to the criterion of incoherence should not be downplayed. Yet, as long as coherence is recognized as a valid positive criterion, it appears obligatory to include incoherence among the negative criteria. For both criteria assume that Jesus' behaviour was by and large consistent. If it is argued that Jesus was no more consistent than any other human being, or even programmatically inconsistent, this diminishes the corroborative value of both criteria. Similarly, if incoherence is, to some extent, in the eye of the beholder, and if it is also both socially and culturally conditioned, so too is coherence. Therefore, to adhere only to one of these criteria is methodologically illicit.[104]

A model for explaining inauthentic elements in the sources

As noted above, the current study will not content itself with identifying secondary elements in the sources and their underlying traditions, but also aims at providing a plausible explanation of how such accretions originated. This requires consideration of different models for understanding the transmission and growth of gospel tradition. I will first of all bring attention to the influential theories bound up with older form criticism and then propose an alternative model, one that to the best of my knowledge has not been employed consistently in combination with the criteria-oriented approach in previous historical Jesus studies.

An older form-critical model

Bultmann stands as the inaugurator of a paradigm that views the gospel tradition as evolving in an uncontrolled fashion, ever open to being changed, enlarged and abbreviated by an anonymous mass of primitive Christians. Viewing the synoptic Gospels primarily as expressions of the life of the community, rather than as reminiscences of the life of Jesus, Bultmann repeatedly asserts that episodes about Jesus and sayings

---

[104] *Pace* Meier, *A Marginal Jew*, vol. I, p. 177, and Shin, *Textual Criticism*, pp. 190–5.

attributed to him were really formed to serve as vehicles for the Church's standpoints.[105] Largely along the same line of thinking, Theissen has offered a more precise delineation of the transmitters of gospel tradition and reflected on the phenomenon that some traditions are preserved while others are not. According to the early work of Theissen, it is unlikely that sayings of ethical purport will be transmitted further, unless the transmitters agree with their contents. He draws the conclusion that the radical sayings of Jesus were transmitted by itinerant radicals, and he thus goes further than Bultmann, even though the underlying principle is the same, namely that there is a close correspondence between the needs of the transmitters and the material transmitted.[106]

It has been a widely held conviction among form-critical scholars that additions to the tradition can be explained as the work of Christian prophets. According to Bultmann, the community would not have distinguished between the traditional sayings of the earthly Jesus and the oracles of the Spirit delivered by prophets, since in all these words it was the risen Lord who spoke. Prophetic oracles were therefore placed on the lips of Jesus in the Gospels.[107] The most fully argued case for the impact of primitive Christian prophetic oracles on the tradition has been presented by Eugene Boring. Like Bultmann and others, Boring advocates the view that some of the sayings of Jesus in the Gospels were originally isolated sayings of the risen Lord, delivered by Christian prophets. Only gradually would these oracles have been placed within a narrative framework, merged with sayings of the historical Jesus, and eventually integrated into the Gospel narratives so as to be perceived as sayings of the earthly Jesus. Boring does not argue that this accounts for the entire growth of tradition, since there were also non-prophetic additions. Neither does he claim that any prophetic oracle could indiscriminately have been accepted as a saying of Jesus, since the community would have exercised a controlling function by accepting and rejecting purported sayings of the Lord. Even so, in some instances oracles that militated against the tradition were accepted as genuine and authoritative sayings.[108] While this scenario is not altogether inconceivable, there are

---

[105] Bultmann, *Die Geschichte der synoptischen Tradition*, pp. 4–6 and *passim*.

[106] G. Theissen, 'Wanderradikalismus: Literatursoziologische Aspekte der Überlieferung von Worten Jesu im Urchristentum', *ZTK* 70 (1973), 245–71 (247–8). For criticism of the theory of *homeostasis* that underlies Theissen's reconstruction, see S. Byrskog, 'A New Perspective on the Jesus Tradition: Reflections on James D. G. Dunn's *Jesus Remembered*', *JSNT* 26 (2004), 459–71 (468–70).

[107] Bultmann, *Die Geschichte der synoptischen Tradition*, pp. 134–6.

[108] M. E. Boring, *Sayings of the Risen Jesus: Christian Prophecy in the Synoptic Tradition* (Cambridge University Press, 1982), pp. 67–9, 110, 210; M. E. Boring, *The*

elements in Boring's hypothesis that seem unverifiable, superfluous or even unlikely. Each of these points will now be considered in turn.

Firstly, it appears well-nigh impossible to identify those sayings which originated with Christian prophets, although Boring's criteria are more helpful than the purely form-critical procedure suggested by Käsemann.[109] Not accepting the formal characteristics of prophecy as a sufficient indication that a certain saying originated with a Christian prophet rather than with Jesus himself, Boring demands that in order to be considered a possible product of Christian prophecy, a saying should at once be detachable from its immediate narrative context and judged unhistorical on grounds other than only its prophetic form.[110] This is methodologically sound, but it can only establish a possibility. Sayings that meet Boring's criteria are possibly, but not necessarily, prophetic sayings of the risen Lord.

Secondly, at times the role of prophets in this reconstruction appears to be superfluous. As stated above, Boring holds that some expansion of the traditional material was carried out by teachers and scribes who were not prophets. At the same time he maintains that prophets 'also functioned as interpreters of the sayings of Jesus within the church, elaborating and modifying traditional sayings to express the word of the risen Lord more clearly to the present situation'.[111] It is not evident how this aspect of the prophetic function is thought to have differed from that of non-prophetic scribes. Boring's insistence that some elaborative work was performed by prophets seems to be founded on the notion that certain sayings attributed to the earthly Jesus would in fact have been perceived, for instance in the Q community, as sayings of the risen Lord speaking in the present.[112] This reasoning is circular and unnecessarily complex: some traditional sayings are held to have been modified so that they could be presented as sayings of the risen Jesus, and only then were they incorporated again into the Gospels as sayings of the earthly Jesus.

Continuing Voice of Jesus: Christian Prophecy and the Gospel Tradition (Louisville, KY: Westminster/John Knox, 1991), pp. 106–7, 132, 154, 251.

[109] E. Käsemann, 'Sätze heiligen Rechtes im Neuen Testament', *NTS* 1 (1955), 248–60.

[110] Boring, *The Continuing Voice of Jesus*, pp. 189–90.

[111] *Ibid.*, p. 154. The notion that 'charismatic exegesis' was characteristically done by prophets is questioned by D. E. Aune, *Prophecy in Early Christianity and the Ancient Mediterranean World* (Grand Rapids, MI: Eerdmans, 1983), pp. 339–46; C. Forbes, *Prophecy and Inspired Speech in Early Christianity and Its Hellenistic Environment*, WUNT 2:75 (Tübingen: Mohr Siebeck, 1995), pp. 229–37.

[112] Boring, *The Continuing Voice of Jesus*, pp. 231–2.

Thirdly, detailed analysis of synoptic material has revealed that in a number of places the evidence is unsupportive of, or even contradicting, Boring's hypothesis. The inconclusiveness of his argument in specific cases has been demonstrated.[113] Synoptic comparison of the expanded sayings material in Matthew and the pre-Matthean tradition demonstrates that the evangelist creatively crafted new sayings from elements already extant in the tradition, but this does not indicate either that Matthew took the liberty to form sayings that would deviate from, or contradict, the tradition that he had received, or that some of these sayings in fact originated with prophets.[114] The same case has been made for Luke, Mark and Q.[115] If these sources are representative of the development of gospel tradition even at the pre-literary stage, there is reason to doubt the validity of the prophetic model for understanding how the tradition was extended and modified.

A new rhetorical-critical model

Against the perception that the gospel tradition was open to constant modification to suit the needs of the earliest Christians, Birger Gerhardsson and others have remarked that the milieu in which the gospel tradition was transmitted, and the prominent place of teachers in primitive Christianity, should make us expect that the tradition has been handed over in accordance with more restrained and conservative principles.[116] Source-internal features confirm this expectation. When Paul occasionally refers to commands of 'the Lord', he quotes sayings known to us from the synoptic Gospels, and he is careful to distinguish them from his own opinions (1 Cor 7.10–13). The Gospels also include traditions that seem to contradict Christian practice and conviction (e.g. Matt

---

[113] Aune, *Prophecy in Early Christianity*, pp. 240–2.

[114] G. Stanton, 'Matthew as a Creative Interpreter of the Sayings of Jesus', in P. Stuhlmacher (ed.), *Das Evangelium und die Evangelien: Vorträge vom Tübinger Symposium 1982*, WUNT 28 (Tübingen: Mohr Siebeck, 1983), pp. 273–87; S. Byrskog, *Jesus the Only Teacher: Didactic Authority and Transmission in Ancient Israel, Ancient Judaism and the Matthean Community*, CBNTS 24 (Stockholm: Almqvist & Wiksell, 1994), pp. 350–60.

[115] E. Rau, *Jesus – Freund von Zöllnern und Sündern: Eine methodenkritische Untersuchung* (Stuttgart: Kohlhammer, 2000), pp. 50–9.

[116] B. Gerhardsson, *Memory and Manuscript: Oral Tradition and Written Transmission in Rabbinic Judaism and Early Christianity*, ASNU 22 (Uppsala: Almqvist & Wiksell, 1961); B. Gerhardsson, *The Gospel Tradition*, CBNTS 15 (Lund: Gleerup, 1986); R. Riesner, *Jesus als Lehrer: Eine Untersuchung zum Ursprung der Evangelien-Überlieferung*, WUNT 2:7, 3rd edn (Tübingen: Mohr Siebeck, 1988); S. Byrskog, 'The Transmission of the Jesus Tradition', in T. Holmén and S. E. Porter (eds.), *Handbook for the Study of the Historical Jesus*, 4 vols. (Leiden: Brill, 2011), vol. II, pp. 1465–94.

3.13–15; Mark 2.18–20; John 4.1–3). That such traditions were transmitted, despite their limited usefulness in the life of the churches, indicates that a purported origin with the earthly Jesus was sufficient grounds for the transmitters to preserve the tradition.

While it is evident that the process of transmission and adaptation of the Jesus tradition led to the addition of new material to the corpus of sayings, it is more reasonable to view this accretion as the result of a development – or an evolution – than to see it as the outcome of free creation. Recently, Samuel Byrskog has suggested that an important motivation for the development of the sayings tradition was rhetorical, and that the handbook patterns of chreia manipulation and elaboration can shed light on how the sayings of Jesus were expanded by the evangelists and in the gospel tradition.[117] As the present investigation will explore the possibility of using this model in order to reconstruct the prehistory of Mark 2.1–12, some introductory remarks on the chreia (χρεία) and apomnemoneuma (ἀπομνημόνευμα) in antiquity must now follow.

The chreia is a literary form, widely distributed throughout ancient Greek and Latin literature. In his first- or second-century *Progymnasmata*, Aelius Theon defines the chreia as 'a concise statement or deed, aptly attributed to some specific character or to what is analogous to a character' (201.17–19). It is closely related to the apomnemoneuma; actually, ancient textbooks sometimes claim that the chreia is a kind of apomnemoneuma.[118] However, they also frequently point out the distinction between proper apomnemoneumata and chreiai. According to Theon, this difference is twofold. First, the chreia 'is concise, but the apomnemoneuma is sometimes expanded'; secondly, the chreia 'is attributed to some character, but the apomnemoneuma is also remembered on its own'.[119] If a chreia is expanded according to the pattern prescribed by the textbooks, it will be turned into an apomnemoneuma, and, conversely, an apomnemoneuma may be compressed into a chreia proper.

---

[117] S. Byrskog, 'The Early Church as a Narrative Fellowship: An Exploratory Study of the Performance of the *Chreia*', *TTK* 78 (2007), 207–26; S. Byrskog, 'The Transmission of the Jesus Tradition: Old and New Insights', *EC* 1 (2010), 1–28. See the seminal study of B. L. Mack and V. K. Robbins, *Patterns of Persuasion in the Gospels* (Sonoma, CA: Polebridge, 1989).

[118] Hermogenes, *Prog.* 6.4; Aphthonius, *Prog.* 3.21; Vatican Grammarian, *De Chria* 1–2; PSI 1.85 4–7.

[119] Theon, *Prog.* 202.12–15. What is meant by the apomnemoneuma being remembered 'on its own' or 'for its own sake' (καθ' ἑαυτό) is not entirely clear; see R. F. Hock and E. N. O'Neil, *The Chreia in Ancient Rhetoric*, vol. I: *The* Progymnasmata, SBLTT 27 (Atlanta: Scholars, 1986), pp. 109–10 n. 5. Hermogenes, *Prog.* 6.15–17, and Nicolaus, *Prog.* 19.13–14; 26.1–8, mention length as the only trait distinguishing apomnemoneuma from chreia.

Later in this study (Chapter 6), I will discuss some evidence that gospel tradition was transmitted in the form of chreia, at least occasionally. While it cannot be demonstrated that the transmitters of gospel tradition consciously expanded the sayings of Jesus in accordance with a pattern represented by the rhetorical handbooks, this hypothesis nevertheless appears to be fully plausible. What we can infer about the literary and rhetorical abilities of first-century Christians at a general level allows us to think that the evangelists would have been familiar with the *Progymnasmata* and would thus have been capable of expanding chreiai. They were, as is now commonly recognized, able to compose biographies[120] and, as we shall see, the handling of chreiai was a skill of great value to ancient biographers. The sparse attestation of chreiai and apomnemoneumata in early Jewish literature indicates that any familiarity with these forms and the rhetorical exercises associated with them would have derived from Hellenistic schooling.[121] We can be fairly certain that Paul, one of the few transmitters of gospel tradition known to us by name, would have learnt how to copy, decline and elaborate chreiai as part of his education in the Hellenistic school. Whether or not this also applies to other transmitters, such as the Twelve, we do not know; but the Gospels do indeed contain what can be recognized as chreiai and apomnemoneumata, which largely correspond to what NT scholarship has usually termed 'apophthegmata' or 'pronouncement stories'. Chreiai proper are to be found only in Luke (6.4 D; 17.20; 19.45–6). Apomnemoneumata are more numerous: for example, the synoptic episode about the plucking of grains on a Sabbath (Mark 2.23–8 par.) has been analyzed as an expanded chreia.[122] Justin Martyr's designation of the Gospels as 'the apomnemoneumata of the apostles' – one of the earliest attempts at generic classification of these writings – may thus be quite to the point.[123]

---

[120] R. A. Burridge, *What Are the Gospels? A Comparison with Graeco-Roman Biography*, 2nd edn (Grand Rapids, MI: Eerdmans, 2004); D. Frickenschmidt, *Evangelium als Biographie: Die vier Evangelien im Rahmen antiker Erzählkunst*, TANZ 22 (Tübingen: Francke, 1997); M. Reiser, 'Die Stellung der Evangelien in der antiken Literaturgeschichte', *ZNW* 90 (1999), 1–27.

[121] C. Hezser, 'Die Verwendung der hellenistischen Gattung Chrie im frühen Christentum und Judentum', *JSJ* 27 (1996), 371–439 (374).

[122] R. Parrott, 'Conflict and Rhetoric in Mark 2:23–28', *Semeia* 64 (1994), 139–70.

[123] See L. Alexander, 'Memory and Tradition in the Hellenistic Schools', in W. H. Kelber and S. Byrskog (eds.), *Jesus in Memory: Traditions in Oral and Scribal Perspectives* (Waco, TX: Baylor University Press, 2009), pp. 113–53; S. Byrskog, 'From Memory to Memoirs: Tracing the Background of a Literary Genre', in M. Zetterholm and S. Byrskog (eds.), *The Making of Christianity: Conflicts, Contacts and Constructions*, CBNTS (Winona Lake, IN: Eisenbrauns, in press).

The place of the new model in the present study

In the present study, the rhetorical model as outlined above will be applied to one of the synoptic episodes which relates how Jesus forgives sins (Mark 2.1–12). Diachronic analysis of chreiai and apomnemoneumata requires a considerable amount of caution. Theoretically, if it were possible to establish with certainty that the synoptic apomnemoneumata are indeed the product of chreia expansion, one might attempt to reverse the process known to us from the *Progymnasmata*, by identifying and removing the added elements. This would then leave us with the chreia proper in its simple, concise, 'original' form.[124] But while the rhetorical textbooks of antiquity focus on the expansion and elaboration of chreiai, Theon remarks that students should practise not only how to expand chreiai, but also how to compress them, that is, to reverse the procedure of expansion (210.5; 213.13–14). Thus the student could be presented with an apomnemoneuma and instructed to compress it into a chreia proper. We cannot exclude *a priori* the possibility that some of the synoptic pericopes were originally told as apomnemoneumata, in which case the compressed chreia form would be secondary, as indeed a comparison of synoptic passages sometimes indicates.[125] What we do have are, with a few exceptions, apomnemoneumata, and these may or may not have begun their career as chreiai proper.

Moreover, even if it could be demonstrated that the concise form of some synoptic chreia was indeed primary to its added elements, this would naturally be insufficient in order to claim that the saying or deed as depicted in the chreia proper was actually spoken or done by the historical Jesus. Ronald Hock has discussed the problems inherent in the use of chreiai as sources of historical information and has come to the conclusion that 'the burden of proof properly falls on those claiming historicity for any one chreia or for chreiai in general'. Not only were copyists at liberty to paraphrase the wording of a given chreia, but the same chreia could also be attributed to different characters and placed in varying circumstances.[126] This means that the insight that many Gospel episodes are actually chreiai or apomnemoneumata has not enhanced the likelihood that they originate from the historical Jesus. If rhetorical analysis cannot, by itself, prove Gospel material to be the result of expansion

---

[124] Cf. the tendency in Mack and Robbins, *Patterns of Persuasion*, pp. 65–6, 122–3, 200–8.

[125] See, e.g., Mark 11.15–17 = Luke 19.45–6; cf. Hock and O'Neil, *The Chreia*, pp. 40–1. See also Dibelius, *Die Formgeschichte des Evangeliums*, 2nd edn, pp. 149–64.

[126] Hock and O'Neil, *The Chreia*, pp. 42–6 (the quotation is from p. 46).

and thus unhistorical, it cannot prove that such material is historical either. In the present study, the function of rhetorical analysis will be restricted to explaining the formation of material already established as unhistorical by other criteria. Put differently, the order of procedure will be identical to that suggested by Boring: I will undertake the first sifting of the material with the aim of distinguishing between historical and unhistorical elements in the Gospel episodes by applying the criteria for authenticity already specified. Only after that will I make the attempt to account for the accretion of unhistorical elements. However, unlike Boring I regard the growth of tradition to have been influenced by the mechanics of disciplined progymnastic rhetoric rather than by charismatic prophetic creativity.

Outline of the study

The main body of the present study will be structured around the criteria for authenticity applicable to the components of gospel tradition dealing with Jesus and forgiveness, primarily Mark 2.1–12. The criterion of embarrassment does not appear to apply to these texts at all – the Gospels contain no trace of any attempts to downplay or to explain away the theme – and it will consequently be left out of further consideration.

Chapter 2 is intended as a discussion of the applicability of the criterion of multiple attestation to the forgiveness sayings in the Gospel. The nature of the relationship between the episodes in Matt 9.1–8, Mark 2.1–12 and Luke 5.17–26 will be pondered along with the possible connection of extra-synoptic texts to these episodes. The question of whether or not the forgiveness sayings in Luke 7.36–50 constitute an independent attestation will receive due attention. I will also discuss gospel traditions in which Jesus makes general statements about forgiveness, as well as sayings that have been interpreted as investing Jesus' disciples with an authority to forgive sins.

Chapter 3 will explore the potential gains in applying the criterion of discontinuity to some of the forgiveness sayings. Previous proposals that the theme in its entirety is derived either from the belief of primitive Christians that their risen and glorified Lord could forgive sins, or from the Church's own practice of forgiving sins, will be reassessed in the light of a comprehensive investigation of the topic of forgiveness in all extant Christian literature up to *c*. 135 CE.

Chapter 4 brings in the negative criterion of implausibility. From a study of the place of human mediation of forgiveness in early Judaism, I will discuss whether or not the controversy over forgiveness as depicted in Mark 2.6–10 par. is historically plausible in a first-century Galilean setting.

Chapter 5 aims at testing the coherence of the forgiveness sayings with a broader reconstruction of the activity of the historical Jesus as a healer and of his identity as a prophet. By relating Jesus' proclamation of forgiveness and the self-understanding that it expresses to overall reconstructions of his mission and identity, I mean to take seriously the call for interaction between analytic and synthetic approaches in historical Jesus research.

Chapter 6 takes its point of departure in the results yielded by the preceding chapters and seeks to explain the development of the earliest account of how Jesus forgave sins into the episode in Mark 2.1–12. At this point, progymnastic chreia elaboration will be brought in as a possible explanation for the accretion of secondary material.

Chapter 7 is the conclusion, in which I will summarize the results of the preceding chapters and extract some implications of these results for historical Jesus research.

2

FORGIVENESS IN THE GOSPEL TRADITION

The investigation will begin by setting out the primary evidence from the Gospels, and by identifying and excluding from further consideration any elements that stem from the evangelists' redactional activity, the word 'redaction' being used here in a sense that is more metaphorical than literal, that is, as a means of visualizing in literacy-focused terms quite complex processes and phenomena, which often operate according to principles of orality.[1] In this way, I hope to be able to clarify to what extent the notion of the earthly Jesus as someone who forgave sins is multiply attested in the tradition.

The concern will be with those texts which, directly as in Mark 2.1–12 par., or indirectly as in John 20.19–23, attribute or may attribute a forgiving activity to the earthly Jesus. 'Forgiving activity' is a deliberately vague expression, which draws attention to an important aspect of the criterion of multiple attestation that was mentioned in Chapter 1: what, exactly, are we expecting to find attested? If it is a general attitude of forgiveness in Jesus' mission, or an emphasis on the theme in his preaching, then 'forgiving activity' can be taken in a broad sense to include not only every mention of forgiveness in the sayings of Jesus, but also his table-fellowship with sinners, his parables and so on. If, on the other hand, our interest lies in determining the plausibility of Jesus claiming for himself an authority to forgive sins, then the criterion of multiple attestation is met only if multiple sources agree that Jesus did lay claim to such an authority. What is general cannot count as attestation for what is specific.

To keep this distinction clear, the evidence will be divided into three categories. First of all, I will deal with the Gospel episodes involving specific announcements of forgiveness, said to have been directed by Jesus to particular individuals, and with other material possibly related

---

[1] See J. D. G. Dunn, 'Altering the Default Setting: Re-Envisaging the Early Transmission of the Jesus Tradition', *NTS* 49 (2003), 139–75.

to these episodes. Secondly, attention will be turned to other forgiveness statements, in which Jesus announces the general possibility of and requirements for gaining God's forgiveness, either in the present or in the future. Thirdly, I come to the statements in which Jesus possibly commissions his disciples to forgive sins.

Specific announcements of forgiveness

The healing of a paralytic (Mark 2.1–12 par.)

It is natural to begin with an analysis of the three synoptic episodes in which Jesus makes his most overt claim that 'the Son of Man has authority to forgive sins on earth' (Matt 9.6/Mark 2.10/Luke 5.24). I will then move to John 5 in order to determine its relationship to the synoptic episodes, and, finally, the possibility that the Letter of James alludes to gospel tradition somehow related to the synoptic episodes will be considered.

The synoptic episodes

Mark 2.1–12. Standing at the beginning of the first Markan cycle of controversies (2.1–3.6), this episode presents us with the first encounter between Jesus and his adversaries in the Gospel. Their silent accusation of blasphemy foreshadows the high priest's charge against Jesus at his trial (14.64) and turns Mark 2.1–12 into a worthy opening of a ministry that will be characterized by conflict and opposition throughout.[2] It is also in this episode that Jesus refers to himself as the Son of Man for the first time in Mark's Gospel. The conflict revolves around authority (ἐξουσία), which is a characteristic earlier associated with Jesus but denied to his opponents (1.22, 27), and this contributes to the impression that this episode is essential to the unfolding of Mark's plot.

The widespread scholarly opinion that the episode stems from a pre-Markan source, which corresponds to (most of) what is now Mark 2.1–3.6, is plausible and will be discussed in Chapter 6 below. As we do not have access to the hypothesized source, it is imperative to take a minimalist approach to the identification of Markan redaction, in order not to run the risk of dispensing too briskly with elements that could after all turn out to be traditional and possibly historical.

---

[2] M. Hengel, 'Probleme des Markusevangeliums', in Stuhlmacher (ed.), *Das Evangelium und die Evangelien*, pp. 221–65 (pp. 230–1).

The episode takes place in a house in Capernaum. It cannot be determined whether the reference to Capernaum is itself redactional or whether it is derived from tradition.[3] However, both the adverbial qualifier 'again' and the remark that Jesus was 'at home' (2.1) may be taken as a link back to Jesus' latest sojourn in Capernaum and the house of Simon and Andrew (1.21–34).[4] Hence there is reason to believe that some of the elements in 2.1 derive from Markan redaction. Similarly, the vivid depiction of how many had gathered (συνήχθησαν) at the door (πρὸς τὴν θύραν, 2.2) is suggestive of the previous mention of the entire town being gathered at the door (ἐπισυνηγμένη πρὸς τὴν θύραν, 1.33), and the phrase 'he was speaking the word to them' (ἐλάλει αὐτοῖς τὸν λόγον, 2.2) is distinctly Markan (cf. 4.33; 8.32).[5] It cannot be demonstrated beyond reasonable doubt that any of the elements in 2.3–4, which narrates the arrival of the paralytic and his being lowered through the roof, derive from Mark's hand, although some expressions are quite typical of the Gospel and thus could be redactional.[6]

In 2.5 Jesus pronounces the first of two forgiveness sayings in this episode. The introductory 2.5a is likely to be traditional: elsewhere in Mark, the noun 'faith' (πίστις) occurs exclusively on Jesus' lips and in no case is it demonstrably redactional (4.40; 5.34; 10.52; 11.22), while the vocative and non-literal 'child' (τέκνον) to introduce a saying attributed to Jesus is only found here and in the parallel in Matthew.[7] In 2.5b, the reading 'are (being) forgiven' in the present tense (ἀφίενται) seems original, despite the fact that the perfect tense 'are forgiven' (ἀφέωνται) is supported by an impressive array of textual witnesses. Since the latter variant is universally attested in Luke 5.20, 23, and thus certainly original to Luke, it probably crept in from there and contaminated the textual traditions of both Mark and Matthew. The perfect may be regarded as more natural in Greek (John 20.23; 1 John 2.12), whereas the Markan present

[3] Bultmann, *Die Geschichte der synoptischen Tradition*, pp. 68–9. See also Chapter 6 below.

[4] J. Dewey, *Markan Public Debate: Literary Technique, Concentric Structure and Theology in Mark 2:1 to 3:6*, SBLDS 48 (Chico, CA: Scholars, 1980), p. 67.

[5] W. Weiss, *'Eine neue Lehre in Vollmacht': Die Streit- und Schulgespräche des Markus-Evangeliums*, BZNW 52 (Berlin/New York: de Gruyter, 1989), p. 128; D. Burkett, *Rethinking the Gospel Sources*, vol. I: *From Proto-Mark to Mark* (New York/London: T & T Clark, 2004), pp. 27–8.

[6] I. Maisch, *Die Heilung des Gelähmten*, SBS 52 (Stuttgart: KBW, 1971), pp. 16–20; J. Gnilka, 'Das Elend vor dem Menschensohn (Mk 2,1–12)', in R. Pesch and R. Schnackenburg (eds.), *Jesus und der Menschensohn*, FS A. Vögtle (Freiburg: Herder, 1975), pp. 196–209 (pp. 200–1).

[7] Cf. Mark 10.24 (τέκνα); John 13.33 (τεκνία).

form comes more easily as the reflection of an underlying Aramaic imperfect such as ישתבקון חטאיך.

A common reading of the phrasing 'your sins are (being) forgiven' construes it as a divine or theological passive, of which the implied agent is God.[8] As Hofius maintains, the implied agent could as well be Jesus himself, irrespective of whether the phrase is read in its present context, is assigned to a hypothetical original episode corresponding to 2.1–5, 11–12, or is taken in isolation. The strongest argument marshalled by Hofius is a number of Hebrew and Aramaic texts, in which similar formulae are used with clear reference to the human speakers themselves.[9] As Hofius points out, this renders the passive form ambiguous: its implied agent could be either God or Jesus himself.

It is not Jesus but his adversaries who indicate how the passive of 2.5b should be understood according to Mark. The scribes who are present accuse Jesus of blasphemy, since he infringes on God's own prerogative to forgive sins (2.6–7). Jesus' response in 2.8–10 matches the scribal accusation closely. 'Why do you think these things in your hearts?' (2.8b) counters 'Why does this one speak like this?' (2.7a), while 'the Son of Man has authority to forgive sins on earth' (2.10) is a direct answer to 'Who can forgive sins except one, God?' (2.7c).[10] The correspondence of 'Which is easier…?' (2.9) to 'He blasphemes' (2.7b) is less obvious, as is the answer to this rhetorical question; for it to function as part of the argumentation it must, however, be presumed either that it is easier to pronounce a word of forgiveness than to command a paralytic to rise and walk, or that both are equally difficult.

To decide whether 'go' (ὕπαγε) or 'walk' (περιπάτει) is original in 2.9 is difficult, since both readings are well attested. It could be argued that the latter reading has a claim to priority, since both Matthew and Luke appear to have taken it over from Mark, and 'go' could be the result of assimilation to 'go to your home' (2.11). Even so, this assimilation would only be partial, and Matthew's and Luke's 'walk' could equally well be due to their turning of the concrete statement into a general principle.

Various scholars have suggested that 2.10 should be construed as the narrator's comment.[11] However, here, as in the rest of Mark, it is Jesus

---

[8] Jeremias, *Neutestamentliche Theologie*, p. 116.

[9] Hofius, 'Jesu Zuspruch der Sündenvergebung', pp. 131–9.

[10] Maisch, *Die Heilung des Gelähmten*, pp. 79–81.

[11] C. S. Patton, 'Did Jesus Call Himself the Son of Man?', *JR* 2 (1922), 501–11 (502); C. P. Ceroke, 'Is Mk 2,10 a Saying of Jesus?', *CBQ* 22 (1960), 369–90; W. L. Lane, *The Gospel of Mark* (Grand Rapids, MI: Eerdmans, 1974), pp. 98, 120.

who speaks of the Son of Man.[12] His saying in 2.10 confirms the scribal understanding of the passive in 2.5b: they have identified the implied agent correctly as Jesus. In addition, the Markan Jesus introduces another christological dimension by his claim to be 'the Son of Man' who 'has authority ... on earth'. Jesus presents himself in categories of a high christology, by appropriating traits that – as will be argued in Chapter 4 below – may be labelled angelomorphic or even divine.

With this claim, the heated exchange between Jesus and the scribes has come to an end, and the attention is now redirected to the paralytic. Jesus commands him to rise, to take his pallet and to go to his home (2.10b–11). The paralytic obeys, and this results in the episode's choral ending, which reports that 'all' were amazed, that they glorified God and acknowledged the extraordinary character of what they had just witnessed (2.12). One may wonder whether the scribes are included among those who express astonishment over the healing, but a continued reading of the Markan narrative will reveal that this is not likely.

Matt 9.1–8. On the two-source hypothesis, Matthew has rearranged and combined material from Mark and Q with his own redaction into a continuous series of miracle episodes (8.1–9.34). As a result, the healing of the paralytic comes not as the opening of a sequence of controversies, but as one in a series of 'mighty acts' performed by Jesus.

Like Mark, Matthew has set the scene in Jesus' 'own town' (9.1), that is, in Capernaum (4.13). By strongly abbreviating and rewording his source for 9.2a, Matthew has achieved the double purpose of linking the episode to the miracles of the preceding chapter and of sharpening the focus on the question of authority.[13] Among other things, Mark's reference to the gathering of 'many' is eliminated by Matthew; however, at the end of the episode, Matthew betrays his dependence on Mark by suddenly introducing 'the crowds' (οἱ ὄχλοι, 9.8).[14] A close bond between this episode and the previous healings is established by the appearance of the paralytic as 'lying on a bed' (ἐπὶ κλίνης βεβλημένον), which is reminiscent of the healing of the centurion's servant, who was lying par-

---

[12] Klauck, 'Die Frage der Sündenvergebung', 227–8.
[13] H. J. Held, 'Matthäus als Interpret der Wundergeschichten', in G. Bornkamm, G. Barth and H. J. Held (eds.), *Überlieferung und Auslegung im Matthäusevangelium*, WMANT 1 (Neukirchen: Neukirchener, 1960), pp. 155–287 (pp. 165–7).
[14] W. D. Davies and D. C. Allison, *A Critical and Exegetical Commentary on the Gospel according to Saint Matthew*, ICC, 3 vols. (Edinburgh: T & T Clark, 1988–97), vol. II, pp. 68, 95.

alyzed (βέβληται παραλυτικός, 8.6) and the healing of Peter's mother-in-law, who was lying sick in bed (βεβλημένην, 8.14).[15] With two minor exceptions, 9.2b reproduces Mark 2.5 exactly: an aorist replaces Mark's historical present, and the forgiveness saying is introduced with 'Take heart' (θάρσει). Since Matthew has deleted Mark's mention of the faith act of breaking up the roof, but retains his reference to Jesus 'seeing their faith', the mere bringing of the paralytic to Jesus can be seen as the fulfilment of the requirement of faith, frequently assumed in Matthew's healing episodes.[16]

Matthew is less extensive in his introduction of the scribes (9.3) than is Mark. More significantly, the scribal accusation as redacted by Matthew consists of one pregnant sentence, 'This one is blaspheming' (οὗτος βλασφημεῖ). Matthew's deletion of the question 'Who can forgive sins except one, God?' eliminates Mark's focus on the uniqueness of Jesus' claim and prepares for the extension of his authority that will come to the fore in 9.8.[17] Furthermore, the concise charge is consonant with Matthew's tendency to portray the religious leaders as evil.[18] The Matthean scribes are neither bewildered nor anxious about God's prerogatives. Their accusation of blasphemy is simply an evil rejoinder to a benevolent deed; Jesus explicitly brands their thoughts as 'evil' (πονηρά, 9.4). The following rhetorical question (9.5) is developed into a general statement by dropping both Mark's reference to the paralytic and the phrase 'and take up your pallet'. As in the Markan episode, the 'Son of Man' saying in Matt 9.6a should be read as a word of the Matthean Jesus, which is clearly marked off from the narrator's brief comment 'he said to the paralytic' by the addition of 'then' (τότε).[19] The saying replicates Mark 2.10 almost verbatim, but the qualifier 'on earth' (ἐπὶ τῆς γῆς) is placed before 'to forgive sins' (ἀφιέναι ἁμαρτίας) and thus drawn closer to the concepts of authority and the Son of Man.

Jesus' command to the paralytic (9.6b) differs only stylistically from Mark's version. In keeping with his tendency to abbreviate, Matthew concentrates on the healed paralytic's act of rising and leaving (9.7), but dispenses with Mark's reference to his taking up his pallet. More substantial

---

[15] On Matthew's (and Luke's) choice of 'bed' (κλίνη) for Mark's 'pallet' (κράβαττος), see *ibid.*, pp. 87–8.

[16] Matt 8.10, 13; 9.22, 28–9; 15.28. See B. Gerhardsson, *The Mighty Acts of Jesus according to Matthew*, Scripta minora Regiae Societatis humaniorum litterarum Lundensis 1978–9:5 (Lund: Gleerup, 1979), pp. 45–51.

[17] Klauck, 'Die Frage der Sündenvergebung', 246.

[18] J. D. Kingsbury, 'The Developing Conflict between Jesus and the Jewish Leaders in Matthew's Gospel: A Literary-Critical Study', *CBQ* 49 (1987), 57–73 (65–6).

[19] *Pace* Davies and Allison, *Matthew*, vol. II, pp. 93–4.

changes occur in 9.8. The vague Markan mention of 'all' is replaced by 'the crowds', which eliminates the impression that even the scribes may have joined in glorifying God. To denote the crowds' reaction, Matthew deviates from Mark's 'be amazed' (ἐξίστασθαι) and instead has 'they feared' (ἐφοβήθησαν) or 'they marvelled' (ἐθαύμασαν).[20] Most importantly, the onlookers' direct speech 'We never saw anything like this' is abandoned by Matthew in favour of the indirect 'glorified God who had given such authority to human beings' (τὸν δόντα ἐξουσίαν τοιαύτην τοῖς ἀνθρώποις).

It is reasonable to construe this authority as the authority to forgive sins already mentioned in 9.6, and the dative expresses the notion that this authority has been given to human beings, which is in keeping with Matthew's standard use of language.[21] I concur with the majority of interpreters who see in the 'human beings' a reference to the circle of disciples and, by extension, to the Church.[22] Suggestions that 9.8 claims the authority to forgive sins for all people, or that the 'Son of Man' expression in 9.6 reflects an original Aramaic בר (א)נשׁ in the sense of 'human being', are improbable in the light of Matthew's theology as a whole, and of his apparent dependence on Mark.[23] It is to the Twelve that the Matthean Jesus gives authority to expel unclean spirits and to heal (10.1), and to Peter he will give the keys (16.19). In view of the tightened relationship between 'authority' and 'on earth' in 9.6, it is notable that the two sayings about binding and loosing speak of an activity on earth (ἐπὶ τῆς γῆς) that will be confirmed in heaven (16.19; 18.18).[24] And while perhaps not concerned directly with the pronouncement of forgiveness, the second of these sayings appears to grant to the congregation an authority to exclude and to readmit members who have sinned (18.18). Taken together, these considerations invite the conclusion that Matthew has reworked the exclusively christological Mark 2.1–12 into

---

[20] See J. R. C. Cousland, *The Crowds in the Gospel of Matthew*, NovTSup 102 (Leiden/ Boston/Cologne: Brill, 2002), pp. 130–2, on the textual uncertainty.

[21] Matt 10.1; 21.23; 28.18. Cf. W. Schenk, '"Den Menschen" Mt 9,8', *ZNW* 54 (1963), 272–5, and recently T. Costin, *Il perdono di Dio nel vangelo di Matteo: Uno studio esegetico-teologico*, Tesi Gregoriana Serie Teologia 133 (Rome: Editrice Pontificia Università Gregoriana, 2006), pp. 120–2, for the unlikely understanding of τοῖς ἀνθρώποις as *dativus commodi*.

[22] See, e.g., H. Leroy, *Zur Vergebung der Sünden: Die Botschaft der Evangelien*, SBS 73 (Stuttgart: Katholisches Bibelwerk, 1974), pp. 56–7; Gerhardsson, *The Mighty Acts of Jesus*, pp. 76–84.

[23] Cf., e.g., Meyer, *Jesu Muttersprache*, p. 94; Dunn, *Jesus Remembered*, pp. 146–7 (cautiously).

[24] See Klauck, 'Die Frage der Sündenvergebung', 247.

an episode that expresses both his christology and his ecclesiology with equal emphasis.

Luke 5.17–26. In contradistinction to Mark and Matthew, Luke does not provide a specific geographical setting for the episode. His carefully crafted opening introduces the characters at the beginning of the episode (5.17). His statement that Jesus 'was teaching' corresponds to Mark's 'was speaking the word to them' but, in the Lukan version, the primary audience is a group that represents the religious elite of the Jewish homeland. By noting the presence of the power of the Lord, Luke portrays Jesus with a prophetic characteristic (cf. 1.17; 4.14–15, 36), which both indicates that a healing is about to take place and foreshadows the polemical question that the scribes and Pharisees will pose.

The narration about how the paralyzed man is brought to Jesus (5.18–19) utilizes Markan material that has been reworked above all for stylistic purposes. In describing the men who carry the bed and how they lower it 'through the tiles' (διὰ τῶν κεράμων) rather than digging through the roof as in Mark, Luke has made the scenario more comprehensible to an audience accustomed to Hellenistic urban architecture.[25]

Luke has also improved on his source in 5.20 where, apart from changing Mark's historical present into an aorist 'he said' (εἶπεν) and deleting a superfluous dative 'to the paralytic', he has added an explicating dative 'for you' (σοι). Moreover, he apparently found the vocative 'man' (ἄνθρωπε, cf. 12.14; 22.58, 60) preferable to Mark's 'child', which has clearly patronizing connotations elsewhere in Luke (2.48; 15.31; 16.25). In the pronouncement of forgiveness, Luke's change of the present 'are (being) forgiven' into the perfect 'are forgiven' (ἀφέωνται) is probably also stylistic rather than material.[26] Though the choice of the perfect tense might facilitate a reading of the verb as an indication that something which has already been decreed is now being proclaimed, the words of the Lukan Jesus provoke reactions that are as strong as those caused by the present-tense formulations in Mark and Matthew.

Since the religious leaders were introduced at the beginning of the episode, Luke can refer to them simply as 'the scribes and the Pharisees' in 5.21, where 'scribes' copies Mark's language rather than Luke's own redactional 'teachers of the Law'.[27] By reformulating their accusation,

---

[25] C. C. McCown, 'Luke's Translation of Semitic into Hellenistic Custom', *JBL* 58 (1939), 213–20 (213–16).

[26] A. Loisy, *Les évangiles synoptiques*, 2 vols. (Montier-en-Der: Ceffonds, 1907–8), vol. I, p. 476.

[27] J. A. Fitzmyer, *The Gospel according to Luke I–IX*, AB 28 (New York: Doubleday, 1970), pp. 581, 583.

he achieves smoother Greek, but he also destroys the correspondence between the scribal questions and Jesus' counter-questions as reported in Mark. Instead, the phrasing 'Who can (δύναται) forgive sins...?' provides a link back to Luke's introductory mention of the power (δύναμις) of the Lord: Jesus has power both to heal and to forgive sins. Like Matthew, Luke has turned the rhetorical question in 5.23 into the statement of a general principle, where saying 'your sins are forgiven' is compared with saying 'rise and walk'. The 'Son of Man' saying (5.24a) differs only in word order from the Markan and Matthean forms: as in Matthew, 'on earth' is drawn closer to 'Son of Man' and to 'authority', but it is a peculiarity of Luke to place 'Son of Man' before the mention of authority. Since Luke's Gospel has a clearly defined narratee, who is addressed in the second person singular (1.3–4), the proposal that 5.24a should be read as the narrator's comment rather than as a word of Jesus must be deemed unlikely.[28]

Like Matthew, Luke has the paralyzed man performing exactly what he is told to do, including going 'to his home' (5.25); in addition, the healed man glorifies God. Two terms introduced by Luke serve to portray Jesus as a Hellenistic miracle-worker: the man was healed 'instantly' (παραχρῆμα) and the onlookers profess to have seen 'wondrous things' (παράδοξα, 5.26).[29] The Pharisees and scribes may be included among the 'all' who were taken by amazement (ἔκστασις) and fear, just as the teachers were amazed as a result of their encounter with Jesus earlier in the narrative (2.47).

A variant in John 5?

As I noted in Chapter 1, Crossan has argued that Mark 2.1–12 and John 5.1–9a, 14b are ultimately variants of one oral tradition, which reached the Gospel authors through a common written collection of miracles.[30] Similarly, the Jesus Seminar holds that Mark 2.1–12, John 5.1–18 and Acts 3.1–10 all derive from the same oral tradition. The common denominator of the episodes is the command to rise and walk, around which different settings and characters were developed.[31] In both reconstructions, the explicit mention of forgiveness must have entered the chain of oral or

---

[28] See *ibid.*, p. 579.
[29] L. T. Johnson, *The Gospel of Luke*, Sacra Pagina (Collegeville, MN: Liturgical, 1991), p. 95.
[30] Crossan, *The Historical Jesus*, pp. 324–5.
[31] R. W. Funk, R. W. Hoover and the Jesus Seminar, *The Five Gospels: The Search for the Authentic Words of Jesus* (New York: Polebridge, 1993), pp. 44–5, 414.

written transmission at some stage subsequent to the parting of Markan and Johannine lines. In the following, I will argue that the hypothesis of a common tradition underlying the two episodes is not plausible. Certainly there are reasons for viewing the substance of John 5.2–9a as pre-Johannine. The absence of the Sabbath motif, which is exploited in the subsequent controversy (5.9b–18), indicates that this material was taken over from an oral tradition or from a written source and inserted into the Gospel's narrative context.[32] In this process, a distinctively Johannine colouring of the episode took place.[33] On the other hand, the agreements between Mark 2.1–12 par. and John 5.2–9a are hardly significant enough to posit their origin within a single common tradition. Quite a number of dissimilarities can be pointed out.[34] As a matter of fact, only two points of agreement between the Markan and the Johannine episodes stand out. First of all, if John 5.14b originally belonged to 5.2–9a, the conjunction of sin and illness is presupposed in both cases. Taken by itself, this agreement could be due merely to indebtedness to a common early Jewish and Christian heritage of viewing illness as resulting from sin. Secondly, and more strikingly, the formulae used by Jesus in Mark and John are nearly identical, if the reading advocated by NA27 in Mark 2.9 is original: 'Rise, [Mark: and] take up your pallet and walk' (ἔγειρε [καὶ] ἆρον τὸν κράβαττόν σου καὶ περιπάτει, Mark 2.9/John 5.8). Any reconstruction which assumes that as widely differing episodes as Mark 2.1–12 and John 5.2–9a could have been created on the sole basis of this sentence, which could not possibly have been transmitted as an independent saying, must be dismissed. Nevertheless, a crucial question persists: is the verbal agreement in Mark 2.9/John 5.8 coincidental, or does it indicate that these episodes are somehow related to each other?

Dodd offered the most extensive argument against a tradition-historical or literary interdependence between Mark 2.9 and John 5.8. He compared the sentence to other healing formulae employed in the NT and found that each type of healing has its own recurrent and appropriate phrase. Thus, the effective word in the healing of a deaf mute is 'Be opened!' (εφφαθα/διανοίχθητι, Mark 7.34); lepers are healed through

---

[32] E. Haenchen, 'Johanneische Probleme', *ZTK* 56 (1959), 19–54 (48); E. Lohse, 'Jesu Worte über den Sabbath' in W. Eltester (ed.), *Judentum, Urchristentum, Kirche*, FS J. Jeremias, BZNW 26 (Berlin: Töpelmann, 1960), pp. 79–89 (pp. 79–80).

[33] L. Th. Witkamp, 'The Use of Traditions in John 5.1–18', *JSNT* 25 (1985), 19–47 (21–31).

[34] R. E. Brown, *The Gospel according to John I–XII: A New Translation with Introduction and Commentary*, AB 29 (Garden City, NY: Doubleday, 1966), pp. 208–9; Meier, *A Marginal Jew*, vol. II, pp. 680–1.

'Be cleansed!' (καθαρίσθητι, Mark 1.41 par.; *EgerG* 41); and exorcisms take place through 'Get out!' (ἔξελθε, Mark 1.25 par.; 5.8; 9.25).[35] To Dodd's examples could be added, in the case of healing a withered hand, 'Stretch out your hand!' (ἔκτεινον τὴν χεῖρα, Mark 3.5 par.), in the case of healing a blind person, 'Regain your sight!' (ἀνάβλεψον, Luke 18.42; Acts 22.13), and in the case of reviving a dead person, 'Rise!' (κουμ/ἔγειρε/ἐγέρθητι/ἀνάστηθι, Mark 5.41/Luke 8.54; Luke 7.14; Acts 9.40). In arguing that 'Rise, take up your pallet and walk' is an analogous stock phrase that is appropriately employed in cases of healing a paralytic, which would explain its recurrence in Mark 2.9 and John 5.8, Dodd has received considerable assent.[36] Nevertheless, while *prima facie* an attractive suggestion, this explanation fails to do justice to the evidence.

First of all, at a general level, stereotyped phrases of healing characteristically focus on the reversal of the malfunctioning condition. This means that the command to a 'closed' ear or mouth is to be opened; to an impure person it is to be cleansed; to an evil spirit that has invaded a person it is to get out; to an immobile hand it is to be stretched out; to a blind person it is to see again; and to a dead person it is to rise.[37] It is this word that effectuates the healing. Further commands by the healer serve either as a dismissal (Mark 5.19; cf. Acts 22.16) or to provide evidence that the miracle has indeed occurred (Mark 1.44 par.; 5.43; Acts 9.41; *EgerG* 43–6). These are usually separated from the healing word itself, though on some occasions the phrase of healing and the formula of dismissal are fused into one, so that the latter is integral to the healing (Mark 10.52; Matt 8.13; Luke 17.14; John 4.50; 9.7, 11). From this, one would expect also the stereotyped phrase of healing a paralytic to focus on the reversal of the state of paralysis, while it may certainly at times be merged with a formula of dismissal or with a command to demonstrate the reality of the healing.

Secondly, this expectation is confirmed by the formulae employed in the NT episodes that narrate how lame or crippled people are healed. Apart from Matt 8.5–13, where a 'paralytic' is healed without a command by the healer to rise and/or to walk (obviously because the healing is performed at a distance), the stereotypical formula appears to be 'Rise!' or 'Rise and walk!', with some variations in accordance with the

---

[35] C. H. Dodd, *Historical Tradition in the Fourth Gospel* (Cambridge University Press, 1963), p. 176.
[36] *Ibid.*, pp. 176–7. See Brown, *John I–XII*, p. 208; Meier, *A Marginal Jew*, vol. II, p. 680.
[37] See also Q 7.22; Matt 10.8; 15.31.

different circumstances.[38] The textual witnesses are divided as to whether Peter tells the crippled man at the Beautiful Gate simply to 'Walk!' (περιπάτει) or to 'Rise and walk!' (ἔγειρε καὶ περιπάτει, Acts 3.6). Paul, when healing a crippled man in Lystra, employs the formula 'Stand up straight on your feet' (14.10). The specific mention of the feet has been prepared for by the introductory remark that the man was 'unable to use his feet' (14.8). Similarly, Peter's directive to Aeneas, 'Stand up and make your bed' (9.34), is prepared for through the detail of this paralyzed man lying 'on a pallet' (9.33). In like manner, the mention of a pallet in 'Rise, take up your pallet and walk/go to your home' (Mark 2.9, 11) appears to be prompted by the specific circumstance of the paralytic, who has been brought to Jesus on a pallet (2.4). It is telling that, as they turn the rhetorical question in Mark 2.9 into a general principle, both Matthew and Luke leave out not only the Markan reference to the paralytic, but also the injunction to him to take up his pallet. As a result, they both provide what can truly be regarded as a stereotyped phrase for this type of healing, 'Rise and walk' (ἔγειρε καὶ περιπάτει, Matt 9.5/Luke 5.23). And, not surprisingly, Gospel passages that summarize Jesus' miracles (Q 7.22; Matt 15.31) draw attention to the fact that the crippled are now able to walk (περιπατεῖν), and not to their ability to carry around pallets or to make their beds.

In John 5.8, however, Jesus commands the infirm man to take up his pallet, even though no such thing has been mentioned earlier in the episode, and the man's illness has not even been specified. In the subsequent controversy, the carrying of the pallet is essential, since it is considered a violation of the Sabbath (5.10). The act of rising recedes into the background, so that what is left of Jesus' order in 5.8 is now 'Take up your pallet and walk' (5.11) or even 'Take up and walk' (5.12). Accordingly, Barnabas Lindars suggested that John 5.2–9a 'is a fusion of a non-Synoptic Jerusalem tradition and the well-known Galilean story in Mk 2.1–12'.[39] While 5.2–7 reproduces a pre-Johannine miracle story set in Jerusalem, 5.8–9a is a pastiche of the source or the tradition that underlies Mark 2.1–12, here brought in to introduce the pallet as a link to the Sabbath controversy of 5.9b–18. The original conclusion of the Jerusalem miracle story has been lost.[40]

---

[38] Witkamp, 'The Use of Traditions', 42 n. 64.
[39] B. Lindars, *The Gospel of John*, NCB (London: Oliphants, 1972), p. 52. See also Witkamp, 'The Use of Traditions', 25–6.
[40] Lindars, *John*, pp. 209–10, 215–16.

Lindars' suggestion seems to account best for the evidence. John appears to be acquainted with the synoptic episode, either from oral tradition or from a pre-Markan source, or, indeed, from the very Gospel of Mark.[41] Themes present in Mark 2.1–12 may be echoing throughout John 5, but some of the purported echoes are very difficult to assess. To the dubious echoes belongs first of all Jesus' admonition 'Sin no more' (μηκέτι ἁμάρτανε, 5.14), linking the illness with sin in a manner presupposed also in the Markan episode, and thus possibly derived from there.[42] However, it is more likely either that 5.14b formed the original ending of the Jerusalem miracle story[43] or that it is the evangelist's composition (see Chapter 5 below). The accusation of blasphemy in Mark 2.7 may be reflected in the charge against the Johannine Jesus that he has made himself equal to God (5.18).[44] But it has been correctly pointed out that the motivations for the charges are different.[45] A final possible but uncertain echo of the Markan episode is Jesus' later pronouncement to the effect that 'you marvel' (θαυμάζετε, 7.21) at the healing, which could indicate that John has Mark 2.12 in mind. A stronger case could be made for identifying John 5.27 as an echo of Mark. The sudden appearance of the expression 'Son of Man' (υἱὸς ἀνθρώπου) stands out against Jesus' references to himself as 'the Son' (eight times) or 'the Son of God' (once) in 5.19–29.[46] The juxtaposition of 'Son of Man' and 'authority' (ἐξουσία) brings 5.27 remarkably close to Mark 2.10, and 'to execute judgement' might well correspond to the ministry of forgiving and retaining sins that forms part of Jesus' mission (John 20.21–3). John 5.27, thus, could well be explained as a Johannine reformulation of the Markan Son of Man's claim to the authority to forgive sins.

To conclude this discussion of the relationship of John 5 to Mark 2.1–12, I repeat that the hypothesis of a single common tradition behind the two episodes is not plausible, and that the close verbal agreement

[41] See P. Borgen, 'John and the Synoptics', in D. L. Dungan (ed.), *The Interrelations of the Gospels: A Symposium Led by M.-É. Boismard – W. R. Farmer – F. Neirynck: Jerusalem 1984*, BETL 95 (Leuven University Press, 1990), pp. 408–58 (pp. 431–2), whose argument against the dependence of John 5.1–18 on Mark operates on an all too static conception of orality vs literacy. For the notion of 're-oralization', see Byrskog, *Story as History*, pp. 138–44. See also F. Neirynck, 'John and the Synoptics: Response to P. Borgen', in Dungan (ed.), *The Interrelations of the Gospels*, pp. 438–50.

[42] Lindars, *John*, pp. 216–17; Witkamp, 'The Use of Traditions', 27–8 (both cautiously); Neirynck, 'John and the Synoptics', p. 446.

[43] Haenchen, 'Johanneische Probleme', 48–9; Witkamp, 'The Use of Traditions', 26–7.

[44] Lindars, *John*, p. 219 (cautiously); Neirynck, 'John and the Synoptics', pp. 446–7.

[45] Borgen, 'John and the Synoptics', 430.

[46] R. Bultmann, *Das Evangelium des Johannes*, KEK (Göttingen: Vandenhoeck & Ruprecht, 1941), pp. 195–6.

between Mark 2.9 and John 5.8 is most readily explained by positing that John drew on a pre-Markan tradition or source, or even on Mark's Gospel. The fact that the themes of authority and the Son of Man occur in close conjunction with the Johannine healing is significant, since this indicates that John knew and used the synoptic episode in a form not substantially different from what is now found in Mark 2.1–12, whether in oral or in written shape.

An allusion in Jas 5.13–18?

Luke Timothy Johnson has pointed out that the 'only possible exception' from the rule that the Letter of James does not allude to any narrative gospel material is provided by 'the intriguing echo of gospel healing accounts' in Jas 5.15. To 'raise (up)' (ἐγείρειν) is a term that frequently occurs in the healing episodes.[47] Furthermore, the statement that 'the prayer of faith (πίστεως) will save (σώσει)' the person who is ill is reminiscent of Jesus' declaration 'your faith (πίστις) has saved (σέσωκεν) you' in the synoptic Gospels.[48] To these remarks could be added the observation that both Jas 5.15 and Mark 2.1–12 par. combine the theme of forgiveness with Jesus' ability to 'raise up' those who are ill. In Jas 5.15, 'the Lord' who will raise up the person affected by illness ought to be Jesus Christ, in whose name both the prayer and the anointing are carried out (5.14).[49] The change from the active 'will raise up' (ἐγερεῖ) to the passive 'will be forgiven' (ἀφεθήσεται) indicates a change of acting subjects: while it is Jesus who restores the ill person to health, his or her sins are forgiven by God. A similar passive is also employed in Mark 2.5 par., and the topic of saving faith is also at least implied by the synoptic episodes. Therefore, *if* a specific gospel story is alluded to in Jas 5.15, it could be the episode about the healing of a paralytic at Capernaum.

---

[47] Mark 1.31; 9.27; John 12.1, 9, 17; cf. Mark 2.9 par.; 2.11 par.; Mark 2.12/Matt 9.7; Mark 3.3/Luke 6.8; Mark 5.41/Luke 8.54; Mark 10.49; Matt 8.15; 9.25; Luke 7.14; John 5.8. See Johnson, *James*, p. 55.

[48] Mark 5.34 par.; Mark 10.52/Luke 18.42; Luke 7.50; 17.19. See L. T. Johnson, *Brother of Jesus, Friend of God: Studies in the Letter of James* (Grand Rapids, MI: Eerdmans, 2004), p. 23 n. 51. Cf., however, Chapter 5 below.

[49] M. Dibelius and H. Greeven, *James: A Commentary on the Epistle of James* (Philadelphia: Fortress, 1975), p. 253 n. 67; F. Mussner, *Der Jakobusbrief*, HTKNT 13, 5th edn (Freiburg: Herder, 1987), pp. 220–3. On the ambiguity of 'the Lord' in 5.14, see C. Burchard, 'Zu einigen christologischen Stellen des Jakobusbriefes', in C. Breytenbach and H. Paulsen (eds.), *Anfänge der Christologie*, FS F. Hahn (Göttingen: Vandenhoeck & Ruprecht, 1991), pp. 353–68 (p. 364 n. 61).

There is nothing in the rest of the letter to indicate James' dependence on specifically Markan material, let alone on the written synoptic Gospels. Moreover, neither Mark 2.1–12 nor its parallels in Matthew and Luke contain the formula 'your faith has saved you', and all three synoptic versions of the episode present forgiveness as granted by the Son of Man rather than by God. As a matter of fact, James declares that any sin will be forgiven (gnomic future) for the 'doer of sin' much as Jesus in Mark 2.5 par. declares that the sins of the paralytic are forgiven, without any indication that this is a matter of potential controversy. This irenic atmosphere and James' reservation of the prerogative to forgive sins for God himself indicate that James does not allude to the dialogue in Mark 2.6–10 par. He could still, of course, be alluding to the episode in a more primitive form that lacked the controversy dialogue, such as has been frequently hypothesized. I will argue in Chapter 6 below that the story did most probably exist in this less elaborated form. Thus it is possible – but only just possible – that the Letter of James does allude to this more primitive form of the episode.

The sinful woman (Luke 7.36–50)

Luke's episode about Jesus, a sinful woman and Simon the Pharisee poses a series of difficulties to be dealt with prior to any attempt at evaluating the historicity of the pericope. First of all, how should this episode be understood as it now stands within the Gospel of Luke? Secondly, what is the relationship of this pericope to the episodes in Matthew, Mark and John that relate the anointing of Jesus in Bethany and that have some striking features in common with this Lukan episode?[50] And, thirdly, what part or parts of Luke 7.36–50 can safely be attributed to Lukan redaction, and can thus be excluded from the authentication of the episode? These three questions will be discussed in the following.

Interpretation of Luke 7.36–50

Luke 7.36–50 is a three-part drama starring Jesus (in his role as party-goer and associate of disreputable people, see 7.34), Simon the Pharisee (who represents 'this generation' of experts in the Law, see 7.30–2) and

---

[50] M. Myllykoski, 'The Sinful Woman in the *Gospel of Peter*: Reconstructing the Other Side of P.Oxy. 4009', *NTS* 55 (2009), 104–15, suggests that POxy 4009 contains a different version of Luke 7.45–9. If this proposal is correct, the *Gospel of Peter* is probably dependent on the Gospel of Luke for this episode.

the anonymous woman (who represents the collective of notorious sinners, see 7.29).[51] The theme of contrast and opposition described in general in 7.29–35 is concretely exemplified in 7.36–50.

Jesus, as the expected main character, accepts an invitation to eat in
the house of 'one of the Pharisees' (7.36). This latter figure is referred to
simply as 'the Pharisee' throughout the first part of the episode (7.37, 39)
until Jesus addresses him by his personal name, 'Simon', which is then
also adopted as the narrator's designation for him (7.40, 43, 44). The
meal appears already to be under way when 'a woman who was a sinner
in the town' (7.37) arrives. The wording indicates that the woman is a
public sinner, quite probably a prostitute.[52] The Pharisee's assumption
that Jesus is not aware of what kind of woman she is (7.39) implies that
Jesus is a temporary visitor to the town, which may be Nain (see 7.11).

How should the woman's actions towards the feet of the dining Jesus –
moistening them with her tears, wiping them with her hair, kissing them
and anointing them – be understood? There are two major options. The
first is to view them as acts of repentance. Charles Cosgrove observes
that the woman's loosening of her hair and weeping were interpreted as
penitential acts already in the early Church, and that literary evidence
confirms that, in antiquity, Greek and Roman women would sometimes
unbind their hair as a sign of grief.[53] Expressions of penitence in early
Judaism were frequently derived from mourning rituals, and Luke's portrayal of the woman could serve to characterize her as mournful and
penitent. However, Cosgrove also points out that there are other ways to
understand the social significance of the woman's actions.[54] This takes
us to the second option, namely to understand them as expressions of
love and gratitude. Foot-washing is construed as a demonstration of love
in some early Jewish and Christian stories.[55] The sinful woman may be
showing her love for Jesus, the 'friend of toll-collectors and sinners' (see
7.34). Somewhat simplistically, therefore, the woman's actions could
be read either with an emphasis on her weeping, and accordingly as a

---

[51] J. J. Kilgallen, 'John the Baptist, the Sinful Woman, and the Pharisee', *JBL* 104
(1985), 675–9 (677–8).

[52] K. E. Corley, *Private Women, Public Meals: Social Conflict in the Synoptic Tradition*
(Peabody, MA: Hendrickson, 1993), p. 124.

[53] C. H. Cosgrove, 'A Woman's Unbound Hair in the Greco-Roman World, with Special
Reference to the Story of the "Sinful Woman" in Luke 7:36–50', *JBL* 124 (2005), 675–92
(677–8, 682–4).

[54] *Ibid.*, 689–92.

[55] *JosAsen* 20.1–5; John 13.1–17 (cf. 13.34–5). See O. Hofius, 'Fußwaschung als
Erweis der Liebe: Sprachliche und sachliche Anmerkungen zu Lk 7,44b', *ZNW* 81 (1990),
171–7.

request for forgiveness, or with an emphasis on Jesus' feet being washed, kissed and anointed, and thus as a demonstration of thankfulness for forgiveness already received. The ensuing dialogue between Jesus and the Pharisee (7.39–47) appears to support the latter interpretation. Simon's assumption that Jesus has to be a prophet in order to know that the woman is a sinner indicates that he does not perceive her behaviour as a penitential act.[56] Furthermore, Jesus' parable (7.41–3) and its application (7.44–7) centre on the theme of love in response to forgiveness already granted.[57] In line with Jesus' remark that 'the one for whom little is forgiven, loves little', the clause 'for she loved much' (ὅτι ἠγάπησεν πολύ, 7.47) will have to be taken as giving the reason for knowing that the woman's sins have been forgiven, and not as giving the reason for the granting of forgiveness.[58] This far in the episode, it is most natural to understand Jesus as speaking of a forgiveness that has occurred prior to the point at which the woman entered Simon's house in order to demonstrate her gratitude.

At the end of the episode, complications set in, as Jesus addresses the woman with the phrase 'Your sins are forgiven' (ἀφέωνταί σου αἱ ἁμαρτίαι, 7.48). In isolation, it could be interpreted along the lines of 7.47a.[59] Several objections must, however, be raised against such an understanding of 7.48. If the woman came to Jesus to express her gratitude for a forgiveness already experienced, it appears superfluous for Jesus to tell her something that she already knows. Also, the parallels between 5.20–1 and 7.48–50 suggest that the latter passage should be read in the light of the former. In both cases, faith (πίστις) is the ground for forgiveness (5.20; 7.50); Jesus' word of forgiveness elicits a comment from those present, commencing with 'Who is this who…?' (5.21; 7.49); and the bystanders do not hear the pronouncement of forgiveness as a divine passive, but draw the conclusion that Jesus claims for himself the ability to forgive sins (5.21; 7.49). It is hardly possible to view the diners' reaction as a misunderstanding; on the contrary, it expresses the implied author's conviction.[60] Therefore, unlike 7.39–47, 7.48–50 cannot

---

[56] Cosgrove, 'A Woman's Unbound Hair', 688–9.

[57] J. J. Kilgallen, 'Forgiveness of Sins (Luke 7:36–50)', *NovT* 40 (1998), 105–16 (111–12).

[58] U. Wilckens, 'Vergebung für die Sünderin', in P. Hoffmann (ed.), *Orientierung an Jesus: Zur Theologie der Synoptiker*, FS J. Schmid (Freiburg: Herder, 1973), pp. 394–424 (pp. 404–7); Fitzmyer, *Luke I–IX*, pp. 686–7; J. B. Green, *The Gospel of Luke*, NICNT (Grand Rapids, MI: Eerdmans, 1997), pp. 313–14.

[59] Kilgallen, 'John the Baptist', 678.

[60] Cf. *ibid.*, 678.

easily be read as interpreting the woman's actions as an expression of gratitude, but appears rather to portray her as a penitent. A reading of the episode that is fully coherent and free from tension can hardly be achieved.

Relationship to Mark 14.3–9/Matt 26.6–13/John 12.1–8

Mark and Matthew narrate an anointing of Jesus' head by an unnamed woman in Bethany shortly prior to the passion (Mark 14.3–9/Matt 26.6–13). John includes what must be a variant of the same episode, although in his version the woman is named Mary and anoints Jesus' feet (John 12.3–8). That Luke 7.36–50 is also related to the Bethany episodes in one way or another can be concluded from two facts. First of all, as Luke does not reproduce Mark 14.3–9 but skips directly from Mark 14.1–2 to 14.10–11 (Luke 22.1–6), he evidently viewed this pericope as the doublet of an episode which he had already related, and, in keeping with his common practice, he chose not to include the doublet.[61] Secondly, the similarities between the Lukan and the Markan episodes cannot possibly be accidental. Especially striking are two minor verbal agreements: the reference to 'an alabaster jar of myrrh' (ἀλάβαστρον μύρου, Mark 14.3; Luke 7.37) and the proper name 'Simon' (Mark 14.3; Luke 7.40, 43, 44).[62]

Some have taken the view that Mark and Luke represent different versions of a common oral tradition, and John is sometimes thought to provide a third version of the same traditional story.[63] Mack has suggested that the Markan and the Lukan episodes are distinct elaborations of a single chreia which, he argues, involved an objection to the woman's action from the bystanders and concluded with Jesus' 'plausibly clever', 'aphoristic' rejoinder. Primitive Christian communities made use of the Hellenistic pattern of chreia elaboration and replaced both the original objection and the original rejoinder with a dialogue that was more useful for their concerns.[64] But it is difficult to see how progymnastic elaboration of a single chreia could have resulted in such diverse narrations as

---

[61] H. Schürmann, *Traditionsgeschichtliche Untersuchungen zu den synoptischen Evangelien: Beiträge* (Düsseldorf: Patmos, 1968), pp. 280–1.

[62] See further J. Delobel, 'Lk 7,47 in Its Context: An Old Crux Revisited', in F. Van Segbroeck et al. (eds.), *The Four Gospels 1992*, FS F. Neirynck (Leuven University Press, 1992), pp. 1581–90 (pp. 1582–3); K. E. Corley, 'The Anointing of Jesus in the Synoptic Tradition: An Argument for Authenticity', *JSHJ* 1 (2003), 61–72 (63).

[63] R. Holst, 'The One Anointing of Jesus: Another Application of the Form-Critical Method', *JBL* 95 (1976), 435–46; Fitzmyer, *Luke I–IX*, p. 686.

[64] Mack and Robbins, *Patterns of Persuasion*, pp. 89–92.

Mark 14.3–9 and Luke 7.36–50. According to Mack's hypothesis, the communities would have preserved practically unaltered the woman's action of anointing together with some details in the description of the circumstances, while taking the liberty to replace the pronouncement or chreia proper with entirely different sayings. Certainly, the rhetorical textbooks allow, or even instruct, the student to adapt and to improve the wording of a given chreia (see Chapter 6 below), but they constantly presuppose that the paraphrased chreia will remain substantially faithful to what Theon labels the 'point' (κῦρος, *Prog.* 202.21). And empirical study of how chreiai were used in antiquity shows that what tended to be altered liberally were their attribution to certain individuals and their descriptions of circumstances, while their points were normally preserved fairly intact.[65] Thus, if indeed the Markan and Lukan episodes originated with the same brief story, they were altered and expanded in a procedure manifestly different from the standard way of chreia elaboration.

Another view of the relationship between the episodes holds that Luke 7.36–50 is a reworking of Mark 14.3–9 and that Lukan redaction can account for the differences.[66] Yet there remain a number of discrepancies that are not so easily explained. Luke's purported relocation of the episode in time and space, his change of the Markan anointing of Jesus' head into a washing and anointing of Jesus' feet, and his introduction of the dominant themes of sin, forgiveness and love are all unexpected features which, in view of how Luke normally handles his sources, cannot simply be ascribed to free redaction. Once again, it would be remarkable if Luke had opted to rework the Markan episode so extensively in order to suit his own interests, but had still retained such an unimportant detail as the name of the host.

As many scholars have concluded, the most plausible scenario is that at the core of the Lukan episode is a story originally distinct from Mark's episode about the anointing at Bethany, but at some point elements of the (pre-)Markan episode were blended into the (pre-)Lukan episode.[67] Consequently, as Luke encountered Mark 14.3–9 in the composition of

[65] Hock and O'Neil, *The Chreia*, pp. 37–46.

[66] L. Schottroff and W. Stegemann, *Jesus von Nazareth – Hoffnung der Armen*, 3rd edn (Stuttgart: Kohlhammer, 1990), p. 142; Theissen and Merz, *Der historische Jesus*, p. 459; Corley, 'The Anointing of Jesus', 68–71; Fiedler, 'Gottes Vergebungsbereitschaft', p. 168.

[67] A. Legault, 'An Application of the Form-Critique Method to the Anointings in Galilee (Lk 7, 36–50) and Bethany (Mt 26, 6–13; Mk 14, 3–9; Jn 12, 1–8)', *CBQ* 16 (1954), 131–45 (143–4); Brown, *John I–XII*, pp. 450–1; Wilckens, 'Vergebung für die Sünderin', pp. 398–400; Delobel, 'Lk 7,47 in Its Context', pp. 1584–6; Dunn, *Jesus Remembered*, p. 523.

his own Gospel, he found that he had already included an episode that was similar enough to be regarded a doublet of the Bethany episode, and he therefore avoided a repetition. Finally, while John 12.1–8 appears to be based primarily on Mark 14.3–9, the mention of Jesus' feet and specifically the phrase 'she wiped with her hair' (John 12.3; cf. Luke 7.38) seem to be imported either from Luke or from pre-Lukan tradition.[68] This rather complex hypothesis about the relationship between the episodes in Mark, Luke and John seems to do better justice to the evidence than any other suggestion.

Lukan redaction of the episode

Opinions vary also concerning which parts of Luke 7.36–50 should be assigned to Lukan redaction. Bultmann thought that the parable in 7.41–3 was the kernel of the episode, around which Luke had modelled the rest on the basis of the Bethany episode.[69] A more common view, which is also more convincing in the light of the considerations above, includes 7.36–8 in the oral or written story, which Luke chose to incorporate into his Gospel. Kim Paffenroth's detailed study of the hypothetical L source identifies several significant deviations from typical Lukan vocabulary and style in 7.36–47 and concludes that this section was taken over from L.[70] Others have argued that the episode existed in a shorter form in Luke's source. Ulrich Wilckens thinks that, while 7.36–43, 47 is pre-Lukan, 7.44–6 is an expansion made by Luke himself. The expansion applies the general principles expressed in 7.41–3, 47 specifically to Simon and highlights the conflict between Jesus and the Pharisee, which the pre-Lukan pericope did not do. Wilckens also suggests that the expansion was inspired by Mark 14.6.[71] This is possible but far from evident. If 7.44–6 is indeed a secondary elaboration of the argument presented in 7.41–3, 47, at least 7.44–5 could have been present already in Luke's source.

There is more agreement on 7.48–50, which is commonly held to have been crafted by Luke.[72] As pointed out above, 7.48 introduces an

---

[68] J. A. Bailey, *The Traditions Common to the Gospels of Luke and John* (Leiden: Brill, 1963), pp. 1–5; A. Dauer, *Johannes und Lukas: Untersuchungen zu den johanneisch-lukanischen Parallelperikopen Joh 4,46–54/Lk 7,1–10 – Joh 12,1–8/Lk 7,36–50; 10,38–42 – Joh 20,19–29/Lk 24,36–49*, FzB 50 (Würzburg: Echter, 1984), pp. 126–206.

[69] Bultmann, *Die Geschichte der synoptischen Tradition*, pp. 19–20.

[70] Paffenroth, *The Story of Jesus*, pp. 74–84, 86–94.

[71] Wilckens, 'Vergebung für die Sünderin', pp. 399–406, 417.

[72] T. Schramm, *Der Markus-Stoff bei Lukas: Eine literarkritische und redaktionsgeschichtliche Untersuchung*, SNTSMS 14 (Cambridge University Press, 1971), pp. 44–5.

understanding of the relationship between love and forgiveness that differs from 7.41–7. It is probable that Luke is responsible for this attempt
to bring the episode into harmony with 5.17–26, and that he modelled
the phrase 'Your sins are forgiven' (7.48) on 5.20. Similarly, the diners'
amazed question 'Who is this who even forgives sins?' (7.49) strongly
echoes 5.21 but is not dressed in polemical language.[73] It also shares with
5.21–4 the presupposition that the implied agent of forgiveness is Jesus
himself, and thus voices a christology which is not found in 7.36–47.[74]
And the conclusion 'Your faith has saved you; depart in peace' (7.50) is
a stereotypical formula, which ultimately derives from Mark 5.34, but
which is here given in a slightly polished Lukan form (cf. 8.48). To sum
up, there are quite persuasive reasons to view 7.48–50 as a composition
created by the evangelist in order to make the episode more congruent
with the Gospel's theology of sin, repentance and forgiveness. The passage is ultimately dependent on Mark and cannot therefore be held to
contribute independent attestation of Jesus' forgiving activity.

By contrast, 7.36–43, 47 (possibly also 7.44–6) appears to come from
a source other than Mark and could be invoked as an independent witness to this theme. It must however be pointed out that even this part
of the episode has not been reproduced verbatim without alterations by
Luke. I have already mentioned that a few details in the narrative seem
to have been influenced by a recollection of Mark 14.3–9. Moreover,
some elements are characteristically Lukan, notably the identification of
Simon as a Pharisee.[75] Another such element is the implicit characterization of Jesus as a prophet.

A crucial question is whether 7.47 has been modified in comparison
with its source, and if so, to what extent. Joël Delobel's analysis of the
phrase 'Therefore I tell you, her many sins are forgiven; for she loved
much' (7.47a) is inconclusive: the terminology is neither characteristically Lukan nor is it very un-Lukan. The perfect 'are forgiven' (ἀφέωνται)
does, however, bring suspicion about Lukan redaction, since Luke shows
a preference for this form elsewhere (5.20, 23; 7.48). Delobel suggests
that 7.47a has been reworked by Luke, while 7.47b has been imported

---

[73] Cf. D. L. Bock, 'Jesus as Blasphemer', in S. McKnight and J. B. Modica (eds.), *Who
Do My Opponents Say that I Am? An Investigation of the Accusations against Jesus*, LNTS
327 (London: T & T Clark, 2008), pp. 76–94 (p. 81), who alleges that the reaction of 'the
Jewish theologians' is the same in Luke 7.36–50 as in Mark 2.1–12.

[74] Michl, 'Sündenvergebung in Christus', 33–4; J. J. Kilgallen, 'What Does It Mean to
Say that there Are Additions in Luke 7,36–50?', *Bib* 86 (2005), 529–35 (531–3).

[75] Holst, 'The One Anointing of Jesus', 438–9 n. 20.

from the source without modification.[76] If 'for she loved much' is taken to express the reason why forgiveness is granted, it seems necessary to assume Lukan redaction here, just as in 7.48. But as stated above, I am inclined to view the clause as a statement of the reason for knowing that the woman's sins have been forgiven, so that 7.47a stands no less than 7.47b in perfect harmony with the parable of 7.41–3.

It is actually likely that the episode in its pre-Lukan shape contained the distinctive feature of 7.47a, that is, its specific application of the parable's general principle to the woman. Klaus Berger has classified 7.40–3 as belonging to the category of 'paradigmatic legal decisions' (*paradigmatische Rechtsentscheide*). In this type of narrative, the speaker tells a short parable, which normally presents a legal case between two parts, and then leaves it to his interlocutor(s) to judge the case.[77] Berger has pointed out that the parable in Luke begins on a note strikingly similar to the parable told by Nathan to David in 2 Sam 12.1–7.[78] Simon's ironically flawed opinion that Jesus cannot be a prophet (7.39) should also be noticed in conjunction with the fact that the main speaker in this literary type is often precisely a prophet.[79] Jesus' invitation of Simon to give a verdict (7.42b) is paralleled in most other instances of the same type.[80] And his laudatory remark 'You have judged correctly' (ὀρθῶς ἔκρινας, 7.43) comes close to Uriel's 'You have judged well' (*bene iudicasti*, 2 Esd 4.20). The narratives in this category typically conclude with the main speaker's application of the paradigmatic decision to the specific case, which reveals to the interlocutor that he has judged himself.[81] David learns that he himself is the rich man who has slaughtered the poor man's only lamb (2 Sam 12.7); the inhabitants of Judah and Jerusalem are told that they are the Lord's unproductive vineyard (Isa 5.7); the religious leaders of Jerusalem realize that they are the disobedient son of the Father (Matt 21.31–2); and Ezra hears 'You have judged well, so why have you not judged yourself?' (2 Esd 4.20). Thus, the concrete application of the parable is always made explicit, and such was probably also the case from the beginning in what is now Luke 7.40–7: in the pre-Lukan version, Jesus probably stated the woman's correspondence

---

[76] Delobel, 'Lk 7,47 in Its Context', pp. 1588–9.
[77] K. Berger, *Formen und Gattungen im Neuen Testament*, UTB 2532 (Tübingen: Francke, 2005), p. 107; also K. Berger, 'Materialien zu Form und Überlieferungsgeschichte neutestamentlicher Gleichnisse', *NovT* 15 (1973), 1–37 (20–5).
[78] Berger, 'Materialien', 23.
[79] 2 Sam 12.1; Isa 5.1–7; *ApocrEzek* frg 1.
[80] Isa 5.3–4; 2 Esd 4.18; *ApocrEzek* frg 1; Matt 21.31; Luke 10.36.
[81] K. R. Snodgrass, *Stories with Intent: A Comprehensive Guide to the Parables of Jesus* (Grand Rapids, MI: Eerdmans, 2008), p. 34.

to the debtor explicitly, and the correspondence between the sins and the monetary debt in the parable. As a matter of fact, the failure to identify Simon as the one for whom little has been forgiven in 7.47b is more contrary to expectation. To sum up the discussion of Luke 7.36–50, whereas 7.48–50 is likely to be the evangelist's own creation, 7.36–43, 47 stems largely from a source (L) or from pre-Lukan tradition; this is possibly also the case with 7.44–6. Most importantly, I have found no reason to suspect that Luke has substantially changed what was in his source for 7.47. On the contrary, the source is likely to have contained a statement to the fact that the woman's sins had been forgiven. Independently of Mark, Luke 7.47 therefore attests to Jesus' announcement of forgiveness for specific individuals. But it should be emphasized that this announcement of forgiveness differs from Mark 2.1–12 par. in some important respects: whatever its exact wording was in the source, Luke 7.47a is not directed towards the sinner herself, but towards another person, and the announcement concerns a forgiveness that has already taken place. Luke 7.47a thus lacks the performative force of the saying in Mark 2.5 par. The passive is naturally taken to imply that the agent of forgiveness is God, and Jesus functions as his prophet, endowed with the ability to infer correctly from the woman's behaviour that her sins have been forgiven.

Other forgiveness statements

Forgiveness for those who forgive (Mark 11.25 par.)

When the Markan Jesus delivers his teaching on the relationship between faith and prayer (11.22–4), he appends what seems to be a loosely connected remark about prayer for forgiveness: 'And when you stand and pray, forgive if you have a complaint against someone, so that your Father in heaven may also forgive your transgressions' (11.25).[82] Rather than reproducing this saying at the corresponding point in his Gospel (21.22), Matthew gives an antithetical parallelism to conclude his version of the Lord's Prayer: 'For if you forgive the human beings their transgressions, your heavenly Father will forgive you also; but if you do not forgive the human beings, your Father will not forgive your transgressions either' (6.14–15). In association with the petition for forgiveness in 6.12, Matthew underlines the importance of mutual forgiveness

---

[82] On 11.25 as part of Mark's original text, see V. Auvinen, *Jesus' Teaching on Prayer* (Åbo Akademi University, 2003), pp. 172–3.

for prayers to be effectively heard.[83] Luke does not take up the saying at all but passes over it together with the rest of Mark 11.19–25.

While Q apparently did not contain this saying, it may have included the Lord's Prayer, the fifth petition of which is a prayer for forgiveness (Matt 6.12/Luke 11.4/*Did* 8.2). It is virtually impossible to decide what was the original shape of this petition, if indeed there ever existed a single original form, but Luke's 'forgive us our sins' (ἄφες ἡμῖν τὰς ἁμαρτίας ἡμῶν) is widely recognized as secondary to Matthew's 'forgive us our debts' (ἄφες ἡμῖν τὰ ὀφειλήματα ἡμῶν) and to the *Didache*'s 'forgive us our debt' (ἄφες ἡμῖν τὴν ὀφειλὴν ἡμῶν).[84] Whereas the present tense is employed in the second clause, both in Luke's 'for we ourselves also forgive (ἀφίομεν) everyone in debt to us' and in the *Didache*'s 'as we also forgive (ἀφίεμεν) our debtors', Matthew appears to be using the aorist: 'as we also have forgiven (ἀφήκαμεν) our debtors'. The latter wording brings out with unambiguous clarity the Matthean tenet that mutual pardon is a precondition for receiving God's forgiveness (see also 5.23–4).

Another echo of this teaching on the relationship between divine and human forgiveness can be heard in two of the Apostolic Fathers (*1 Cl* 13.2; Pol *Phil* 2.3). Both passages quote Jesus as having advised his audience to forgive in order that they themselves may be forgiven. The two forms of this saying are obviously related to both Q 6.37–8 and Mark 4.24b (see Table 2). The nearly invariable core of the saying is 'By the measure which you use to measure up, it will be measured up for you', which occurs in all of the variants. In addition, all of them except Mark 4.24b specify that this general principle has ramifications for a correct attitude towards the judgement of other people. Matthew and Luke probably drew these elements from Q, and the longer form which is preserved by Luke is probably the original version.[85] But Q apparently did not contain the explicit mention of forgiveness that Clement and Polycarp have in common alongside the counsel to be merciful. Accordingly, there is much to be said for the opinion that Clement and Polycarp, independently of one another, recall this saying from a collection of sayings other than the synoptic Gospels and Q, quite possibly one that only existed in

---

[83] See K. Stendahl, 'Prayer and Forgiveness', *SEÅ* 22–3 (1957–8), 75–86.

[84] See, e.g., Meier, *A Marginal Jew*, vol. II, pp. 354–5 n. 9. On the relationship between Matthew and *Didache*, see J. A. Draper, 'The Jesus Tradition in the Didache' in J. A. Draper (ed.), *The* Didache *in Modern Research*, AGJU 37 (Leiden: Brill, 1996), pp. 72–91 (p. 86).

[85] Davies and Allison, *Matthew*, vol. I, pp. 667–8.

Table 2 *'Forgiveness for those who forgive'*

Matt 7.1–2	Luke 6.37–8	Mark 4.24b	1 Cl 13.2	Pol Phil 2.3
Μὴ κρίνετε, ἵνα μὴ κριθῆτε·	Καὶ μὴ κρίνετε, καὶ οὐ μὴ κριθῆτε· καὶ μὴ καταδικάζετε, καὶ οὐ μὴ καταδικασθῆτε. ἀπολύετε, καὶ ἀπολυθήσεσθε·			Μὴ κρίνετε, ἵνα μὴ κριθῆτε·
			Ἐλεᾶτε, ἵνα ἐλεηθῆτε· ἀφίετε, ἵνα ἀφεθῇ ὑμῖν·	ἀφίετε, καὶ ἀφεθήσεται ὑμῖν· ἐλεᾶτε, ἵνα ἐλεηθῆτε·
			ὡς ποιεῖτε, οὕτω ποιηθήσεται ὑμῖν· ὡς δίδοτε, οὕτως δοθήσεται ὑμῖν· ὡς κρίνετε, οὕτως κριθήσεσθε· ὡς χρηστεύεσθε, οὕτως χρηστευθήσεται ὑμῖν·	
	δίδοτε, καὶ δοθήσεται ὑμῖν·			
	μέτρον καλὸν πεπιεσμένον σεσαλευμένον ὑπερεκχυννόμενον δώσουσιν εἰς τὸν κόλπον ὑμῶν·			
ἐν ᾧ γὰρ κρίματι κρίνετε κριθήσεσθε,				

Table 2 (cont.)

Matt 7.1–2	Luke 6.37–8	Mark 4.24b	1 Cl 13.2	Pol Phil 2.3
καὶ ἐν ᾧ μέτρῳ μετρεῖτε μετρηθήσεται ὑμῖν.	ᾧ γὰρ μέτρῳ μετρεῖτε ἀντιμετρηθήσεται ὑμῖν.	ἐν ᾧ μέτρῳ μετρεῖτε μετρηθήσεται ὑμῖν καὶ προστεθήσεται ὑμῖν.	ᾧ μέτρῳ μετρεῖτε, ἐν αὐτῷ μετρηθήσεται ὑμῖν.	ᾧ μέτρῳ μετρεῖτε ἀντιμετρηθήσεται ὑμῖν.

oral form.[86] The saying seems to have been remarkably elastic from the beginning, and to have allowed for a virtually limitless application of the general principle. It cannot therefore be excluded that the specific topic of forgiveness was secondarily introduced in the document, or oral tradition which underlies both *1 Cl* 13.2 and Pol *Phil* 2.3, and maybe this took place under the influence of other synoptic sayings, such as Mark 11.25.

It turns out that the topic of 'forgiveness for those who forgive' is well attested in the gospel tradition, even if the origins of *1 Cl* 13.2/Pol *Phil* 2.3 are so uncertain that this saying cannot count as evidence. Both Mark 11.25 and the Lord's Prayer (Q?) testify that suppliants who have forgiven their fellow human beings can count on God's forgiveness. That this notion belongs to the heritage of early Judaism is evident from Ben Sira's statement on this point: 'Forgive the wrongdoing of your neighbour, and then as you pray your sins will be loosened' (Ecclus 28.2). While drawn by Ben Sira (28.3–5), the negative conclusion that God withholds his forgiveness from those who do not forgive their neighbours is only implicit in Mark 11.25 and in the Lord's Prayer. It is Matthew who elaborates this consequence of Jesus' teaching (6.15; 18.35).[87] In general, however, primitive Christians seem to have been reluctant to maintain mutual forgiveness as a strict precondition for receiving God's forgiveness, no doubt because they held on to the conviction that it was Jesus' death and resurrection that had made forgiveness possible, and that sins were forgiven through the baptismal rite and through faith in Jesus (see Chapter 3 below). Thus, reciprocal forgiveness was regarded as a consequence of, and response to, God's forgiveness in Christ, rather than as its prerequisite (Eph 4.32; cf. Col 3.13).[88] It may be in line with this primitive Christian view of forgiveness as christologically and sacramentally grounded that Luke, in his version of the Lord's Prayer, avoids reproducing Mark 11.25 and puts less emphasis on the appeal to pardon one's debtors prior to receiving forgiveness. To some extent, there

---

[86] K. Berding, *Polycarp and Paul: An Analysis of Their Literary and Theological Relationship in Light of Polycarp's Use of Biblical and Extra-Biblical Literature*, VCSup 62 (Leiden: Brill, 2002), pp. 53–9; A. F. Gregory, '*1 Clement* and the Writings that Later Formed the New Testament', in A. Gregory and C. Tuckett (eds.), *The New Testament and the Apostolic Fathers*, vol. I: *The Reception of the New Testament in the Apostolic Fathers* (Oxford University Press, 2005), pp. 129–57 (pp. 131–4).

[87] J. Park, 'Sündenvergebung: Ihre religiöse und soziale Dimension im Matthäusevangelium', unpublished Ph.D. thesis, University of Heidelberg (2001), pp. 143–6.

[88] V. Taylor, *Forgiveness and Reconciliation: A Study in New Testament Theology* (London: Macmillan, 1946), pp. 14–15.

is discontinuity between Jesus and Christianity about the relationship between human and divine forgiveness.

Forgiveness for all blasphemies except one (Mark 3.28–9/Q 12.10)

The saying which declares that all blasphemies will be forgiven except blasphemy against the Spirit is preserved in two forms that may in part represent different Greek translations of a single Aramaic original.

In Mark's version, the saying is prompted by the scribal accusation against Jesus of exorcizing by the power of Beelzebul (Mark 3.22, 30). Jesus first declares that all sins and all blasphemies will be forgiven 'for the sons of men' (3.28), and then he makes one exception: anyone who blasphemes against the Holy Spirit 'has no forgiveness (οὐκ ἔχει ἄφεσιν) forever, but is guilty of everlasting sin' (3.29). This saying is markedly eschatological, unlike 11.25 and the petition for forgiveness in the Lord's Prayer, which both concern the habit of asking for forgiveness regularly. Matthew has retained the saying within the setting taken over from Mark and has reworded it slightly. Among other things, Matthew has replaced Mark's phrase 'has no forgiveness' with 'will not be forgiven' (οὐκ ἀφεθήσεται, 12.31b). Moreover, Matthew has clarified Mark's mention of 'everlasting sin' as a reference to sin that cannot be forgiven 'either in this age or in the age to come' (12.32b), and he has thus retained the saying's eschatological focus. Finally, it appears quite obvious that the *Didache* alludes to this saying, although it is not explicitly attributed to Jesus: 'every sin will be forgiven, but this sin will not be forgiven' (11.7). The *Didache* is either dependent on the Gospel of Matthew or reflective of a tradition very close to that employed by Matthew. Like Matt 12.31, the *Didache* mentions 'sin' and states that there is one sin which 'will not be forgiven' (οὐκ ἀφεθήσεται).[89] This sin is, however, identified as putting to test or as judging a prophet who speaks 'in the Spirit' (ἐν πνεύματι). And the *Didache* does not preserve the unmistakably eschatological character of the saying found in

---

[89] Among those who hold that *Did* 11.7 presupposes Matthean redaction of the saying are E. Massaux, *The Influence of the Gospel of Saint Matthew on Christian Literature before Saint Irenaeus*, vol. III: *The Apologists and the Didache*, NGSt 5:3 (Leuven: Peeters, 1993), p. 165; C. M. Tuckett, 'Synoptic Tradition in the Didache', in Draper (ed.), *The Didache in Modern Research*, pp. 92–128 (pp. 104–5). By contrast, Draper, 'The Jesus Tradition in the Didache', p. 79, finds no evidence of literary dependence.

Mark and Matthew, since the future 'will (not) be forgiven' could well be construed as gnomic.[90] A rather different form of the saying seems to have been contained in Q. In Luke, it is part of a block of paraenetic teaching on heavenly support for courageous witnesses during the persecution to come (Luke 12.1–12). Immediately preceded by a 'Son of Man' saying (12.8–9) and followed by a promise of the assistance of the Holy Spirit (12.11–12), the saying on forgiveness mentions both the Son of Man and the Holy Spirit in antithetical parallelism: 'everyone who speaks a word against the Son of Man, for him it will be forgiven (ἀφεθήσεται); but for the one who blasphemes against the Holy Spirit, it will not be forgiven (οὐκ ἀφεθήσεται)' (12.10). Matthew has integrated the Q saying into the Markan saying, so that the eschatological qualifier follows on the formulation imported from Q (Matt 12.32). At some minor points, Matthew and Luke differ, which makes it difficult to establish the exact wording of the saying in Q.

There are good reasons to view the corresponding saying in *GThom* 44 as derived from the canonical Gospels, or at least from Matthew. It is commonly recognized that the trinitarian structure, according to which blasphemies against the Father and the Son 'will be forgiven' (ϲⲉⲛⲁⲕⲱ ⲉⲃⲟⲗ ⲛⲁϥ), but those against the Holy Spirit will not, represents a later stage of theological development than the 'Son of Man' saying in Q.[91] Moreover, the qualification that blasphemy against the Spirit will not be forgiven 'either in earth or in heaven' (ⲟⲩⲧⲉ ϩⲙ̄ ⲡⲕⲁϩ ⲟⲩⲧⲉ ϩⲛ̄ ⲧⲡⲉ) seems to be a clear case of Thomasine redaction of what is in itself a Matthean redaction of the Markan saying.[92] In keeping with its non-eschatological tendency, *Thomas* apparently substituted 'earth' and 'heaven' for Matthew's 'in this age' (ἐν τούτῳ τῷ αἰῶνι) and 'in the [age] to come' (ἐν τῷ μέλλοντι) respectively. As Wolfgang Schrage pointed out, this results in the rather awkward expression 'in (the) earth'.[93] It also

---

[90] A total of ninety-three future verb forms are found in the *Didache*. Among these, the eighteen future verbs in 16.1–8 and possibly also the four occurrences in 1.5 and 3.7 are eschatological, while sixty-nine futures may be labelled 'imperative' or 'gnomic' (the distinction is sometimes impossible to make). If one excludes from consideration the 'Two-Way Treatise' of chapters 1–6 and the apocalyptic chapter 16, there are eleven futures in addition to those in 11.7b, all of which are imperative or gnomic (11.5, 7*abis*, 8, 9, 11, 12; 12.1*bis*, 2; 13.3).

[91] R. Valantasis, *The Gospel of Thomas* (London/New York: Routledge, 1997), p. 120.

[92] *Pace* B. H. Gregg, *The Historical Jesus and the Final Judgment Sayings in Q*, WUNT 2:207 (Tübingen: Mohr Siebeck, 2006), pp. 197–8.

[93] W. Schrage, *Das Verhältnis des Thomas-Evangeliums zur synoptischen Tradition und zu den koptischen Evangelienübersetzungen: Zugleich ein Beitrag zur gnostischen Synoptikerdeutung*, BZNW 29 (Berlin: Töpelmann, 1964), p. 99 n. 1.

results in the untypical word order 'earth – heaven' (cf. *GThom* 12; 91).
Both these curious phenomena are conveniently explained by positing
that *Thomas* is dependent on Matthew, and accordingly it would be futile
to attempt to recover a separate tradition behind the Thomasine logion.

The two forms of the saying in Mark and Q agree that all blasphemies
(or hostile words), except the one against the Spirit, will be forgiven. By
contrast, the extension of the promised forgiveness to cover all kinds of
sin seems to be a Markan peculiarity, which is also reflected in Matthew
and the *Didache*, but absent from Q. On the other hand, Q spoke of the
Son of Man, who is not mentioned in the Markan form. Finally, it should
be noticed that the Q form of the saying is not explicitly eschatological.
Neither Luke nor the *Didache* include the eschatological qualifier present
in Mark, emphasized by Matthew, and de-eschatologized in *Thomas*; the
Greek future forms do not, by themselves, necessitate an eschatological
interpretation.

Mark's 'sons of men' and Q's 'Son of Man' are conveniently explained
as translation variants of the Aramaic (א)נש(א) לבר, but whether a reconstruction of the presumed Aramaic original saying should be based primarily on Mark or Q has been debated. Boring's argument in favour
of the eschatological Markan form as more primitive than the Q form
is dependent on his identification of the saying as the utterance of a
primitive Christian prophet.[94] To my mind, Lindars has made a more
convincing case for the primitiveness of the Q form. He reconstructs the
Aramaic saying behind Q 12.10 as follows:

וכל די יאמר מלה לבר אנשא
ישתבק לה
וכל די יאמר לרוחא דקדשא
לא ישתבק לה [95]

Whether the imperfect forms ישתבק were intended to have a present or a
future meaning would not be immediately clear apart from the context of
the saying. This does not change significantly even if one prefers to follow one of the Aramaic retranslations that are based on the Markan form
of the saying, for these also assume that an Aramaic imperfect, such as
ישתבק, underlies ἀφεθήσεται.[96] It is only the second half of the Markan

---

[94] M. E. Boring, 'The Unforgivable Sin Logion Mark III 28–29/Matt XII 31–32/Luke
XII 10: Formal Analysis and History of the Tradition', *NovT* 18 (1976), 258–79 (272).

[95] B. Lindars, *Jesus Son of Man: A Fresh Examination of the Son of Man Sayings in the
Gospels in the Light of Recent Research* (London: SPCK, 1983), pp. 34–8.

[96] C. Colpe, 'ὁ υἱὸς τοῦ ἀνθρώπου', in *TWNT*, vol. VIII, pp. 403–81; Boring, 'The
Unforgivable Sin Logion', 276.

saying that contains an eschatological qualifier, whereas the core of the first half agrees with the Q form by announcing universal forgiveness without any indication of temporality. To sum up, in Mark 3.28–9/Q 12.10 Jesus announces the general terms of forgiveness in the present or in the future. The saying's hypothesized Aramaic *Vorlage* is multiply attested and coheres well with other authentic traditions.[97] This holds true not only for the promise of universal forgiveness, but also for the negative part of the saying, which warns that there is one blasphemy that will not be forgiven. The historical Jesus did not proclaim unconditional forgiveness but, as argued above, preached forgiveness of one's neighbours as a prerequisite for gaining God's forgiveness.[98] This saying adds an additional requirement: in order to count on God's forgiveness, human beings must not blaspheme against the Spirit, that is, they must not reject the power of God, present and active on earth. Jesus, like Moses before him, is a vehicle of the Spirit.[99] Those who reject him will not be forgiven by God.

Forgiveness for outsiders? (Mark 4.10–12)

When questioned about his parables, the Markan Jesus alleges that everything comes in parables to those who are outside, 'lest they turn around and it be forgiven for them' (Mark 4.12; cf. Isa 6.10). A natural reading of Mark 4.10–12 suggests that both ἵνα and μήποτε carry final force, giving Jesus an active role in the hardening of the minds of the outsiders and thus preventing them from being forgiven. This fits well within the Gospel narrative which, after describing the acceptance of John's baptism for the forgiveness of sins by 'the entire Judean country and all Jerusalemites' (1.4–5), quickly turns to divergent appraisals of Jesus and their consequences for forgiveness. On the one hand, there are those who, like the paralytic, respond to Jesus with 'faith' and who are thus assured of forgiveness (2.5). On the other hand, the scribes from Jerusalem accuse him of being possessed by Satan and those who react

---

[97] Gregg, *The Historical Jesus and the Final Judgment Sayings*, pp. 203–5.

[98] *Pace* Boring, 'The Unforgivable Sin Logion', 276–7. See Hengel and Schwemer, *Jesus und das Judentum*, p. 413.

[99] E. Lövestam, *Spiritus blasphemia: Eine Studie zu Mk 3,28f par Mt 12,31f, Lk 12,10*, Scripta minora Regiae Societatis humaniorum litterarum Lundensis 1966–7:1 (Lund: Gleerup, 1968), pp. 58–68; J. D. G. Dunn, *Jesus and the Spirit: A Study of the Religious and Charismatic Experience of Jesus and the First Christians as Reflected in the New Testament* (London: SCM, 1975), pp. 52–3; Lindars, *Jesus Son of Man*, pp. 36–7.

like that will never be forgiven (3.22, 28–30). Now that Jesus deliberately speaks in parables that are incomprehensible 'to those outside' (ἐκείνοις ... τοῖς ἔξω), he includes in this group those who do not recognize his authority, namely his close relations who were previously said to be standing 'outside' (ἔξω, 3.31, 32) and the scribes who have blasphemed against the Holy Spirit.[100] They are already beyond any possibility of forgiveness.

That the passage is coherent with the narrative development in Mark's story does not necessarily imply that it was created by Mark. It is widely recognized that Mark 4.12 quotes Isa 6.9–10 in a form that exhibits a striking concurrence with the *Targum Jonathan* over against the MT and LXX. While the Hebrew of Isa 6.10 ends 'and he will heal it' (ורפא לו) and the Greek similarly 'and I will heal them' (καὶ ἰάσομαι αὐτούς), *Tg*Isa 6.10 and Mark 4.12 agree in saying 'and it will be forgiven for them' (וישתביק להן/καὶ ἀφεθῇ αὐτοῖς).[101] As Mark elsewhere uses the LXX, this conformity with a line of interpretation, which was later to be included in the Targum, indicates that this form of the quotation is pre-Markan.[102] And since the quotation cannot syntactically stand on its own, and must also have been included in a saying of Jesus in order to be remembered and transmitted by primitive Christianity, it is most likely that 4.11–12 came down to Mark as a unit.[103]

The authenticity of the passage is notoriously difficult to assess. On the one hand, that primitive Christians used Isa 6.9–10 to explain their failed mission to Israel is attested elsewhere (Acts 28.26–7; cf. Rom 11.8).[104] On the other hand, as far as I can see, nothing in this passage militates against its derivation from the historical Jesus, and it is indeed coherent with Jesus' prophetic identity.[105] Moreover, when detached from its Markan setting, 4.11–12 becomes difficult to interpret, especially if an underlying Aramaic version is postulated. In Aramaic the quotation may have functioned simply to state that there are outsiders

---

[100] M. D. Goulder, 'Those Outside (Mk. 4:10–12)', *NovT* 33 (1991), 289–302 (291–2).

[101] B. Chilton and C. A. Evans, 'Jesus and Israel's Scriptures', in Chilton and Evans (eds.), *Studying the Historical Jesus*, pp. 281–335 (pp. 300–4).

[102] T. W. Manson, *The Teaching of Jesus: Studies of Its Form and Content* (Cambridge University Press, 1931), pp. 77–8.

[103] B. Chilton, *A Galilean Rabbi and His Bible: Jesus' Own Interpretation of Isaiah* (London: SPCK, 1984), pp. 90–8, does not acknowledge these difficulties in his case for 4.12 as an independent saying of the historical Jesus.

[104] Meier, *A Marginal Jew*, vol. II, pp. 491–2.

[105] See C. A. Evans, *To See and Not Perceive: Isaiah 6.9–10 in Early Jewish and Christian Interpretation*, JSOTS 64 (Sheffield: JSOT Press, 1989), pp. 103–6; Snodgrass, *Stories with Intent*, pp. 157–64.

'who (ד), when they see, see but do not understand, and when they hear, hear but do not comprehend, so that they do not turn around (or: unless they turn around) and it is forgiven for them (ויתובון וישתביק להון)'.[106] Or it may have expressed the notion that Jesus' preaching was intended to harden the hearts of an unwilling people, which would be consonant with the function of the passage both in Isaiah and in Mark. The uncertainty precludes the building of a reconstruction of the historical Jesus' preaching about forgiveness on this item of gospel tradition.

Forgiveness in the parables

The unforgiving servant (Matt 18.23–35)

Bringing the Matthean discourse about relationships within the church to an end, the parable of the unforgiving servant follows on the dialogue between Jesus and Peter about repeated forgiveness (18.21–2). As the latter item appears to be related to Luke 17.4, it contains at least some pre-Matthean elements, and the appendage of the parable (18.23–35) is most probably the evangelist's own working.[107] Robert Gundry has argued that the parable was composed in its entirety by Matthew himself on the basis of the parable of the two debtors (Luke 7.41–3).[108] But besides the fact that Luke 7.41–3 and Matt 18.23–35 seem to make quite different points, and also the fact that the similarities in vocabulary are not very remarkable, the slight discrepancy between 18.21–2 (concerning the necessity to forgive an unlimited number of times) and 18.23–35 (concerning mutual forgiveness as a consequence of, and precondition for, God's forgiveness) indicates that the parable antedates the Gospel of Matthew.[109]

As the parable now stands, some elements are likely to be the result of redaction. Above all, the concluding 18.35 is strongly coloured by distinctly Matthean language ('my heavenly father', ὁ πατήρ μου ὁ οὐράνιος) and theological emphasis (a refusal to forgive one's fellow believer will make God withdraw his forgiveness). It was probably added

[106] For various proposals, see J. Jeremias, *Die Gleichnisse Jesu*, 7th edn (Göttingen: Vandenhoeck & Ruprecht, 1965), pp. 13–14; Taylor, *Mark*, pp. 256–8.

[107] W. G. Thompson, *Matthew's Advice to a Divided Community: Mt. 17,22 – 18,35*, AnBib 44 (Rome: Biblical Institute Press, 1970), pp. 208, 234–6.

[108] R. H. Gundry, *Matthew: A Commentary on His Handbook for a Mixed Church under Persecution*, 2nd edn (Grand Rapids, MI: Eerdmans, 1994), pp. 371–2.

[109] E. Linnemann, *Gleichnisse Jesu: Einführung und Auslegung*, 6th edn (Göttingen: Vandenhoeck & Ruprecht, 1975), p. 111.

by Matthew in order to bring out the parable's allegorical potential.[110] Moreover, the introductory formula in 18.23, 'Therefore the kingdom of heavens has become like…', is characteristically Matthean, as is the designation of one of the characters as 'a man who was a king'. As this character is simply labelled 'master' (κύριος) throughout the rest of the parable, it is possible that Matthew turned him into a king as a means of inviting an allegorical interpretation.[111] It is quite possible that the pre-Matthean parable was about a master and his servants, and that it did not identify the master as a king, nor as a cipher for God.

The suspicions that the neat allegorical scheme in 18.23–35 derives from Matthew and that the pre-Matthean parable was more ambiguous can be bolstered by some observations on how Matthew incorporates Q 12.58–9 into the Sermon on the Mount. This piece of moral exhortation addresses the same general topic as 18.23–35 – the dreadful consequences of failing to come to terms with one's neighbour – but locates all initiatives with the two contending parts while the role of the third part is subordinate. While, in Luke's version, the third part involves a 'magistrate' (ἄρχων), a 'judge' (κριτής), and a 'constable' (πράκτωρ), Matt 5.25 mentions only the 'judge' (κριτής) and the 'servant' (ὑπερέτης), who can now be seen as ciphers for God and for the angel of judgement.[112] Q 12.58–9 and the traditional parable behind Matt 18.23–34 both appear to have functioned as exhortations to forgive one's neighbour, since failure to do so will result in judgement and in a punishment here portrayed in monetary terms, 'until you have paid back the last penny' (Q 12.58, cf. Matt 18.34). I find the implicit notion of divine forgiveness being limited well enough attested to go back to the historical Jesus, but it is Matthew who has brought it out explicitly and emphasized it.

The prodigal son (Luke 15.11–32)

Luke introduces his arrangement of three parables on the theme of being lost and found by relating that the Pharisees and scribes 'were murmuring' on seeing that Jesus associated and ate together with toll collectors and sinners (15.1–2). The parable of the lost sheep (15.3–7) is evidently pre-Lukan, since it has a variant in Matt 18.12–14. Luke's version of

---

[110] M. C. de Boer, 'Ten Thousand Talents? Matthew's Interpretation and Redaction of the Parable of the Unforgiving Servant', *CBQ* 50 (1988), 214–32 (219–21).

[111] W. Michaelis, *Die Gleichnisse Jesu: Eine Einführung*, 3rd edn (Hamburg: Furche, 1956), p. 191.

[112] G. Strecker, *Die Bergpredigt: Ein exegetischer Kommentar* (Göttingen: Vandenhoeck & Ruprecht, 1984), p. 72.

the parable is elaborated with a concluding scene, in which the sheep's owner exclaims 'Rejoice with me!' (συγχάρητέ μοι, 15.6). This elaboration may be pre-Lukan, as Jeremias argued on philological grounds.[113] In its present context, the scene evokes the banquet of joy to which the Pharisees and scribes have objected, and Luke interprets both the parabolic rejoicing and Jesus' association with sinners as celebrations of repentance (μετάνοια). Repentance is something for which Luke shows a special concern throughout the Gospel and Acts.[114] The parable of the lost coin (15.8–10) also seems to be pre-Lukan. It too contains a mention of common rejoicing (15.9) and a final application of the parable to repentance (15.10).

The parable of the prodigal son is the Lukan Jesus' third and most forceful response to the objections. At first glance, it seems to fit the immediate context and Luke's purposes so well that the entire parable could have been authored by the evangelist.[115] However, philological analyses of the parable have demonstrated that it contains features that are uncharacteristic of Luke.[116] Furthermore, in a recent study of the parable, Vesa Ollilainen has demonstrated that it more likely than not originated with the historical Jesus, since it both coheres well with authentic material about Jesus and cannot convincingly be relocated to an 'alternative homeland' within primitive Christianity.[117]

Since there is no repentance terminology within the parable, commentators have frequently doubted that it is about repentance at all. Ollilainen maintains that the parable as told by the historical Jesus did not concern repentance. The son's decision to return to his father is not prompted by contrition, but by his acute lack of sustenance and his hope that a return will bring about material gains.[118] Correct as these observations are, the conclusion that repentance is not involved presumes that feelings of remorse are integral to the concept of repentance and that it must be free from ulterior motives. Some early Jewish descriptions of repentance

---

[113] J. Jeremias, 'Tradition und Redaktion in Lukas 15', *ZNW* 62 (1971), 172–89 (182).

[114] Luke 3.3, 8; 5.32; 10.13; 11.32; 13.3, 5; 16.30; 17.3, 4; 24.47; Acts 2.38; 3.19; 5.31; 8.22; 11.18; 13.24; 17.30; 19.4; 20.21; 26.20. See G. D. Nave, *The Role and Function of Repentance in Luke-Acts*, Academia Biblica 4 (Atlanta: SBL, 2002), pp. 159–91.

[115] For this view, see L. Schottroff, 'Das Gleichnis vom verlorenen Sohn', *ZTK* 68 (1971), 27–52.

[116] Jeremias, 'Tradition und Redaktion', 174–9; C. E. Carlston, 'Reminiscence and Redaction in Luke 15:11–32', *JBL* 94 (1975), 368–90 (378–83); V. Ollilainen, 'Jesus and the Parable of the Prodigal Son', unpublished Ph.D. thesis, Åbo Akademi (2008), pp. 78–86.

[117] Ollilainen, 'Jesus and the Parable of the Prodigal Son', pp. 115–36.

[118] *Ibid.*, pp. 103–6, 132, 181.

do indeed mention remorse alongside moral improvement and public confession (e.g. Philo *PraemPoen* 163), but in other cases the motivation for turning back to God seems to be the temporal benefit supposed to result from such an act.[119] Accordingly, the prodigal son's behaviour in 15.17–21 is well within the boundaries of an early Jewish conception of repentance, involving the resolution to 'return' and the confession of one's failings. Such a confession naturally implies a request for forgiveness.

Forgiveness is not explicitly mentioned in this parable either, but the father's behaviour indicates that he forgives his son. The theology of forgiveness expressed in this parable agrees well with an uncontroversial tenet of early Judaism: there is forgiveness for all who repent (e.g. Ecclus 17.24; *PsSol* 9.6–7). If representative of Jesus' message, this parable grants no distinctive characteristics to his preaching of forgiveness.

The Pharisee and the toll-collector (Luke 18.10–14)

This short exemplary parable takes Lukan criticism of Pharisaic self-righteousness even further. Not only does Luke introduce the parable by stating that Jesus told it 'to some who trusted that they themselves were righteous (δίκαιοι) and who despised others' (Luke 18.9), but the climactic point also employs language of righteousness: 'I tell you, this one went back to his home having been made righteous (δεδικαιωμένος) rather than that one' (18.14a). This raises suspicion that both 18.9 and 18.14a were composed by Luke, in line with other Lukan formulations that use similar vocabulary in order to characterize religious authorities (10.29; 16.14–15; 20.20).[120] If this is so, Luke may well have constructed the entire parable, possibly as a concrete application of the traditional saying about elevation and humiliation in 18.14b (cf. Q 14.11). There are additional reasons, primarily the conventional concept of repentance presupposed in the parable, that make me hesitant to ascribe it to the historical Jesus.[121] Even if this assessment is mistaken, the parable does not add much to our knowledge about Jesus' view of forgiveness. It seems reasonable to

---

[119] Tob 13.8 and Josephus, *Bell* V.415 employ repentance terminology (ἐπιστρέφειν and μετανοεῖν respectively) to recommend concrete actions that will bring deliverance from national crises (cf. *LAB* 30.4–5, without explicit mention of repentance).

[120] F. G. Downing, 'The Ambiguity of "The Pharisee and the Toll-Collector" (Luke 18:9–14) in the Graeco-Roman World of Late Antiquity', *CBQ* 54 (1992), 80–99 (96–7).

[121] M. D. Goulder, *Luke: A New Paradigm*, JSNTS 20 (Sheffield Academic Press, 1989), pp. 668–70; T. Hägerland, 'Jesus and the Rites of Repentance', *NTS* 52 (2006), 166–87 (185–7).

assume that 18.14a means that the toll-collector's prayer for forgiveness (18.13b) was granted. In this way, 18.10–14 confirms the basic conviction found in Mark 11.25 and Matt 6.12/Luke 11.4, namely that God's forgiveness is granted as a response to prayer. Like Luke 15.11–32, this passage (if authentic) reaffirms Jesus' place within first-century Judaism, but it contains no special qualifications or preconditions that give any distinct flavour to the historical Jesus' preaching on forgiveness.

Forgiveness as a result of Jesus' death

The strong tendency in primitive Christianity to associate forgiveness with the death of Jesus will be dealt with in Chapter 3. Here I will draw attention to the few Gospel passages in which Jesus himself makes proleptic mention of his death as explicitly or implicitly bringing about forgiveness. The question concerning what significance the historical Jesus may have attached to his impending death is so complex that the treatment here can only be quite cursory.

The ransom saying (Mark 10.45 par.)

Forming the climax of Jesus' ethical instruction in Mark 10.41–5, the so-called ransom saying seems to draw on the depiction of the Servant of the Lord in Isaiah 53: 'For thus the Son of Man has not come to be served, but to serve and to give his life as a ransom for many (λύτρον ἀντὶ πολλῶν)' (10.45).[122] Forgiveness is not mentioned, but may be implied by association with the Isaianic statements about the Servant, who 'carried the sins of many and was handed over because of their sins' (Isa 53.12; cf. 53.4, 5, 6, 8, 11).

Whereas Matt 20.28 reproduces the saying from Mark, Luke appears to give it in a shorter form in the context of his narration of Jesus' last supper: 'But I am in your midst as one who serves' (Luke 22.27b). It is possible that this form of the saying is more primitive and that the Markan form represents a later development influenced by Christian reflection on Jesus' death.[123] On the other hand, it cannot be excluded that the form in Luke 22.27b is the result of an abbreviation of the Markan saying.[124] The

---

[122] See R. E. Watts, 'Jesus' Death, Isaiah 53, and Mark 10:45: A Crux Revisited', in W. H. Bellinger, Jr. and W. R. Farmer (eds.), *Jesus and the Suffering Servant: Isaiah 53 and Christian Origins* (Harrisburg, PA: Trinity, 1998), pp. 125–51, and the literature cited therein; S. McKnight, *Jesus and His Death: Historiography, the Historical Jesus, and Atonement Theory* (Waco, TX: Baylor University Press, 2005), pp. 167–8.
[123] Bultmann, *Die Geschichte der synoptischen Tradition*, p. 154.

deutero-Pauline confession of 'the human being Jesus Christ, who gave himself as a ransom for all (ἀντίλυτρον ὑπὲρ πάντων)' (1 Tim 2.5–6), seems to presuppose the saying in its Markan form. The authenticity of the saying continues to be an unresolved problem. Stuhlmacher's argument for authenticity employs the criterion of dissimilarity in its dubious double form (see Chapter 1 above) and fails to establish discontinuity between the saying and primitive Christian theology.[125] Moreover, the notion that predictions of Jesus' untimely death formed a prominent part of his teaching is difficult to reconcile with the confusion and disappointment apparently following on the event itself and with the indications that the disciples attributed a preordained significance to it only in retrospect (Luke 24.25–7, 44–6; John 2.19–22; 20.9).[126] Since forgiveness is at most implied by Mark 10.45, the problem of the saying's authenticity is in any case hardly central to the present investigation.

The last supper (Matt 26.28)

Another tradition arguably betraying influence from Isaiah 53 is the last supper narrative, where in Mark Jesus identifies the cup as 'my covenantal blood which is being poured out for many (ὑπὲρ πολλῶν)' (Mark 14.24). Matthew extends this formula into 'my covenantal blood which is being poured out for many for the forgiveness of sins (περὶ πολλῶν εἰς ἄφεσιν ἁμαρτιῶν)' (Matt 26.28). Here the link between Jesus' violent death and forgiveness is explicit. The mention of forgiveness is consonant with the redactional outline of Matthew's Gospel (cf. 1.21), and the phrase appears to have been relocated to this place from the pre-Matthean description of John's baptism of repentance 'for the forgiveness of sins' (Mark 1.4; Luke 3.3; cf. Matt 3.1).[127] One could certainly argue that, with this addition, Matthew has simply brought out what is already implicit in the Markan allusion to the death of the Servant at this point. It is not impossible that at least shortly before his execution – as opposed to during the main part of his career – Jesus had come to think of his death as salvific and even involving the forgiveness of sins. It must still be kept in mind how uncertain is the reconstruction of an original

---

[124] R. Riesner, 'Back to the Historical Jesus through Paul and His School (The Ransom Logion—Mark 10.45; Matt 20.28)', *JSHJ* 1 (2003), 171–99.

[125] Stuhlmacher, *Biblische Theologie*, vol. i, p. 121.

[126] Theissen and Merz, *Der historische Jesus*, pp. 377–8.

[127] Leroy, *Zur Vergebung der Sünden*, pp. 30–7.

form of the tradition behind the Pauline (1 Cor 11.23–5; Luke 22.19–20) and Markan (Mark 14.22–4; Matt 26.26–8) versions. The allusion to the Servant motif is absent from the tradition reproduced by Paul and Luke and may have originated with Mark or with the tradition he used.

Forgiveness as part of the commission of the disciples of Jesus

A commission to forgive and retain sins (John 20.19–23)

As part of the second appearance of the risen Jesus in the Gospel of John, the disciples receive the Holy Spirit and are commissioned to forgive and retain sins. Elsewhere, I have offered an extensive synchronic interpretation of this episode, which I will summarize here.[128] The Johannine Jesus' declaration 'As the Father has sent me, I too send you' (20.21), in conjunction with his breathing the Spirit into his disciples (20.22), constitutes a commissioning of the disciples as prophets, just as the Gospel portrays Jesus as a prophet (4.19; 9.17) or as 'the prophet like Moses' (cf. 6.14; 7.40). John grants, to both Jesus and his disciples, mantic and prophetic characteristics that are especially prominent in the LXX Balaam cycle and in its earliest interpretations.[129] Not of themselves (5.19; 15.4–5), but rather by the Spirit (1.32–3; 16.13), do they testify (3.11; 15.27) about the hidden things which they have seen and heard (3.32; 14.7–9, 24). Yet another aspect of this prophetic mission is to forgive and retain sins, in the sense of proclaiming sinfulness and forgiveness in accordance with a pneumatic insight. The Johannine Jesus displays his ability to identify abiding sinfulness (8.21, 24; 9.41), and so he fulfils his mission to execute judgement (5.22). Now, after the glorification of Jesus, his disciples are invested with the same prophetic authority.[130] The commissioning formula 'If you forgive the sins of any they are forgiven for them, if you retain [the sins] of any they are retained' (20.23) strongly echoes Balak's words to the mantic Balaam, 'whoever you bless is blessed, and whoever you curse is cursed' (Num 22.6). Both Balaam and the disciples of Jesus have, for all the differences that exist

---

[128] T. Hägerland, 'The Power of Prophecy: A Septuagintal Echo in John 20:19–23', *CBQ* 71 (2009), 84–103.

[129] Num 22.1–24.25; Josephus *Ant* IV.102–30; Philo *Mos* I.263–99; cf. *LAB* 18.10–12.

[130] Bultmann, *Johannes*, p. 537; R. E. Brown, *The Gospel according to John XIII–XXI: A New Translation with Introduction and Commentary*, AB 29A (Garden City, NY: Doubleday, 1970), pp. 1042–3; S. E. Hansen, 'Forgiving and Retaining Sin: A Study of the Text and Context of John 20:23', *HBT* 19 (1997), 24–32 (28–9).

between them, an infallible prophetic ability to proclaim and to effectuate blessing/forgiveness and curse/retention according to the mind of
God. None of them is, however, entrusted with an autonomous power to
bless, to curse, to forgive or to retain at will. John 20.23 should therefore
be taken as saying that the disciples can rest assured of the Spirit's presence to inform them about what God has already decided.

That John 20.19–23 is somehow related to Luke 24.36–43 is obvious,
although it is uncertain whether Luke 24.36b, 40 belonged to the text
originally or entered it at a very early stage from John 20.19b–20.20a.[131]
Most scholars have thought that Luke and John here used a common
tradition and that there is no literary dependence in either direction.[132] In
this specific case, John's independence of Luke is supported by the fact
that the elements in Luke 24.36–43 which are most clearly characteristic of Lukan redaction – the expression 'becoming terrified' (24.37) and
the noun 'thoughts' (24.38) – have left no imprint on John 20.19–23.[133]
From Johannine redaction stem in all probability at least the qualification 'for fear of the Jews' (20.19), the mention of Jesus' 'side' (20.20)
and the statement 'As the Father has sent me, I too send you' (20.21).[134]
In view of these indications that John has reworked the tradition quite
extensively, and taking into account the fact that the commission in 20.23
is fully coherent with the Gospel's theology and narrative plot at large, it
might seem plausible at first sight to consider 20.23 as also purely redactional. Two observations nevertheless disqualify such a position.

First of all, the passage includes vocabulary that is atypical of
the Gospel of John.[135] In the thirteen occurrences of ἀφιέναι outside
20.23, this verb never denotes 'to forgive'. The Lamb of God is the one
'who takes away (αἴρων) the sin of the world' (1.29), not the one who

---

[131] See Dauer, *Johannes und Lukas*, pp. 209–16, on the textual uncertainty.

[132] Bultmann, *Johannes*, pp. 534–5; Dodd, *Historical Tradition*, pp. 144–5; Brown, *John XIII–XXI*, pp. 1028–9.

[133] The phrase ἔμφοβος γενόμενος occurs three more times in Luke (24.5, where it is preferred to the Markan ἐκθαμβεῖσθαι) and Acts (10.4; 24.25); the single non-Lukan NT use of ἔμφοβος is in Rev 11.13. The noun διαλογισμός is more frequent in the NT, occurring fourteen times in all, but Luke shows a special preference for it. Twice the nom-inal form replaces Mark's διαλογίζεσθαι (5.22; 9.47); twice it has no counterpart in the synoptic parallels (6.8; 9.46); and once it occurs in a programmatic passage peculiar to Luke (2.35).

[134] The phrase διὰ τὸν φόβον τῶν Ἰουδαίων occurs also in John 7.13; 19.38; cf. 9.22. πλευρά links the episode back to the crucifixion (19.34). Jesus' being sent by the Father is referred to forty-two times in John with either of the verbs ἀποστέλλειν and πέμπειν (cf. twice in Matthew; once in Mark; four times in Luke), and 17.18 comes close to 20.21 both in form and in content. See also Dauer, *Johannes und Lukas*, pp. 221–2, 234–7.

[135] Bultmann, *Johannes*, p. 535; Dauer, *Johannes und Lukas*, pp. 242–4.

Table 3 *The syntactic structure of Num 22.6; John 20.23; Matt 16.19; 18.18*

	Num 22.6	John 20.23	Matt 16.19	Matt 18.18
A Conditional or conditional relative	οὓς ἐὰν εὐλογήσῃς σύ,	ἄν τινων ἀφῆτε τὰς ἁμαρτίας	ὃ ἐὰν δήσῃς ἐπὶ τῆς γῆς	ὅσα ἐὰν δήσητε ἐπὶ τῆς γῆς
B Apodosis	εὐλόγηνται,	ἀφέωνται αὐτοῖς,	ἔσται δεδεμένον ἐν τοῖς οὐρανοῖς,	ἔσται δεδεμένα ἐν οὐρανῷ,
A´ Conditional or conditional relative	καὶ οὓς ἐὰν καταράσῃ σύ,	ἄν τινων κρατῆτε	καὶ ὃ ἐὰν λύσῃς ἐπὶ τῆς γῆς	καὶ ὅσα ἐὰν λύσητε ἐπὶ τῆς γῆς
B´ Apodosis	κεκατήρανται.	κεκράτηνται.	ἔσται λελυμένον ἐν τοῖς οὐρανοῖς.	ἔσται λελυμένα ἐν οὐρανῷ.

'forgives'. Moreover, the juridical language applied to dealings with sin in John includes the notions that Jesus will 'judge' (κρίνειν, 8.24–6) and the Spirit will 'convict' (ἐλέγχειν, 16.8); but 20.23 says 'retain' (κρατεῖν), another un-Johannine choice of vocabulary that is probably prompted by the need for an antonym to ἀφιέναι.[136]

Secondly, the relationship between John 20.23 and Matt 16.19; 18.18 cannot be ignored. Together with Num 22.6, these sayings belong to a group of syntactically parallel formulae, of which no further specimen seems to exist within early Jewish and primitive Christian literature (see Table 3). A saying in this group consists of two members, each of which is made up of a conditional clause or conditional relative (A and A´) followed by an apodosis (B and B´). The predicate of A is also the predicate of B, and that of A´ is also that of B´; the verb employed in the first member is semantically the opposite of that employed in the second member. In A and A´, the verb is active and in the second-person subjunctive,

---

[136] Cf. Ecclus 28.1 (διατηρεῖν). See Bultmann, *Johannes*, p. 537 n. 4. S. M. Schneiders, 'The Raising of the New Temple: John 20.19–23 and Johannine Ecclesiology', *NTS* 52 (2006), 337–55 (352–4), proposes a radically different understanding of κρατεῖν in 20.23; for criticism, see J. Lambrecht, 'A Note on John 20,23b', *ETL* 83 (2007), 165–8; Hägerland, 'The Power of Prophecy', 99–100 n. 46.

while in B and B´, the verb is in the passive third-person simple perfect or periphrastic future-perfect indicative.[137] It is unlikely that these closely aligned sayings came about in total isolation from each other, although the nature of their relationship is open to discussion. I will have to postpone this discussion until the end of the section below on the Matthean commissions, but it can be concluded already at this point that Matt 16.19; 18.18 indicate that John 20.23 should not be ascribed in its entirety to the evangelist.

As a final remark, it is important to bear in mind that John 20.23 does not pretend to be a saying of the earthly Jesus, but of the risen one. Its attribution to the historical Jesus could therefore be maintained only on the premise that it has been relocated from a traditional setting in the earthly life of Jesus to its present position as part of an appearance of the risen Lord – an unlikely assumption, as we shall see.

Commissions to bind and loose (Matt 16.13–20; 18.15–20)

The Matthean commissions in their contexts

The two Matthean commissions to 'bind' and 'loose', given by Jesus to Peter and to the disciples respectively, are nearly identical in formulation (Matt 16.19; 18.18). As William Thompson has pointed out, when Matthew gives a saying twice, it may well be that it is employed with two different meanings.[138] This appears to be the case also with 16.19/18.18.

Matt 16.13–20. Peter's confession of Jesus at Caesarea Philippi and Jesus' subsequent macarism follow a scene in which Jesus warns his disciples about 'the leaven of the Pharisees and the Sadducees' (16.6, 11), which turns out to be a warning against their 'teaching' ($\delta\iota\delta\alpha\chi\dot{\eta}$, 16.12). This mention of teaching is significant for the interpretation of 16.13–20. Here human and inadequate opinions about the identity of the Son of Man (16.13–14) are contrasted with Simon Peter's recognition of Jesus as 'the Messiah, the Son of the living God' (16.16). As a response to Peter's words, Jesus declares that he will build his Church 'on this rock' and will give to Peter 'the keys of the kingdom of heaven' (16.18–19). Both the giving of the keys and the commission to bind and loose are to be viewed as Jesus' declaration that he will grant a teaching authority to Peter in the future, when he builds his Church.

---

[137] Hägerland, 'The Power of Prophecy', 97–9.
[138] Thompson, *Matthew's Advice*, p. 194.

'To bind' (δεῖν) and 'to loose' (λύειν) here mean to pronounce halakhic rulings, that is, to forbid and to permit.[139] Not only is this, as pointed out earlier, the most likely reading of the commission in the immediate context of Matthew 16, but it also agrees well with the Gospel of Matthew as a whole, where the terminology of closing, binding and loosing has to do with the authority to teach.[140] Moreover, the verbs שרא and אסר are frequently used with these connotations in rabbinic literature.[141] There is, accordingly, much to be said for the majority opinion that Matt 16.19 is not a commission to forgive sins, but a commission to teach authoritatively, a task that will be performed by Peter and the rest of the disciples after Jesus' death and resurrection (28.20).

Against the majority view, Hans Kvalbein has recently defended the interpretation of 16.19 as a reference to the authority to forgive sins. In Kvalbein's construal of the structure of the Gospel, the phrase 'From that time Jesus began…' (ἀπὸ τότε ἤρξατο ὁ Ἰησοῦς) signals a new beginning in the Gospel in 4.17 and 16.21, but in both these instances the phrase includes the immediately preceding episode. In other words, the occurrence of the phrase in 16.21 highlights that something new has been introduced with 16.13–20. As a result of this understanding of the structure, 16.13–20 is marked off sharply from 16.5–12, and there is no warrant for interpreting the commissioning of Peter in the light of the mention of 'teaching' in 16.12. Kvalbein argues instead that λύειν is a synonym of ἀφιέναι.[142] While it is clear that λύειν may indeed be used in the sense of 'to forgive', Kvalbein's case for it doing so in Matt 16.19 is, in my opinion, seriously weakened by his neglect of how Matthew employs the vocabulary outside of 18.18. Furthermore, Kvalbein's argument depends on the purported function of the phrase in 16.21 as a sharp divider between different parts of the Gospel. One may wonder how the original recipients of the Gospel, encountering the text aurally rather than visually, could have been expected to recognize such a definite break between 16.12 and 16.13 in retrospect, when they encountered the

---

[139] Davies and Allison, *Matthew*, vol. II, pp. 638–9; Byrskog, *Jesus the Only Teacher*, pp. 246–9.

[140] Matt 5.19 (λύειν, cf. 5.17); 23.4 (δεσμεύειν, cf. 23.2); 23.13 (κλείειν).

[141] H. L. Strack and P. Billerbeck, *Kommentar zum Neuen Testament aus Talmud und Midrasch*, vol. I, 9th edn (Munich: Beck, 1986), pp. 739–41; J. D. M. Derrett, 'Binding and Loosing (Matt 16:19; 18:18; John 29:23 [sic])', *JBL* 102 (1983), 112–17.

[142] H. Kvalbein, 'The Authorization of Peter in Matthew 16:17–19: A Reconsideration of the Power to Bind and Loose', in J. Ådna (ed.), *The Formation of the Early Church*, WUNT 183 (Tübingen: Mohr Siebeck, 2005), pp. 145–74. Kvalbein's perception of Matthew's structure reflects J. D. Kingsbury, *Matthew: Structure, Christology, Kingdom*, paperback edn (Minneapolis: Fortress, 1989), pp. 7–25.

crucial phrase in 16.21. More plausibly, they would have heard 16.13–20 with the discussion of 'teaching' in 16.2–12 still ringing in their ears, and would have interpreted it accordingly.

Matt 18.15–20. The instructions concerning the treatment of an erring brother conclude with two sayings which promise unfailing harmony between the disciples' collective behaviour on earth and the Father's action in heaven: the commission to bind and loose (18.18) and the promise that their prayer will be heard (18.19–20). Placed in this context, the saying about binding and loosing seems to have a more specific meaning than in 16.19, that is, a meaning which relates to the topic of dealing with sinners in the congregation.

When predicated of the disciples, 'to bind' (δεῖν) here appears to be used in the sense of 'to expel' from the congregation, and 'to loose' (λύειν) denotes the act of readmitting the penitent sinner to the congregation. Also, this use of the verbs is paralleled by אסר and שרא in rabbinic literature, though the attestation is sparse.[143] It cannot be strictly separated from the meaning 'to forgive', given not only to the Greek λύειν in the LXX but apparently also to the Aramaic שרא in *Targum Neofiti*.[144] From the perspective of the congregation, to readmit a member would entail regarding the past sin as forgiven.[145] It is also more natural to construe the binding and loosing that will take place in heaven simultaneously with the disciples' decisions on earth as references to the retaining and forgiving of sins.

The future perfects of 18.18 should not be taken to say that the binding and loosing in heaven precedes that on earth temporally.[146] Matt 18.18 is closely followed by 18.19, which clearly expresses the notion that the Father will concur with whatever two disciples agree on. Yet this is due to Jesus' presence among the assembled believers (18.20), which ensures that they will only ask for such things as are compatible with the Father's will.

A traditional commission

According to Gundry, Matt 16.17–19 is an entirely redactional expansion of the episode of Peter's acknowledgement of Jesus as the

---

[143] *bMoedQat* 16a. See Thompson, *Matthew's Advice*, p. 190; Davies and Allison, *Matthew*, vol. II, p. 636.

[144] Job 42.9; Isa 40.2; Ecclus 28.2; *TgNeof*Gen 4.7.

[145] Gundry, *Matthew*, p. 369.

[146] *Pace* J. R. Mantey, 'Distorted Translations in John 20:23; Matthew 16:18–19 and 18:18', *RevExp* 78 (1981), 409–16.

Messiah.[147] But there are so many features uncharacteristic of Matthew in this passage that the hypothesis of redactional origin seems untenable.[148] Moreover, 18.18 may be secondary over against 16.19, since it is being cast in slightly Mattheanized language: the singular 'heaven' in contrast with 'the earth' is more typical of Matthew than the plural employed in 16.19.[149] If this is correct, it is likely that the plural in 16.19 stems from a pre-Matthean form of the saying. Finally, Dodd has argued convincingly that John 20.23 is not dependent on either of the Matthean sayings, but represents a separate strand of tradition.[150] This corroborates the pre-Matthean origin of Matt 16.19.

An influential explanation of the origin of the Matthean and Johannine commissions was offered by J. A. Emerton. He suggested that the traditional saying was based on the Isaianic promise to Eliakim, on whose shoulder the Lord 'will put the key of David's house ... and he will open, and there is no one who closes, and he will close, and there is no one who opens' (Isa 22.22). Emerton thinks that the Matthean and Johannine sayings may be translation variants of a common Aramaic original which, as he conjectures, ran 'and whatsoever thou shalt shut (אחד) shall be shut: and whatsoever thou shalt open (פתח) shall be opened', and which was interpreted differently on the basis of the semantic potential of the Aramaic verbs.[151] Despite the attractiveness of a hypothesis that can account for the saying in all its variants, Emerton's proposal is not fully convincing. First of all, as Emerton himself grants, his tentative reconstruction of the translation process involves some extremely hypothetical steps. He argues that the process has led from 'open' (פתח) in the original saying via its being reinterpreted as 'release' as an antonym of 'hold' (itself a reinterpretation of 'close', אחד) to 'forgive' (ἀφιέναι) in John 20.23, in the light of another verb, which means both 'to release' and 'to forgive' (שרא). Secondly, Num 22.6 constitutes a closer formal parallel to the sayings in Matthew and John than Isa 22.22 does. John 20.23 especially, which lacks the reference to the keys, seems far removed from Isa 22.22 if Num 22.6 LXX is brought into the picture. Thirdly, there seems to be some point of contact between the Matthean and Johannine

---

[147] Gundry, *Matthew*, pp. 330–6.

[148] Davies and Allison, *Matthew*, vol. II, p. 605.

[149] Thompson, *Matthew's Advice*, pp. 193–4; Byrskog, *Jesus the Only Teacher*, pp. 359–60.

[150] Dodd, *Historical Tradition*, pp. 347–9. See now also M. Theobald, *Herrenworte im Johannesevangelium*, HBS 34 (Freiburg: Herder, 2002), pp. 174–96.

[151] J. A. Emerton, 'Binding and Loosing – Forgiving and Retaining', *JTS* 13 (1962), 325–31.

sayings at the level of the Greek, which renders it unlikely that they owe their similarities exclusively to an Aramaic original. The fact that the apodoses of both the Matthean and the Johannine variants employ verbs in the perfect tense cannot be explained on the basis of Isa 22.22, but is more understandable if the sayings derive from a Greek original that employed the perfect tense.

If there existed a saying in Greek, modelled on Num 22.6 LXX and corresponding to the structure of Matt 16.19; 18.18 and John 20.23, its precise wording may be irrecoverable. As far as the pre-Matthean tradition is concerned, the motif of the keys may have been blended into the saying from Isa 22.22, but no such influence is detectable in John 20.23. There is much to be said for the *opinio communis* that the traditional commission was a saying of the risen Jesus, as it is in John.[152] For, although the saying occurs on the lips of the earthly Jesus in the pre-Matthean tradition, Matt 16.19 is placed in a context that refers to the time of the Church, and both the Matthean versions of the saying employ the future perfect tense in the apodoses to indicate their applicability in the future. It is not unlikely that the simple perfects in the original saying, which can still be found in John 20.23, were turned into future perfects as the saying was transferred to a point in time before Easter. Meier also points out that, while there is a tendency to retroject post-Easter gospel tradition into the life of the earthly Jesus, there is no 'flow' in the other direction. He believes that this is also applicable in the case of Matt 16.19/John 20.23.[153] In all likelihood, then, the commission to forgive/loose and retain/bind cannot tell us anything about how the historical Jesus viewed forgiveness.

Conclusion

From the foregoing investigation can be drawn a number of conclusions regarding the attestation of proclamations of and about forgiveness attributed to Jesus in the gospel tradition.

First of all, the commissioning of Jesus' disciples to forgive sins cannot be traced back to the historical Jesus. The traditional saying behind Matt 16.19; 18.18; John 20.23 was originally ascribed to the risen Jesus. It cannot, therefore, be used to form a view of the preaching of forgiveness by the historical Jesus. Only Matt 9.8 provides a link between the

---

[152] U. Luz, 'Das Primatwort Matthäus 16:17–19 aus Wirkungsgeschichtlicher Sicht', *NTS* 37 (1991), 415–33 (415–16).

[153] Meier, *A Marginal Jew*, vol. II, pp. 899–901; vol. III, pp. 234–5.

earthly Jesus' claim to have the authority to forgive sins on the one hand and, on the other, the subsequent authority of the Church to forgive sins. This is clearly due to Matthean redaction.

Secondly, Jesus' proclamation of forgiveness in general terms is attested in multiple sources (Mark; Q; possibly L). Several traditional items agree in attributing to Jesus forgiveness statements which employ similar wording: 'your Father in heaven may forgive' (Mark 11.25); '(it) will be forgiven' (Mark 3.28; Q 12.10; Pol *Phil* 2.3?). It is important to note that, while many such statements are routinely interpreted in eschatological terms, the Greek formulae generally allow for the construal of the futures as gnomic. And if they existed in Aramaic, the verbs were most likely in the imperfect tense, so that the distinction between the present and the future could only have been made on contextual grounds. There is also multiple attestation of Jesus' preaching about the preconditions for forgiveness. Far from proclaiming the universal and unconditional forgiveness of sins, he, according to gospel tradition, put forward two requirements for being forgiven by God: to have forgiven one's neighbour (Mark 11.25; the Lord's Prayer (Q 11.4?); Pol *Phil* 2.3/*1 Cl* 13.2?) and not to have denied the active presence of the Spirit of God in Jesus' mission (Mark 3.29; Q 12.10). The tradition sometimes seems to take for granted that, when God forgives, it is in response to prayer (Mark 11.25; the Lord's Prayer (Q 11.4?); Luke 15.21?; 18.10–14?).

Thirdly, announcements of forgiveness for specific individuals are found in Mark 2.5 and Luke 7.47 (from L) and thus multiply attested. The Aramaic formula that possibly underlies Mark 2.5, 'your sins are forgiven' (חטאיך ישתבקון), would come remarkably close to the purported Aramaic original behind Mark 3.28/Q 12.10. While I have argued that Luke 7.47 was substantially taken over from L, the exact phrasing appears to be genuinely Lukan, and the precise wording in L cannot be retrieved. The differences that exist between Mark 2.5 and Luke 7.47 should not be overlooked: while the former announcement is addressed to the sinner himself and is – at least in its Markan context – clearly meant to be performative, Luke 7.47a speaks of the sinner in the third person and concerns a forgiveness that has already taken place.

Fourthly, Mark 2.5 is unique in the gospel tradition in that it has Jesus pronounce the forgiveness directly to a specific individual with performative force. It is this function of the pronouncement that enables a construal of the implied agent of the passive as Jesus himself, and not as God. This is how the statement is interpreted by the characters in the Markan narrative (2.6–10). Luke 7.48–50, which contains a similarly functioning performative pronouncement of forgiveness and which also interprets the implied agent as Jesus, is a secondary accretion by Luke. Thus, the criterion of multiple attestation can be employed in this case only to demonstrate the likelihood that the historical Jesus made pronouncements of forgiveness, for categories of people as well as for specific individuals. It can be invoked to argue neither that the historical Jesus explicitly claimed to have the 'authority to forgive sins' (Mark 2.10), nor that he announced forgiveness by performative statements to specific individuals.

3

FORGIVENESS AND PRIMITIVE
CHRISTIAN THEOLOGY

The arguments of scholars who deny that the historical Jesus forgave sins can, somewhat simplistically, be grouped together in two basic hypotheses. According to the first hypothesis, which dates back to Bauer, the Gospel episodes reflect a tenet of christology: the risen and living heavenly Christ forgives sins. According to the second, originally proposed by Bultmann, the rationale is ecclesiological: primitive Christians sought to anchor their own authority in the earthly life of Jesus. Either hypothesis will gain plausibility only if it can be demonstrated that primitive Christians did harbour these christological or ecclesiological convictions, and if it can be shown that they were likely to express them in the form of narrative about Jesus. It is therefore remarkable that no thorough investigation of the topic of forgiveness in primitive Christian literature seems to have been made. The present chapter seeks to fill the gap by reviewing the topic as treated in all extant sources of primitive Christianity up to *c*. 135 CE, whether canonical or non-canonical, (proto-)orthodox or (proto-)gnostic.

Methodologically, what will be tested in this chapter is the applicability of the criterion of discontinuity. As pointed out in Chapter 1, this is to be understood as pertaining only to the question of continuity and discontinuity between Jesus and Christianity. It cannot be demonstrated beyond doubt that primitive Christianity as a whole did not view the risen Jesus as the forgiver of sins, but it may be demonstrated that the evidence that primitive Christians did do so is far too meagre to allow any hypotheses to be built on that foundation. To avoid circular reasoning, the Gospels will normally be bracketed out from the material considered. Exception from this rule will only be allowed for some Gospel material that seems clearly to point beyond the narrative time frame of the life of the earthly Jesus: the synoptic missionary discourses and the commissions in John 20.19–23; Matt 16.13–20; 18.15–20.

The body of the chapter will be divided into two parts. Firstly, the place of forgiveness in primitive christology will be delineated, and, secondly, the self-understanding of the primitive Church in relation to forgiveness will come under scrutiny.

Forgiveness and primitive christology

That the declaration that 'the Son of Man has authority to forgive sins' (Mark 2.10) is a retrojection of a christological tenet into the earthly life of Jesus has been stated frequently in critical scholarship.[1] But when it comes to finding evidence for this christological notion outside the synoptic episodes, the same scholars have usually been content to make rather sweeping statements. That first-century Christians thought that their risen Lord forgave sins appears to be taken for granted. According to Wrede, 'the entire passage has the flavour of primitive christology … Jesus … may claim for himself also this divine prerogative since, as his miracle shows, he is no "human being", but a being vested with superhuman power, the "Son of God"'.[2] 'The community wants … to make a christological statement concerning the authority of Jesus. As a special example Jesus' authority to forgive sins is selected, since it is capable of illustrating the divine superiority of Jesus in a particular way', writes Ingrid Maisch.[3] Johann Michl suggests, albeit cautiously, that 'what was expected of the exalted Lord, the synoptic Gospels tell already of the earthly one, namely that he forgave sins … Such an expectation can only be understood against the backdrop of early christology and from the belief that Jesus is the Son of God in a unique sense.'[4] It remains to be seen whether or not an investigation of the evidence for primitive christology lends support to this hypothesis.

The evidence will be grouped into three categories: first of all, those passages which assert that God forgives sins without any intermediary; secondly, those according to which God grants forgiveness 'through' or

---

[1] Bauer, *Kritik der evangelischen Geschichte*, pp. 91–3; Wrede, 'Zur Heilung des Gelähmten', 354–8; A. Loisy, *L'Évangile selon Marc* (Paris: Nourry, 1912), pp. 82–9; Maisch, *Die Heilung des Gelähmten*, pp. 97–101; K. Kertelge, 'Die Vollmacht des Menschensohnes zur Sündenvergebung (Mk 2,10)', in Hoffmann (ed.), *Orientierung an Jesus*, pp. 205–13 (p. 207); Michl, 'Sündenvergebung in Christus', 28–31; Fiedler, *Jesus und die Sünder*, pp. 115–16; W. Thissen, *Erzählung der Befreiung: Eine exegetische Untersuchung zu Mk 2,1–3,6*, FzB 21 (Würzburg: Echter, 1976), pp. 127–43.
[2] Wrede, 'Zur Heilung des Gelähmten', 357 (my translation).
[3] Maisch, *Die Heilung des Gelähmten*, pp. 98–9 (my translation).
[4] Michl, 'Sündenvergebung in Christus', 34–5 (my translation).

'because of' Jesus; and, thirdly, the few passages which do attribute a forgiving activity to the heavenly Jesus.

God as the agent of forgiveness

In a majority of cases, primitive Christian literature speaks of the granting of forgiveness by virtue of Jesus or through his mediation, but there are also passages about forgiveness which do not mention Jesus. These passages can be divided into three subgroups: statements referring to a singular act of forgiveness at the moment of conversion and/or of baptism; passages that concern the forgiveness of sins committed by believers after their conversion; and, finally, passages in which a future granting of forgiveness at the end-time is expected.

A singular act of forgiveness

Paul's epistolary production does not give a prominent place to traditional forgiveness terminology. The verb ἀφιέναι, 'to forgive', occurs only once in the genuinely Pauline letters, and this time in a quotation from the LXX Psalms: 'Blessed are those whose iniquities have been forgiven (ἀφέθησαν) and whose sins have been covered! Blessed is the man for whom the Lord will never take sin into account' (Rom 4.7–8 = Ps 32.1–2). Paul introduces the quotation by saying that 'even David pronounces a macarism on the human being to whom God reckons righteousness apart from works' (Rom 4.6). From this it is evident that Paul views the OT language of forgiveness as somehow related to his own concept of how God makes sinners righteous.[5] This is not to say that 'to make righteous' (δικαιοῦν) is the exact Pauline equivalent of 'to forgive'; indeed, the former concept appears to be wider than the latter, which may be the reason why Paul prefers it.[6] Yet it can be taken for granted that those who have been made righteous have, among other things, experienced the forgiveness of sins.

When making general statements about being made righteous, Paul repeatedly employs the verb δικαιοῦν in the present (Gal 2.16; 3.8, 11; 5.4; Rom 3.24, 26, 28; 4.5; 8.33) or future tense (Gal 2.16; Rom 2.13; 3.20, 30). However, when he becomes specific, he normally employs the

---

[5] C. E. B. Cranfield, *A Critical and Exegetical Commentary on the Epistle to the Romans*, ICC, 2 vols. (Edinburgh: T & T Clark, 1975–9), vol. I, p. 233; J. D. G. Dunn, *Romans 1–8*, WBC 38A (Dallas: Word Books, 1988), pp. 206–7.

[6] Taylor, *Forgiveness and Reconciliation*, pp. 29–31.

verb in the aorist (Rom 4.2; 5.1, 9; 8.30*bis*; Gal 3.24), indicating that to be made righteous is a once-and-for-all experience, something that happens at the decisive moment of one's transformation from unbeliever into believer.[7] There can be no doubt that the one who makes Jews and Gentiles righteous is God.

Acts similarly acknowledges an eradication of sins at the moment of conversion. In Luke's narration, Peter exhorts his audience to 'repent and turn around, in order that your sins may be wiped out (ἐξαλειφθῆναι)' (Acts 3.19). Semantically, 'to wipe out' sins overlaps with 'to forgive' sins (see Jer 18.23). As the agent is not mentioned explicitly, it is natural to assume that it is God.

The *Shepherd of Hermas* also testifies to the notion of an initial bestowal of forgiveness, as the hypostasized Church speaks of 'the mercy of the Lord, who instilled righteousness into you, in order that you should be made righteous (ἵνα δικαιωθῆτε) and be sanctified from all evil and from all deceit' (*Vis* 3.9.1). Throughout the *Shepherd of Hermas*, 'the Lord' (ὁ κύριος or ὁ δεσπότης) is normally used of God and only exceptionally, if ever, of Jesus.[8] Thus it was God who granted righteousness to the believers, plausibly through baptism, at which they received forgiveness (ἄφεσις) of past sins and the obligation to lead a pure and sinless life (cf. *Man* 4.3.1–2).

Three second-century works mention God's forgiveness for the sins of those who are converted. Firstly, the *Preaching of Peter* was extant by the middle of the second century and may have been composed prior to 135 CE.[9] It is possible but not certain that the *Preaching of Peter* is the source of a citation in Clement of Alexandria, which says that all sins committed in ignorance will be forgiven (ἀφεθήσεται) for those who recognize them and repent (*Preaching of Peter* 8 = Clement, *Strom.* 6.48.6). Secondly, the Syriac text of the *Apology of Aristides* (possibly authored in 124–5 CE)[10] depicts conversion as involving a confession of past sins committed in ignorance. The convert thereby purifies his heart, and his sins are forgiven (ܡܫܬܒܩܝܢ, *ApolArist* 17.2). Thirdly, Clement alludes to a statement similar to the two already mentioned, which

---

[7] E. P. Sanders, *Paul and Palestinian Judaism: A Comparison of Patterns of Religion* (London: SCM, 1977), pp. 500–1.

[8] C. Osiek, *The Shepherd of Hermas: A Commentary* (Minneapolis: Fortress, 1999), p. 56 n. 14.

[9] B. Pouderon, 'Introduction', in B. Pouderon et al. (eds.), *Aristide: Apologie: Introduction, textes critiques, traductions et commentaire*, SC 470 (Paris: Cerf, 2003), pp. 21–180 (pp. 78–9).

[10] *Ibid.*, pp. 32–7.

purportedly belongs to the doctrine taught by Basilides during the reign of Hadrian (117–38 CE). Clement is discussing baptism, which in his view deletes all sins of whatever kind that were committed before coming to faith; but Basilides, Clement asserts, says that not all sins are forgiven (ἀφίεσθαι) but only those committed involuntarily and prompted by ignorance (Basilides, frg 10 = Clement, *Strom.* 4.153.3–4). While Clement accuses Basilides of underrating God's gift, Winrich Löhr has suggested that Basilides might have viewed all pre-baptismal sins as the result of ignorance and unconsciousness, and accordingly he subscribed to the notion of an offer of total forgiveness in baptism.[11] If this is correct, Basilides would be in substantial agreement about this question, not only with Clement, the *Preaching of Peter*, and *Aristides*, but also with Paul and Luke.

Forgiveness of sins committed after conversion

First Clement normally gives a christological foundation for God's offer of forgiveness, but there are two passages in which the author leaves out any reference to Jesus. Recalling the golden days of the Corinthian Christians, the author tells them, 'you used to stretch out your hands to Almighty God in good readiness with pious confidence, imploring him to forgive (ἵλεων γενέσθαι), if you had unintentionally committed some sin' (*1 Cl* 2.3).[12] What is envisaged here is a continuous habit of confessing sins committed after baptism with a conviction that God will repeatedly forgive. The communal prayer included in 59.4–61.1 contains a petition for forgiveness that is indebted to early Jewish penitential prayers: 'forgive us our lawless deeds and wrongdoings and offences and errors (ἄφες ἡμῖν τὰς ἀνομίας ἡμῶν καὶ τὰς ἀδικίας καὶ τὰ παραπτώματα καὶ πλημμελείας). Do not take account of any sin of your servants and handmaids' (60.1–2).[13] Like early Jewish prayers for forgiveness, the prayer suggested by *First Clement* implores God to forgive all kinds of sins that human beings habitually commit.

[11] W. A. Löhr, *Basilides und seine Schule: Eine Studie zur Theologie- und Kirchengeschichte des zweiten Jahrhunderts*, WUNT 83 (Tübingen: Mohr Siebeck, 1996), pp. 163–5.
[12] ἵλεω γίνεσθαι with a recipient of forgiveness in the dative is used in the LXX to translate נשא (Num 14.19), כפר (Deut 21.8) and סלח (Num 14.20; Jer 5.7; 50.20), all of which can also be rendered with ἀφιέναι (נשא, e.g. Exod 32.32; כפר, Isa 22.4; סלח, e.g. Lev 4.20).
[13] On this petition, see H. Löhr, *Studien zum frühchristlichen und frühjüdischen Gebet: Untersuchungen zu 1 Clem 59 bis 61 in seinem literarischen, historischen und theologischen Kontext* (Tübingen: Mohr Siebeck, 2003), pp. 224–59.

Also expressive of the Jewish heritage of primitive Christianity is the description of the martyrdom of James, the brother of the Lord, in the (*Second*) *Apocalypse of James* from the Nag Hammadi library.[14] Facing his death by stoning, James invokes God, 'Do not give me into the hand of a judge harsh on sin (ⲡⲛⲟⲃⲉ)! Forgive me all my debts (ⲕⲱ ⲛⲁⲓ ⲉⲃⲟⲗ ⲛ̅ⲛ̅ⲏ ⲉⲧⲉⲣⲟⲓ ⲧⲏⲣⲟⲩ) of [my] days!' (*2 ApocJas* (NHC V,4) 63.15–19). Here, again, it is presumed that even a saintly believer, such as James, will need to confess the sins he has committed in his lifetime and beg God to forgive them.

Some works speak of a second, but limited, opportunity to repent of grave sins committed after baptism. While the basic contents of the *Book of Elchasai* are known only through allusions made in early patristic sources, critical scholarship affirms the existence of such an apocalyptic writing with some characteristically Jewish traits already in the reign of Trajan and probably by 116 CE.[15] This book seems to have contained an assertion that the angelic Son of God 'announced to human beings the gospel of a new remission of sins (καινὴν ἄφεσιν ἁμαρτιῶν)' (Hippolytus, *Ref.* 9.13.3). Third-century heterodox groups in Rome and Palestine apparently held that acceptance of the message of the *Book of Elchasai* would secure God's forgiveness, a promise that must have been contained within the book itself.[16]

Such an opportunity to repent and to receive forgiveness for post-baptismal sins is also the main theme of the *Shepherd of Hermas*. This offer is bound up with the acceptance of the message which Hermas receives from the Church, and it will be valid only for a short period of time (*Herm Vis* 2.2.4–5; *Man* 4.3.3–6). Forgiveness will be secured only after rigorous repentance, which must include, among other things, a decision to forgive the shortcomings of fellow human beings (*Sim* 7.1.4–5; 9.23.4–5; 9.33.3). Even the ultimate sin of apostasy will be forgiven (*Vis* 2.2.8–2.3.1). With remarkable clarity, the Angel of Repentance stresses twice that to forgive sins is a divine prerogative. The angel first distinguishes between, on the one hand, his own role in assisting the former sinner in his effort to lead a sinless life, and, on the other hand, God's capacity to forgive previously committed sins: for previous sins 'there

---

[14] S. K. Brown, 'Jewish and Gnostic Elements in the Second Apocalypse of James (CG V, *4*)', *NovT* 17 (1975), 225–37.

[15] G. P. Luttikhuizen, *The Revelation of Elchasai: Investigations into the Evidence for a Mesopotamian Jewish Apocalypse of the Second Century and Its Reception by Judeo-Christian Propagandists* (Tübingen: Mohr Siebeck, 1985), pp. 88, 121–2, 190–2.

[16] Hippolytus, *Ref.* 9.13.3–4; Eusebius, *Hist. Eccl.* 6.38 (quoting Origen). See Luttikhuizen, *The Revelation of Elchasai*, pp. 62, 90–1, 217.

is one who can offer healing (ἔστιν ὁ δυνάμενος ἴασιν δοῦναι), for he is the one who has authority over everything (ὁ ἔχων πάντων τὴν ἐξουσίαν)' (*Man* 4.1.11). This doctrine is later restated in slightly different words: 'For the earlier ... sins of ignorance it is possible for God alone to grant healing, for his is all the authority (τῷ θεῷ μόνῳ δυνατὸν ἴασιν δοῦναι· αὐτοῦ γὰρ πᾶσά ἐστιν ἡ ἐξουσία)' (*Sim* 5.7.3).[17] Curiously, these statements combine the motives of sin, healing and authority in a manner similar to the controversy in Mark 2.6–10. But the dissimilarities are also conspicuous. Whereas the Markan episode narrates an actual healing of paralysis, in *Hermas* 'healing' is a metaphor of forgiveness.[18] And whereas Mark attributes the authority to forgive sins to the Son of Man, these passages in *Hermas* explicitly reserve this ability for God.

Eschatological forgiveness

Contrary to what might be expected, primitive Christian literature hardly contains any references at all to an expected bestowal of forgiveness at the end-time. Early Judaism looked forward to such an ultimate eschatological forgiveness by God.[19] This would usher in an era of sinlessness.[20] The simplest explanation for the virtual absence of this expectation from primitive Christianity is that Christians held the end-time to have begun already: the promised bestowal of forgiveness had taken place through Jesus' death and resurrection, and believers were now both enabled and obliged to lead a sinless life.

Paul may nevertheless be envisaging a final gift of forgiveness from God for the people of Israel, as he invokes a pastiche of Isa 59.20–1 and 27.9 as evidence for the coming salvation of Israel in its entirety (Rom 11.26–7). That 'the deliverer will turn away ungodliness from Jacob' may not indicate that he will forgive the people's sins, but the explication of God's covenant as 'when I take away (ἀφέλωμαι) their sins' does evoke the notion of forgiveness. The verb employed here, ἀφαιρεῖν,

---

[17] *Herm Vis* 1.1.9–1.2.1; 1.3.1; 2.2.8; *Man* 12.6.2; *Sim* 5.7.4; 7.1.4; 8.11.3; 9.23.4–5 all predicate the act of forgiveness of God.

[18] *Herm Vis* 1.1.9; 1.3.1; *Man* 12.6.2; *Sim* 5.7.4; 7.1.4; 8.11.3; 9.23.5.

[19] Jer 31.34; 33.8; 50.20; Ezek 37.23 (all with reference to Israel's return from exile); *1 En* 5.6 (in the Greek text; with reference to the 'elect'); 11Q13 ii 5–6 (with reference to the 'sons of light'?).

[20] 2 Esd 6.26–7; *ApocMos* 13.3–5; Book of the Watchers: *1 En* 5.8; Epistle of Enoch: *1 En* 91.14, 17; Book of Parables: *1 En* 49.2; *Jub* 50.5; *TLevi* 18.9. Cf. the references to a postdiluvian era of sinlessness in the Book of the Watchers (*1 En* 10.20–2), the Epistle of Enoch (*1 En* 107.1) and *Jub* 5.12.

is employed in the sense of 'to forgive' a number of times in the LXX, though normally in the active voice (see Chapter 4 below). It is possible that Paul found it apt to allude to the early Jewish notion of eschatological forgiveness when he discussed the ultimate destiny of Israel. In addition, the *Didache* may also refer to God's eschatological act of forgiveness (*Did* 11.7). I commented in Chapter 2 on the uncertainty involved in deciding whether the future tense used should be construed as gnomic or as eschatological future, and in any case the formula ultimately stems from the gospel tradition.

Jesus as the mediator of forgiveness

According to the common pattern of primitive Christian theology, forgiveness of sins is ultimately bestowed by God but somehow mediated by Jesus. The mediation takes place in manifold ways: through Jesus' suffering and death, through his intercession, through baptism, repentance and faith in his name. All of these will be considered here, as will the unique portrayal of the heavenly Jesus as a messenger of forgiveness in the *Shepherd of Hermas*.

Forgiveness by virtue of Jesus' suffering and death

Within twenty years of Jesus' death, the belief that his death somehow dealt with sins was already widespread. Paul can quote 'Christ died for our sins according to the scriptures' (1 Cor 15.3) as part of received tradition. Primitive Christian literature elaborates the theme by expressing, through various metaphors and sometimes in conjunction with the explicit mention of forgiveness, the fundamental conviction that Jesus' death involved the abolition of sins. These expressions will be reviewed briefly in the following.

He who died 'for our sins'. If the pre-Pauline formulation 'Christ died for our sins according to the scriptures' (1 Cor 15.3) is meant to refer to a specific OT passage, there is no better candidate than the description by Second Isaiah of how the Servant of the Lord took upon himself 'the sin of all of us' (Isa 53.6 MT) or 'the sin of many' (53.12 MT).[21] The same tradition may be echoed in Paul's formulaic reference to Jesus

---

[21] H. Merklein, 'Paulus und die Sünde', in Frankemölle (ed.), *Sünde und Erlösung im Neuen Testament*, p. 149; O. Hofius, 'Das vierte Gottesknechtslied in den Briefen des Neuen Testamentes', in B. Janowski and P. Stuhlmacher (eds.), *Der leidende Gottesknecht: Jesaja 53 und seine Wirkungsgeschichte*, FzAT 14 (Tübingen: Mohr Siebeck, 1996), pp. 107–28 (pp. 118–21).

Christ as the one 'who gave himself up for our sins' (Gal 1.4). Another passage, probably influenced by Isa 52.13–53.12, is Paul's statement that Jesus 'was handed over because of our trespasses' (παρεδόθη διὰ τὰ παραπτώματα ἡμῶν, Rom 4.25), which may also be traditional. This formula seems to presuppose the LXX: unlike the MT, the LXX twice says that the Lord 'handed over' (παραδιδόναι) his servant (Isa 53.6, 12); the LXX also says that the Servant suffered 'because of' (διά) sins (53.5*bis*, 12).[22] While the notion that Jesus' suffering and death took place 'for our sins' indisputably antedates Paul's letters, these pregnant formulations do not reveal whether the death of Jesus was thought to effectuate forgiveness.

Paul himself elaborates the theme of Jesus' death 'for our sins'. While we were still sinners, Christ died 'for us' (Rom 5.8; cf. 5.6–7; 2 Cor 5.15, 21). The result was that we 'were made righteous' (Rom 5.9, cf. 5.19) – as noted above, a concept preferred by Paul over against that of forgiveness. At other times he employs the vocabulary of reconciliation to denote the changed relationship between God and human beings through the death of Jesus, being constantly unambiguous about God as the agent of reconciliation (Rom 5.10–11; 2 Cor 5.18–19).[23]

In other primitive Christian writings, the traditional formula surfaces occasionally. First Peter says that 'Christ suffered once for sins, a righteous one for unrighteous ones' (1 Pet 3.18). Ignatius employs the formula to insist that the Eucharist is 'the flesh of our Saviour Jesus Christ, which [*sic*] suffered for our sins and which the Father raised up in his goodness' (Ign *Smyrn* 7.1). And in the opening of his letter to the Philippians, Polycarp speaks of 'Jesus Christ, who endured death for our sins' (Pol *Phil* 1.2). These instances from the early second century may indicate that the formula retained its established position in oral tradition far beyond the time of Paul.

The suffering Servant. Going beyond the formulaic use of phrases such as the above, some primitive Christian authors draw more extensively on the portrayal of the Servant of the Lord in Second Isaiah. The emphasis is sometimes on the exemplary function of the Servant's suffering (*1 Cl* 16.1–17), but already First Peter portrays the suffering of Jesus as both exemplary and vicarious (1 Pet 2.21–5). Drawing clearly on Isa 53.4, 12, the letter describes Jesus as him 'who himself

---

[22] Taylor, *Forgiveness and Reconciliation*, p. 42; Hofius, 'Das vierte Gottesknechtslied', pp. 121–2.

[23] On Paul's notion of reconciliation, see C. Breytenbach, *Versöhnung: Eine Studie zur paulinischen Theologie*, WMANT 60 (Neukirchen-Vluyn: Neukirchener, 1989).

carried our sins in his body on the pole, in order that we might be freed from our sins (ταῖς ἁμαρτίαις ἀπογενόμενοι) and live for righteousness; by whose wound you were healed' (2.24; cf. Pol *Phil* 8.1). The imagery presupposes that sins are viewed in physical categories, not as 'forgiven', but rather destroyed (cf. Col 2.13–14, on which see below).

A passage in First John also appears to echo Isaiah 53 (1 John 3.5; cf. John 1.29).[24] There is no discernible influence from the LXX here, since Jesus is said to 'take' (αἴρειν) sins rather than 'carry' ((ἀνα-)φέρειν) them (see Isa 53.4, 11, 12). Attention is drawn to the lack of sin in Jesus (see Isa 53.9) and the author expresses his conviction that those who remain in Jesus cannot sin (1 John 3.4–6). The focus is on the exemplary behaviour of the Servant.

The servant imagery can be merged with the metaphor of Jesus as the sacrificial victim. Hebrews speaks of Jesus as 'having been offered once to carry the sins of many' (Heb 9.28; cf. Isa 53.12),[25] and *Barnabas* quotes key phrases from Isa 53.5, 7 as scriptural proof that 'the Lord endured handing over his flesh to destruction, in order that we might be purified through the forgiveness of sins (τῇ ἀφέσει τῶν ἁμαρτιῶν), that is, in the sprinkling of his blood' (*Barn* 5.1–2). In neither of these instances can the agent of forgiveness be the sacrificed servant himself: the agent must be God.

Finally, the *Letter to Diognetus* appears to be echoing the Servant imagery in a rather unexpected manner: God, rather than Jesus, is said to have 'taken on himself our sins' (τὰς ἡμετέρας ἁμαρτίας ἀνεδέξατο, *Diogn* 9.2), thus appropriating a trait of the Servant.[26] Even in *Diognetus*, it is Jesus' righteousness that 'could cover our sins', that could 'make many lawless people righteous' (9.3, 5); we have been made righteous 'only in the Son of God' (9.4). Here, as frequently elsewhere, Jesus' role is instrumental.

The sacrificial victim. In rudimentary form the understanding of the death of Jesus as expiatory goes back to Paul. Here it is impossible to go profoundly into the questions raised by Paul's much-discussed statement that the faithful are 'made righteous for free, by [God's] grace, through the redemption in Christ Jesus, who God put forward as an atoning sacrifice through faith, in his blood, as proof of his righteousness because of

[24] Michl, 'Sündenvergebung in Christus', 26–7.
[25] Hofius, 'Das vierte Gottesknechtslied', p. 124.
[26] H. E. Lona, *An Diognet: Übersetzt und erklärt*, KfA 8 (Freiburg: Herder, 2001), pp. 265–6.

his passing over the previously committed sins' (Rom 3.24–5).[27] God's 'passing over' (πάρεσις) sins could be tantamount to his forgiving them, but it is more likely that Paul refers to sins that God left temporarily unpunished until the sacrificial death of Jesus, which expiated them.[28] In any case, the acting subject in Rom 3.25 is God, while the sacrificial death of Jesus is the means of atonement (cf. 8.3).

The same pattern is visible in First John. God 'sent his Son as an atoning sacrifice (ἱλασμόν) for our sins' (1 John 4.10; cf. 2.2), and the blood of Jesus 'purifies us from all sin' (2.7). The one who will 'forgive us our sins and purify us from all iniquity' (2.9) is God.[29] Again, the role played by Jesus is subordinate and instrumental.

Hebrews and *Barnabas* both make extensive use of the sacrificial metaphor. Though high-priestly typology dominates the christology of Hebrews, Jesus is also described as the perfect sacrifice. Arguing that 'there is no forgiveness without the shedding of blood' (Heb 9.22), the author emphasizes that Christ offered his own blood once and for all (9.12, cf. 9.14, 25–6; 10.10). The blood of animals cannot remove sins (10.4); but Jesus offered a single sacrifice for sins (10.12) that rendered any further sin offering obsolete (10.18). The *Letter of Barnabas* identifies several OT sacrifices as types for the salvific death of Jesus. The sprinkling of the blood of Jesus brings about forgiveness (*Barn* 5.1). Similarly, the author reads the Day of Atonement ritual in Leviticus 16 as a foreshadowing of Jesus, who offered his flesh as a sacrifice 'for (our) sins' (*Barn* 7.3, 5). A third image is taken from the red heifer ritual in Numbers 19, which is read allegorically: the slaughtered heifer, designated as a sin-offering in Num 19.9, is Jesus; the sinful men are those responsible for Jesus' death; the children, who sprinkle the people so that they may be purified from their sins, are the twelve apostles (*Barn* 8.1–3). Jesus is the victim whose death brings forgiveness, but he is not portrayed as forgiving.

The high priest. While Jesus is occasionally said to have 'purified' (καθαρίσαι) his people, in terms evocative of OT priestly rituals (Eph 5.25–7; Tit 2.14; cf. Lev 16.30), it is in Hebrews that the typology of the high priest is extensively applied to Jesus and explicitly related to forgiveness. At the opening of the treatise, the Son of God is said to

---

[27] On the translation of ἱλαστήριον as 'atoning sacrifice', see Dunn, *Romans 1–8*, pp. 170–2.

[28] J. A. Fitzmyer, *Romans: A New Translation with Introduction and Commentary*, AB 33 (London: Geoffrey Chapman, 1993), pp. 351–2.

[29] R. E. Brown, *The Epistles of John: A New Translation with Introduction and Commentary*, AB 30 (New York: Doubleday, 1982), p. 209.

have made 'purification for sins' (καθαρισμὸν τῶν ἁμαρτιῶν, Heb 1.3), a phrase seemingly taken from the reference to the high-priestly ritual for the Day of Atonement in Exod 30.10 LXX. The same ritual is typologically expounded in Heb 9.23–8: through his death, Jesus entered the heavenly sanctuary 'to invalidate sin' (εἰς ἀθέτησιν τῆς ἁμαρτίας, 9.26). This he did 'to atone for (ἱλάσκεσθαι) the people's sins' (Heb 2.17). The author's use of ἱλάσκεσθαι is rather unexpected, since the unprefixed verb always takes God as its subject in the LXX, where it is employed in the sense of 'to forgive'.[30] But the overt exploitation of high-priestly typology makes it likely that the author does not attribute the activity of forgiving sins to Jesus, but rather that of offering an atoning sacrifice, for which the LXX uses ἐξιλάσκεσθαι. The role of forgiving sins is reserved for God alone (Heb 8.12; 10.17).

The liberator from sin. A very different conceptualization of sin is presupposed by primitive Christian authors who portray Jesus as the liberator from sin. Far from being visualized as a juridical guilt, economic debt or cultic defilement, sin is in these cases thought of as a powerful dominion, which rules those who are not 'in Christ'.[31] Paul claims that Jesus 'gave himself for our sins, in order to rescue us from the present evil age' (Gal 1.4) and speaks of 'the redemption in Christ Jesus' which resulted from God's putting forward Jesus as an atoning sacrifice (Rom 3.24–5). In a similar vein, the Letter to Titus states that Jesus 'gave himself for us, to redeem us from all lawlessness' (Tit 2.14). The underlying idea is that believers have been freed from the power of sin in order to serve God by leading a life that is not marked by sin (see also 1 Pet 1.18–19).

A very close relationship, or even equivalence, between redemption and forgiveness is expressed by Colossians and Ephesians. In the former letter, the author gives thanks to God, who has rescued the believers from the power of darkness and transferred them to the kingdom of his Son, 'in whom we have redemption, the forgiveness of sins' (Col 1.13–14). The author of Ephesians takes over this formula with two minor changes: 'transgressions' replaces 'sins' and redemption is qualified as available 'through his blood' (Eph 1.7; cf. Col 1.22). Redemption and forgiveness are 'in Jesus', that is, worked by God and available to the believers through Jesus as the mediator. In Ephesians, the same pattern

---

[30] Exod 32.14; 2 Kgs 5.18; 24.4; 2 Chron 6.30; Ps 24.11; 64.4; 77.38; 78.9; Lam 3.42; Dan 9.19; Greek Esth 4.17h; cf. Luke 18.13.

[31] H.-J. Klauck, 'Heil ohne Heilung? Zu Metaphorik und Hermeneutik der Rede von Sünde und Vergebung im Neuen Testament', in Frankemölle (ed.), *Sünde und Erlösung im Neuen Testament*, pp. 18–52 (pp. 26–9); Merklein, 'Paulus und die Sünde', pp. 151–2.

is presupposed in the exhortation of the believers to forgive one another, 'as also God forgave (ἐχαρίσατο) you in Christ' (Eph 4.32). The role of Jesus is clearly subordinated to that of God (on Col 3.13, see below).

Finally, the doxology that opens John's letter to the seven churches in Revelation gives glory to Jesus, 'who loves us and freed us from our sins (λύσαντι ἡμᾶς ἐκ τῶν ἁμαρτιῶν ἡμῶν) with his blood' (Rev 1.5). According to David Aune, '[i]n effect, λύειν ἐκ τῶν ἁμαρτιῶν means "to forgive sins"'.[32] However, several reasons prevent the conclusion that the author of Revelation depicts Jesus as having forgiven sins. The phrase 'to free from sins' does not seem to be used in the sense of 'to forgive sins' in the LXX. Probably, 'to loose (λύειν) sin' in Job 42.10 means 'to forgive sin' but, in this case, unlike Rev 1.5, the direct object is 'sin'.[33] Furthermore, there is, as Elisabeth Schüssler Fiorenza has pointed out, a close structural and theological correspondence between the doxology in 1.5–6 and the hymn of praise in 5.9–10, which describes redemption in terms of Christ 'buying' believers for God, that is, ransoming them from their captivity as prisoners of war.[34] Aune himself has drawn attention to the structural correspondence between Rev 1.5–6 and Tit 2.14,[35] and, as has been noted above, the latter passage does not speak of forgiveness, but of the transferral from the dominion of sin to the dominion of God. It appears natural to interpret Rev 1.5 along the same lines, so that the reference there is to the believers' liberation from being held captive by their sins.

Forgiveness through the intercession of Jesus

While not as universally attested as the view of his death as salvific, the notion of Jesus' continuous intercession for those who have sinned surfaces in a number of texts that otherwise differ widely in theological

---

[32] D. E. Aune, *Revelation 1–5*, WBC 52A (Dallas: Word Books, 1997), p. 47.

[33] Job 42.10 LXX, 'and he loosed the sin for them on account of Job' (καὶ ἔλυσεν τὴν ἁμαρτίαν αὐτοῖς διὰ Ιωβ) comes curiously close to the Targum of Job from Qumran: 'and God listened to the voice of Job and forgave them their sins on his account (ושמע א[ל]ה[א בקלה די איוב ושבק להין חטאיהון בדילה, 11Q10 38.2–3). In 42.9, ἀφιέναι and שבק could be intended to correspond to נשא in the MT, according to which 'the Lord accepted Job's prayer' (וישא יהוה את־פני איוב), but this is not certain, *pace* E. Hatch and H. A. Redpath, *A Concordance to the Septuagint and the Other Greek Versions of the Old Testament (Including the Apocryphal Books)*, 2 vols. (Oxford: Clarendon, 1897). (ἀνα-)λύειν occurs elsewhere in the passive form with ἁμαρτία(ι) as its subject (Isa 40.2; Ecclus 3.15; 28.2), corresponding to an active form of the verb with 'sin(s)' as its direct object.

[34] E. Schüssler Fiorenza, *The Book of Revelation: Justice and Judgment* (Philadelphia: Fortress, 1985), pp. 68–81.

[35] Aune, *Revelation 1–5*, pp. 45–6.

character. Paul expresses his conviction that Jesus 'is at the right hand of God' and 'intercedes (ἐντυγχάνει) for us' (Rom 8.34), but he does not mention sins specifically. Likewise, the author of Hebrews states that Jesus 'can also save forever those who come to God through him, since he always lives to intercede (ἐντυγχάνειν) for them' (Heb 7.25). It is possible in view of his subsequent discussion of the high-priestly sacrifice for sins (7.26–7) that the author here envisages a ministry of praying specifically for sins to be forgiven, but he does not say so explicitly.

First John clearly associates Jesus' intercessory work with forgiveness, claiming that 'if somebody sins, we have an advocate (παράκλητον) with the Father, Jesus Christ who is righteous' (2.1). The notion that the righteous departed pray for the forgiveness of the sins of the living is firmly rooted in several variants of early Judaism, and the phrasing in First John is strikingly evocative of Philo's articulation of this conception.[36] What Philo predicated of the ancient saints of Israel, First John attributes to Jesus: the continuing ministry of praying before God on behalf of sinners, at least on behalf of those sinners who have not committed mortal sin (see 5.16–17).

Luke's narration of the death of Stephen (Acts 7.54–60) also assigns the role of advocate to Jesus.[37] Scholars have frequently taken Stephen's invocation of Jesus, 'Lord, do not hold (μὴ στήσῃς) this sin against them' (7.60) as equivalent to saying 'Lord, forgive this sin for them' and thus as expressing the notion that the heavenly Jesus forgives sins.[38] But this interpretation appears to be based on the misunderstanding of 'to establish' (ἱστάναι) and 'to remit' (ἀφιέναι) as antonyms in 1 Macc 13.36–40; 15.2–9, where a careful reading reveals that these verbs are by no means antonymous.[39] A more relevant philological background for Stephen's prayer is provided by the regulations concerning vows and pledges in Num 30.11–15 LXX, which allow a husband either to

---

[36] *PraemPoen* 166. See R. Le Déaut, 'Aspects de l'intercession dans le judaïsme ancien', *JSJ* 1 (1970), 45 n. 1; H. Thyen, *Studien zur Sündenvergebung: Im Neuen Testament und seinen alttestamentlichen und jüdischen Voraussetzungen*, FRLANT 96 (Göttingen: Vandenhoeck & Ruprecht, 1970), p. 125; Klauck, 'Heil ohne Heilung?', pp. 33–4.

[37] For an extensive discussion of what follows in this paragraph, see T. Hägerland, '"Ge inte giltighet åt denna deras synd!" Stefanos förbön och den tidiga kristologin', in G. Samuelsson and T. Hägerland (eds.), *Så som det har berättats för oss: Om bibel, gudstjänst och tro: En hyllning till Lennart Thörn på hans 65-årsdag* (Örebro: Libris, 2007), pp. 91–105.

[38] See, e.g., D. L. Bock, *Proclamation from Prophecy and Pattern: Lucan Old Testament Christology*, JSNTS 12 (Sheffield: JSOT Press, 1987), pp. 224–5.

[39] *Pace* H. J. Cadbury, *The Beginnings of Christianity, Part I: The Acts of the Apostles*, vol. IV: *English Translation and Commentary*, ed. F. J. Foakes Jackson and K. Lake, paperback edn (Grand Rapids, MI: Baker, 1979 (1st edn 1933)), p. 86; *s.v.* ἵστημι BDAG.

nullify (περιαιρεῖν) his wife's vows and pledges by speaking out, or to validate (ἱστάναι) them by keeping silence. In the former case, 'the Lord will forgive (καθαρίσει (MT: יסלח))' the woman (30.13). In Acts 7.60, Stephen analogously petitions Jesus not to validate the sin of the assassins, but to nullify it by speaking on their behalf, reserving for God the prerogative of properly forgiving their sin. This also explains better why Jesus is standing, rather than sitting, at the right hand of God in Stephen's vision (7.55–6): Jesus is not functioning as a judge, but as the advocate of his faithful witness (cf. Luke 12.8–9), who exemplarily asks him to speak also in favour of the enemies.

This understanding of Acts 7.60 affects the construal of Peter's advice to Simon Magus, 'ask the Lord that, if possible, the intention of your heart may be forgiven for you' (Acts 8.24). The identity of 'the Lord' is obscure. If it refers to God, a post-baptismal sin may be forgiven by God without Jesus playing any instrumental role (cf. 3.19). If, by contrast, it refers to Jesus, then his function could be understood in either of two ways: as the one who actually forgives sins, or as the heavenly advocate, who intercedes for the sinner before God. The contextual nearness between 7.60 and 8.22 speaks for the latter alternative, as does the passive construction 'will be forgiven' (ἀφεθήσεται), which may indicate that the implicit agent of forgiveness is not identical with 'the Lord' to whom the prayer is addressed.

Mention should also be made of a curious passage in the *Apocryphon of James* where the risen Lord promises to pray on behalf of James and Peter: 'I intercede for you with the Father, and he will forgive you much (ϥⲛⲁⲕⲉ ϩⲁϩ ⲛⲏⲧⲛ̄ ⲁⲃⲁⲗ)' (*ApJas* 11.4–6). As soon as James and Peter express their joy about these words – as they have in fact just been told to do – the Lord reproaches them harshly:

> Woe to you who lack an advocate (ⲛ̄ⲛⲟⲩⲡⲁⲣⲁⲕⲗⲏⲧⲟⲥ)! … Or do you perhaps think that the Father is someone who loves humanity or who is convinced through prayers or who forgives (ⲉϣⲁϥⲣ̄ ⲭⲁⲣⲓⲍⲉ) someone because of another or who bears with someone who asks? … Amen, I tell you, He will not forgive the sin (ⲛ̄ϥⲛⲁⲕⲁ ⲡⲛⲁⲃⲉⲓ ⲉⲛ ⲁⲃⲁⲗ) of the soul in any way, nor the guilt of the flesh.
>
> (*ApJas* 11.11–12.13)

This latter passage may be a piece of gnostic polemic against the proto-orthodox notions expressed by the former. But it is not necessary to resolve this tension in order to conclude that, in the *Apocryphon of James*, the role of Jesus is not to forgive sins. His function is, at the most, that of a heavenly intercessor.

Forgiveness appropriated through the name of Jesus

Whereas primitive Christians generally thought that forgiveness was available by virtue of the death of Jesus, they also attributed to Jesus a role in the appropriation of this forgiveness by each believer individually. This is often expressed in vague terms, such as being forgiven 'through Jesus', 'in his name' and so on. Only a provisional and pragmatic division of these passages can be attempted.

Baptism in the name of Jesus. Paul reminds his Corinthian address-ees of their transition from vicious unbelievers into saintly believers: 'but you had yourselves washed, but you were sanctified, but you were made righteous in the name of the Lord Jesus Christ and in the Spirit of our God' (1 Cor 6.11). Sanctification and righteousness, which for Paul implies the forgiveness of past sins, are associated with the moment of initiation, namely with the baptismal 'washing'.[40] Paul seems to refer to the invocation of the name of Jesus over the person who is baptized (see 1.13, 15) and to the reception of the Spirit through baptism (12.13). The one who has ultimately washed the Corinthian believers, who has sanc-tified them and who has made them righteous, is God, although he is not explicitly mentioned in the text.

In Acts, Peter summons his Jerusalem audience to repent and to be baptized 'in the name of Jesus Christ for the forgiveness of your sins'; thereby they will receive the gift of the Holy Spirit (Acts 2.38). Similarly in Acts, Paul recalls how Ananias commanded him, 'Rise, be baptized, and have your sins washed off, calling on his name' (Acts 22.16). The Spirit is not mentioned here and it seems that Paul himself is expected to invoke the name of Jesus at his baptism, but the role of Jesus still remains instrumental.

Colossians offers a 'mystical' interpretation of baptism, according to which the baptized share in the death and resurrection of Jesus (Col 2.11–12). The moments of crucifixion, revivification and baptism are indistinguishable as the author claims that the entire event involved God's act of 'forgiving (χαρισάμενος) us all our trespasses' (2.13). In Jesus'

---

[40] A. C. Thiselton, *The First Epistle to the Corinthians: A Commentary on the Greek Text*, NIGTC (Grand Rapids, MI: Eerdmans, 2000), pp. 453–4. Cf. J. D. G. Dunn, *The Theology of Paul the Apostle* (Grand Rapids, MI: Eerdmans, 1998), p. 454, who sees no reference to baptism here.

death, the decree of indebtedness was nailed to the cross and blotted out (2.14).[41] As noted above, 1 Pet 2.24 presupposes a similar conceptual framework, but it is also instructive to notice a significant difference: according to First Peter, Jesus actively 'carried our sins' upon the cross in his capacity as the Servant, but this is not equated with the forgiveness of sins. In Colossians, where the acting subject is God throughout 2.11–15, the blotting out of the decree in crucifixion is explicitly identified as an act of forgiveness. This is consistent with the dominant pattern: to forgive sins is God's own prerogative.

The Letter to Titus also points to baptism as the moment at which believers were made righteous. God 'saved us through the bath of rebirth and through renewal in the Holy Spirit, which he poured out on us richly through Jesus Christ, our saviour, in order that we should be made righteous by his grace and become heirs of eternal life, according to hope' (Tit 3.5–7). In this passage, Jesus' role is not that of being invoked by name, but that of a mediator through whom the Spirit was given to the baptized. Whether 'by his grace' (τῇ ἐκείνου χάριτι) is a reference to the grace of God (see 2.11) or that of Jesus (see 1.4) cannot be settled, but it is natural to take God as the implied agent of 'being made righteous' (δικαιωθέντες), in accord with the standard pattern.

In the *Letter of Barnabas*, baptism is similarly described as a re-creation, which involves the forgiveness of past sins (see *Barn* 6.11; 11.1; 16.8). According to the author, God has dwelt in the believers ever since the moment when they 'received the forgiveness of sins and put (their) hope in the Name' (16.8). In his exposition of a catena of prophecies about baptism, the author unequivocally states that it is baptism 'which brings forgiveness of sins' (11.1). 'We go down into the water filled with sins and filth, and we come up, bearing fruit in the heart, with fear and hope in Jesus in our spirit' (11.11). Faith and hope in Jesus are constitutive elements of the ritual that brings forgiveness, but there is no indication that Jesus is thought of as someone who forgives sins.

Repentance preached in the name of Jesus. In the Gospel of Luke, the risen Jesus himself says that it is written that the Messiah should suffer and rise again, and 'that repentance for the forgiveness of sins will be preached in his name to all the nations' (Luke 24.47). Similarly, Peter and the apostles confess before the Sanhedrin that God has raised Jesus and 'has exalted (him) to his right hand as leader and saviour, to give repentance and the forgiveness of sins to Israel' (Acts 5.31). In the latter case, it cannot be decided on grammatical grounds whether the

---

[41] R. Yates, 'Colossians 2,14: Metaphor of Forgiveness', *Bib* 71 (1990), 248–59.

implied subject of 'to give' ((τοῦ) δοῦναι), and accordingly whether
the dispenser of forgiveness, is God or Jesus. A few textual witnesses
add a qualifying 'in him' (ἐν αὐτῷ) to the phrase and thus support the
former alternative. Also in Acts, Paul claims to have been commissioned
by Jesus to open the eyes of the Gentiles so that they turn from Satan to
God and 'receive ... forgiveness of sins and a share among those sanc-
tified through faith in me' (Acts 26.18). The repentance preached in the
name of Jesus and received through belief in him is a conversion that
includes among its effects the forgiveness of past sins.

In what appears to be a post-resurrectional instruction to the apostles
in the *Preaching of Peter*, Jesus says, 'Now if someone of Israel is willing to repent and believe in God through my name, his sins will be forgiven for him (ἀφεθήσονται αὐτῷ αἱ ἁμαρτίαι)' (*Preaching of Peter*
6 = Clement, *Strom.* 6.43.3). This saying, evidently modelled on Luke
24.47, envisages that forgiveness will be granted through repentance,
brought about by the apostolic preaching.

First Clement also associates Jesus with an offer of repentance and subsequent forgiveness. The author prefaces an array of scriptural *exempla*
in praise of repentance (*1 Cl* 7.5–8.5) with a christological exhortation:
'Let us look intently at the blood of Christ and realize, how precious it
is to his Father, for having been shed for our salvation, it has brought the
grace of repentance to the entire world' (7.4). Having reviewed God's
previous offers of repentance throughout history, the author then encourages repentance, both in the sense of praying to God (see 2.3; 48.1; 51.1)
and in the sense of 'leaving behind the fruitless toil, the strife, and the
zeal that leads to death' (9.1). When believers repent of such sins, they
enter through the 'gate of righteousness', which is 'in Christ' (48.1–4).
But the one who is asked to forgive, as mentioned already, is God (2.3;
60.1–2).

Anointing in the name of Jesus. The only glimpse of a primitive
Christian ritual of anointing those who are ill is provided by the passage
in James that was discussed in Chapter 2. Faithful prayer and anointing
with oil 'in the name of the Lord' will result in bodily healing and forgiveness (Jas 5.14–15). As I noted previously, while the activity of 'raising up' the ill is predicated of Jesus, the agent of forgiveness is probably
God.

Faith in the name of Jesus. Some passages name forgiveness as an
effect of belief in Jesus, without mentioning either a ritual (baptism or
anointing) or moral repentance. In Acts, Peter claims that 'all the prophets
testify that everyone who believes in him will receive the forgiveness of
sins (ἄφεσιν ἁμαρτιῶν λαβεῖν) through his name' (Acts 10.43). The

aorist indicates that a single bestowal of forgiveness is meant. Much the same message is presented in semi-Pauline language as Luke narrates Paul's speech in the synagogue of Antioch in Pisidia: 'through him the forgiveness of sins is proclaimed to you, and from everything in which you were not able to be made righteous through the law of Moses, everyone who believes is made righteous in him' (13.38–9).

The author of First John also connects faith in Jesus with forgiveness: 'I write to you, my children, because [or: that, ὅτι] your sins have been forgiven for you because of his name' (1 John 2.12). It is probably faith that has led to forgiveness, since the 'name' of Jesus elsewhere constitutes the object of faith in First John.[42] Finally, *First Clement* employs Pauline expressions to describe the relationship between faith and righteousness: 'having been called through his will in Christ Jesus, we are also being made righteous, neither through ourselves, nor through our own wisdom or understanding or piety or through some works that we have done in the purity of our heart, but through the faith, through which the Almighty God has made all from eternity righteous' (*1 Cl* 32.4). And the macarism of Ps 32.1–2 is said to have been pronounced 'on those chosen by God through Jesus Christ our Lord' (50.5–7).

Forgiveness announced by Jesus

The *Shepherd of Hermas* is unique in its portrayal of the heavenly Jesus appearing to announce the conditions for God's forgiveness. The angelomorphic Son of God, called the Most Revered Angel, appears to Hermas and tells him 'that you should observe these commandments, and you will have healing for your sins (*remedium peccatorum habebis*)' (*Herm Sim* 10.2.4). Not only the Son of God, but also the Angel of Repentance, announces the general preconditions for receiving God's forgiveness: sinners will be forgiven if they repent.[43] Such proclamation of the terms of forgiveness appears to be an aspect of the 'authority over repentance' (ἡ ἐξουσία τῆς μετανοίας/*paenitentiae potestas*, *Man* 4.3.5; *Sim* 10.1.3) exercised by the Angel of Repentance. This is consonant with early Jewish angelology, which sometimes assigned to angels the function of announcing forgiveness (see Chapter 4 below). That the Son of

---

[42] 1 John 3.23; 5.13; cf. John 1.12; 2.23; 3.18; 20.31.
[43] *Herm Man* 12.6.2; *Sim* 5.7.4; 7.1.4–5; 8.11.3; 9.23.4–5; 9.33.3. Similar announcements are attributed to the deceased Rhoda (*Vis* 1.1.9) and the hypostasized Church (*Vis* 1.3.1; 2.2.4; 2.2.8–2.3.1; 3.2.2; 3.8.11).

God also performs this function ought to be seen as one of the angelo-morphic traits in the christology of *Hermas*.

Jesus as the agent of forgiveness

From the textual passages reviewed so far, there has emerged a predominant pattern of remarkable consistency, in spite of the wide variety of metaphors involved: the active subject who forgives sins is God, the Father of Jesus Christ. It is not always explicitly stated that Jesus is involved in the bestowal of forgiveness, though most often that is the case. However, his role remains subordinate and instrumental.

I will now draw attention to the few passages in pre-135 CE Christian literature that deviate from the standard pattern. These passages actually seem to say that the heavenly Jesus does forgive or has forgiven sins.

'As the Lord has forgiven you' (Col 3.13)

Colossians, as mentioned earlier, says that forgiveness is available 'in' Jesus (Col 1.14), that is, by virtue of the death and resurrection of Jesus (2.12–14; cf. 1.20, 22) and through baptism (2.12). This conforms to the expected pattern: the agent of forgiveness is God. But there is one passage which appears to assign this role to Jesus:

> Therefore, as holy and beloved elect of God, clothe yourselves with lenient compassion, gentleness, humility, tenderness, and patience. Have forbearance with one another and forgive (χαριζόμενοι) each other, whenever somebody has a complaint against another. As also the Lord forgave you (καθὼς καὶ ὁ κύριος ἐχαρίσατο ὑμῖν), so you (should do) too.
>
> (Col 3.12–13)

A number of uncertainties, which pertain to the original reading of 3.13, the identity of 'the Lord' and the moment of forgiveness, surround the interpretation of this passage. I will consider these points in turn.

Fluctuation between the divine names 'God' (θεός), 'Christ' (Χριστός) and 'Lord' (κύριος) among the textual witnesses is not uncommon in the latter part of Colossians.[44] In 3.13, the manuscripts exhibit four different readings which vary the subject of forgiveness. The singularly attested

---

[44] Col 3.15 (Χριστοῦ-θεοῦ), 16 (Χριστοῦ-κυρίου-θεοῦ and θεῷ-κυρίῳ); 4.3 (Χριστοῦ-θεοῦ). The use of *nomina sacra* (ΘΣ, ΚΣ, ΧΣ) may have contributed to the confusion.

reading 'God forgave you in Christ' (ὁ θεὸς ἐν Χριστῷ ἐχαρίσατο ὑμῖν, 33) is an adaptation to Eph 4.32. Further, the support for 'God forgave you' (ὁ θεὸς ἐχαρίσατο ὑμῖν, ℵ *prima manus*, Vulg. mss) is too weak to be original. It is more challenging to decide between the two remaining readings. The majority text has 'Christ forgave you' (ὁ Χριστὸς ἐχαρίσατο ὑμῖν). This variant is not without considerable external support and could also be regarded as the *lectio difficilior* in view of the tendency already noticed.[45] But, on the other hand, the less precise 'the Lord forgave you' (ὁ κύριος ἐχαρίσατο ὑμῖν) is the reading which can account for all the other variants, and it has the strongest support from the manuscripts (including p[46], B and D *prima manus*). The editors of NA27 seem correct in judging this reading to be the original.

This invites the next question, that is, whether the title 'the Lord' in 3.13 refers to God or to Jesus. In favour of the former option, it may be relevant to point out that Colossians has already described God as the forgiver of sins, and especially that God is without doubt the grammatical subject of 'to forgive' (χαρίζεσθαι) in 2.13.[46] Still, this is no absolute obstacle to the assignment of the act of bestowing forgiveness to Jesus this time, just as peace can be said to come first from God (1.2) and then from Christ (3.15), and the kingdom belongs first to the Son (1.13) and then to God (4.11). In fact, Paul's habit of reserving the title 'Lord' for Christ speaks for seeing a reference to Jesus in this passage.[47] When 'the Lord' is explicitly identified in Colossians, it is always Jesus (1.3; 2.6; 3.17, 24), and it is therefore likely that Jesus is meant also in 3.13.

Col 3.13 does not say that the heavenly Jesus forgives sins on a continual basis. Rather, the aorist ἐχαρίσατο confirms that the Lord's forgiveness has already been granted, once and for all, while believers are encouraged to forgive each other continually. The moment at which they were forgiven by the Lord can only be inferred from 2.11–15, where, as already stated, the death and resurrection of Jesus are not kept apart from the believers' burial and revivification in baptism. In similar manner, 3.13 envisages a forgiveness which is indistinguishably located in the death and resurrection of Jesus and in the initiation of the believers through the

[45] J. M. Ross, 'Further Unnoticed Points in the Text of the New Testament', *NovT* 45 (2003), 209–21 (219).

[46] Taylor, *Forgiveness and Reconciliation*, pp. 5–6, puts the translation of χαρίζεσθαι as 'forgive' into question. There is evidence, however, for the verb being used as a synonym of ἀφιέναι: 'I sacrificed for them, and the Lord forgave (ἀφῆκεν) the sin for them. Then, as Eliphas, Baldad and Sophar realized that the Lord had forgiven (ἐχαρίσατο) their sin for them…' (*TJob* 42.8–43.1).

[47] J. D. G. Dunn, *The Epistles to the Colossians and to Philemon: A Commentary on the Greek Text* (Grand Rapids, MI: Eerdmans, 1996), p. 231.

baptismal rite. 'The Lord forgave' the believers at Colossae – in his death and when they were baptized.

Quite clearly, then, Col 3.13 deviates from the standard pattern by assigning the act of forgiveness to Jesus. That this is hardly indicative of a tendency to give this divine attribute to Jesus can be seen from the use made of the passage in Ephesians, where the unusual statement 'the Lord forgave you' is seemingly corrected to the more conventional phrase 'God forgave you in Christ' (ὁ θεὸς ἐν Χριστῷ ἐχαρίσατο ὑμῖν, Eph 4.32). One gets the impression that the author of Ephesians, realizing that the expression in Col 3.13 diverged from the standard way of speaking of forgiveness, replaced it with a formula that better articulated what was perceived to be christological orthodoxy.[48]

'They were made righteous by the Most Revered Angel' (Herm Man 5.1.7)

To find further expressions of the notion that Jesus has forgiven the sins of believers it is necessary to move beyond the NT to the Apostolic Fathers. In the *Shepherd of Hermas*, the Angel of Repentance is asked to give Hermas advice on how to avoid the vice of bad temper (ὀξυχολία). The conversation continues as the angel responds:

> 'Indeed', he said, 'if you do not avoid it, you and your house, you have lost all your hope. But avoid it, for I am with you. Yes, even all who repent with all their heart will abstain from it, for I will be with them and preserve them. For they were all made righteous by the Most Revered Angel (ἐδικαιώθησαν γὰρ πάντες ὑπὸ τοῦ σεμνοτάτου ἀγγέλου).'
>
> (*Herm Man* 5.1.7)

The Angel of Repentance claims that those who repent were made righteous by the Most Revered Angel, that is, by Jesus. Since *Vis* 3.9.1 employs the verb δικαιωθῆναι with reference to the believers' experience of forgiveness and holiness at their initiation through baptism, this may actually imply that Jesus forgave their sins, despite the repeated assertion in *Hermas* that only God can bring healing for past sins (*Man* 4.1.11; *Sim* 5.7.3). In this case, the reference is not to the first offer of forgiveness in the baptismal rite, but to the second offer of forgiveness through repentance. But since there will be only one such offer of repentance (*Man*

---

48   Ross, 'Further Unnoticed Points', 219.

4.3.6), Jesus is not depicted as forgiving sins on a continual basis, but only through a single and unrepeatable act.

Finally, it should be noticed that a passage in the *Similitudes* possibly links forgiveness with the passion and death of Jesus:

> 'God planted the vineyard, that is, he created the people and handed it over to his Son. And the Son installed the angels over them, to preserve all of them, and himself purified (ἐκαθάρισε) their sins through toiling and enduring many hardships; for no vineyard can be dug without toil and labour. Now that he had purified (καθαρίσας) the people's sins he showed them the paths of life, having given to them the law, which he had received from his Father.'
>
> (*Herm Sim* 5.6.2–3)

The 'toil and labour' that the Son of God has endured for the sake of the vineyard are probably those of his passion, which entailed a 'purification' of sins.[49] Here the choice of vocabulary may be influenced by the vineyard imagery (cf. John 15.1–3). However, since the direct object of purification is the sins, not the vineyard or people, 'to purify' (καθαρίζειν) may be employed here in the sense of 'to forgive' (cf. Num 30.6, 9, 13 LXX). If so, *Hermas* depicts Jesus as one who forgives sins, not only through the singular offer of repentance, but also through his passion and death.

'The Lord forgives all who repent' (*Ign* Phld 8.1)

Ignatius of Antioch is the first author to express the notion that the heavenly Jesus forgives sins repeatedly. This he states as part of his exhortation of the Philadelphian Christians to flee division:

> But where there is division and anger, God does not dwell. Now the Lord forgives all who repent (πᾶσιν οὖν μετανοοῦσιν ἀφίει ὁ κύριος), if they repent to the unity of God and the council of the bishop. I trust in the grace of Jesus Christ, who will loose every bond from you.
>
> (*Ign Phld* 8.1)

In view of Ignatius' language elsewhere in his letters, 'the Lord' (ὁ κύριος) who forgives those who repent is in all probability Jesus.

---

[49] Osiek, *The Shepherd of Hermas*, pp. 178–9.

While 'the Lord' never occurs as an unambiguous reference to God the Father in Ignatius' letters, the expression clearly denotes Christ at least eleven times.[50] The present tense ἀφίει indicates that, unlike the passages from Colossians and *Hermas* discussed above, Ignatius does not limit the forgiving activity of Jesus to a single event in the past, but envisages it as ongoing. There is no mention either of the death of Jesus or of baptism, and Ignatius does not propose the singular offer of repentance preached by *Hermas*, but seems to speak of a general opportunity to repent of sins (cf. Ign *Eph* 10.1; *Smyrn* 9.1). For Ignatius, this must be coupled with a return to the divinely instituted unity made visible through the episcopal 'council' (συνέδριον, *Phld* 8.1; cf. 3.2).

For Ignatius, then, Jesus has appropriated a prerogative normally reserved for God in early Judaism and in nascent Christianity of the first century. Why does this take place here? An explanation may be provided by pointing to the 'monarchian' theology of Ignatius, which operates on the principle that was later labelled *communicatio idiomatum*. What Ignatius predicates of God, he can also predicate of Jesus, and vice versa: thus he speaks of Jesus as 'God'.[51] His reference to Christ's ability to forgive sins is therefore another expression of the christology which enables him to write of 'the blood of God' (*Eph* 1.1).

'If we ask the Lord to forgive us' (Pol Phil 6.2)

A similar understanding of the heavenly Jesus' continuous forgiving activity is mediated by the letter allegedly written by Polycarp of Smyrna to the church at Philippi. The integrity and authorship of this letter are the objects of a debate that need not be entered into here.[52] As discussed in Chapter 2 above, the exhortation 'forgive, and it will be forgiven for you' belongs to the teaching that the author attributes to the Lord (Pol *Phil* 2.3). In the same way as Ignatius does, the *Letter to the Philippians* frequently and consistently refers to Jesus as 'the Lord' (ὁ κύριος).[53]

---

[50] Ign *Eph* 10.3; 15.3; 17.1, 2; 19.1; *Magn* 7.1; 13.1; *Trall* 8.1; *Smyrn* 4.2; 5.2; *Pol* 5.2. Cf. the expression '[our/the] Lord Jesus Christ' (*Phld* 1.1; 4.1; 9.2; 11.2; *Smyrn* 1.1; *Pol inscr.*).

[51] For example Ign *Pol* 8.3. For further references, literature and discussion, see W. R. Schoedel, *Ignatius of Antioch: A Commentary on the Letters of Ignatius of Antioch* (Philadelphia: Fortress, 1995), pp. 20, 39.

[52] See P. N. Harrison, *Polycarp's Two Epistles to the Philippians* (Cambridge University Press, 1936); cf. P. Hartog, *Polycarp and the New Testament: The Occasion, Rhetoric, Theme, and Unity of the Epistle to the Philippians and Its Allusions to New Testament Literature*, WUNT 2:134 (Tübingen: Mohr Siebeck, 2002), pp. 148–69.

[53] Pol *Phil* 5.2; 6.3*bis*; 7.1, 2; 9.2. Cf. the expressions '[our/the] Lord Jesus Christ' (1.1, 2; 2.1; 12.2*bis*; 14.1) and 'our Lord' (1.1; 13.2).

This is likely to be the case in the second passage expressing the notion that divine forgiveness is conditioned by a person's willingness to forgive other human beings:

> Now if we ask the Lord (τοῦ κυρίου) to forgive us (ἵνα ἡμῖν ἀφῇ), we are also obliged to forgive. For we are before the eyes of the Lord and God (τοῦ κυρίου καὶ θεοῦ), and we must all stand before the tribunal of Christ and each one must give an account for himself. So now let us serve him with fear and all reverence, as he himself commanded us, and the apostles who proclaimed the gospel to us, and the prophets who preached in advance the coming of our Lord.
>
> (Pol *Phil* 6.2–3)

The author can presuppose that the addressees habitually ask Jesus, the Lord, for forgiveness of sins committed subsequently to their initiation into the Church. Similarly to Ign *Phld* 8.1, Pol *Phil* 6.2 also does not link the forgiveness bestowed by the heavenly Jesus to his death, although elsewhere the author clearly states that Jesus suffered and died for sins (1.2; 8.1). Neither is there a reference to baptism, but what is presumed is rather the practice of directing penitential prayer to Jesus.

In quoting Rom 14.10–12, the author shows acquaintance with the textual tradition that speaks of 'the tribunal of Christ' rather than 'the tribunal of God', possibly due to influence from 2 Cor 5.10.[54] He thereby envisages Jesus as the future judge, but also as the one who forgives, probably already in the present, since this is what the addressees are supposed to do. Is this an effect of the equation of Jesus with God, as it is in Ignatius? If 'the Lord and God' (τοῦ κυρίου καὶ θεοῦ) is taken as a reference to a single entity, the answer will be affirmative: according to this reading, Pol *Phil* 6.2 does not only label Jesus 'the Lord', but also calls him 'God'. However, it is just as possible that the expression refers to two distinct entities, the Lord Jesus and God, his Father, as does the juxtaposition 'God and Christ,' which recurs three times in the letter.[55] Perhaps the temporal and theological proximity between this letter and those of Ignatius is enough to account for the fact that they share a common view of Jesus' relationship to forgiveness.

---

[54] Berding, *Polycarp and Paul*, p. 85; Hartog, *Polycarp and the New Testament*, pp. 180–1.

[55] Pol *Phil* 3.3; 5.2, 3. In addition, the isolated 'God' (θεός) stands anarthrous in Pol *Phil inscr.*; 1.1, 3; 4.3; 5.1, 3; 6.1; cf. the presence of the article in *inscr.*; 1.2; 2.1*bis*, 3; 4.2; 7.2; 9.2.

The synoptic episodes in relation to primitive christology

It is now time to consider the synoptic episodes in the light of the previous review of primitive Christian thinking about forgiveness. Since
advocates of a christological origin for the Gospels' narration about
Jesus as one who forgives sins have tended to focus on Mark 2.1–12,
sometimes at the expense of Luke 7.36–50, I will in the following make
the Markan episode the main object. The elements of the Lukan episode
found to be traditional in the previous chapter will, however, also receive
some consideration.

Mark 2.1–12 and primitive christology

The clearest result of the investigation conducted in this chapter so far
has been that the subject of whom forgiveness is routinely predicated in
primitive Christianity is God.[56] The role of Jesus is subordinate, instrumental and mediatory: sins are forgiven *because of* Jesus or *through*
Jesus, but not normally *by* Jesus. If these Christians did expect the risen
Lord to forgive their sins, as critical scholars have suggested, this is not
so evident from the sources. With the exception of the Gospels, only four
or five passages in pre-135 CE Christian literature do appear to describe
Jesus as one who forgives sins. Apart from Col 3.13, all these passages are
relatively late, being contained in writings authored in the early second
century: the *Shepherd of Hermas*, Ignatius' *Letter to the Philadelphians*
and Polycarp's *Letter to the Philippians*. Thus, Colossians provides the
only first-century evidence outside the Gospels of the notion that Jesus
forgives sins, while the Apostolic Fathers who express the same notion
are about half a century later than Mark.

The lack of references to a timeless and universal authority to forgive
sins being attributed to the heavenly Jesus before the time of Ignatius
and Polycarp is also noteworthy. In Col 3.13, there is no question of
Jesus forgiving the sins committed by the Colossian believers after their
conversion; what is referred to is a single act of forgiveness in the past,
seemingly located in the death of Jesus and in the believers' baptism.
Similarly, if the metaphor of purification in *Herm Sim* 5.6.2–3 does
indeed refer to forgiveness, it is clear that this forgiveness was wrought
at a specific point in the past, probably through the passion and death
of Jesus. *Herm Man* 5.1.7 says that Jesus has made repentant believers
righteous, which plausibly involves his forgiveness for their sins. Again,

---

[56] For a similar conclusion, see Michl, 'Sündenvergebung in Christus', 27.

this is not something that takes place continually but is limited to a singular offer of repentance. For all the differences between Colossians and *Hermas*, these two writings actually agree in their understanding of a forgiveness bestowed by Jesus, which is intrinsically bound up, on the one hand, with his death and, on the other, with what could anachronistically be categorized as a 'sacrament'.

Further, one can hardly take Col 3.13 as evidence for a strong and clear tendency to attribute the divine prerogative of forgiving sins to the heavenly Jesus. I noted above that Colossians indistinguishably collocates 'peace' and 'kingdom' with 'God' (1.2; 4.11) and 'Christ' (3.15) or 'the Son' (1.13), and thus expresses a form of binitarianism at some points.[57] Turning now to Ephesians, one finds the binitarian pattern preserved, even carried further: peace here comes simultaneously 'from God (our) Father and the Lord Jesus Christ' (Eph 1.2; 6.23), and the kingdom is that 'of Christ and God' (5.5). By contrast, the statement in Colossians about the forgiveness bestowed by the Lord Jesus in the past becomes, in Ephesians, a statement about forgiveness bestowed by God 'in Christ' (Eph 4.32). Despite the tendency of Ephesians to retain and to emphasize the divine attributes given to the heavenly Jesus by Colossians, the author turned the unusual claim in Col 3.13 into a more conventional phrase about God's forgiveness in Christ. The author of Ephesians appears to have recognized that Col 3.13 diverged from typical christological formulations.

Beginning with Ignatius, there may be a tendency to attribute the function of forgiving sins continually to Jesus by virtue of a developing christology, according to which Christ is equal to his Father and thus shares in all divine qualities without exception. Ignatius, who elsewhere unhesitatingly calls Jesus 'God', holds that the Lord Jesus forgives those who repent of their post-baptismal sins (Ign *Phld* 8.1). For Polycarp, it is natural to assume that the believers at Philippi would normally ask Jesus to forgive their sins (Pol *Phil* 6.2).

In view of what has been said so far, the scholarly assertions that Mark 2.1–12 'has the flavour of primitive christology', that forgiveness 'was expected of the exalted Lord' and that the notion 'can only be understood against the backdrop of early christology' do not appear well founded. Conversely, there is discontinuity between, on the one hand, the Markan episode and, on the other, primitive Christianity as it can be known to us. I will conclude this section by spelling out three discontinuous features

---

[57] For the term 'binitarian', see L. W. Hurtado, *Lord Jesus Christ: Devotion to Jesus in Earliest Christianity* (Grand Rapids, MI: Eerdmans, 2003), pp. 151–3.

of this episode that demonstrate, to my mind, that the topic of forgiveness in Mark 2.1–12 cannot be derived in its entirety from primitive christology.

Firstly, as stated in Chapter 2 above, Mark 2.1–12 unambiguously portrays Jesus as the one who forgives the sins of the paralytic. This is dissimilar to the tendency of first-century christology, which reserves this activity for God alone. The sole exception (Col 3.13) is hardly sufficient to change this impression.

Secondly, the climax of the Markan episode consists of the saying in 2.10, according to which the Son of Man 'has authority' (present) to forgive sins. Even in Col 3.13 – or in *Herm Sim* 5.6.2–3 – there is no mention of such a general, timeless authority to forgive. On the contrary, in these christological expressions, Jesus 'has forgiven' or 'purified' (aorist) sins once and for all through his suffering and death. In dissociating forgiveness from the death of Jesus, indeed depicting it as available and offered by Jesus prior to his death, Mark 2.1–12 is again dissimilar to primitive Christianity.

Thirdly, the only ground for the Markan Jesus to forgive the sins of the paralytic is his 'seeing their faith'. There is no mention of baptism or of any other 'sacramental' ritual. This is also dissimilar to the passages from Colossians and *Hermas*, which link Jesus' forgiving activity with baptism and with the special offer of repentance respectively.

Luke 7.36–47; Mark 2.1–5, 11–12 and primitive christology

In the previous chapter I argued that the substance of Luke 7.36–47, with the possible exception of 7.44–6, is pre-Lukan and once existed apart from Luke's appendage of 7.48–50. Thus reconstructed, the pre-Lukan episode will have described Jesus as declaring that the sins of the sinful woman have been forgiven, thereby displaying his status as a prophet. In other words, the pre-Lukan episode does not specify Jesus as the agent of forgiveness; and without 7.48–50, which Luke added in order to bring the episode into conformity with 5.17–26, it would be most natural to assume that the implicit agent of 'her many sins are forgiven' (7.47a) is God.

A similar claim could be made for the pre-Markan episode, which some scholars have hypothesized behind Mark 2.1–5, 11–12. If 2.6–10 is excised from the Markan episode, the agent of the passive 'your sins are forgiven' (2.5b) could be construed as God, which is also how several proponents of this hypothesis interpret the statement in its pre-Markan setting.[58] Can the criterion of discontinuity be applied to Mark 2.5b (apart from 2.6–10) and Luke 7.47a? The answer should be affirmative. While Mark 2.1–12 differs from the predominant pattern of primitive Christian forgiveness theology by enhancing, as it were, Jesus' role into that of one who forgives sins, the pre-Markan and pre-Lukan episodes differ from the same pattern by reducing his role to that of one who proclaims God's forgiveness. In primitive christology, as laid out above, Jesus generally functions as the mediator of God's forgiveness: God forgives sins because of the suffering and death of Jesus, since he intercedes for those who have sinned, and because believers have faith in him and are baptized in his name. However, the heavenly Jesus does not normally announce God's forgiveness. *Hermas* provides the single exception in its depiction of how the Most Revered Angel appears to announce the conditions for forgiveness (*Herm Sim* 10.2.4). But it is unlikely that the hypothesized episodes behind Mark 2.1–5, 11–12 and Luke 7.36–47 originated as retrojections of such angelomorphic christology into the life of the earthly Jesus, since there is nothing else in these episodes to suggest the presence of any angelomorphism. Thus, the historicity of Mark 2.5b and Luke 7.47a in their putative pre-Gospel contexts is corroborated through the criterion of discontinuity.

Forgiveness and primitive ecclesiology

An alternative line of reasoning has been taken by those scholars who find in Mark 2.1–12, or at least in 2.5b–10, a primitive Christian attempt to justify the community's practice of offering the forgiveness of sins. Bultmann stated his conviction that 'the Palestinian church ... by way of this composition traced its prerogative back to an archetypal deed of Jesus' and argued that Matt 9.8 correctly represents the original import of Mark 2.5b–10. The controversial dialogue between Jesus and the scribes echoes a controversy in the life of the community, according to Bultmann, who did not identify the contending parts explicitly.[59] Strobel saw therein a Christian apology, designed to defend the practice

---

[58] Strobel, *Erkenntnis und Bekenntnis*, pp. 59–61; M. Trautmann, *Zeichenhafte Handlungen Jesu: Ein Beitrag zur Frage nach dem geschichtlichen Jesus*, FzB 37 (Würzburg: Echter, 1980), pp. 244–5; Klauck, 'Die Frage der Sündenvergebung', 241; J. Gnilka, *Jesus von Nazaret* (Freiburg: Herder, 1992), pp. 116–17.

[59] Bultmann, *Die Geschichte der synoptischen Tradition*, pp. 13–14 (quotation from p. 13, my translation).

of offering forgiveness in the name of Jesus in the face of Jewish accusations of blasphemy.[60] Reginald Fuller asserted that it had been aimed at 'Pharisaic criticisms'.[61] Others have argued that it is more realistic to envisage a conflict within primitive Christianity, since the appeal to christology and to an authoritative saying of Jesus could hardly have made an impression on non-Christian Jews. One should therefore view the Markan scribes as representatives of Jewish Christians who were reluctant to extend God's prerogative of forgiving sins to Jesus.[62]

As regards the occasions at which forgiveness was concretely bestowed in the primitive Church, the Jesus Seminar, for example, is content to lay down that '[t]he early church was in the process of claiming for itself the right to forgive sins'.[63] Other scholars are more precise. Bultmann proposed that the Palestinian community thought that its practice to forgive sins was legitimate because of the miracles of healing performed in the community.[64] Fuller and Wilckens, commenting on Mark 2.6–10 and Luke 7.36–43, 47 respectively, both identified baptism as the ritual through which the community mediated God's forgiveness.[65] And Hartwig Thyen detected in both Mark 2.5b and Luke 7.48 a 'tendency towards the development of the Church's sacramental institution of penance'.[66] In the following I will investigate the evidence for these alleged activities and their relationship to forgiveness. I will also evaluate the aforementioned suggestions concerning the *Sitz im Leben* of the synoptic forgiveness episodes.

Miracle and forgiveness

According to Bultmann's hypothesis, the Palestinian community held that its power to perform miracles of healing substantiated its claim to have authority to forgive sins. The only external pieces of evidence

[60] Strobel, *Erkenntnis und Bekenntnis*, p. 59.

[61] R. H. Fuller, *The Foundations of New Testament Christology* (New York: Scribner, 1965), p. 149.

[62] H.-W. Kuhn, *Ältere Sammlungen im Markusevangelium*, SUNT 8 (Göttingen: Vandenhoeck & Ruprecht, 1971), p. 96; Klauck, 'Die Frage der Sündenvergebung', 244. See also D. J. Doughty, 'The Authority of the Son of Man (Mk 2,1–3,6)', *ZNW* 74 (1983), 161–81 (166–8).

[63] Funk, Hoover and the Jesus Seminar, *The Five Gospels*, p. 44. Similar statements are made on pp. 163, 283–4.

[64] Bultmann, *Die Geschichte der synoptischen Tradition*, p. 13; R. Bultmann, *Theologie des Neuen Testaments*, 7th edn (Tübingen: Mohr Siebeck, 1977), p. 65.

[65] Fuller, *Foundations of NT Christology*, p. 149; Wilckens, 'Vergebung für die Sünderin', pp. 417–21.

[66] Thyen, *Studien zur Sündenvergebung*, p. 242 n. 2 (my translation).

engaged by Bultmann here were Matt 16.19 and 18.18, which he held to testify that the Palestinian community claimed for itself the authority to forgive sins; that the community employed healings to corroborate this belief is hypothesized solely from Mark 2.1–12.[67] In the following, I will review briefly the data concerning primitive Christian healing, with the intent of assessing the hypothesis that it was somehow associated with a purported authority to forgive sins. First, I will scan the literary evidence for explicit pronouncements of forgiveness in conjunction with healings, and then I will come to the notion of forgiveness as implicitly bestowed through healing.

Explicit forgiveness in healing miracles

Due to the character and focus of primitive Christian literature, few narrations about purported healings performed by followers of Jesus in this era exist. Only the Acts of the Apostles provide some details, narrating eight miracles of healing: three healings of crippled or paralyzed people (Acts 3.1–10; 9.32–5; 14.8–10), two resuscitations (9.36–43; 20.7–12), the healing of a man suffering from dysentery (28.7–8), the healing of Paul's blindness (9.17–19; 22.12–16) and the exorcism of a pythonic spirit (16.16–18).

With the exception of 20.7–12 and 28.7–8, each of these episodes culminates in a verbal command, which effectuates the healing, sometimes accompanied by an action or a gesture, such as raising up the person by his or her hand (3.7; 9.41), laying one's hands on the person (9.17) or praying (9.40). As noted previously in Chapter 2, the healing formula is normally an imperative order that the malfunctioning condition should be restored. Thus, the crippled men at the Beautiful Gate and in Lystra, the paralyzed Aeneas and the deceased Tabitha are all commanded to rise (3.6; 9.34, 40; 14.10), while Ananias bids Paul regain his eyesight (22.13; cf. 9.17) and Paul charges the pythonic spirit to get out of the slave girl in Philippi (16.18). In some cases, however, the constituent formula is preceded by a supplementary phrase. Since these phrases correspond structurally to what I will term the 'faith formula' of Mark 2.5b in relation to the healing formula in Mark 2.11 (see Chapter 5 below), they deserve attention here.

---

[67] Bultmann, *Die Geschichte der synoptischen Tradition*, pp. 12–14. In the original edition of his book (1921), Bultmann made no reference to Matt 9.8; 16.19; 18.18, but nonetheless arrived at the same conclusion as he did ten years later in the second edition (1931), where the Matthean references have been added.

The correspondence is most striking in Peter's words to Aeneas, 'Aeneas, Jesus Christ heals you. Stand up and make your bed' (Acts 9.34), in which a declaration with performative force is intercalated between the address and the healing formula. It functions to point the attention away from the mediator of the healing, in this case Peter, to its source, Jesus.[68] The same purpose is accomplished through the phrases 'in the name of Jesus Christ' (3.6; 16.18) and 'the Lord has sent me' (9.17). Maisch's argument that the formulae in 3.6 and 9.34 are undoubtedly Lukan creations is unconvincing, although it is certainly true that 3.6 serves well to prepare for the repeated mention of 'the name of Jesus' in Acts 3–4.[69] As the notion that miracles are performed by the power of the name of Jesus is present in a variety of primitive Christian sources, it cannot be reduced to a Lukan special concern.[70] The case for seeing 9.34 as pre-Lukan is especially strong, since this formula is found nowhere else in Acts. A pronouncement of forgiveness here would have added credibility to the hypothesis that Mark 2.1–12 reflects a Christian practice of bestowing forgiveness in conjunction with healing miracles, but forgiveness is not mentioned.

From this lack of explicit pronouncements of forgiveness in conjunction with the healing miracles in Acts, one cannot, naturally, demonstrate that such pronouncements never took place, but only that there is no evidence that they did. It is also significant that in the places where pronouncements of forgiveness would have been expected to occur, there may instead be formulae which attribute the healing to the heavenly Jesus, and which thus de-emphasize the importance of the earthly healer.

Implicit forgiveness in healing miracles

In any of the episodes from Acts studied above, it remains *a priori* possible that forgiveness is thought of as being bestowed through the healing act, without being explicitly proclaimed by the healer. To examine this possibility one needs to take into account also those textual passages which mention primitive Christian healing in a more general or cursory manner.

---

[68] J. A. Hardon, 'The Miracle Narratives in the Acts of the Apostles', *CBQ* 16 (1954), 303–18 (306–7).

[69] Maisch, *Die Heilung des Gelähmten*, pp. 66–7, 69.

[70] Mark 9.38–9; Matt 7.22; Jas 5.14 attest to this notion independently of Luke 10.17; Acts 4.30; 19.13; cf. Mark 16.17.

The only positive indication that healing may have implied forgiveness comes from Jas 5.14–16, which has already received attention from other angles above. Here forgiveness is first mentioned as a side effect of the presbyterial prayer for the person who is physically ill in case that person has indeed sinned (5.15). The promotion of the mutual confession of sins then leads immediately back to the topic of bodily healing (5.16). It is crucial to note, however, that the notion of an ecclesial 'authority to forgive sins' is absent from this passage. The presbyters do not forgive sins; it is God who will do this in response to their prayers.[71] It is difficult to see how this could have lead to the kind of controversy that Bultmann and others have seen at the roots of Mark 2.5–10.

Paul, listing 'gifts of healing' among the endowments of the Spirit (1 Cor 12.9, 28, 30), merely affirms that healing was an ingredient of primitive Christian communal life. Luke narrates successful healing ministries as part of the missionary endeavours of Peter and the Twelve (Acts 5.12–16; cf. 4.30), Philip (8.5–8) and Paul (28.7–10). In none of these cases is forgiveness mentioned.

A final clue to the first-century Christian understanding of healing may be found in the synoptic Gospels' missionary discourses. In Mark, Jesus grants 'authority (ἐξουσία) over the unclean spirits' when he sends out the Twelve (Mark 6.7); having departed, they not only preach repentance and expel demons, but they also anoint with oil many who are ill and heal them (6.13). In Matthew, the authority given to the Twelve is also to 'heal every illness and every infirmity' (Matt 10.1), and Jesus instructs them in direct speech: 'Heal the sick, raise the dead, cleanse the lepers, expel the demons' (10.8). In Luke Jesus similarly grants 'power and authority' (δύναμιν καὶ ἐξουσίαν) to the Twelve so that they should, besides expelling demons and preaching the kingdom, 'heal the ill' and 'cure the infirm' (Luke 9.1–2). Accordingly, they leave to evangelize and heal (9.6). The Seventy(-Two) are commanded to heal the sick in any town that receives them (10.9). If indeed the authority to forgive sins was such a prominent and controversial aspect of primitive Christian healing, one might have expected it to be mentioned in these contexts.

Once again, while this brief survey of the material has demonstrated that evidence is lacking for the notion that the church had any authority to forgive sins in conjunction with healing, one must certainly avoid arguing *e silentio* that such a notion could not have been current. It is clear, however, that Bultmann's proposal remains based chiefly on inference

[71] J. Michl, 'Sündenbekenntnis und Sündenvergebung in der Kirche des Neuen Testaments', *MThZ* 24 (1973), 189–207 (193–5).

from Mark 2.1–12 and that there is little if any support for it from other texts.[72] Unless high confidence is placed in the capability of classic form-criticism to reconstruct the *Sitz im Leben* of any pericope, the proposal is unconvincing.

Baptism and forgiveness

Fuller agreed with Bultmann that Mark 2.6–10 had originated in the Palestinian church in order to defend a criticized practice. This practice was identified by Fuller as baptism: '[t]he early Palestinian church would be particularly concerned to vindicate against Pharisaic criticisms their claim to mediate the eschatological remission of sin through baptism'.[73] I have drawn attention earlier in this chapter to the fact that several primitive Christian texts do associate baptism in the name of Jesus with forgiveness. Those texts, and a few others, will now be studied from a different angle.

The bestowal of forgiveness in baptism

As mentioned above, Paul once identifies baptism as the point at which believers are made righteous (1 Cor 6.11). While at times he mentions the baptismal rite without reference to the abolition of sin (Gal 3.26–7; 1 Cor 12.12–13), he draws a similar link between being baptized and being made righteous in his letter to the Roman Christians (Rom 6.1–11). Paul appears to have inherited the notion that baptism has the function of doing away with past sins from earlier tradition.[74] Writing to Corinth, he certainly acknowledges that a human agent is required in order that baptism may take place, but he also expects his addressees to consent with him that the role of the baptizer is merely instrumental (1 Cor 1.12–17).[75] It is foreign to Paul to claim that he himself, or any other baptizers, have forgiven sins in baptism.

Other primitive Christian texts tend to confirm both these tenets: that baptism involves the forgiveness of past sins, and that the baptizer plays a subsidiary role. There are indeed passages which mention baptism

---

[72] Hampel, *Menschensohn und historischer Jesus*, p. 193, arrives at a similar conclusion.

[73] Fuller, *Foundations of NT Christology*, p. 149.

[74] L. Hartman, *'Into the Name of the Lord Jesus': Baptism in the Early Church* (Edinburgh: T & T Clark, 1997), pp. 68–78.

[75] L. Hartman, 'Baptism "Into the Name of Jesus" and Early Christology: Some Tentative Considerations', *ST* 28 (1974), 21–48 (35).

without bringing in the topic of forgiveness (e.g. Heb 6.2; Acts 10.47; John 3.5), but the explicit linkage is nonetheless widespread (e.g. Col 2.11–13; Tit 3.4–7; Acts 2.38; *Barn* 11.1; *Herm Man* 4.3.1). It was shown earlier in this chapter that, while baptism is said to be performed 'in the name of Jesus', it is God who grants forgiveness. Much less, of course, is the significance attributed to the baptizer, who is seldom mentioned at all. Instructions to baptize and regulations concerning baptism certainly recognize the minister's active function (Matt 28.19; *Did* 7.1–4; Ign *Smyrn* 8.2), as Luke also does occasionally (Acts 8.38). However, in Acts, the act of baptizing is normally referred to in the passive voice, even in narrative contexts where a phrasing in the active would not have been out of place.[76] In this way, the focus on God as the real supplier of grace is maintained.

Forgiveness was thus linked to baptism from very early on in primitive Christianity. It seems less probable that the baptismal ritual itself included a declaration of forgiveness. As Lars Hartman suggests, the wide attestation of the otherwise odd formula 'in(to) the name of the Lord Jesus' is quite explicable if 'the phrase was used in the rite in such a way that it stuck in the mind of the participants'.[77] No corresponding consistency can be discerned when it comes to the choice of vocabulary by which to refer to the forgiveness bestowed at baptism.[78] As a consequence, it is groundless to assume that primitive Christian baptism involved a declaration of forgiveness – such as 'your sins are forgiven' – or that it was perceived as an exploitation of the 'authority to forgive sins'.[79] God alone forgave sins at baptism.[80] It is consistent with this that, as far as we know, no minister of baptism claimed to be forgiving sins by performing the ritual.

---

[76] Acts 2.41; 8.12–13, 36; 9.18 (cf. 22.16); 10.47–8; 16.15, 33; 18.8; 19.5; cf. 2.38; 8.16.

[77] Hartman, '*Into the Name of the Lord Jesus*', p. 49. For a less cautious assessment, see G. R. Beasley-Murray, *Baptism in the New Testament* (Grand Rapids, MI: Eerdmans, 1962), pp. 100–2.

[78] The vocabulary includes ἀπολούειν (1 Cor 6.11; Acts 22.16); ἀφιέναι/ἄφεσις (Acts 2.38; *Barn* 6.11; 11.1; 16.8; *Herm Man* 4.3.1–2); δικαιοῦν (1 Cor 6.11; Rom 6.7; Tit 3.7; *Herm Vis* 3.9.1); καθαρισμός (2 Pet 1.9?; cf. 1 Pet 3.21); χαρίζεσθαι (Col 2.13; cf. 3.13; Eph 4.32).

[79] John 20.23 is not applied unequivocally to baptism until the mid third century (Cyprian, *Ep.* 73.7; 69.11; 75.16 (=Firmilian, *Ep. ad Cyprianum* 16)). See Michl, 'Sündenbekenntnis und Sündenvergebung', 203 n. 59; Hägerland, 'The Power of Prophecy', 101 n. 48.

[80] Hartman, '*Into the Name of the Lord Jesus*', p. 45.

Baptism as a potential source of controversy

It is highly doubtful that this mediating and expressly subordinate role of those who administered primitive Christian baptism would have provoked the strong criticism, Pharisaic or other, that Fuller suggests. Textual passages that refer explicitly to baptism and its capacity to mediate forgiveness contain no traces of such controversies. This holds true both for the baptism of John and for primitive Christian baptism.

John's baptism was intrinsically linked with forgiveness, although the precise relationship between repentance, forgiveness and baptism cannot be recovered with certainty.[81] While John's call to baptism was apparently rejected by some (Luke 7.29–30) and his own status seems to have been questioned (Q 7.33), the material at hand does not indicate that his claim to mediate or to confirm forgiveness was made the object of specific criticism.[82] As to Pharisees who made contact with John, the sources depict their attitude as ranging from dismissive (Luke 7.29–30) via neutrally curious (John 1.19–28) to sympathetic (Matt 3.7).[83] While John's legitimacy as a prophet would certainly have been a point of debate among his contemporaries (see Mark 11.30–3), his claim to be offering the means of gaining forgiveness and of escaping the eschatological judgement seems not to have been perceived as either blasphemous or controversial in principle.

The extant data concerning reactions towards the baptismal practice and the preaching of the primitive Palestinian church all come from Acts. When religious authorities respond negatively to primitive Christian activity in Judaea, their hostility often seems to be directed against the belief and the practice as a whole (4.7, 17–18; 5.2–18, 40; 23.1–2, 12–15). Specific topics of conflict are sometimes singled out: the belief in Jesus' resurrection (4.1–2; cf. 22.3–22; 24.20–1; 25.18–19), in his

---

[81] Josephus, *Ant* XVIII.117 denies that John's baptism could be used to ask for forgiveness (μὴ ἐπί τινων ἁμαρτάδων παραιτήσει) and states that those who underwent it had already been purified in their souls. Mark 1.4/Luke 3.3 (βάπτισμα μετανοίας εἰς ἄφεσιν ἁμαρτιῶν) is ambiguous as to whether repentance or baptism effectuates forgiveness, but Mark 1.5 (ἐβαπτίζοντο ... ἐξομολογούμενοι) is difficult to harmonize with Josephus' account. Cf. *GosHeb* 10 = Jerome, *Adv. Pelag.* 3.2 (*baptizat in remissionem peccatorum*). For discussion and varying proposals, see H. Thyen, 'Βάπτισμα μετανοίας εἰς ἄφεσιν ἁμαρτιῶν', in E. Dinkler (ed.), *Zeit und Geschichte*, FS R. Bultmann (Tübingen: Mohr Siebeck, 1964), pp. 97–125 (pp. 97–9); R. L. Webb, *John the Baptizer and Prophet: A Socio-Historical Study*, JSNTS 62 (Sheffield: JSOT Press, 1991), pp. 190–4; Meier, *A Marginal Jew*, vol. II, pp. 53–5; J. E. Taylor, *The Immerser: John the Baptist within Second Temple Judaism* (Grand Rapids, MI/Cambridge: Eerdmans, 1997), pp. 93–100.

[82] Pace W. R. G. Loader, *Jesus' Attitude towards the Law: A Study of the Gospels*, WUNT 2:97 (Tübingen: Mohr Siebeck, 1997), p. 48.

[83] Taylor, *The Immerser*, pp. 192–203.

being the Messiah or Son of God (9.19–23, 27–9), and in his status as
the glorified Son of Man or as an object of worship (7.56–7; 9.14, 21);
the repeated accusations against the authorities that they were responsible for Jesus' death (5.27–8; 7.51–4); and the alleged antinomian, anti-
temple and anti-Israelite contents of the preaching (6.11–14; 21.27–30;
25.7–8). Regardless of the extent to which these controversies took place
historically, it is clear that Luke does not betray any awareness that baptism had ever been a point of conflict between the primitive Church and
the religious authorities of Judaea. The only passage that could possibly
be taken to suggest the contrary is Acts 5.27–33, where repentance and
the forgiveness of sins are mentioned as part of the apostolic testimony
that provokes rage among members of the Sanhedrin. But these aspects
are not highlighted, and, in view of the initial question put by the high
priest, it appears that what is really offensive is once again the keryg-
matic insistence on the centrality of Jesus, and especially the charge
that the authorities were responsible for his death. And ironically, in
view of Fuller's hypothesis, it is precisely at this point that Gamaliel,
the Pharisee, articulates his preference for an irenic attitude towards the
Jerusalem church and his deliberations that its proclamation may be of
divine origin (5.34–9)!

It turns out that the hypothesis forwarded by Fuller is founded on the
same form-critical principle as Bultmann's, and thus it suffers from the
same weakness: besides the inference from the Markan pericope itself,
there is no evidence that the alleged controversies ever took place.
Therefore they cannot satisfactorily explain the origin of the synoptic
forgiveness episodes.

Penance and forgiveness

The third proposal to be considered is Thyen's suggestion that a 'tendency towards the development of the Church's sacramental institution
of penance (*des sakramentalen kirchlichen Bußinstitutes*)' is manifest in
the synoptic forgiveness sayings.[84] Already Bultmann, connecting Mark
2.5b–10 with Matt 16.19 and 18.18, may have aimed at a similar hypothesis. Unlike baptism, which formed a constituent part of Christianity
from its earliest phase and for which the ritual seems to have been relatively well established from the beginning, the 'sacramental institution of
penance' took several centuries to develop and to achieve a broadly recognized form with regard both to its external shape and to its theological

---

[84] Thyen, *Studien zur Sündenvergebung*, p. 242 n. 2.

contents.[85] In the period of interest here, the referent of the expression is not unequivocal. Nevertheless, the phenomenon that formed the basis for all later definitions of the sacrament of penance, namely the forgiveness of post-baptismal sins, is dealt with in pre-135 CE texts and will be scrutinized in the following. Special attention will be given to those passages in which this is coupled with the readmission of excommunicated members of the church.

Firstly, the general evidence for primitive Christian strategies designed to define 'the limits of the community' – to make use of Göran Forkman's expression – will be reviewed.[86] I will employ the term 'limit-defining practices' in order to include not only formal excommunications and readmissions, but also some practices that are less marked by institutionalization. Then I shall turn to the notion of post-baptismal forgiveness and investigate how this was sometimes explicitly linked to such strategies. I will concentrate on whatever evidence may be detected that these practices were perceived as involving an ecclesial authority to forgive sins, which could form a backdrop for the forgiveness sayings attributed to Jesus.

Limit-defining practices

Already Paul recommends and orders measures to be taken against members of the churches who refuse to adjust to the halakhic traditions transmitted by him. In some cases, what appears to be implied is social ostracism, practised in order to bring deviant members into conformity with the conduct of the majority (2 Thess 3.6, 14–15; 1 Cor 5.9–11). A more distinct ritual of excommunication, which exhibits notable similarities with some Qumran texts, seems to be indicated in 1 Cor 5.1–8. Paul here puts his general threats of anathema (Gal 1.8–9; 1 Cor 16.22) into practice and prophetically judges an impenitent sinner to be 'handed over to Satan' at a liturgical assembly in Corinth; his concern is not primarily the repentance of the sinner, but the preservation of the church as the undefiled spiritual temple.[87] When, in 2 Cor 2.5–11, Paul encourages

---

[85] B. Poschmann, *Paenitentia secunda: Die kirchliche Buße im ältesten Christentum bis Cyprian und Origenes: Eine dogmengeschichtliche Untersuchung*, Theophaneia 1 (Bonn: Hanstein, 1940).

[86] G. Forkman, *The Limits of the Religious Community: Expulsion from the Religious Community within the Qumran Sect, within Rabbinic Judaism, and within Primitive Christianity*, CBNTS 5 (Lund: Gleerup, 1972).

[87] T. Hägerland, 'Rituals of (Ex-)Communication and Identity: 1 Cor 5 and 4Q266 11; 4Q270 7', in B. Holmberg and M. Winninge (eds.), *Identity Formation in the New Testament*, WUNT 227 (Tübingen: Mohr Siebeck, 2008), pp. 43–60 (with literature).

the Corinthians to 'forgive' (χαρίσασθαι) a person who had previously offended him, it is difficult to know to what type of sanctions the offender's 'punishment by the majority' (2.6) refers, but they seem to have been imposed by some formal decision.[88] In this case Paul exerts authority in a way that is in essential agreement with his behaviour in 1 Cor 5.1–8.[89] But it does not seem that he views the lifting of the bans on the punished member as tantamount to mediation of divine forgiveness: the sin dealt with in 2 Cor 2.5–11 had not been committed against God, but was an offence which was directed against Paul.

Both ostracism and judicial excommunication are limit-defining practices that recur in the works of other authors. At the least institutionalized level, one finds injunctions against any dealings with manifest sinners. It is uncertain whether this is implied by the deutero-Pauline warnings not to share in the sins of others (Eph 5.3–14; 1 Tim 5.22), but other texts are clear enough. Greeting an unorthodox teacher constitutes participation in his evil works (2 John 9–11). One should refrain from speaking to someone who is guilty of offence until he has repented (*Did* 15.3). Hermas should stay away from an impenitent sinner, lest he incur his guilt (*Herm Man* 4.1.9). According to Ignatius, relations are to be severed with those who fail to accept catholic doctrine and episcopal authority (Ign *Smyrn* 4.1; 5.3; 7.2; *Phld* 3.2–3). Exclusion can also be applied more narrowly to *communicatio in sacris* (*Did* 14.1–2; cf. 4.14).

Another limit-defining strategy, which aims to bring back a sinful member to conformity with the majority, is the practice of reproof. A number of textual passages, beginning with Paul's letters, appear to presume that every member of the church has the right and duty to rebuke and discipline an erring coreligionist.[90] As Christianity becomes more institutionalized, reproving is increasingly viewed as a presbyterial function.[91] Timothy and Titus are urged to reprove and to discipline those who sin (1 Tim 5.20; 2 Tim 2.25; Tit 3.10–11). While recognizing the practice of mutual admonition (*1 Cl* 56.2), the author of *First Clement* does not only write himself in order to admonish the Corinthians (7.1), but also to encourage them to submit to the presbyters and to be disciplined

[88] Forkman, *The Limits of the Religious Community*, pp. 179–80.
[89] Hägerland, 'Rituals of (Ex-)Communication and Identity', pp. 56–7.
[90] 1 Thess 5.14; 2 Thess 3.15; Gal 6.1; Eph 5.11; Matt 18.5; *Did* 15.3; *1 Cl* 56.2; *Herm Man* 8.10; Pol *Phil* 11.4.
[91] 1 Thess 5.12 may indicate that already Paul presupposed the local church leadership to have a special responsibility for reproving. See B. Holmberg, *Paul and Power: The Structure of Authority in the Primitive Church as Reflected in the Pauline Epistles*, CBNTS 11 (Lund: Gleerup, 1978), pp. 113–14.

(παιδευθῆναι, 57.1). Similarly, *Second Clement* presupposes that presbyters admonish believers who need to repent (2 *Cl* 17.3; cf. 19.1–2). Only very few passages describe or allude to formal processes of excommunication. Forkman suggests that 1 Tim 1.20 is a literary imitation of Paul's authentic voice and does not refer to a procedure actually practised in the author's church.[92] It is more likely that the instruction given to Titus as one of his pastoral duties, that he should 'dismiss (παραιτεῖσθαι) any person who causes divisions after a first and second admonition' (Tit 3.10), reflects realities. A similar procedure is proposed in Matt 18.15–20, where excommunication, however, appears to be the responsibility of the church as a whole, rather than of an individual office holder. This passage is among those to be considered shortly below.

Post-baptismal forgiveness mediated by the church

Primitive Christian literature has relatively little to say about the means by which the community of believers can procure and mediate God's forgiveness for sins committed by an already baptized member of the church. To begin with, the forgiveness of the gravest post-baptismal sin, apostasy, was by no means universally held possible. The Letter to the Hebrews excludes the possibility of repentance and forgiveness for apostates (Heb 6.4–6; 10.26–7; cf. 12.17). Its author would thus qualify among those teachers, from whom Hermas has learnt 'that there is no other repentance than that [which took place] when we went down into water and received forgiveness for our previous sins' (*Herm Man* 4.3.1). While the *Shepherd of Hermas* accepts this tenet to be basically correct, the book nonetheless alleges that a special and limited offer of forgiveness for grave post-baptismal sin is currently available.

That post-baptismal sins should be confessed is sometimes mentioned, but explicit references to public confession during an assembly of the church are found only in two writings: in the Letter of James, where believers are encouraged to 'confess [their] sins to one another' (Jas 5.16), and in the *Didache*, which prescribes a confession of failings in the assembly, prior to the liturgical celebration (*Did* 4.14; 14.1).[93] While

---

[92] Forkman, *The Limits of the Religious Community*, p. 183.

[93] *Barn* 19.12 is commonly recognized as containing a more primitive version of *Did* 4.14, lacking the liturgical setting; see K. Niederwimmer, 'Der Didachist und seine Quellen', in C. N. Jefford (ed.), *The* Didache *in Context: Essays on Its Text, History and Transmission*, NovTSup 77 (Leiden: Brill, 1995), pp. 15–36. Concerning the form of confession envisaged in the *Didache*, A. Milavec, 'The Purifying Confession of Failings Required by the Didache's Eucharistic Sacrifice', *BTB* 33 (2003), 64–76 (67), argues that it was individual and varied (*contra* W. Rordorf, 'La rémission des péchés selon la Didachè',

James assigns to the presbyters of the church a special role of praying for forgiveness in conjunction with the anointing of those who are sick (Jas 5.14–15), the letter also suggests that the community as a whole should take part in mutual prayers for forgiveness (5.16). This practice is also mentioned elsewhere in primitive Christian texts.[94] Only the Gospels of Matthew and John mention an authority that goes beyond the practice of intercession for those who have sinned and who repent.[95]

Matthew. What Matt 18.18 calls 'binding' and 'loosing' – that is, exclusion from and readmission into the church – takes place through an assembly of worship, at which Jesus is present to guarantee the harmony between earth and heaven in the disciplinary decisions (18.19–20).[96] As was mentioned in Chapter 2 above, Matthew seems to intimate that ecclesial readmission and divine forgiveness are concomitant. That the commission to 'loose' is practically equivalent to a commission to forgive sins is also implied by Matthew's insistence that God has given the authority to forgive sins to human beings (9.6, 8).

Whether this 'loosing' practised in the post-Easter church as envisioned by Matthew would also involve an announcement of forgiveness along the lines of Matt 9.2 cannot be known.[97] Equally uncertain is the hypothesis that the church would bestow forgiveness indirectly by readmitting a member to the Eucharist, which Matthew links explicitly with forgiveness (26.28).[98] It is nevertheless clear that the communal prayer used to readmit a repentant member to the church cannot be reduced to a humble plea for God's mercy and forgiveness, but is infallibly efficacious by virtue of the presence of the risen Jesus among those who pray.

John. In Chapter 2, I epitomized my interpretation of John 20.19–23 as a commissioning of the disciples of Jesus for their prophetic ministry of announcing God's retention and forgiveness of sins. In view of the close relationship between the Gospel and the Letters of John, it is natural to turn to these letters in order to see how the commission would have been put into practice by a segment of primitive Christianity.

Irénikon 46 (1973), 283–97 (287)). 1 John 1.6; *1 Cl* 51.3; *2 Cl* 8.1–3 do not specify whether confession is public or private, and *Herm Vis* 1.1.3; 3.1.5–6; *Sim* 9.23.4 portray it as private.

[94] 1 John 5.16; *1 Cl* 56.1; Ign *Eph* 10.1; *Smyrn* 4.1; *Herm Vis* 1.1.9.

[95] 1 Tim 5.22 mentions an imposition of hands that has been identified as a ritual of reconciliation, but this interpretation is uncertain. See J. Murphy-O'Connor, 'Péché et communauté dans le Nouveau Testament', *RB* 74 (1967), 161–93 (173–5).

[96] Stendahl, 'Prayer and Forgiveness', 78.

[97] Cf. Davies and Allison, *Matthew*, vol. II, p. 96.

[98] Cf. Klauck, 'Die Frage der Sündenvergebung', 247.

Several verbal links between 1 John 1.1–5 and the characterization of Jesus' disciples in the Gospel of John indicate that the letter's authorial 'we', clearly distinguished from its addressees, lay claim to some continuity with the disciples of the earthly Jesus as portrayed in the Gospel.[99] After 1.5 the distinction between 'we' and 'you' apparently breaks down, and further uses of the first person plural seem to include the church in its entirety. Prophetic characteristics are now applied to the members of the church as a whole.[100] What emerges from First John is the picture of a church, the identity of which is essentially prophetic and which recognizes the Gospel story in its Johannine shape as its foundational 'myth of origin'. There are two discernible ways in which this church defines its limits by employing the prophetic authority granted to it by Jesus in John 20.23.

Firstly, having received the Spirit of prophecy, the church has an infallible ability to know and to declare who remains in God/Jesus and who does not. Remaining in God/Jesus entails the forgiveness of sins; thus the author of First John proclaims to his 'children' that their sins have been forgiven (1 John 2.12). In doing so, he uses his prophetic power, not only to assure the addressees of God's forgiveness, but also to confirm their position as 'insiders', for communion with God and Jesus cannot be separated from communion with the church (cf. 1 John 1.3, 6–7), and to remain in God or in Jesus, and to remain in the church, would be virtually synonymous (cf. 2.9–11; 3.14; 4.11–13).[101] Conversely, the sharp judgement on the children of the devil, who continue in their sin, and who thus remain in death (3.4–15), functions to retain the sins of the antichrists (2.18–19) and to reinforce their status as 'outsiders'. Since the antichrists have apparently left the church and its received doctrine voluntarily, it is not necessary for the church actively to expel members who have strayed from its beliefs and morals, although there are indications that the Johannine literature knows of active excommunication also.[102]

---

[99] ἀκούειν (1 John 1.1, 3, 5; cf. John 14.24); ἑωρακέναι (1 John 1.1, 2, 3; cf. 14.7, 9); μαρτυρεῖν (1 John 15.27).

[100] ἀκούειν (1 John 2.7, 18, 24; 3.11; 4.3; cf. 2 John 6); ἑωρακέναι/τεθεᾶσθαι (1 John 3.6; 4.14; cf. 3 John 11 – but cf. 1 John 4.12, 20); μαρτυρεῖν (4.14). They are also recipients of the 'anointing' (2.20, 27), that is, the Spirit (3.24; 4.6), just like the earthly Jesus (John 1.32–3; 7.39–40) and his disciples (7.39; 14.16–17; 20.22).

[101] Poschmann, *Paenitentia secunda*, pp. 65–6.

[102] See Forkman, *The Limits of the Religious Community*, pp. 174–5; W. Horbury, 'Extirpation and Excommunication', *VT* 35 (1985), 13–38 (22–5), on the possibly technical usage of βληθῆναι ἔξω (John 15.6) and ἐκβάλλειν (3 John 10) respectively to denote expulsion.

Secondly, as Marianne Meye Thompson cogently argues, intercession and abstention from intercession are also the means by which the church carries out the commission to forgive and retain sins.[103] Despite the repeated statements concerning the perfect sinlessness of believers (1 John 3.4–10; 5.18), the author takes for granted that members of the church may indeed sin (1.8–10; 2.1), something which does not merit expulsion. In 5.13–17, a distinction is introduced between 'sin to death' and 'sin not to death', which helps to relieve the apparent contradiction between the two attitudes. Non-deadly sin, for which intercession should be made, is any wrongdoing committed by a member of the church, who does not depart from the faith in Jesus as the author understands it. When such believers commit a sin, their coreligionists can restore life to them through prayer: their sins are not mortal, as long as they have not defected from the faith. Deadly sin is, by contrast, the refusal to believe in Jesus in accordance with Johannine standards.[104] Those who fail to accept the Johannine orthodoxy remain in death (see 3.14) and the author discourages prayer for them. In a sense, by holding back their prayers, the Johannine Christians merely affirm that such non-believers, or heretics, are already 'out', yet they thereby also distance themselves further from the 'outsiders' and reinforce their commitment not to be in 'communion' with them (see 2 John 11). What Donald Carson writes about the retention of sins in the Gospel of John holds true also for the withholding of intercessory prayer suggested in 1 John 5.16: it is 'both description and condemnation'.[105]

Would a returning secessionist be forgiven? Thompson thinks so.[106] But the Johannine literature is silent on the subject and seems to assume that apostasy is definitive. Therefore, while the Johannine authority to forgive sins would function as a limit-defining practice, it would primarily be employed to reinforce the position of insiders as such, and not to readmit repentant apostates.

---

[103] M. M. Thompson, 'Intercession in the Johannine Community: 1 John 5.16 in the Context of the Gospel and Epistles of John', in M. J. Wilkins and T. Paige (eds.), *Worship, Theology and Ministry in the Early Church*, FS R. P. Martin (Sheffield Academic Press, 1992), pp. 225–45 (pp. 235–6); also Michl, 'Sündenbekenntnis und Sündenvergebung', 203–4.

[104] Brown, *The Epistles of John*, pp. 617–19.

[105] D. A. Carson, *The Gospel according to John*, The Pillar New Testament Commentary (Grand Rapids, MI: Eerdmans, 1991), p. 656.

[106] Thompson, 'Intercession in the Johannine Community', pp. 244–5.

The synoptic episodes in relation to primitive ecclesiology

Mark 2.1–12 and primitive ecclesiology

The foregoing search for primitive Christian claims to an ecclesiastic 'authority to forgive sins' has yielded the following results: as far as miracles of healing are concerned, the evidence that they were thought to communicate forgiveness is far too scanty to allow for the conclusion that the link between healing and forgiveness was generally emphasized in primitive Christianity. By contrast, baptism was widely recognized to involve a bestowal of forgiveness. However, as with the healing miracles, there is nothing to indicate that the administration of baptism was seen as an exertion of a personal or corporate authority; on the contrary, the texts constantly play down the role of baptizers as well as that of miracle-workers. Only in the case of 'limit-defining practices' does one find the notion of an ecclesial authority to forgive sins, bound up either with the readmission of repentant sinners to the church (Matt 9.8; 18.18) or with prophetic intercession and assurance of forgiveness (John 20.23; cf. 1 John 2.12; 5.16). Thus, if a plausible setting in the life of the primitive Church should be identified as the ultimate origin of the claim to this authority, and for the controversy narrated in the Markan episode, it should be looked for in these limit-defining practices.

Furthermore, no traces have been found of any conflict over the claim that forgiveness was bestowed in baptism, either within Christianity or between Christianity and traditional Judaism. In limit-defining practices, the offer of forgiveness does not seem to have been a point of controversy in relation to non-Christian Jews, although it did cause some internal conflict, as reflected in *Hermas*. If the scribes of Mark 2.6–7 should indeed be construed as representatives of actual people in pre-70 CE Christianity, no other activity of the primitive Church, apart from these practices, can plausibly have given rise to the theme of conflict in this Markan episode.

In spite of these observations, it appears unlikely that limit-defining practices form the background of Mark 2.1–12. For this verdict, the following reasons can be given.

Firstly, the focus of Mark 2.1–12 – and indeed of Mark's Gospel in its entirety – is christological rather than ecclesiological. In general, the form-critical hermeneutic of construing the narrative Jesus as a mouthpiece of the 'community' leads to conclusions that are speculative or flawed.[107] The few glimpses of primitive church life that can reasonably be identified in Mark are contained in instructions aimed at the disciples.[108] Nothing indicates that the authority claimed for Jesus as the Son of Man in 2.10 is shared by anyone else. Only Matthew added an ecclesiological dimension to the episode by reformulating its conclusion (Matt 9.8) and, as has been remarked above, it is unlikely that he would have done so merely in order to bring out what was already in the Markan episode.

Secondly, the limit-defining practices are not simply retrojected into the earthly life of Jesus even in the Gospels that do have an interest in ecclesiology and in such practices. In Matthew, despite the subtle change in 9.8, the commission to bind and to loose belongs to a context that explicitly presupposes the existence of the church (Matt 18.17), although the founding of the Church will take place at a future date (16.18), plausibly subsequent to the resurrection (cf. 28.18–20). In the commission itself, the future perfect forms also indicate that the practice of binding and loosing does not apply to Jesus' earthly lifetime (18.18). In John, the commission to forgive and retain sins is given by the risen Jesus (John 20.23). Neither of these Gospels simply traces the limit-defining practices 'to an archetypal deed of Jesus'.

Thirdly, while there is evidence that conflicting opinions about the possibility of post-baptismal forgiveness existed already in pre-135 CE Christianity, it is difficult to see these conflicts reflected in the Markan episode. The historical controversy did not involve representatives of traditional Judaism. While the Markan episode depicts a conflict over Jesus' right to forgive sins, the historical controversy concerned the legitimacy of a second offer of forgiveness in addition to baptism, nothing of which can arguably be found in the episode.

Luke 7.36–47 and primitive ecclesiology

Of a quite different nature is the hypothesized episode that underlies Luke 7.36–47. Jesus' pronouncement of forgiveness is not described as

---

[107] For an example, see Bultmann, *Die Geschichte der synoptischen Tradition*, pp. 17–18, who infers a non-fasting primitive community from Mark 2.18b–19a. In reality, primitive Christianity was fasting (Matt 6.16–18; *Did* 1.3; 7.4–8.1; *2 Cl* 16.4; Pol *Phil* 7.2; *Herm Vis* 2.2.1; 3.10.6–7; *Sim* 5.1.1–5.3.9; cf. Mark 9.29 *v.l.*; Acts 13.2–3; 14.23; *GPet* 7.27 – only *GThom* 14.1 rejects it), and it is far more reasonable to see this practice referred to in Mark 2.20, while 2.19a stems from the historical Jesus. See Meier, *A Marginal Jew*, vol. II, pp. 439–50; T. Holmén, *Jesus and Jewish Covenant Thinking*, BIS 55 (Leiden: Brill, 2001), pp. 134–57.

[108] Maisch, *Die Heilung des Gelähmten*, p. 102; Gnilka, 'Das Elend', p. 207.

the exertion of any personal authority to forgive sins, but as an expression of his status as a prophet. Moreover, unlike the Markan episode which is markedly conflict-oriented, the element of controversy is not in focus in this episode. According to the interpretation I have offered in Chapter 2 above, the pre-Lukan episode is not primarily about forgiveness, but about the love and gratitude that result from being forgiven. In view of this, it is quite unlikely that the episode was forged in order to legitimize an ecclesial practice that involved the bestowal of forgiveness. Wilckens' suggestion that the episode may have been recited, and thus preserved, in conjunction with baptism loses much of its force, once it is recognized that the interpretation of the woman's actions in penitential terms derives from Luke's handling of the episode.[109] The same insight rules out the conceivable proposal that the pre-Lukan episode derives from limit-defining practices.

As a matter of fact, it is not likely that primitive Christians – as always to the extent that we know their tendencies and convictions – composed freely a paradigmatic episode, in which Jesus accepts and defends the presence of a public sinner, who has not unambiguously repented of her grave sin, at a meal. Paul emphasizes the need to avoid commensality with grave sinners (1 Cor 5.11) and so displays an attitude which is diametrically opposed to that ascribed to Jesus in the Gospels (Mark 2.15–17 par.); the practice of open table-fellowship is more characteristic of the historical Jesus than of primitive Christianity.[110] Accordingly, the criterion of discontinuity can be applied in order to argue in favour of the general historicity of this pre-Lukan episode.

Conclusion

The discussion in this chapter has produced the following conclusions regarding the extent to which the synoptic forgiveness episodes are congruent with primitive Christian theology.

First of all, Mark 2.1–12 is not representative of primitive christology, since it identifies Jesus as the acting subject of forgiveness. With few, and predominantly late, exceptions (Col 3.13; *Herm Man* 5.1.7; *Sim* 5.6.2–3; Ign *Phld* 8.1; Pol *Phil* 6.2) pre-135 CE Christian texts consistently attribute the act of forgiveness to God rather than to Jesus. Furthermore, of those passages that do indeed seem to attribute the act to Jesus, only those that come from Ignatius and Polycarp can be taken to assume that

---

[109] Cf. Wilckens, 'Vergebung für die Sünderin', pp. 418–21.
[110] Corley, 'The Anointing of Jesus', 72, argues similarly.

Jesus has a timeless authority to forgive sins, while the earlier texts link the act of forgiveness to his death and to baptism. All this makes it rather unlikely that Mark 2.1–12 could have originated as an expression of faith in the authority of the risen Jesus to forgive sins.

Secondly, the hypothesized pre-Gospel episodes of Luke 7.36–47 and Mark 2.1–5, 11–12 are also dissimilar to primitive christology, since they describe Jesus as a prophet or a messenger of forgiveness, while primitive Christianity in general tended to view him as the mediator because of whose suffering and death God forgives sins, as the intercessor for those who have sinned, and as the object of the faith that procures divine forgiveness. Thus, none of these episodes is likely to have originated as an expression of a Christian tenet.

Thirdly, ecclesiology cannot account for the origin of the forgiveness episodes. Neither the Markan, nor the pre-Lukan, episode contains any trait of ecclesiological orientation. Only with the Matthean redaction of Mark 2.1–12 is the authority to forgive sins applied to the Church. This authority is expressed in primitive Christian limit-defining practices, which caused some internal conflict, but it is not plausible that this conflict is reflected in the Markan episode. And Luke 7.36–47 reflects an attitude that is typical of the historical Jesus, but foreign to primitive ecclesiology.

4

MEDIATORS OF FORGIVENESS
IN EARLY JUDAISM

At least since the 1840s, when Bauer published his insightful critique of the Gospels, scholars have been aware that Mark 2.6–7, where the omniscient narrator claims knowledge of the scribes' unspoken criticism, can hardly be acknowledged as historical in the strict sense. Despite this recognition, it has in fact been commonly held that the scribal protest brings a first-century Jewish tenet to expression fairly well: God alone could forgive sins. Fiedler summarized the consensus approvingly in 1976: 'Any expectation of an act of forgiving by anyone else than God himself was missing; not only that: such an activity could only be understood as an attack upon God's own prerogative – as far as it would be taken seriously at all.'[1] The present chapter will challenge this statement both by re-examining the texts already mentioned in the debate, and by highlighting some passages that seem not to have received scholarly attention in this context, but which are of acute importance to the question. In addition to this assessment of the plausibility of the scribal *protest*, I will consider a point of almost equal consequence, namely the apparent *silence* of the scribes as they are faced with Jesus' argument in 2.8–10. This feature, too, has implications for my verdict about the historicity of 2.6–10.

The criterion of implausibility, which comes into play in this chapter, has a number of limitations already discussed in Chapter 1. It assumes a reconstruction of (in this case) early Judaism, which is built on incomplete evidence that has to be generalized. Even if none of the extant sources agrees with the sentiment expressed in 2.7, as I will argue is in fact the case, the possibility that individual scribes in Capernaum held to it can never be excluded with certainty. This is a natural limitation of historiography: we do not have all the facts, so our reconstructions have to be based on the most reasonable interpretation of the facts that we do have.

---

[1] Fiedler, *Jesus und die Sünder*, p. 115 (my translation).

The upcoming survey of early Jewish literature will take into account all early Jewish references that predicate of a subject other than God an activity that could be considered as bestowing, mediating or pronouncing forgiveness. To what extent these should actually be considered as analogous to the forgiveness sayings in the gospel tradition will be discussed at the end of each part of the chapter. In order to acquire as full a picture as possible of 'early Judaism', I shall include all texts possibly stemming from Israelite/Jewish pre-135 CE authors – noting, of course, the uncertainties of provenance and dating when such occur. It should go without saying that the Gospels, or other primitive Christian writings, cannot be used to affirm the veracity of their own portrayal of non-Christian Jewish belief.[2] As the primary interest of the investigation lies in notions current in the first century, older texts such as the books of the OT should preferably be read through the lens of later expositors – so that, for example, Josephus' rewriting of the Samuel narrative will be of greater value to this study than the critically established 'original sense' of the deuteronomistic history.

Those who have previously proposed analogies for the synoptic forgiveness sayings have usually drawn them from the depiction of priests and prophets in the OT and in early Judaism and less frequently from Jewish angelology. Most of the evidence, including those textual passages which have hitherto gone unnoticed, can indeed be placed in one or the other of these categories. I will first deal with the alleged evidence for priestly forgiveness of sins, and then with forgiveness as an activity of prophets and angels respectively.

Priestly forgiveness

Since the OT and early Jewish literature frequently associate forgiveness with the temple, its sacrificial cult and the priesthood, it is only natural that analogies to the synoptic forgiveness sayings have been sought in this area. Developing earlier form-critical suggestions, Koch enunciated a hypothesis in 1966 that has since exerted some influence on historical Jesus research. According to him, priests of the second temple would pronounce the forgiveness of sins when they officiated at guilt- and sin-offerings.[3] This hypothesis came under severe criticism from Hofius in 1983, and in 1992 Sanders, who at first had seemed to be sympathetic to

---

[2] Cf. D. L. Bock, 'The Son of Man in Luke 5:24', *BBR* 1 (1991), 109–21 (117–18).
[3] K. Koch, 'Sühne und Sündenvergebung um die Wende von der exilischen zur nachexilischen Zeit', *EvT* 26 (1966), 217–39 (226–7, 231).

it, also deemed it unlikely.[4] Recently (2007), Crispin Fletcher-Louis has reopened the discussion on the relationship between the priesthood and forgiveness, arguing that not any priest at the temple, but the high priest specifically, was believed in some circles to be endowed with an authority to forgive sins.[5]

These two proposals will now be evaluated in turn. Firstly, I will assess the evidence that forgiveness was pronounced by priests, either in conjunction with the offering of sacrifices or in other cultic contexts. Secondly, Fletcher-Louis' reading of passages concerning the high priest will be scrutinized.

Priestly pronouncements of forgiveness

Koch's suggestion that sins were declared forgiven by priests in order to consummate a sin- or a guilt-offering built on Gerhard von Rad's earlier proposal that the expression 'it will not be accepted' (Lev 7.18; 19.7; 22.23, 25) over faulty sacrifices would have been pronounced aloud by the officiating priests and, correspondingly, that priests would also have declared when an offering had been accepted.[6] Koch took the 'סלח–כפר formula', widely attested in Leviticus, to indicate that forgiveness was effectuated by a priestly word of absolution: 'And the priest shall atone for him for his sin; and it will be forgiven for him (ונסלח לו)' (Lev 4.26). While the passive formula 'it will be forgiven' indicates that God is the implicit agent of forgiveness, Koch finds it plausible that the phrase refers to a priestly declaration that announced the offering to be valid.[7] Given the relative stability of rituals such as these, one would expect this practice to have been continued at the Jerusalem temple into the first century. Critique of Koch's hypothesis has, however, shown that it is not only unsupported, but indeed conflicts with some of the evidence.

Hofius points to the fact that there is no reference to a priestly pronouncement of forgiveness in early Jewish literature. Allegations that passages in the Samaritan literature do predicate forgiveness of priests are shown to be based on faulty interpretation of the texts. Significantly,

---

[4] Hofius, 'Vergebungszuspruch und Vollmachtsfrage', pp. 115–27; E. P. Sanders, *Judaism: Practice and Belief 63* BCE–*66* CE (London: SCM, 1992), p. 109. Cf. Sanders, *Jesus and Judaism*, pp. 273–4, 301; E. P. Sanders, *Jewish Law from Jesus to the Mishnah: Five Studies* (London: SCM/Philadelphia: Trinity, 1990), p. 62.

[5] Fletcher-Louis, 'Jesus as the High Priestly Messiah', 72–4.

[6] G. von Rad, *Theologie des Alten Testaments*, vol. I: *Die Theologie der geschichtlichen Überlieferungen Israels*, 6th edn (Munich: Kaiser, 1969), pp. 261, 274–5.

[7] Koch, 'Sühne und Sündenvergebung', 226–7, 231. Lev 4.20, 31, 35; 5.10, 13, 16, 18, 26; 19.22; Num 15.25–6, 28 also contain the formula.

the few more detailed descriptions of sacrificial rituals that have survived do not mention any formula of absolution. Ben Sira's vivid portrayal of a high-priestly liturgy concludes with the pronunciation of the blessing (Ecclus 50.20–1). It is possible that this was thought to imply an optative plea for forgiveness but, as Hofius remarks, that remains an assumption.[8] The corresponding silence in the Mishnaic description of the ritual for the Day of Atonement may also be pertinent, for on this day, as Lev 16.1–34 repeatedly says, the high priest 'atones' for sins. In the Mishnah, we find spelt out the high priest's confessions (*mYoma* 3.8; 4.2; 6.2) and his verbal declaration of the scapegoat as 'a sin-offering to the Lord' (4.1). He is also reported to have said a short prayer after having put incense on the pan in the inner sanctuary (5.1) and to have counted aloud (?) the sprinklings of blood (5.3–4). At the end of the worship, the high priest would read parts of the Torah, pronounce blessings and say a prayer (7.1). In view of this detailed account, the lack of any recollection of a word of absolution is noteworthy.

Sanders draws attention to the description in the *Letter of Aristeas* of how sacrifices were offered in the Jerusalem temple: 'And there is complete silence, so that one would assume that not even a single human being was present in the place, although about seven hundred officials are present' (*EpArist* 95; cf. 92).[9] There is no reason to doubt the veracity of this report. Priests sacrificed in silence, wherefore, as Sanders argues, it is unlikely that they would have pronounced a formula of forgiveness.[10] At least with regard to the first century, then, Koch's hypothesis seems untenable.

High-priestly authority to forgive sins

As part of an endeavour to highlight what he believes to be a neglected but crucial aspect of the self-understanding of the historical Jesus, Fletcher-Louis argues that Jesus thought of himself as the eschatological high priest, and that this identity is expressed at several points in Mark 1–6. One of these points is his claim to have the authority to forgive sins in 2.10 which, in Fletcher-Louis' words, 'can be derived straightforwardly from biblical statements about the high priest'.[11] But none of the evidence can support the argument, as will be seen on closer examination.

[8] Hofius, 'Vergebungszuspruch und Vollmachtsfrage', pp. 120–5.
[9] Sanders, *Judaism*, pp. 80–1.
[10] *Ibid.*, p. 109.
[11] Fletcher-Louis, 'Jesus as the High Priestly Messiah', 72–3.

The Pentateuchal passages in the Hebrew Bible

A proper evaluation of Fletcher-Louis' thesis will begin in the Hebrew OT. It should be noted that, besides the instances noted by Fletcher-Louis as saying that Aaron and his sons should 'remove/forgive' (נשא) guilt or sin (Exod 28.38; Lev 10.17), there are two more Pentateuchal passages that predicate 'bearing/removing' (נשא) guilt or sin of Aaron and his sons (Num 18.1) or of the Levites (18.23). Taking these passages into consideration will help us to see how questionable are his assertions that 'where נשא is used with sin as its direct object the meaning is usually "forgive"' and 'it is natural to understand the priests' action as a form of forgiveness'.[12] To begin with, נשא with a noun that denotes 'sin' does *not* translate as 'forgive' in a majority of cases. Apart from the passages already mentioned, the verb can readily be translated 'forgive' in sixteen cases out of a total of forty-five instances of this construction.[13] In the remaining twenty-nine cases, some other translation must be found: to 'incur' guilt due to one's own transgression, to 'bear responsibility' or to 'bear' someone else's sin vicariously.[14] As a matter of fact, 'to forgive' does not come as a natural translation in any of the twelve occurrences in Leviticus.[15]

Num 18.22–3 contrasts the sons of Israel with the Levites: while the former will no longer approach the tabernacle 'to contract sin (לשאת חטא) and die', the latter 'will bear their guilt (ישאו עונם)'. Neither use of נשא can be construed as a reference to forgiveness; this passage is about taking responsibility for the sanctuary.[16] It is not difficult to see that 18.1–5 is an expression of the same notion, except that this time, the distinction is between the priests and the Levites. In order to save the Israelites from divine wrath, the Lord tells Aaron, 'you [pl.] shall bear (תשאו) the guilt of the sanctuary … you shall bear (תשאו) the guilt of your priesthood' (18.1). That this has nothing to do with forgiveness is evident from the

---

[12] *Ibid.*, 73.

[13] Gen 50.17; Exod 10.17; 23.21; 32.32; 34.7; Num 14.18; Josh 24.19; 1 Sam 15.25; 25.28; Isa 33.24; Mic 7.18; Ps 25.18; 32.1, 5; 85.3; Job 7.21. Cf. Gen 18.26; Num 14.19, where a direct object is lacking.

[14] Gen 4.13; Exod 28.43; Lev 5.1, 17; 7.18; 16.22; 17.16; 19.8, 17; 20.17, 19, 20; 22.9; 24.15; Num 5.31; 9.13; 14.34; 18.22; 30.16; Isa 53.12; Ezek 4.4, 5, 6; 14.10; 18.19, 20; 23.49; 44.10; Hos 14.3.

[15] J. Milgrom, *Leviticus 1–16: A New Translation with Introduction and Commentary*, AB 3 (New York: Doubleday, 1991), p. 295.

[16] J. Milgrom, *Studies in Levitical Terminology*, vol. I: *The Encroacher and the Levite: The Term* 'Aboda (Berkeley: University of California Press, 1970), pp. 22–33; B. A. Levine, *Numbers 1–20: A New Translation with Introduction and Commentary*, AB 4A (New York: Doubleday, 1993), pp. 439–40, 451.

references to inanimate things to qualify the 'guilt': neither the sanctuary nor the priesthood can, of course, be forgiven in any meaningful sense of that word. And in fact the same holds true for Exod 28.38. It is Fletcher-Louis' failure to take seriously the fact that this passage says that 'Aaron will take the guilt of the holy things', and *not* 'the people's sins', that enables him to see a reference to forgiveness here. Lev 10.17 remains the only instance in which the verb could possibly be rendered 'to forgive'. Rebuking Aaron's sons for not having eaten their portion of the sin-offering, Moses explains that 'he gave it to you to bear/remove/forgive (לשׂאת) the guilt of the congregation, to atone for them before the Lord'. Several considerations nevertheless speak against interpreting this passage in terms of a commission to Aaron's sons to forgive sins. Firstly, it seems reasonable to construe it analogously with the other passages, in which the verb is never used in the sense of 'to forgive'. Secondly, Moses' criticism in 10.16–18 recalls earlier stipulations concerning the sin-offering, which entrust the priests with the task of atoning for sins, but not to forgive sin. Thirdly, 'to bear the guilt of the congregation' and 'to atone for them before the Lord' appear to be juxtaposed in synonymous parallelism, and, as seen above, there is a distinction between priestly atonement and divine forgiveness. In its original context Lev 10.17, therefore, does not seem to refer to any priestly authority to forgive sins.

The Pentateuchal passages in LXX and the Targums

One of the keys to understanding how these passages were interpreted in early Judaism is provided by the ancient translations of the OT and especially by the LXX. Again, Fletcher-Louis' characterization of ἀφιέναι as 'a normal translation' of נשׂא does not tell the full story. It is true that in eight of the cases where נשׂא is used in the sense of 'to forgive', the LXX translates it with ἀφιέναι.[17] However, there are nine other instances, in which the Hebrew verb seems to be employed in the same sense but where it is rendered in Greek by some other verb.[18] To this should be added the twenty-seven passages in which נשׂא has something to do with sin, but where it cannot reasonably mean 'to forgive' – with the possible exception of Gen 4.13, the LXX never employs ἀφιέναι here, but opts

---

[17] Gen 18.26; 50.17; Exod 32.32; Isa 33.24; Ps 25.18; 32.1, 5; 85.3.

[18] Exod 34.7; Num 14.18 (both ἀφαιρεῖν); Exod 10.17 (προσδέχεσθαι); Num 14.19 (ἵλεω γίνεσθαι); Josh 24.19 (ἀνιέναι); 1 Sam 15.25; 25.28 (both αἴρειν); Mic 7.18 (ἐξαίρειν); Job 7.21 (ποιεῖν λήθην). Cf. Exod 23.21 (οὐ γὰρ μὴ ὑποστείληταί σε).

for other vocabulary, mostly λαμβάνειν.[19] One may conclude that the Greek translators were quite sensitive to the different senses in which נשא is employed in the OT, and that they used ἀφιέναι as an equivalent of the Hebrew verb only in a minority of cases.

It is significant that the LXX does not render נשא with ἀφιέναι in any of the Pentateuchal passages under discussion. The Greek verb employed in Num 18.1, 23 is λαμβάνειν, which indicates that the translator understood the expression as a reference to the priests and the Levites who had contracted or incurred guilt. The verbs used in Exod 28.38 (ἐξαίρειν) and in Lev 10.17 (ἀφαιρεῖν) are hardly more semantically precise than נשא. Only the latter verb is sometimes used to translate standard Hebrew terminology of forgiveness.[20] Considerations of the context nevertheless militate against the translation of this verb as 'to forgive' in Lev 10.17.

When it comes to the Targums, Fletcher-Louis correctly remarks that '[w]hilst נשא does occur in Aramaic, other verbs translate the Hebrew in the Targums to Exodus and Leviticus'.[21] None of the Targums employs a verb that lends support to Fletcher-Louis' interpretation in any of the Pentateuchal passages. Instead they may render נשא literally as 'bear', 'take up' or 'receive'.[22] They also use סלח pa., a verb sometimes predicated of God in the sense of 'to forgive', but which also takes on the causative meaning 'to bring forgiveness'.[23] Only the latter sense can be intended in these passages, where the preposition על follows the verb and thus secures the meaning 'to bring forgiveness for sins' rather than 'to forgive sins' – this is especially clear in *TgOnq*Lev 10.17, where 'to bring forgiveness for (לסלחא על) the sins of the congregation' and 'to atone for them' occur in synonymous parallelism.[24]

The Pentateuchal passages in early Jewish literature

As regards the interpretation of Exod 28.38 and Lev 10.17 in post-biblical early Judaism, Fletcher-Louis claims that from *Second Enoch* '[w]e know that some Jews took these passages to mean that the high priest's

---

[19] Exod 28.43 (ἐπάγεσθαι πρὸς ἑαυτόν); Lev 5.1, 17; 7.18; 16.22; 17.16; 19.8, 17; 24.15; Num 5.31; 9.13; 14.34; 18.22; 30.16; Ezek 4.4, 5, 6; 14.10; 18.19, 20; 23.49; Hos 14.3 (all λαμβάνειν); Lev 20.17 (κομίζεσθαι); Lev 20.19; 22.9 (both ἀποφέρειν); Isa 53.12 (ἀναφέρειν).

[20] Exod 34.7; Num 14.18 (both translating נשא), Exod 34.9 (סלח).

[21] Fletcher-Louis, 'Jesus as the High Priestly Messiah', 74.

[22] *TgNeof*Exod 28.38 (נטל); *TgOnq*Exod 28.38; *TgPsJon*Exod 28.38 (both נטל); *TgNeof* Lev 10.17 (טען); *TgOnq* Num 18.22–3; *TgPsJon* Num 18.1, 22–3 (all קבל).

[23] *TgOnq*Lev 10.17; *TgOnq* Num 18.1. See *s.v.* סְלַח Jastrow.

[24] Hofius, 'Vergebungszuspruch und Vollmachtsfrage', p. 122.

job was to take away – to forgive – sin'.[25] In this literary work, Enoch is taken up to God and undergoes what can be interpreted as his investiture with heavenly high priesthood (*2 En* 22.8–10) before he returns to earth for a short period of time. As he is about to be taken up definitely, Enoch is greeted by the people at Akhuzan as 'the one who carried away the sin of mankind' (64.5).[26] According to Fletcher-Louis, Enoch thereby implements the Pentateuchal commission to remove or to forgive sin. This conclusion is, in my opinion, doubtful.

First of all, that *Second Enoch* actually portrays its hero as a celestial high priest rests mainly on an interpretation of *2 En* 22.8–10 that is not universally acknowledged.[27] Even if the validity of this reading is postulated, there is no reason to assume that its author thought that every trait associated with Enoch also applied to the current high priest in Jerusalem.

Secondly, the intertextual relationship posited by Fletcher-Louis between *2 En* 64.5 and Exod 28.38; Lev 10.17 is by no means evident. If present at all, the high-priestly character of Enoch is quite marginal in *Second Enoch*, and apart from chapters 64–7 being set in Akhuzan/Jerusalem, there is nothing to indicate that to take away sins is an exertion of this specific capacity. In fact, it appears more plausible that 64.5 echoes Second Isaiah's depiction of the Servant of the Lord by drawing together several passages distributed across Isa 40–55. Like the Servant, Enoch 'will be glorified before the face of the Lord' since he is 'the one whom the Lord chose'.[28] His appointment 'to be the one who makes a written record of all [the Lord's] creation' is elsewhere stated to be for the purpose of letting his house 'read and understand that there is no other God apart from myself' (*2 En* 36.1; cf. 33.8; 47.2–3), just as the Lord, according to Second Isaiah, chose his servant 'so that you may know, believe me and understand that *I am*: before me, there is no other god, and after me, none will be' (Isa 43.10).[29] And when Enoch is said to be 'the one who carried away the sin of mankind' this is again reminiscent of the righteous Servant, who 'will bring righteousness ... to the many, and their guilt he will carry (יסבל) ... and he took (נשא) the sin of

[25] Fletcher-Louis, 'Jesus as the High Priestly Messiah', 73.

[26] For *Second* (Slavonic) *Enoch*, I use F. I. Andersen's translation of the longer recension in *OTP*, vol. i, pp. 101–213.

[27] See C. Böttrich, 'The Melchizedek Story of *2 (Slavonic) Enoch*: A Reaction to A. Orlov', *JSJ* 32 (2001),445–70 (456–7).

[28] Cf. Isa 49.2; 52.13 (glorification); 41.8, 9; 42.1; 43.10; 44.1, 2; 45.4; 49.7 (election).

[29] Cf. Isa 44.6; 45.5; 46.9. See also Isa 40.12, 22; 42.5; 44.24, possibly echoed in *2 En* 47.4–6.

the many' (Isa 53.11–12). This is not the place to investigate in depth the intertextual relationship between Second Isaiah and *Second Enoch*, but it should be clear that any allusion to the Pentateuchal passages in *2 En* 64.5 must be argued for more extensively than Fletcher-Louis has done.

Thirdly, the phrasing 'who carried away the sin of mankind' in *2 En* 64.5 is hardly less obscure than the Pentateuchal passages. If we should indeed recognize Enoch's high-priestly image, the phrase 'to take away sins' would, in the light of other Enochic traditions, be more readily understood as a reference to his offering of sacrifices to atone for sins (*Jub* 4.23–6) or to his intercession for sinners (*1 En* 13.4–7) – though at least the latter would not seem to fit well into the overall theology of the book (cf. *2 En* 53.1–2). Another interpretation is offered by Andrei Orlov, who suggests that Enoch's first ascension and metamorphosis had the function of 'taking away sin'.[30] I suggest a simpler and somewhat less spectacular way of reading *2 En* 64.5, namely that it is precisely by being 'the one who makes a written record' that Enoch has 'carried away the sin of mankind'. For, as Enoch tells his sons as he hands over the books in his handwriting: 'If you hold on firmly to them, you will not sin against the Lord' (47.2). Put differently, Enoch has not taken away any previously committed sins, but he has brought the means by which human beings will be able to lead a sinless life in the future. To sum up the discussion of *2 En* 64.5, it is not evident that it portrays Enoch as a high priest, that it echoes the Pentateuchal passages or that it speaks about the forgiveness of sins.

Mark 2.1–12 in relation to priestly typology

There is, then, no firm indication either that priests declared sins to be forgiven at the offering of sacrifices, which would constitute an analogy to Jesus' proclamation of forgiveness in Mark 2.5b, or that the high priest – earthly, heavenly or eschatological – was thought to have an authority to forgive analogous to that claimed by the Markan Jesus in 2.10. Neither the assertion that 'your sins are forgiven' was 'something the priest could say in the Temple to everyone who had brought a sin-offering'[31] nor the claim that in 2.10 'Jesus appeals to the high priestly

---

[30] A. Orlov, *The Enoch-Metatron Tradition*, TSAJ 107 (Tübingen: Mohr Siebeck, 2005), pp. 232–4.

[31] J. D. G. Dunn, *The Partings of the Ways: Between Christianity and Judaism and Their Significance for the Character of Christianity*, 2nd edn (London: SCM, 2006), p. 60.

Son of Man's authority to "forgive" – to remove – sins'[32] is sufficiently supported by early Jewish evidence.

Even if there were indeed a priestly practice of declaring the forgiveness of sins, this could not have prompted the conflict narrated in Mark 2.6–10. For the Galilean scribes to have reacted with such vehemence against Jesus' alleged appropriation of priestly language, they must have believed not only that the priests did have such a right to proclaim forgiveness, but also that *only* the priests had this right. According to James Dunn, Jesus was offensive, since 'he pronounced the man's sins forgiven *outside the cult and without any reference* (even by implication) *to the cult*', while 'man could only promise and pronounce the forgiveness of sins when he operated within the terms and structures provided by God – the Temple, priesthood and sacrifice'.[33] A longstanding scholarly tradition interprets Jesus' declaration of forgiveness as an indication of some kind of opposition to, or competition with, the cultic practices of the Jerusalem temple, with the ultimate reason for this opposition having been allegedly found in Jesus' deep religious consciousness,[34] in his eschatology[35] or in his political involvement.[36]

But, as Sanders remarks, the sources give 'no indication that they [the priests] considered forgiveness to be their exclusive right'.[37] Broer's important study demonstrates convincingly that forgiveness was not generally held to be restricted to the cult.[38] I will corroborate these insights further below by drawing attention to prophetic declarations of forgiveness. Neither the suggestion that 'to forgive sins' was an exclusive prerogative of the priests (if a priestly task at all), nor the hypotheses concerning Jesus' allegedly cult-critical declaration of forgiveness seem to be compatible with the evidence.

Moreover, the suggestion that the controversy in 2.6–10 is about a priestly prerogative is not compliant with the phrasing of the scribal accusation of blasphemy.[39] Dunn claims that disregard for the

---

[32] Fletcher-Louis, 'Jesus as the High Priestly Messiah', 74.

[33] Dunn, *The Partings of the Ways*, p. 61 (original emphasis). See Dunn, *Jesus Remembered*, pp. 787–8.

[34] D. F. Strauss, *Das Leben Jesu für das deutsche Volk bearbeitet*, 18th edn (Stuttgart: Alfred Kröner, n.d. (1st edn 1864)), p. 106.

[35] Weiss, *Die Predigt Jesu vom Reiche Gottes*, pp. 206–8; Wright, *Jesus and the Victory of God*, pp. 435–6, 647.

[36] Crossan, *The Historical Jesus*, p. 324.

[37] Sanders, *Jewish Law*, p. 62.

[38] Broer, 'Jesus und das Gesetz', pp. 83–97.

[39] F. Hahn, *Christologische Hoheitstitel: Ihre Geschichte im frühen Christentum*, 5th edn (Göttingen: Vandenhoeck & Ruprecht, 1995), p. 239.

divinely commissioned sacrificial cult could have merited such a charge. Accordingly, while Dunn acknowledges a 'christological emphasis' in Mark 2.7, 10, he nevertheless appears to accept the basic historicity of the charge of blasphemy.[40] Yet, in Mark, the scribes' rhetorical question even appears to rule out the notion of any delegated priestly authority to forgive sins: *only God* can forgive sins (see 2.7). On a comparison between John the Baptist's offer of forgiveness and that of Jesus, the former lends itself to an anti-temple interpretation far more easily than the latter.[41] Still, as pointed out in Chapter 3 above, nothing indicates that John was accused of blasphemy.

Prophetic forgiveness

Analogies to the synoptic forgiveness episodes have also, and more accurately, been identified in prophetic literature and narrative material about prophets. Theodor Keim (1871) remarked that, while several OT passages identify forgiveness as a divine prerogative, the prophets of old nevertheless proclaimed forgiveness in God's name. He pointed specifically to Second Isaiah's proclamation of post-exilic forgiveness (Isa 40.2) and Nathan's prophetic words to David (2 Sam 12.13).[42] More recently, scholars have reiterated the suggestion in order to explain how Jesus' announcement of forgiveness would have been heard in the context of early Judaism.[43] Others have denied the relevance of these parallels.[44] Surprisingly, though, a more detailed investigation of whatever role forgiveness may have played in first-century notions of prophecy seems not to have been attempted.

As stated in the introduction to this chapter, the most pertinent analogies would be those which can be found in early Jewish interpretations of the biblical material. By studying this literature one will see that the notion of prophetic mediation of forgiveness, which is expressed already in the OT texts themselves, was also current in the first century. In the following, the prophets, who are portrayed as bestowing, mediating or announcing God's forgiveness in the OT and early Jewish literature, will be presented one by one, with primary attention given to the

---

[40] Dunn, *The Partings of the Ways*, pp. 60–1; Dunn, *Jesus Remembered*, pp. 787–8.

[41] See Webb, *John the Baptizer*, pp. 203–5.

[42] Keim, *Geschichte Jesu von Nazara*, vol. II, pp. 175–6 n. 5.

[43] Sanders, *Jewish Law*, p. 62; M. Casey, *The Solution to the 'Son of Man' Problem*, LNTS 343 (London: T & T Clark, 2007), p. 156.

[44] Kellermann, 'Wer kann Sünden vergeben außer Elia?', p. 166; Hofius, 'Jesu Zuspruch der Sündenvergebung', pp. 127–8; Bock, 'Jesus as Blasphemer', pp. 81–2.

two prophets of whom the very act of forgiving seems to be predicated, namely Samuel and Daniel.

Samuel the prophet

Samuel in the Hebrew Bible

As the first prophet who can to some extent be said to fill the vacancy after Moses, Samuel is an important character in the biblical narrative. He is variously designated as a 'prophet', 'seer' and 'man of God'.[45] He exercises his office primarily by delivering oracles from the Lord, sometimes exhibiting prognostic abilities and knowledge of rather trivial details (see 1 Sam 9.20). Once he interprets a seemingly incidental event as a prophetic symbolic act (15.27–9). On Samuel's lips are also found prophetic admonitions directed towards the people of Israel (7.3–6; 8.6–20). Moreover, he delivers irrevocable oracles of judgement (3.11–14; 13.13–14; 15.22–3; cf. 28.16–19) and an oracle of salvation (12.20–2). In addition, Samuel functions as the people's representative before God: he prays for the Israelites (7.5, 8–9; 12.19) and he delivers their requests to the Lord (8.6, 21; cf. 9.9).

1 Sam 12.16–25. The body of the chapter is Samuel's speech before Israel at the installation of Saul as the first king of the nation. As Samuel successfully calls upon the Lord to send thunder and rain, the Israelites are seized with fear of both the Lord and of Samuel, and they realize that their petition for a king was a gross sin. They then confess their sin and entreat Samuel to pray for them to God, 'that we may not die' (12.19). To this Samuel responds reassuringly:

> Fear not! You have committed all this evil; yet do not turn away from following the Lord, but serve the Lord wholeheartedly. You will not turn away to follow futile things that give no benefit or rescue, since they are futile. For the Lord, for the sake of his great name, will not abandon his people; for it has pleased the Lord to make you his people.
>
> (1 Sam 12.20–2)

---

[45] 1 Sam 3.20; 2 Chron 35.18; cf. 1 Sam 9.9; 19.20 (נביא); 1 Sam 9.11, 18, 19; 16.14 (cf. 4Q52; LXX); 1 Chron 9.22; 26.28; 29.29; cf. 1 Sam 9.9 (רֹאֶה); 1 Sam 9.6, 7, 8, 10 (אִישׁ־אֱלֹהִים). On the terminology, see G. L. Keown, 'Prophecy in 1 and 2 Samuel', *RevExp* 99 (2002), 175–84 (176–8).

The marker 'Fear not!' (אל־תיראו) by which Samuel's oracle commences is, apart from the plural number, identical with the assuring imperative that forms a constitutive part of Second Isaiah's oracles of salvation.[46] Although delivered in response to the people's confession of their sin, the oracle is not tantamount to an explicit declaration of forgiveness; the Israelites actually do not ask to be forgiven, but that their lives may be spared – and Samuel's reply indicates that their request has been accepted.

Samuel then declares that he will continue to pray for the people (12.23). His intercession for the people is mentioned here in a way reminiscent of 7.2–11, where the prophet also begs the Lord to preserve the people despite their former sins. In this way Samuel resembles Moses, who interceded on behalf of the people, and who implored God to forgive them several times when they had sinned.[47] An early tendency to juxtapose Moses and Samuel as the two most powerful intercessors in pre-exilic Israel is evident within the OT itself (Jer 15.1; cf. Ps 99.6). It has frequently been assumed that this expresses the notion that intercession is a characteristically prophetic activity, but in reality intercession is neither restricted to prophets nor practised by all – or even by a majority – of those designated prophets.[48] It is therefore significant that Samuel imitates this aspect of the career of the greatest prophet: it serves to portray him as a 'prophet like Moses'.

1 Sam 15.24–5. This is another passage in the Samuel cycle that closely parallels an incident in the narrated life of Moses. As Samuel pronounces the Lord's judgement on Saul, the king answers the prophet: 'I have sinned. For I have transgressed the Lord's command and your word, since I feared the people and listened to their voice. But now, please, forgive my sin (שא נא את־חטאתי) and return with me, so that I may worship the Lord' (1 Sam 15.24–5). In Saul's plea, נשא seems indeed to be employed in the sense of 'to forgive'. Does this imply that the king is begging Samuel to forgive the sin he has committed against the Lord? In view of the similarities between this passage and Exod 10.16–17, where

---

[46] Isa 41.10, 14; 43.1, 5; 44.2; 54.4. On this formula, see C. Westermann, *Das Buch Jesaja: Kapitel 40–66*, ATD 19, 3rd edn (Göttingen: Vandenhoeck & Ruprecht, 1976), pp. 13–15.

[47] Exod 32.11–13, 30–2; 34.8–9; Num 14.13–19; 21.7; Deut 9.18–20; Ps 106.23. See E. Aurelius, *Der Fürbitter Israels: Eine Studie zum Mosebild im Alten Testament*, CBOTS 27 (Stockholm: Almqvist & Wiksell, 1988).

[48] S. E. Balentine, 'The Prophet as Intercessor: A Reassessment', *JBL* 103 (1984), 161–73; Aurelius, *Der Fürbitter Israels*, p. 3; *pace* G. von Rad, *Theologie des Alten Testaments*, vol. II: *Die Theologie der prophetischen Überlieferungen Israels*, 10th edn (Gütersloh: Kaiser, 1993), pp. 59–60.

another impious ruler, Pharaoh, seems to request that Moses and Aaron should, on the one hand, forgive the sin committed against them and, on the other hand, entreat the Lord to suspend the punishment inflicted for the sin committed against him, Saul's plea for forgiveness may well be interpreted to include a reference to his transgression of Samuel's prophetic word, rather than to his violation of the Lord's command. It will become clear below that this is how Josephus understood the passage.

Samuel in early Jewish literature

Before turning to Josephus' retelling of the biblical episodes about Samuel, I will provide a summary of other early Jewish interpretations of this prophetic figure. That the memory of Samuel continued to play a role in Qumran can be seen primarily from the manuscripts of the Books of Samuel from Cave 4, but also from apocryphal works such as the *Vision of Samuel* (4Q160) and the *Apocryphon of Jeremiah* (4Q389). Moreover, Second Esdras (*Fourth Ezra*) mentions Samuel as one of the famous intercessors for the impious (2 Esd 7.106–11). The most pertinent evidence, however, comes from the Wisdom of Ben Sira and from Pseudo-Philo's *Biblical Antiquities*.

Ben Sira. Ben Sira twice labels Samuel a prophet (προφήτης) and ascribes to him the activity of prophesying (Ecclus 46.13–20). His calling upon the Lord is mentioned as a prayer because of the enemies of the nation rather than as a prayer for forgiveness (46.16). Only *post mortem* is Samuel dealing with sin: 'after falling asleep he prophesied and showed to the king his destiny; from the earth he raised his voice in prophecy, to wipe out (ἐξαλεῖψαι) the lawlessness of the people' (46.20). As mentioned in Chapter 3 above, 'to wipe out' sins may imply forgiving them; but the Greek of Ben Sira does not use the verb in this sense (cf. 40.12). The meaning 'to blot out', 'to extinguish' is more appropriate, with reference to the final destruction of Saul (1 Sam 28.16–19).

Pseudo-Philo's Biblical Antiquities. The *Liber antiquitatum biblicarum* emphasizes Samuel's status as a prophet. It designates him a prophet (*propheta*) eight times and predicates of him the act of 'prophesying' (*prophetare, prophetizare*) another five times.[49] It also makes the links between Moses and Samuel more explicit (*LAB* 53.2; 57.2).

After Samuel's death, the Philistines exclaim: 'Behold, Samuel the prophet is dead, and who prays for Israel?' (64.2). This is again

---

[49] *LAB* 49.8; 50.8; 51.6, 7; 57.4*bis*; 59.4; 64.2 (*propheta*); 49.7, 8; 53.12; 54.5 (*prophetare*); 53.11 (*prophetizare*).

reminiscent of the Israelites' concern at the death of Moses (cf. 19.3). The *Biblical Antiquities* portrays Moses as a successful intercessor for his sinful people (12.8–10) and seems to imply that Samuel imitated this ministry, though it never states directly that the latter prayed for forgiveness. As a matter of fact, its retelling of 1 Sam 12 effectively eliminates any mention of the people's sinfulness in demanding a king (*LAB* 57.1–4).

Samuel in Josephus

There is no consensus on either the language or the form of the text(s) employed by Josephus in his rewriting of the Books of Samuel, but there are strong indications that his *Vorlage* was closely aligned with the text-type represented by the proto-Lucianic recension and the Samuel scroll from Qumran.[50] As Louis Feldman points out, Josephus labels Samuel a 'prophet' no less than forty-five times. The amount of space he allots to Samuel, compared with the biblical narrative and the treatment of other prophets in the *Antiquities*, also indicates that, according to Josephus, Samuel is a prophet of utmost importance.[51]

With regard to the prophet's ability to deal with sin, the description is somewhat inconsistent. In his retelling of 1 Sam 7.2–6, Josephus turns Samuel's call for repentance into a more general speech of moral exhortation and he also leaves out the biblical reference to Samuel's intercession (*Ant* VI.19–22). There is a certain tension between the two passages that do refer to the prophet's praying for those who have sinned – passages to which the following paragraphs will draw attention.

Ant VI.91–3. This passage, which contains Josephus' retelling of 1 Sam 12.16–25, is crucial for the understanding of the phenomenon of prophetic forgiveness in early Judaism. Even so, it has been constantly neglected in previous research. In VI.86–94, Josephus introduces the noun 'prophet' three times and the verb 'to prophesy' once, thereby highlighting Samuel's status precisely as a prophet.[52] As in the biblical narrative, Samuel reluctantly installs Saul as king and delivers his farewell speech,

---

[50] E. Ulrich, 'Josephus' Biblical Text for the Books of Samuel', in L. H. Feldman and G. Hata (eds.), *Josephus, the Bible, and History* (Detroit: Wayne State University Press, 1989), pp. 81–96; L. H. Feldman, *Josephus's Interpretation of the Bible* (Berkeley/Los Angeles/London: University of California Press, 1998), pp. 32–4.

[51] L. H. Feldman, 'Prophets and Prophecy in Josephus', *JTS* 41 (1990), 386–422 (390–1); Feldman, *Josephus's Interpretation of the Bible*, pp. 490–1.

[52] C. Begg, 'Samuel's Farewell Discourse according to Josephus', *SJOT* 11 (1997), 56–77 (75).

which he concludes by promising a sign from heaven. Sudden thunder, lightning and hail demonstrate 'the truth of the prophet in all matters' (VI.92) and, as a result, the people are brought to repentance:

> [T]hey confessed that they had sinned and had fallen into this because of ignorance, and they began to implore the prophet as a mild and gentle father, to make God benevolent towards them and to forgive this sin (ταύτην ἀφεῖναι τὴν ἁμαρτίαν), which they had committed in addition to other things by which they had acted insolently and had violated the law. He for his part promised to beg and to persuade God to pardon them for these things (συγγνῶναι περὶ τούτων αὐτοῖς).
>
> (Josephus *Ant* VI.92–3)

The first thing to come to terms with is the syntax of this part of the passage: 'began to implore the prophet ... to make God benevolent towards them and to forgive this sin' (ἱκετεύειν τὸν προφήτην ... τὸν θεὸν αὐτοῖς εὐμενῆ καταστῆσαι καὶ ταύτην ἀφεῖναι τὴν ἁμαρτίαν). While it is unquestionable that the grammatical subject of 'to make benevolent' (καταστῆσαι) is 'the prophet' (τὸν προφήτην), translators have been confused about the subject of 'to forgive' (ἀφεῖναι) and have frequently predicated this infinitive of 'God' (τὸν θεόν).[53] But this is an extremely unlikely interpretation, since it assumes that 'to make' or 'to render' (καταστῆσαι) is here employed in a twofold sense and that it takes as complements to the direct object 'God' both an adjective, 'benevolent' (εὐμενῆ), and a verb, 'to forgive' (ἀφεῖναι) – this is a way of using the verb καθιστάναι which, apart from being quite clumsy, has no parallels in Josephus.[54] Christopher Begg's translation stays closer

---

[53] See Whiston's 1737 translation, 'besought the prophet ... to render God so merciful as to forgive this their sin'; the LCL translation, 'implored the prophet ... to render God gracious to them that He might forgive this sin'; and Feldman's paraphrase, 'call upon him ... to render G-d gracious to them so that He may forgive this sin' (*Josephus's Interpretation of the Bible*, p. 499).

[54] καθιστάναι occurs 347 times in Josephus' writings. In 72 of these instances, the verb takes two accusatives: the complement may then be either a noun, in which case καθιστάναι may generally be translated as 'appoint' (54 times), or an adjective, where it usually denotes 'make' or 'render' (18 times). The construction in *Ant* VI.92 obviously belongs to the latter category and is closely paralleled in *Ant* VII.158; XI.110 (where the adjective is likewise εὐμενής); *Bell* I.206, 358; *Ant* XIII.401; XVII.6 (εὔνους). As for καθιστάναι followed by an infinitive, this construction is uncommon in Greek literature (see *s.v.* LSJ). It does occur in Josephus, but never in the sense proposed for *Ant* VI.92, i.e. 'make somebody do something'. In the only passage where an active form of the verb is followed by an infinitive, καθεστάκει must mean 'he placed' or 'he appointed' (ὁ σκόπος ὃν ὁ βασιλεὺς Ἰώραμος καθεστάκει τοὺς ἐρχομένους εἰς τὴν πόλιν ἀφορᾶν, *Ant* IX.114). Likewise, the two passive participles of καθιστάναι which govern infinitives require the translation

to the original Greek than do its predecessors: 'begged the prophet ... to make God benevolent to them and forgive this offense of theirs'.[55] This translation opens up the possibility of construing 'the prophet' as the grammatical subject of 'to forgive' which, I would argue, is, in view of how Josephus uses the verb καθιστάναι elsewhere, a far more likely understanding of the syntax.[56] Thus, 'to make' and 'to forgive' are at an equal level: both verbs are governed by 'they begged' or 'they began to implore' (ἱκετεύειν), and they both take 'the prophet' as their grammatical subject.

Another difficulty to be addressed is the nature of the sin for which the people ask forgiveness of Samuel. Is it an offence against the prophet, or a sin committed against God? Several factors point to the latter alternative. First of all, Josephus has earlier expressed his view that the request for a king was primarily a rebellion against God. When Samuel is saddened by the demand, God comfortingly reminds him that the people 'had not despised him [the prophet] but himself [God], so that he might not reign alone', although the request was indeed an expression of ungratefulness both to God and to Samuel, 'towards me and your prophecy' (VI.38). Secondly, the speech of Samuel chastises the people for their insolence against God: they are accused of having 'committed great impiety towards God' (VI.88), of being so possessed by madness that they 'flee from God' and, as a result, God is 'enraged and displeased' (VI.91). Nowhere throughout his speech does Samuel intimate that he has taken personal offence. Thirdly, as Begg remarks, the collocation 'to forgive sin' (ἀφιέναι ἁμαρτίαν) occurs nowhere else in the works of Josephus.[57] The word he normally employs for the forgiveness of personal offences by human beings is 'to pardon' (συγγινώσκειν), which is the verb predicated of God in VI.93.[58] Had Josephus wished to portray the crowd as asking Samuel for forgiveness of a crime committed against him personally, it would have been in keeping with his habit to use the

---

'appointed' (ὁ φυλάσσειν τὴν πόλιν ὑπὸ Ἰωσήπου καθεσταμένος, *Bell* II.616; τὸν ὑπὸ τοῦ θεοῦ κατασταθέντα βασιλεύειν, *Ant* VII.265). In *Ant* VI.92, by contrast, the translation of καταστῆσαι as 'to appoint' is excluded, since the verb takes εὐμενῆ as its complement.

[55] C. T. Begg, *Flavius Josephus: Translation and Commentary*, vol. IV: *Flavius Josephus Judean Antiquities 5–7* (Leiden: Brill, 2005), p. 124.

[56] In an e-mail sent to me on 19 December 2008, Prof. Begg explained that he understands 'God' to be the subject of 'forgive'. My reading of the syntax of the passage, therefore, is contrary to the translator's intention.

[57] Begg, 'Samuel's Farewell Discourse', 70 n. 91; Begg, *Judean Antiquities 5–7*, p. 124.

[58] See *Ant* III.23; XI.229; cf. IX.214 (συγγνώην παρασχεῖν); XI.144 (συγγνωμονῆσαι).

same verb. The identification of the sin mentioned in VI.92 as an evil deed against God may explain why another verb is used here: it seems that Josephus can employ ἀφιέναι, but not συγγινώσκειν, with reference to the prophet's act of offering forgiveness *on behalf of God*. This invites the final question to be asked of the passage quoted: in what sense do the people expect Samuel to be able to 'forgive this sin' against God? In view of the prophet's response, it is quite clear that he will comply with their plea by begging God to pardon them, that is, by interceding for them in order to appease the divine wrath. This implies that 'to forgive this sin' and 'to make God benevolent' are to some extent used as synonymous expressions, but the former phrase may carry a sense that goes beyond that of the latter. It is quite possible that the verb ἀφιέναι is used here in the concrete sense of 'to dismiss', 'to send away'. The crowd is, of course, anxious that the terrifying thunderstorm should cease, so the contents of their desperate plea can be paraphrased as a petition 'to make God benevolent towards them and, once this has been done, to send away the punishment for this sin'. When Samuel 'forgives' a sin, he prays for the people in order to placate God and to avert the temporal punishment for the sin committed.

Ant VI.142–54. Josephus' rewriting of 1 Sam 15.10–31 includes a narration of how Samuel's intercession for Saul is rejected by God. The original story's brief remark that Samuel 'cried to the Lord all the night' (15.11) is significantly elaborated by Josephus. Here the prophet begs God 'to be reconciled to Saul and to cease from anger', but the deity refuses to grant 'pardon' (συγγνώμη) for Saul and appeals to the principle 'that it is not just to forgive sins (ἁμαρτήματα χαρίζεσθαι) on the grounds of intercession': to show such compassion would result in the increase of sins (*Ant* VI.143–4). No mention was made of this principle in VI.93, where Samuel seems confident that his intercession will bring about God's forgiveness, nor was the objection raised that to change one's mind is a human, not a divine, characteristic (cf. VI.153).

When Samuel communicates God's judgement on Saul and declares that he will be removed from authority, the king admits his wrongdoing:

> Saul confessed that he had acted unjustly and did not deny his sin, for he had transgressed the prophet's commands. However, it was because of fright and fear of his soldiers that he had neither prevented nor stopped them from plundering the booty. 'But pardon and be mild (συγγίνωσκε καὶ πρᾶος ἴσθι)' [he said], for he would take care not to sin in the future. He begged the prophet to return and perform sacrifices of thanksgiving to

God; but the latter went away to his home, since he saw that
God was not willing to be reconciled.

(Josephus *Ant* VI.151)

While in 1 Sam 15.24 Saul confesses his sin, both against the Lord and
against Samuel, Josephus only reports that 'he had transgressed the
prophet's command'. Saul's plea for pardon accordingly concerns the
disrespect he has shown to Samuel – the verb συγγινώσκειν is appropriately used – whereas he neither confesses to have sinned against God nor
asks for the deity's forgiveness. One may hypothesize that Josephus left
out Saul's confession that he 'had transgressed the Lord's command' in
order to make it understandable why Saul, unlike the crowd in *Ant* VI.92
or unlike David in VII.153, cannot be pardoned: in a crucial sense, Saul
remains unrepentant.

Daniel the prophet

Daniel in the Old Testament

The Book of Daniel does not label its hero as a prophet, but it will become
clear below that he was viewed as such in early Judaism. In the Aramaic
biblical narrative, the Babylonian court acknowledge that 'a spirit of
holy gods' is at work in him (4.5, 6, 15; 5.11; cf. 5.12, 14; 6.4). While his
companions share some of his knowledge and wisdom, Daniel is singled
out as the one who 'had insight about every kind of vision and dreams'
(1.17; cf. 5.12; chapters 7–12), to whom mysteries are revealed (2.19,
30, 47; 4.6). In the wake of his success as an interpreter of dreams, he is
appointed as Nebuchadnezzar's 'chief of the magicians, the enchanters,
the astrologists, and the diviners' (5.11; cf. 4.6).

Daniel's most obvious engagement with forgiveness is his prayer in
9.4–19. It is an excellent example of early Jewish penitential prayer,
offered 'with fasting, sackcloth and ashes' (9.3) and including a lament-
like confession of sins with several elements characteristic of this literary
type.[59] But for the understanding of Daniel's role concerning forgiveness
in early Judaism, the episode about Nebuchadnezzar's insanity in Daniel
4 is of greater importance.

Dan 4.1–34 MT. Nebuchadnezzar has a frightening dream and
requests 'the magicians, the enchanters, the astrologists, and the

---

[59] R. A. Werline, *Penitential Prayer in Second Temple Judaism: The Development of a
Religious Institution*, SBLEJL 13 (Atlanta: Scholars, 1998), pp. 67–82.

diviners' to interpret it for him. Only Daniel – addressed by the king as 'Beltheshazzar, chief of the magicians' – is capable of understanding the vision. He informs Nebuchadnezzar that the enormous tree about to be cut down is the king himself. But a bud of the roots shall be left, fettered on the ground:

> This is the interpretation, o king, and the decree of the Most High which has come upon my lord the king is this: You will be expelled from among human beings, and your dwelling place will be with the wild animals of the field. You will be fed with grass like the oxen and you will be wetted with dew from the sky. Seven years will pass over you, until you realise that the Most High has authority over the kingdom of human beings and that he gives it to whomsoever it pleases him. Now that it was said: 'leave a bud of the roots of the tree': your rule is confirmed for you, as soon as you realise that Heaven is in authority. Therefore, o king, let my advice be acceptable to you! Remove your sin (פרק ... חטאך) with almsgiving, and your guilt (עויתך) by showing mercy to the poor – then your prosperity may be prolonged.

(Dan 4.21–4)

What Daniel delivers is not prophecy, but the interpretation of a mystery already revealed directly to the king (cf. 2.28; 4.6). Nebuchadnezzar will be chastised for his sin. Daniel recommends that he repent, so that his 'prosperity may be prolonged', but this hardly means that, if the king follows Daniel's advice, he will escape punishment.[60] A year later, when Nebuchadnezzar prides himself of Babylon's greatness, a voice from heaven ratifies the verdict and the king is transformed into an animal-like being. Only seven years later is he restored to sanity and to royal power.

Dan 4.1–37 LXX. There is no consensus about the relationship between the MT and the Old Greek version of Daniel 4, but Rainer Albertz's argument that, at several points, the Aramaic text presupposes an earlier version of the story, which the Old Greek reproduces more faithfully, is convincing.[61] Among the numerous discrepancies, the weight placed on Nebuchadnezzar's repentance should be noted here. Whereas in the Aramaic text Daniel advises the king to 'remove' his sin by performing

---

[60] L. F. Hartman and A. A. Di Lella, *The Book of Daniel: A New Translation with Introduction and Commentary*, AB 23 (Garden City, NY: Doubleday, 1978), p. 177.

[61] R. Albertz, *Der Gott des Daniel: Untersuchungen zu Daniel 4–6 in der Septuagintafassung sowie zu Komposition und Theologie des aramäischen Danielbuches*, SBS 131 (Stuttgart: Katholisches Bibelwerk, 1988), pp. 71–6.

deeds of charity, in the LXX his first recommendation is 'Pray to him for your sins!' (Dan 4.27 LXX). And when the seven years of punishment have passed, at the point where the MT has Nebuchadnezzar state tersely that 'I raised my eyes toward heaven', the king narrates in the Old Greek:

> And after seven years I set my soul to prayer and pleaded about my sins before the face of the Lord, the God of heaven, and to the great God of gods I prayed about my faults of ignorance … At the consummation of the seven years, the time of my deliverance came, and my sins and faults of ignorance were complete (ἐπληρώθησαν) before the God of heaven. I prayed to the great God of gods about my faults of ignorance, and then an angel called me from heaven: 'Nebuchadnezzar, pay service to the God of heaven and give glory to the Most High! The kingship over your people is returned to you.'
>
> (Dan 4.33a, 34 LXX)

The introduction of a heavenly messenger to announce the restoration of Nebuchadnezzar's power is unique to the Old Greek, and Daniel plays no further role in the episode.

Daniel in early Jewish literature

As mentioned already, Daniel came to be recognized quite soon as one of the prophets.[62] Only the Hebrew biblical canon denies this status to him and places the Book of Daniel among the Writings rather than among the Prophets. This may be a post-135 CE phenomenon.[63] In the following, I will summarize Daniel's role with regard to sin and forgiveness as described in Josephus and in the *Lives of the Prophets* respectively, before I turn to a detailed study of the *Prayer of Nabonidus* from Qumran.

Josephus. Josephus' portrayal of Daniel reflects the author's identification with the heroic prophet and interpreter of dreams at a Gentile court in the distant past.[64] This, combined with Josephus' desire to present himself in the most positive light possible, may have prompted his characterization of Daniel as 'a prophet of good things' (*Ant* X.268), which in reality contradicts his earlier statement that Daniel had become

---

[62] 4Q174 1–3 ii 3; Josephus, *Ant* X.249; *VitProph* 4; Matt 24.15.
[63] K. Koch, 'Is Daniel Also among the Prophets?', *Int* 39 (1985), 117–30.
[64] See, e.g., R. Gray, *Prophetic Figures in Late Second Temple Jewish Palestine: The Evidence from Josephus* (Oxford University Press, 1993), pp. 74–8.

'a prophet of bad things' for Belshazzar (X.246). Political motives are also likely to be behind the censoring approach to Dan 4.1–34 that Josephus takes as he deletes the figurative details of the king's dream and his loss of sanity (*Ant* X.216–17).[65] On the other hand, Josephus retains the thrust of the biblical narration by mentioning that it was 'because of his insolence against God' (X.241) that Nebuchadnezzar was punished and, like the LXX, he elaborates the topic about the king's repentance by stating that the king regained both his human stature and his royal power only 'after many entreaties and prayers' (*Ant* X.242; cf. X.217). Daniel, however, takes no part in this process of repentance.

Lives of the Prophets. The legendary Life of Daniel focuses almost exclusively on Nebuchadnezzar's insanity and repentance. From the outset, Daniel is characterized as an ascetic intercessor (*VitProph* 4.3). Nothing is said about the king's dream or about Daniel's interpretation thereof, but the sin of Nebuchadnezzar appears to be revealed to the prophet only after the metamorphosis has occurred (4.6). The legend also introduces the non-biblical element of Daniel's intercession for Nebuchadnezzar, which reduces the seven-year punishment to seven months (4.4, 12, 14). During these seven months the king weeps and prays 'all day and during the night forty times' to Israel's God (4.9); having been restored to human form he spends the remainder of the seven years in repentance:

> For the six years and six months he prostrated himself to the Lord God and confessed his impiety; and after the forgiveness of his offence (μετὰ ἄφεσιν τῆς ἀνομίας αὐτοῦ) God returned his royal power to him. As long as he was making confession, he neither ate bread or meat nor did he drink wine, for Daniel had instructed him to propitiate (ἐξιλεοῦσθαι) the Lord by eating soaked pulse and vegetables.
>
> (*VitProph* 4.15–16)

Daniel is thus involved in Nebuchadnezzar's repentance and attainment of forgiveness in several ways: he discerns the reason for the king's punishment, he prays for him, and he instructs him on how to repent properly.

But is the *Lives of the Prophets* a reliable witness to early Jewish conceptions? David Satran's close reading of the Life of Daniel reveals details that point to a setting within Byzantine Christianity rather than within first-century Judaism. The description of Nebuchadnezzar's

---

[65] Feldman, *Josephus's Interpretation of the Bible*, pp. 646–7.

ascetic diet corresponds exactly, and exclusively, to penitential regimen among monastics in the fourth century and later. Satran further notes that the process of prostrations and public confessions in order to attain forgiveness can be derived from fourth- and fifth-century Christian penitential practices. Satran concludes that, whereas early Jewish traditions underlie the legend, it is in its present shape a Christian text.[66] On the other hand, and in favour of a Hellenistic Jewish origin for the Life of Daniel, Anna Maria Schwemer draws attention to the influence of the Old Greek text on the narrative, to the affinities between 4Q242 and the Life, and to the relative unpopularity of Daniel 4 in early Christianity.[67] A prudent attitude, in the face of the uncertain provenance of the Life of Daniel, will be to consider the text as an expression of the interpretative tendency to highlight Nebuchadnezzar's repentance and forgiveness, which can be discerned already in the Greek OT and in Josephus, and also the added tendency to increase Daniel's role in the process, which can be found also in Qumran.

Daniel in Qumran

A few decades after its composition, the Book of Daniel was read and copied at Qumran. This can be seen from the preserved fragments of the book, the earliest of which is dated to the late second century BCE.[68] But the Danielic corpus was larger, including the *Aramaic Apocalypse* or 'Son of God text' (4Q246), which exhibits a close relationship to the biblical book, and *Pseudo-Daniel* (4Q243–5), which contains the prophet's name and includes a narrative framework. Only the *Prayer of Nabonidus* is of direct interest in the present study.

Prayer of Nabonidus (4Q242). This text is extant in four tiny fragments, first published by J. T. Milik in 1956 and forty years later in the definitive edition by John Collins.[69] It fortunately bears the fully legible

---

[66] D. Satran, *Biblical Prophets in Byzantine Palestine: Reassessing the* Lives of the Prophets, SVTP 11 (Leiden/New York/Cologne: Brill, 1995), pp. 88–91, 96.

[67] A. M. Schwemer, *Studien zu den frühchristlichen Prophetenlegenden* Vitae Prophetarum, vol. I: *Die Viten der großen Propheten Jesaja, Jeremia, Ezechiel und Daniel: Einleitung, Übersetzung und Kommentar*, TSAJ 49 (Tübingen: Mohr Siebeck, 1995), pp. 370–1.

[68] P. W. Flint, 'The Daniel Tradition at Qumran', in J. J. Collins and P. W. Flint (eds.), *The Book of Daniel: Composition and Reception*, VTSup 83, 2 vols. (Leiden: Brill, 2001), vol. II, pp. 329–67 (p. 330).

[69] J. T. Milik, '"Prière de Nabonide" et autres écrits d'un cycle de Daniel: Fragments araméens de Qumrân 4', *RB* 63 (1956), 407–15; J. Collins, '4QPrayer of Nabonidus ar', in G. Brooke (ed.), *Qumran Cave 4*, vol. XVII: *Parabiblical Texts, Part 3*, DJD 22 (Oxford: Clarendon, 1996), pp. 83–93.

superscription 'Words of the prayer which king Nabonidus (נבני) prayed' and makes reference to the king's disease and to his location in Teiman. Then follow the much discussed lines which are of importance to the present study. I will argue for this understanding of the preserved parts: 'I was afflicted for seven years, and from … and as for my sin, a diviner forgave it (וחטאי שבק לה גזר); he … a Jew …' (4Q242 1–3 3–4). Next we learn that the king is instructed to make a written proclamation to give glory to the name (of God), and the remainder of the reconstructed text appears to be the beginning of this proclamation. Nabonidus relates how he prayed for seven years to his gods of silver, gold, wood, stone and clay. Finally he mentions his healing.

The similarities between the *Prayer of Nabonidus* and the episode of Nebuchadnezzar's insanity in Daniel 4 are so manifest that some relationship can be taken for granted. In view of the extensive differences that also exist, it is wise not to postulate any direct dependence of one text on the other.[70] Rather, the two texts are variants of the same legend, preserved by the *Prayer of Nabonidus* in a form that seems to exhibit more ancient traits than its counterpart in the biblical canon. Daniel's name, to be sure, is nowhere mentioned in the extant fragments of 4Q242, which allows for the possibility that the 'diviner' (גזר) is an anonymous Jew, not yet identified with Daniel.[71] Although this could be true for the literary work as originally authored, it is unlikely that the Qumran copyist failed to recognize the diviner as Daniel. The copy is commonly dated to the first century BCE, but not earlier than 75.[72] By that time, the Book of Daniel had been in existence for about a century, and it was, as already mentioned, also known and copied at Qumran. Those members of the Qumran community who copied, read and heard the *Prayer of Nabonidus* did, in all probability, identify this 'diviner' of the Jewish exile in the court of a Babylonian king as Daniel, 'the chief of the … diviners' (רב גזרין, Dan 5.11). This is all the more likely to have been the case if line 4 of frags. 1–3 should be restored, as is usually thought, to include the characterization of the diviner as 'a Jewish man among the children of the exile' (cf. Dan 2.25; 5.13; 6.14).[73]

[70] M. Henze, *The Madness of King Nebuchadnezzar: The Ancient Near Eastern Origins and Early History of Interpretation of Daniel 4*, JSJSup 61 (Leiden/Boston/Cologne: Brill, 1999), pp. 64–9.

[71] R. Meyer, *Das Gebet des Nabonid: Eine in den Qumran-Handschriften wiederentdeckte Weisheitserzählung* (Berlin: Akademie-Verlag, 1962), pp. 53–67, 82–94.

[72] F. M. Cross, 'Fragments of the Prayer of Nabonidus', *IEJ* 34 (1984), 260–4 (260).

[73] Milik, '"Prière de Nabonide"', 408; Collins, '4QPrayer of Nabonidus ar', p. 88.

As regards the role of this Jewish diviner in the *Prayer of Nabonidus*, his only function could be to advise the king to make the written proclamation.[74] But I find this less likely. It would be quite unusual for a manifestly Jewish narrative like this to have the king pray to his idols for seven years and then be healed, only to learn after his recovery that it was actually caused by Israel's God – one would expect his restoration to health to follow some act of conversion, such as scholars have suggested was originally part of line 3.[75] If Nabonidus was indeed converted to the worship of the Lord prior to his recovery without the intervention of a human being, it seems awkward to bring in the diviner at this point.[76] The place of the diviner in the narrative is more intelligible if he enters it before Nabonidus is healed and, as in the translation given above, is credited with having 'forgiven' the king's sin.

That a sin has been forgiven, according to line 4, is beyond doubt. Being juxtaposed with 'sin', the verb שבק naturally translates as 'to forgive', and alternative translations are not convincing.[77] The difficulty lies in determining the grammatical subject of the verb. Several interpreters take it to be God, and the plausibility of this reading increases if the restoration of 'God' in line 3 is correct. Yet this restoration is not certain, and there are considerations that speak in favour of construing the 'diviner' as the subject, in line with the suggestion made by André Dupont-Sommer.[78] Florentino García Martínez argues that it is preferable to view the sentence 'and an exorcist pardoned my sin' as 'defined by the two ו which precede וחטאי and והוא'.[79] Since asyndeton is relatively rare in Aramaic, one would have expected 'And a diviner' (וגזר) instead of the simple 'A diviner' (גזר) to introduce a new sentence. There are several exceptions to this rule and this argument is by no means conclusive.[80] Yet it is statistically more probable than not that a noun, which is not preceded by a conjunction or an adverb, should be read with the foregoing verb. One has to agree with García Martínez that the only

---

[74] Henze, *The Madness of King Nebuchadnezzar*, p. 67.

[75] A. Dupont-Sommer, *Les écrits esséniens découverts près de la mer Morte* (Paris: Payot, 1959), p. 532; B. Jongeling, C. J. Labuschagne and A. S. van der Woude, *Aramaic Texts from Qumran: With Translations and Annotations*, SSS 4 (Leiden: Brill, 1976), pp. 126–8.

[76] F. García Martínez, *Qumran and Apocalyptic: Studies on the Aramaic Texts from Qumran*, STDJ 9 (Leiden: Brill, 1992), pp. 125–6.

[77] Cf. Milik, '"Prière de Nabonide"', 408 (*accorder*); E. Vogt, 'Precatio regis Nabonid in pia narratione iudaica (4Q)', *Bib* 37 (1956), 532–4 (*concedere*).

[78] Dupont-Sommer, *Les écrits ésseniens*, pp. 340–1.

[79] García Martínez, *Qumran and Apocalyptic*, p. 125.

[80] H. Bauer and P. Leander, *Grammatik des Biblisch-Aramäischen* (Halle: Max Niemeyer, 1927), § 106 a.

substantial objection against the predication of forgiveness of the diviner is 'the presupposition of the impossibility of sins being pardoned by a man'.[81] Émile Puech, for example, rejects this interpretation because it would make the *Prayer of Nabonidus* express a 'novel theological conception, unknown from the Bible and from ancient Judaism'.[82] I have argued above that the notion is not unknown but quite clearly expressed by Josephus in *Ant* VI.92, which invalidates this objection.

If, then, the *Prayer of Nabonidus* seems to attribute an act of forgiveness to the 'diviner', what does this imply for the understanding of notions of forgiveness and human agency in Qumran? Following an investigation by Giuseppe Furlani, Dupont-Sommer suggested that גזר means 'exorcist' in 4Q242. According to Dupont-Sommer, both 4Q242 and Mark 2.1–12 testify to the Essene view that healers-exorcists may also forgive sins – as opposed to the Pharisaic doctrine that God alone could do so.[83] There are several flaws in this argumentation. The meaning 'exorcist' for גזר, based on a putative etymology, is far from certain.[84] In early Judaism, one knew at least from the Book of Daniel that there had been 'diviners' (גזרין) at the Babylonian court (Dan 2.27; 4.4; 5.7, 11), but their precise function or the way in which they differed from the 'sages', 'magicians', 'enchanters' or 'astrologists' was hardly known. Already the earliest translators were at a loss about how to render the term.[85] The word is not everyday Qumran jargon but specifically Danielic terminology: even if the meaning 'exorcist' is accepted, the occurrence of the word would not evoke the notion of Essenes expelling demons, but rather the picture of the Babylonian court officials, whose chief was Daniel.[86] Much as the Babylonians' attribution of Daniel's abilities to 'the spirit of holy gods' (4.5, 6, 15; 5.11, 14) bestows some realism on the narrative as it bears witness to their supposed polytheistic convictions, so

---

[81] García Martínez, *Qumran and Apocalyptic*, p. 126.

[82] É. Puech, 'La prière de Nabonide (4Q242)', in K. J. Cathcart and M. Maher (eds.), *Targumic and Cognate Studies*, FS M. McNamara, JSOTS 230 (Sheffield Academic Press, 1996), pp. 208–27 (p. 216).

[83] A. Dupont-Sommer, 'Exorcismes et guérisons dans les écrits de Qoumrân', in *Congress Volume: Oxford 1959*, VTSup 7 (Leiden: Brill, 1960), pp. 246–61 (pp. 257–71). See G. Furlani, 'Aram. *Gāzrīn* = Scongiuratori', *Atti della Accademia nazionale dei Lincei: Rendiconti: Classe di Scienze morali, storiche e filologiche: Serie 8* 3 (1948), 177–96.

[84] W. Kirchschläger, 'Exorzismus in Qumran?', *Kairos* 18 (1976), 135–53 (147 n. 74); B. Janowski, 'Sündenvergebung "um Hiobs willen": Fürbitte und Vergebung in 11QtgJob 38 2f. und Hi 42 9f. LXX', *ZNW* 73 (1982), 251–80 (271–2).

[85] Furlani, 'Aram. *Gāzrīn* = Scongiuratori', 177–81.

[86] A. Steinmann, 'The Chicken and the Egg: A New Proposal for the Relationship between the *Prayer of Nabonidus* and the *Book of Daniel*', *RevQ* 20 (2002), 557–70 (563–4); Casey, *The Solution to the 'Son of Man' Problem*, p. 153.

Nabonidus' classification of Daniel as a גזר serves to convince the reader of 4Q242 that this prayer was actually pronounced by the Babylonian king. It is not a Jewish approval of the notion that Daniel was a 'diviner' or an 'exorcist' any more than the mention of 'holy gods' in the Book of Daniel is an endorsement of polytheism on the part of the author.

As mentioned above, the Qumranites viewed Daniel as a prophet and would do so also on encountering the *Prayer of Nabonidus*. Josephus has Daniel categorize himself among 'the other Chaldeans and magicians' when he speaks to King Nebuchadnezzar (*Ant* X.203), but his own conviction is that Daniel was a prophet (X.246, 249, 267–9). It is not too fanciful to imagine that a first-century reader of the *Prayer of Nabonidus* in Qumran would in fact recognize the Jewish 'diviner' as Daniel the prophet, and, although the preserved text does not mention the healing of the king, we may assume that it is implicit in the expression 'a diviner forgave my sin'. The prophet, it seems, acts quite similarly to Samuel in *Ant* VI.92–3: he 'forgives' the penitent sinner by averting the temporal punishment for his sin, presumably by prayer to God, although this is not stated in the text.

Other prophets

As far as I am aware, the only prophets in early Jewish literature of whom the act of forgiving sins is predicated are Samuel and – possibly – Daniel. The theme of prophetic intercession is emphasized in early Judaism, where several prophets and other righteous ancestors are portrayed as praying for those who have sinned.[87] Additionally, a number of prophets are described as mediators of God's forgiveness, mostly through the proclamation of oracles.

Moses

Early Jewish literature perpetuates the OT picture of Moses as an intercessor for the Israelites when they have sinned.[88] Was Moses also thought to have proclaimed God's forgiveness to the people? Two passages, from Josephus and Philo respectively, could possibly be taken as saying so, but neither of them is unambiguous.

---

[87] For example Abraham (*Jub* 22.14; *TAbr* [A] 14.5–6, 10–15; Philo, *ConfLing* 109); Jacob (*TReub* 1.7; 4.4; *TJud* 19.2; *TGad* 5.9; *TBenj* 3.6); Jeremiah (*ParJer* 2.3); Ezra (Josephus *Ant* XI.143–4).

[88] 2 Esd 7.106; *AssMos* 11.11, 17; 12.6; *LAB* 12.8–10; 19.3; 4Q504 1–2 ii 7–10; Artapanus, frag. 3 = Eusebius, *PraepEv* 9.27.21; Philo, *MutNom* 125–9; *Mos* I.47, 187; II.166; *PraemPoen* 56; *QuaestExod* II.49b.

Josephus routinely leaves out the biblical episodes in which Moses prays for forgiveness. Rewriting Num 14.11–25, he alters the narrative so that the theme of Moses' successful prayer for forgiveness is not reproduced; instead Moses refuses to be the 'reconciler' (καταλλάκτης) of the Israelites and his announcement to them is one of judgement (*Ant* III.311–15). Curiously, the only mention in the *Antiquities* that Moses asked God for forgiveness on behalf of the people is part of an addition to the biblical narrative of Exodus 16. Josephus records Moses' prayer for deliverance from hunger and for forgiveness, to which God assents (III.22–3). He then has Moses announce to the crowd 'that he had come with relief from God for the present difficulties' (III.24). This could imply that Moses announced God's forgiveness to the people, but Josephus does not say so explicitly, and the focus in this passage is on the crisis posed by the lack of sustenance.

As he discusses the different names applied to Moses, Philo remarks that in some functions the arch-prophet is called 'god' (*MutNom* 125–8). In this capacity, Moses belongs among the mediators who intercede for those liable to punishment for their sins, and who thereby, 'imitating the merciful power (ἵλεω δύναμιν) of the father, will mete out punishments with special moderation and benevolence' (129). Since Philo attributes to Moses a share in the divine power to punish sinners, but also in God's mercy, one might reason that Moses somehow participates also in the act of forgiveness. Again, this is not overtly stated.

Deborah

The OT labels Deborah a prophetess (Judg 4.4), an epithet seized on by both Josephus and Pseudo-Philo. While the latter enhances Deborah's role and places her between Moses and Samuel as one of the great intercessors of Israel, Josephus' attitude towards her is more ambiguous.[89] Both these literary works include a non-biblical episode of Deborah's intervention in response to the repentance of the suffering Israelites, which indicates their dependence on a common source or tradition.

---

[89] See C. A. Brown, *No Longer Be Silent: First Century Jewish Portraits of Biblical Women: Studies in Pseudo-Philo's* Biblical Antiquities *and Josephus's* Jewish Antiquities (Louisville, KY: Westminster/John Knox, 1992), pp. 39–92; L. H. Feldman, *Studies in Josephus' Rewritten Bible*, JSJSup 58 (Leiden/Boston/Cologne: Brill, 1998), pp. 153–62; M. Roncace, 'Josephus' (Real) Portraits of Deborah and Gideon: A Reading of *Antiquities* 5.198–232', *JSJ* 31 (2000), 247–74 (249–59); L. H. Feldman, 'On Professor Mark Roncace's Portraits of Deborah and Gideon in Josephus', *JSJ* 32 (2001), 193–220 (194–206).

Josephus relates that when the people realized that the hardships under Sisera had resulted from their negligence of the law, 'they began to implore a prophetess called Deborah ... to pray to God that he would take pity (λαβεῖν οἶκτον) on them and not overlook their extermination by the Canaanites' (*Ant* V.200–1). Next, he remarks that God promised to rescue them; Josephus does not tell how this promise was communicated to the crowd, but one may assume that it was delivered by the prophetess. Such a prophetic oracle conveyed by Deborah would imply an announcement of divine mercy and forgiveness for the past sins of the people, but Josephus does not make that explicit.

In Pseudo-Philo's version of the episode, the Israelites decide to keep a seven-day fast, at the completion of which the Lord sends Deborah to them (*LAB* 30.4–5). While Deborah will later be characterized as an intercessor (33.4), her function here is not to pray for the people, but to reproach them (30.5–6). Even so, her address ends with an oracle of promise: 'And now behold: the Lord will take pity on you (*ecce nunc Dominus inviscerabitur vobis*) today, not for your sake, but for the sake of his covenant, which he made with your ancestors, and the oath which he took not to abandon you forever' (30.7). Deborah's announcement, that God will take pity on the people, comes as a response to the repentance of the Israelites and can therefore, in effect, be viewed as an announcement of forgiveness, although the terminology is different.

Nathan

Although Nathan's oracle of consolation in response to David's confession of his sin has been most frequently identified by critical scholars as an antecedent for Jesus' announcement of forgiveness, the interpretation of the biblical passage in terms of forgiveness is slightly misleading. With prophetic insight into David's sin, Nathan proclaims an oracle of judgement on the king. David surrenders and repents: 'David said to Nathan, "I have sinned against the Lord." Nathan said to David, "The Lord also has put away your sin (גַּם־יְהוָה הֶעֱבִיר חַטָּאתְךָ); you will not die. But, since you really have despised the Lord in this matter, the son born to you will indeed die"' (2 Sam 12.13–14). The plot of the narrative seems to militate against the translation of עבר hiph. as 'forgive'. David's sin has not been deleted, but transferred onto his son, who will have to die in the place of his father.[90] The Greek translator's choice of παραβιβάζειν to

---

[90] P. K. McCarter, *II Samuel: A New Translation with Introduction and Commentary*, AB 9 (New York: Doubleday, 1984), p. 301; Leroy, *Zur Vergebung der Sünden*, pp. 18–19.

represent עבר hiph. here and in 24.10, where the notion of a transferral of
the punishment is also present, confirms this interpretation.

This understanding of Nathan's words is modified in early Judaism,
possibly under influence from Ps 32.5, to a reading in terms of forgiveness.[91] Josephus' rewriting of the episode is consonant with this tendency. Josephus has Nathan foretell the impending death of David's son
prior to the king's confession (*Ant* VII.152); as a result, the death of the
son is not a substitution, but part of David's punishment. When David
admits his sin, 'with tears and grief', God is actually placated: 'God
took pity and was reconciled (διαλλάττεται), and promised to preserve
both his life and his kingdom; for, said he, he was no longer angry with
him [David], since he had repented of what had happened. And Nathan,
having prophesied this to the king, returned home' (VII.153). Despite
Nathan's reassuring words, David's son dies, which creates some inconsistency in the narrative (VII.154–5). Josephus' use of the verb 'prophesy' (προφητεύειν) underscores that it is Nathan's status as a prophet
that enables him to announce God's forgiveness.

Shemaiah

In an expansion of the deuteronomistic episode about Shishak's attack
on Jerusalem under Rehoboam, the Chronicler introduces a narration
about the repentance of the Judean leadership and about the favourable
response of the Lord (2 Chron 12.2–12). The Egyptian invasion is interpreted as the result of the people's infidelity to the law, and the prophet
Shemaiah emerges to deliver the talionic judgement in prophetic form:
'Thus says the Lord: You have abandoned me; likewise, I have abandoned you into the hand of Shishak' (12.5). On hearing this, the king
and the princes 'humble themselves' and acknowledge the Lord's righteousness, to which the Lord responds with a second oracle granted to
Shemaiah: 'They have humbled themselves. I will not destroy them, but I
will shortly grant them deliverance, and my wrath will not be poured out
on Jerusalem by the hand of Shishak. But they will become his servants,
so that they will learn [the difference between] serving me and serving
the kingdoms of the earth' (12.7–8). One may reasonably infer that the
prophet also delivered this oracle to the leaders.[92] Forgiveness language
is not employed, but the deity is clearly placated by the repentance of the

---

[91] 4Q398 14–17 ii 1–2; cf. Ecclus 47.11; CD v 6.
[92] S. Japhet, *I & II Chronicles: A Commentary*, Old Testament Library (London: SCM,
1993), p. 680.

rulers and therefore inhibits the punishment. Jerusalem's impending servitude is a pedagogical chastisement rather than an actual penalty.

Josephus' retelling of the episode further emphasizes the penitential actions, which he depicts as being performed by the Jerusalem crowd when faced with the threat of God, through the prophet Shemaiah, to abandon them (*Ant* VIII.256). Rehoboam and the people confess their sin and impiety, for which reason, Josephus says, 'God ... told the prophet that he would not destroy them; however he would subject them to the Egyptians, in order that they might learn whether it is less demanding to serve a human being than God' (VIII.257). The retelling stays close to the Chronicler's account; again it is repentance that induces God's favour, and enslavement to Egypt is for the sake of teaching the people a lesson rather than for punishment. Though not stated explicitly, their repentance seems to have resulted in God's forgiveness, which is announced to the prophet and presumably also communicated by him to the people.

Elijah

A similar course of events, but with a crucial point of difference, is narrated in the episode about Ahab and Elijah (1 Kgs 21.17–29). After the killing of Naboth, the word of the Lord comes to Eiljah, urging him to deliver an oracle of judgement against the king. As Ahab hears the oracle, he rends his clothes, puts on sackcloth and fasts, and the word of the Lord comes again to Elijah: 'since [Ahab] humbles himself before me, I will not bring evil in his days; in the days of his son I will bring evil upon his house' (21.29). Unlike Rehoboam's repentance, that of Ahab does not result in the cancellation of the punishment, but only in its postponement and transferral from Ahab to his son.

Josephus does not change this picture substantially, but adds to the biblical description of Ahab's repentance that the king confessed his sins. He also makes clear that the prophet announced God's altered verdict to the king, which the biblical episode does not say (*Ant* VIII.362). Still, Ahab's repentance works only to delay the punishment, not to annul it. The prophetic oracle delivered by Elijah is not, therefore, an announcement of forgiveness, either in the OT or in Josephus.

Huldah

Both the deuteronomistic history and the Chronicler designate Huldah as a 'prophetess' (2 Kgs 22.14/2 Chron 34.22). She appears in the narrative at the point where the Book of the Law has been rediscovered in the temple. Realizing that Israel and Judah have been unfaithful to the Lord, Josiah repents and sends emissaries to Huldah, to 'inquire of the Lord' concerning the king and the people. The prophetess responds that evil will befall Jerusalem, but Josiah will be spared since he has humbled himself before the Lord (2 Kgs 22.15–20/2 Chron 34.23–8).

Josephus rewrites the episode so that Huldah's role becomes analogous to that of Deborah, the only other character in the *Antiquities* to be called a 'prophetess' (προφῆτις, *Ant* V.200; X.59, 60). Josiah sends his embassy to Huldah not simply to ask God about the future of the people, but to make the prophetess 'propitiate God and attempt to make him benevolent' (ἰλάσκεσθαι τὸν θεὸν καὶ πειρᾶσθαι ποιεῖν εὐμενῆ, X.59). Here Josephus once again exhibits his tendency to introduce the notion of prophetic intercession.[93] The present passage is strongly evocative of the similar requests made to Deborah and Samuel, but the outcome this time is different. Rather than speaking reassuringly as Deborah and Samuel did, Huldah tells the emissaries that God has already made his decision, 'which no one would be able to cancel by prayers' (X.60). The content of this verdict is then given in a row of infinitives, which can be seen as representing the oracle which was delivered in direct speech by the prophetess:

> The deity had ... decided ... to destroy the people, to expel them from the land, and to deprive them of all good things of the present, since they had transgressed the laws without repenting for so long a time, although the prophets had both advised them to act sensibly in this matter and predicted the punishment for their impieties; a punishment which he would definitely inflict on them, in order that they might be convinced that he was God and had not lied in any of those things which he had announced to them through the prophets. Yet, since [Josiah] had become just, [God] would hold back the disasters for some time; but after his death he would send the decided sufferings upon the crowds.
>
> (Josephus *Ant* X.60–1)

Huldah refuses to intercede for the people and announces instead God's non-forgiveness, which makes the episode an inversion of the Deborah episode. The underlying logic may be that, unlike the king, the crowds

---

[93] C. T. Begg and P. Spilsbury, *Flavius Josephus: Translation and Commentary*, vol. v: *Flavius Josephus Judean Antiquities 8–10* (Leiden/Boston: Brill, 2005), p. 224.

have not repented in this case. And Josiah's repentance can only postpone the impending punishment.

Isaiah

Proclamations of forgiveness are also found in the Book of Isaiah. In
one of his prophecies about the future restoration of peaceful Jerusalem,
the prophet declares: 'No inhabitant will say, "I am ill"; the people who
dwell in her, their iniquity is forgiven (נְשֻׂא עָוֹן).' (Isa 33.24). Somewhat
later in the prophetic book, the time of fulfilment for this expectation
seems to have come: 'Speak to the heart of Jerusalem, cry to her, that her
service is completed, that her iniquity has been paid for (נרצה עונה), that
she has received from the Lord's hand a double amount for all her sins'
(40.2). It is not clear to whom the commission to proclaim forgiveness is
directed. Here the LXX explicates: 'Priests (ἱερεῖς), speak to the heart
of Jerusalem, comfort her, for her humiliation is completed, her sin has
been forgiven (λέλυται αὐτῆς ἡ ἁμαρτία); for she has received from
the Lord's hand a double amount for her sins' (40.2 LXX). The Greek
translation introduces a reference to priestly declarations of forgiveness.
This declaration does not take place within the cult, but the priests seem
to function as prophets.[94]

Mark 2.1–12 in relation to prophetic typology

From the foregoing survey of the relationship between prophets and the
bestowal, mediation or pronouncement of forgiveness in early Jewish
texts, it can be concluded that the portrayal of Jesus in Mark 2.5 is not
without parallels. This holds true regardless of whether God or Jesus is
taken to be the implied agent of the passive verb in 2.5b.

If, as Sanders holds, 'Your sins are [being] forgiven' is a so-called divine passive, equivalent of 'God forgives your sins', there are numerous
antecedents in biblical and early Jewish literature.[95] True prophets know
when God forgives, is reconciled, takes pity, and so on; and they are
entitled to communicate this to others, as Deborah, Nathan, Shemaiah,
(Second) Isaiah and perhaps also Moses did. It is true that the exact formula 'Your sins are [being] forgiven' is not found on the lips of a prophet

---

[94] J. Ziegler, *Untersuchungen zur Septuaginta des Buches Isaias* (Münster:
Aschendorffsche Verlagsbuchhandlung, 1934), p. 71.
[95] E. P. Sanders, *The Historical Figure of Jesus* (London: Allen Lane, 1993), pp.
213–14.

or other human being in the literature.[96] Still there is no obvious reason why this expression should have been perceived as more presumptuous than any of those collated in this chapter.

On the other hand, if 'Your sins are [being] forgiven' is taken to mean 'I forgive your sins', this implies that Jesus himself is the subject of forgiveness.[97] I have sought to establish that, contrary to what has commonly been asserted, the notion that a human being can 'forgive sins' is not completely foreign to early Judaism. Josephus' retelling of the Samuel narrative implies the expectation that the prophet is able to 'forgive' a sin in the sense of mediating God's forgiveness – analogously to the way in which 'to bless' is commonly used in the sense of mediating God's blessing (e.g. Num 6.22–7). In the light of *Ant* VI.92, I find it plausible that the *Prayer of Nabonidus* predicates forgiveness of another prophet, that is, to Daniel, although the text is too fragmentary for any argument to depend on it. The evidence from Josephus, even if it should be unique, suffices to invalidate the prevalent opinion that early Jewish literature contains no reference to a human being who 'forgives sins'.

According to either understanding of Mark 2.5b, it is likely that such a pronouncement would have been heard as an implicit claim that the speaker was a prophet, that is, God's mouthpiece. Not all prophets had 'forgiven sins' or announced forgiveness, but those human beings who were thought to have done so were prophets. If Jesus indeed made such a declaration of forgiveness, it is not likely that any subsequent controversy would have concerned the allegedly blasphemous nature of this pronouncement. No such polemic surrounds the literary analogies reviewed above. In his judicious treatment of the issue, Sanders comments that a wicked person who claimed for himself the status of a prophet might conceivably have been accused of blasphemy, but 'there is no sign that Jesus was himself openly wicked'.[98] To Sanders' observation that none of the 'false prophets' of first-century Judaism seems to have been labelled a blasphemer can be added yet another reminder of the case of John the Baptist, whose prophetic self-allegations were doubted and criticized, but which apparently never induced the charge of blasphemy.

Sanders' final remark in *Jewish Law from Jesus to the Mishnah* on the issue of blasphemy in Mark 2.1–12 is worth quoting in full, since it encapsulates several crucial insights:

---

[96] A. Y. Collins, *Mark: A Commentary* (Minneapolis: Fortress, 2007), p. 185.
[97] Hofius, 'Jesu Zuspruch der Sündenvergebung', pp. 131–9.
[98] Sanders, *Jewish Law*, p. 63.

As far as I can see, the best case that can be made for connecting Jesus' statement 'your sins are forgiven' with blasphemy is presumption – not the presumption of forgiving sins in place of God (the text does not say that), nor the presumption of discussing forgiveness even though not accredited (the priesthood did not exercise that kind of control). One might find blasphemous presumption in Jesus' saying that God forgave a man who was not known to have confessed and made restitution. The case for blasphemy, however, is extremely weak (even if one were to have no doubts at all about the pericope).[99]

Sanders' conclusion that the connection between Mark 2.5b and blasphemy is 'extremely weak' is essentially accurate. He also appears to be correct in proposing that if anything was very controversial or indeed blasphemous about this pronouncement of forgiveness, it was Jesus' neglect of customary penitential practices as a prerequisite for obtaining forgiveness.[100] Only his assertion that the text does not depict Jesus as presuming to forgive sins in place of God has to be questioned: the charge of blasphemy in 2.7 is motivated unequivocally by the view that Jesus attempts to do what only God can do. The text seems to be saying something that does not fit with early Judaism according to early Jewish sources.

At the present stage of knowledge about early Judaism, then, the scribal reaction as recorded in 2.6–7 is historically implausible. Jesus' announcement in 2.5b could have instigated the criticism that he had made a false claim that he was a prophet, or that he had disregarded the necessity of repentance as commonly understood, but it could hardly have prompted the accusation that he had blasphemed by infringing a divine prerogative. Moreover, Jesus' counter-argument in 2.8–10 culminates in a stronger claim about his personal authority to forgive sins, but there is no indication of any continued conflict following the 'Son of Man' saying. This abrupt end to the controversy, which serves to corroborate the historical implausibility of the scenario, will now come to the fore in the third part of the chapter.

---

[99] *Ibid.*, p. 63. See also Casey, *The Solution to the 'Son of Man' Problem*, p. 157.

[100] Hägerland, 'Jesus and the Rites of Repentance', 166–87. T. Holmén, 'Jesus and Magic: Theodicean Perspectives to the Issue', in M. Labahn and B. J. Lietaert Peerbolte (eds.), *A Kind of Magic: Understanding Magic in the New Testament and Its Religious Environment*, LNTS 306 (London: T & T Clark, 2007), pp. 43–56 (pp. 53–5), suggests that this neglect may have invited accusations that Jesus was dealing in magic.

Angelic forgiveness

Few scholars have given due attention to the third typology relevant for the purpose of this chapter, namely the concept of angelic mediation of forgiveness. An exception is provided by Berger, who in 1977 claimed that this was 'the only analogy to texts in which Jesus grants the forgiveness of sins to individual human beings'.[101] While hesitant to see these concepts as fully analogous, Ulrich Kellermann added some further references to the notion that heavenly messengers could mediate divine forgiveness (1993).[102] Despite the scholarly interest in early Jewish and Christian angelomorphism in recent years, this concept has not been considered anew as a possible background of the synoptic forgiveness episodes. This part of the chapter seeks to fill the gap.

Angelic mediation of forgiveness

A manifold relationship exists in early Judaism between human sinfulness on the one hand and angels on the other. The scenario ranges from the evil angels, who actively bring about sin,[103] via the mediatory function of recording and reporting any sins committed,[104] to the positive angelic roles of undoing sin by praying for those who have committed it[105] and by purifying the earth from it (*1 En* 10.20). In a few passages, angels are portrayed as bestowing or announcing forgiveness.

The Angel of the Lord forgives sins

Two passages within the Hebrew OT may predicate forgiveness terminology of the Angel of the Lord. Since the OT does not maintain a clearcut distinction between God and the Angel of the Lord (e.g. Exod 3.1–6), it is quite comprehensible that the divine function of forgiving sins may also be attributed to the Angel.

Exod 23.20–1. God concludes the giving of the Covenant Code by promising the continuous presence of his angel: 'I am sending an angel in

---

[101] K. Berger, 'Almosen für Israel: Zum historischen Kontext der paulinischen Kollekte', *NTS* 23 (1977), 180–204 (188, my translation).

[102] Kellermann, 'Wer kann Sünden vergeben außer Elia?', pp. 166–7. Among the passages noted by Kellermann are Isa 6.7; Zech 3.4; *Jub* 41.24, which will be considered below.

[103] *1 En* 9.6; 12.4; 16.3; *Jub* 10.3–11; 12.20; 15.31; cf. 4Q213a 1 i 17; 11Q5 xix 15.

[104] *1 En* 99.3; *Jub* 4.6; cf. *SibOr* 2.214–19; *TAbr* [B] 10.7–8.

[105] *1 En* 15.2; *LAB* 15.5; cf. *1 En* 40.6; *ApocMos* 33.5; 35.2; *TAbr* [A] 14.5–6, 10–15; *TLevi* 3.5–6.

front of you to protect you on the way and to bring you to the place I have prepared. Behave yourself in his presence and obey his voice. Do not provoke him, for he will not forgive your [pl.] transgression (לֹא יִשָּׂא לְפִשְׁעֲכֶם). For my name is in him' (Exod 23.20–1). As the Angel of the Lord is here said *not* to forgive the people's transgression, one could infer that, in principle, this angel has authority to do so.[106]

Alan Segal has drawn attention to a Talmudic text apparently directed against such a reading of Exod 23.21. In *bSanh* 38b, a R. Idi success-fully debates with a 'heretic' or 'schismatic' (מִין), who holds that the Angel of the Lord should be worshipped as an independent deity. The villain points to the fact that it is written of this angel that 'he will not forgive your transgression'. Segal correlates this rabbinic datum with the Markan Jesus' claim to have the authority to forgive sins and he thinks that the interlocutor of R. Idi might have been a Christian.[107] While this does not reveal how Exod 23.21 was interpreted prior to the third century CE, it is noteworthy that the LXX translator rewrote the crucial clause as 'for he will not shrink before you' (οὐ γὰρ μὴ ὑποστείληταί σε), perhaps in order to avoid the inference that the angel is a separate divine being.[108] By contrast, the Targums agree with the MT in predicating for-giveness terminology of the angel.

Zech 3.4. In the Book of Zechariah, the prophet has a vision, in which he sees Joshua the high priest standing accused by Satan before the Angel of the Lord. Joshua is dressed in dirty clothes, but at the angel's command he is undressed and clothed in attire that befits his ministry. In conjunction with this, the Angel of the Lord addresses Joshua directly: 'He said to him, 'Look, I have taken away your iniquity from you (הֶעֱבַרְתִּי מֵעָלֶיךָ עֲוֹנֶךָ), and I will dress you in solemn apparel' (Zech 3.4). As noted above, the verb עבר hiph. with a term for 'sin' as the direct object is ambiguous: it sometimes implies forgiveness, but at other times this interpretation is out of the question (cf. Esth 8.3; Jer 11.15). The LXX translator opted for the Greek verb ἀφαιρεῖν, the import of which is also uncertain. It is therefore not clear whether or not the angel's statement

---

[106] H. Ausloos, 'The "Angel of YHWH" in Exod. xxiii 20–33 and Judg. ii 1–5: A Clue to the "Deuteronom(ist)ic Puzzle?"', *VT* 58 (2008), 1–12 (9–10); C. von Heijne, *The Messenger of the Lord in Early Jewish Interpretations of Genesis* (Uppsala universitet, 2008), p. 109.

[107] A. F. Segal, *Two Powers in Heaven: Early Rabbinic Reports about Christianity and Gnosticism* (Leiden: Brill, 1977), pp. 68–73. See also J. E. Fossum, *The Name of God and the Angel of the Lord: Samaritan and Jewish Concepts of Intermediation and the Origin of Gnosticism*, WUNT 36 (Tübingen: Mohr Siebeck, 1985), pp. 307–8.

[108] J. W. Wevers, *Notes on the Greek Text of Exodus*, SBLCS 30 (Atlanta: Scholars, 1990), p. 370.

'I have taken away your iniquities' can be construed as equal to 'I have forgiven your sins'.

Angels who announce forgiveness

There are two or three passages in which angels announce, through passive formulae, that sins are forgiven. In this context it may be appropriate to mention the notion of a heavenly messenger, who appears in order to announce the completion and acceptance of repentance, as found in Dan 4.34 LXX and in *JosAsen* 15.2–10.[109] Aseneth is visited, upon her penitential prayer, by 'a man from heaven' (*JosAsen* 14.3) who is likely to be identified as Michael (cf. 14.8). The messenger tells Aseneth to do away with all signs of sorrowful repentance (14.12) and then announces that he has heard and seen her penitence and that her name is now written in the book of the living (15.2–4).

The passages which will now be considered display the same basic structure. A confession of sin prompts an angelic word of reassurance; in the following passages, the angel's announcement explicitly mentions forgiveness.

Isa 6.5–7. On seeing the enthroned Lord surrounded by the seraphim, who praise his holiness and glory, Isaiah confesses that he is a 'man of impure lips' who cannot endure the vision of the Lord (Isa 6.5). Analogous to the undressing of Joshua's filthy clothing in Zech 3.4, Isaiah is purified through a symbolic action by one of the angelic beings: 'One of the seraphim flew towards me, and took in his hand, with a pair of tongs, a glowing coal from the altar. He made it touch my mouth and said, "This has touched your lips; your iniquity departs and your sin is forgiven (וְסָר עֲוֺנֶךָ וְחַטָּאתְךָ תְּכֻפָּר)"' (Isa 6.6–7). The seraph thus announces forgiveness to the prophet, and the touching with a glowing coal accompanies this announcement as a symbol consistent with Isaiah's lament over his impure lips. However, in the LXX, the coal itself is depicted as removing the prophet's sin: 'it will take away your iniquities, and your sins it will clean away' (ἀφελεῖ τὰς ἀνομίας σου καὶ τὰς ἁμαρτίας σου περικαθαριεῖ, Isa 6.7 LXX).

Jub 41.24. The retelling of the episode about Judah and Tamar (Gen 38.1–26) in *Jubilees* 41 expounds the biblical account by clearly condemning Judah's immorality and by narrating his repentance through lamentation and prayer. As a result of his penitence, angels appear to Judah with an announcement of forgiveness: 'We told him in a dream

---

[109] Berger, 'Almosen für Israel', 187–8.

that it would be forgiven for him (ይሰረይ ፡ ሎቱ), since he pleaded much and since he mourned and did not do it again' (*Jub* 41.24). It is impossible to determine the precise temporal meaning of the Ethiopic imperfect used to express the action of being forgiven. The verbal form could refer either to the future or to the present; the Ethiopic version of Matt 9.2 employs an imperfect (ይትኀደጉ) to represent the Greek aoristic present 'are (herewith) forgiven' (ἀφίενται).[110] This ambiguity would have been inherent in the Hebrew original of *Jubilees*. Whether an assurance that God will ultimately forgive Judah's sin, or a performative statement with immediate impact, the passage definitely attests to the notion that angels possess and mediate the knowledge of God's readiness to forgive.

TAbr [A] 14.14. Less conspicuous is the reference to the voice from heaven that announces forgiveness to Abraham in the longer recension of the *Testament of Abraham*. Here Michael and Abraham pray together for the forgiveness of the sin of the patriarch: 'As they begged for a long while, a voice came from heaven saying, "Abraham, Abraham! The Lord has heard your prayer and the sin is (being) forgiven for you (ἀφίεταί σοι ἡ ἁμαρτία)..."' (*TAbr* [A] 14.13–14). The source of the heavenly voice is not specified, but the reference to the Lord in the third person could justify an interpretation of the utterance as angelic rather than divine. The voice then switches to the first person, in conformity with the tendency pointed out above to merge God's voice with that of the Angel of the Lord.

Mark 2.1–12 in relation to angelic typology

The preceding review of pertinent passages indicates that Berger was correct to see the notion of angelic forgiveness as analogous to the synoptic portrayal of Jesus as one who forgives sins. Not only are there OT and early Jewish texts that depict angels as announcing God's forgiveness in a manner consonant with the 'divine passive' construal of Mark 2.5b (Isa 6.7; *Jub* 41.24; *TAbr* [A] 14.14?); there are also passages in which the Angel of the Lord may be the grammatical subject of forgiveness, along the lines of Mark 2.10 (Exod 23.21; Zech 3.4?). I will make

---

[110] On the aoristic present, see BDR, § 320. The Syriac Chronicle actually has the perfect ܐܫܬܒܩ to represent either the Greek *Vorlage* of ይሰረይ or the underlying original Hebrew. One should take into account, however, that the Syriac rendition is rather liberal, at times amounting to paraphrase. Thus, in the present passage, the angelic narrator's absence from the Chronicle results in the impersonal wording 'it was told to him' in place of the Ethiopic 'we told him' (see J. C. VanderKam, *The Book of Jubilees*, CSCO 511 (Leuven: Peeters, 1989), p. 275). Further, the Syriac represents the announcement of forgiveness as direct speech, 'it has been forgiven *for you* (ܠܟ)'.

a case that 2.1–12 does express a christology influenced by angelology, largely concentrated in 2.10. This will have to be argued at some length, and only after this will it be possible to consider the implications for the historical assessment of this episode.

Angelomorphic christology in Mark 2.10

Charles Gieschen defines 'angelomorphic christology' as 'the identification of Christ with angelic form and functions ... whether or not he is specifically identified as an angel'.[111] Some scholars have identified the characterization of Jesus in the transfiguration episode (Mark 9.2–8) as clearly angelomorphic.[112] Gieschen acknowledges the portrayal of the Son of Man as an angelomorphic being in three Markan passages.[113] And, most importantly for the present purposes, Fletcher-Louis construes Luke 5.24 as angelomorphic, in line with his overall interpretation of the Lukan 'Son of Man' sayings.[114] A closer look at two key concepts in Mark 2.10 – 'authority on earth' and 'the Son of Man' – will lend support to Fletcher-Louis' construal, which holds true for the saying also in its Markan form and context.

Authority on earth. The saying in Mark 2.10 has a strong Danielic flavour: not only is the Son of Man concept indebted to creative interpretation of the 'one like a son of man' (Dan 7.13), but the entire phrasing of 2.10 strongly echoes Dan 4.14, 'so that those who live may know that the Most High has authority over the kingdom of human beings'. Especially noteworthy are the resemblances between the Greek versions of Dan 4.14 on the one hand, and Mark 2.10 on the other. The syntactical structure of Mark's final clause 'but so that you may know that' (ἵνα δὲ εἰδῆτε ὅτι) corresponds to Theodotion's 'so that those who live may know that' (ἵνα γνῶσιν οἱ ζῶντες ὅτι, 4.17 Theod.), while 'has authority' (ἐξουσίαν ἔχει) and 'on earth' (ἐπὶ τῆς γῆς) is closer to the LXX (ἐξουσίαν ἔχειν ... τῶν ἐπὶ τῆς γῆς, 4.17 LXX; cf. 4.27, 31 LXX). This is not to say that 2.10 utilizes both these Greek versions of Daniel, or indeed any one of them, but it demonstrates that the saying in Mark actually echoes Dan

---

[111] C. A. Gieschen, *Angelomorphic Christology: Antecedents and Early Evidence,* AGJU 42 (Leiden: Brill, 1998), p. 28.

[112] C. Rowland, 'A Man Clothed in Linen: Daniel 10.6ff. and Jewish Angelology', *JSNT* 24 (1985), 99–110 (100); K. P. Sullivan, *Wrestling with Angels: A Study of the Relationship between Angels and Humans in Ancient Jewish Literature and the New Testament,* AGJU 55 (Leiden: Brill, 2004), pp. 114–16.

[113] Mark 8.38; 13.27; 14.62. See Gieschen, *Angelomorphic Christology,* p. 256.

[114] C. H. T. Fletcher-Louis, *Luke-Acts: Angels, Christology and Soteriology,* WUNT 2:94 (Tübingen: Mohr Siebeck, 1997), p. 238.

4.14 more clearly than a direct comparison with the Aramaic might indicate.[115] The passage in Daniel speaks about God's sovereign authority on earth; in Mark 2.10, part of this authority is ascribed to Jesus as the Son of Man. An antecedent for such a relocation of authority is the early Jewish notion of God delegating his authority, especially over earthly matters, to angels.

The Book of the Watchers affirms, in agreement with Dan 4.14, that 'authority (ἐξουσία/ᖺᐊᑊ) over everything' belongs to the Lord (*1 En* 9.5); but it also acknowledges that God has granted to Shemihazah 'authority (ἐξουσία/ᖺᐊᑊ) to rule over those who are together with him' (9.7). *Jubilees* presupposes two types of authority given to angels. On the one hand, the book states that the angels who had been sent to earth by God were expelled 'from all their authority' (ᖺᐊᑊ) as a result of their transgression.[116] This is evidently a reference to an authority which should be exercised for the benefit of human beings. On the other hand, authority to deceive people has also been granted to spirits and angels. Mastema, the diabolic commander-in-chief, exercises a divinely sanctioned 'authority' (ᖺᐊᑊ, *Jub* 10.8) to destroy and lead astray together with his band of spirits, who are specifically said to 'rule (ᑊᐁᑊ) before Satan *on earth* (ᑊᐁ : ᒣᑅᐄ)' (10.11).[117] As Abram turns from idolatry to monotheism, he prays that God would save him 'from the evil spirits who exercise authority (ᑊᐁᑊ) over the thoughts of people's hearts' (12.20). And, most importantly, the angelic narrator speaks of Israel's special status:

> For there are many peoples and many nations, and all are his, and over all he authorized spirits, so that he might lead them astray from following him. But over Israel he did not authorize (ᑊᑊᑊ) any angel or spirit. For he alone is their ruler, and he will guard them and demand them from his angels and from his spirits and from everyone and all his powers, so that he may guard them and bless them, and they may be his and he may be theirs from now and to all eternity.
>
> (*Jub* 15.31–2)

[115] A. Feuillet, 'L'*exousia* du Fils de l'homme', *RSR* 42 (1954), 161–92 (172–3); J. Kiilunen, *Die Vollmacht im Widerstreit: Untersuchungen zum Werdegang von Mk 2,1–3,6*, AASFDHL 40 (Helsinki: Suomalainen Tiedeakatemia, 1985), pp. 118–19.

[116] *Jub* 5.6; cf. *LAB* 34.3 (*quia transgressi sunt, factum est ut angeli in potestate non essent*).

[117] *Jub* 10.11; cf. *1 En* 9.6; 10.20 (of Michael); 12.4 (in the Ethiopic text); 15.8, 10; 64.2.

The notion of God 'authorizing' (שלט) evil spirits over human beings was also current in Qumran. Other early Jewish and Christian literature perpetuates various conceptions of diabolic authority.[118] Angels of good standing are also portrayed as invested with authority over different spheres, things and functions of the heavenly administration.[119] To be sure, not only angels are held to have authority on earth. Adam, and through him all humanity, was given authority over all that is on earth.[120] Earthly kings and rulers exercise authority.[121] And, according to the Epistle of Enoch, the righteous will eventually be given authority over sinners (*1 En* 96.1).

Even so, there is no evident link between the forgiveness of sins and, for example, Adam.[122] What speaks in favour of seeing angelology rather than any of the other typologies as the backdrop of Mark 2.10 is not simply the concept of 'authority on earth', but also its juxtaposition with the theme of forgiveness and with the 'Son of Man'.

The Son of Man. In accordance with the customary division of the 'Son of Man' sayings into three categories of the present, the suffering and the future Son of Man, Mark 2.10 belongs to the group of 'present' sayings. But this category is a mixed bag of widely disparate sayings, held together only by their common use of the present tense or its equivalent (cf. 2.10, 28 with Q 9.58). A more useful approach for the present purpose will be to follow Vermes in grouping the material into Danielic and non-Danielic sayings, depending on each saying's affinity with the motif of the one 'like a son of man' in Daniel 7.[123] Vermes should not be followed, however, in his opinion that Mark 2.10 is a non-Danielic saying that employs the expression 'son of man' as the equivalent of a first person singular pronoun.[124] Nor is Maurice Casey's proposal, that 'son of man' here functions as an indefinite pronoun, convincing.[125] On the contrary, the influence of Daniel 7 on Mark 2.10 seems undeniable.

---

[118] 4Q213a 1 i 17; 11Q5 xix 15; *TJob* 8.2–3; 16.2, 4; 20.3; Luke 4.6; *Barn* 2.1; 4.13.

[119] *3 Bar* 12.3; *TAbr* [A] 9.8; 13.11; Rev 14.18; 18.1; *Herm Man* 4.3.5; *Sim* 8.3.3, 5; 10.1.3.

[120] *Jub* 2.14; *Herm Man* 12.4.2; cf. Gen 1.28. See also J. Marcus, 'Son of Man as Son of Adam', *RB* 110 (2003), 38–61 (59–60).

[121] *EpArist* 206, 253; *TAbr* [A] 2.11; cf. *TJud* 21.2–4.

[122] *Pace* J. Marcus, 'Son of Man as Son of Adam: Part II: Exegesis', *RB* 110 (2003), 370–86 (371–4).

[123] Vermes, *Jesus the Jew*, pp. 177–86.

[124] *Ibid.*, p. 180.

[125] M. Casey, *Son of Man: The Interpretation and Influence of Daniel 7* (London: SPCK, 1979), pp. 159–61, 228–9.

As sayings about the authority of the Son of Man, 2.10 and 2.28 belong closely together in structure, content and intertextual relationship with the Book of Daniel. The connection between these two sayings in the Markan narrative is signalled through the adverbial 'also' in the second saying: 'the Son of Man is lord also (καί) of the Sabbath' (2.28).[126] The two expressions 'to have authority' (ἐξουσίαν ἔχειν) and 'to be lord' (κύριον εἶναι) are interchangeable, as can be seen both from the fact that they are employed to render the Aramaic שליט in the Greek versions of Dan 4.14 and from their juxtaposition in literature originally composed in Greek.[127] Both sayings thus assign a sphere of authority or lordship to the Son of Man, and they do so under the influence of Dan 4.14. It is also difficult to avoid the impression that the collocation of 'the Son of Man' and 'authority' in Mark 2.10 has been inspired by the depiction of the one 'like a son of man', to whom was given 'authority' in Dan 7.14.

The identity of Daniel's one 'like a son of man' is under discussion.[128] Several interpreters have contributed towards the good case for construing the figure as an angel, probably Michael.[129] More importantly, pre-135 CE Jewish texts identify the one 'like a son of man' as the Messiah.[130] While foreign to the Book of Daniel, this identification was most likely prompted by the association of 'kingship' with this humanlike figure. In the Book of Parables, the figure subsequently referred to as 'that son of

---

[126] Cf. B. Schaller, *Fundamenta Judaica: Studien zum antiken Judentum und zum Neuen Testament*, SUNT 25 (Göttingen: Vandenhoeck & Ruprecht, 2001), p. 139 n. 58, who interprets Mark 2.28 in the light of the preceding verse to mean 'the Son of Man is lord [not only of the works of creation but] also of the Sabbath'. Besides neglecting the strong parallelism between 2.10 and 2.28 (see Kiilunen, *Die Vollmacht im Widerstreit*, pp. 197–8), this places too much weight on the linking between 2.27 and 2.28, which appears artificial and is almost certainly secondary. Recognizing the latter point, and noting the absence of a parallel to 2.27 in both Matthew and Luke, scholars have suggested that a shorter parallel tradition existed (S.-O. Back, *Jesus of Nazareth and the Sabbath Commandment* (Åbo Akademi University Press, 1995), pp. 73–7) or that 2.27 belongs to a Markan redactional layer unknown to the two other synoptic evangelists (Burkett, *From Proto-Mark to Mark*, pp. 232–3).

[127] Dan 4.17 LXX; Dan 4.17 Theod.; *EpArist* 253; cf. *Herm Man* 12.4.2–3; *Sim* 9.23.4; 9.28.8.

[128] See J. A. Fitzmyer, *The One Who Is to Come* (Grand Rapids, MI: Eerdmans, 2007), pp. 58–9.

[129] N. Schmidt, 'The Son of Man in the Book of Daniel', *JBL* 19 (1900), 22–8; J. J. Collins, 'The Son of Man and the Saints of the Most High in the Book of Daniel', *JBL* 93 (1974), 50–66; C. Rowland, *The Open Heaven: A Study of Apocalyptic in Judaism and Early Christianity* (London: SPCK, 1982), pp. 178–83; H. Sahlin, 'Wie wurde ursprünglich die Benennung "Der Menschensohn" verstanden?', *ST* 37 (1983), 147–79.

[130] 2 Esd 13.32 (cf. 7.29); *1 En* 48.10; 52.4. Cf. the tradition attributed to R. Aqiba in *bHag* 14a; *bSanh* 38b.

man' is introduced as 'another one, whose face was like the appearance of a man, and full of grace was his face, like one of the holy angels' (*1 En* 46.1–2). Angelomorphism is here explicit, but it also occurs in a more subtle fashion: 'All these things, which you have seen, are for the authority (ᎮᏁᎋ᎗) of his Messiah, so that he may be in command and have power on earth (ᎎ᎖ : ᎖ᎧᎺᎺ : ᎎ᎖᎗Ꭸᎋ : ᎚Ꮂ : ᎎ᎗ᎂ)' (52.4). The authority of the Messiah Son of Man doubtless echoes Dan 7.14, but the Book of Parables emphasizes his angelomorphic character by attributing authority 'on earth' to him.

The Book of Parables is now regularly considered an expression of early Judaism, to be dated in the first century or even earlier.[131] Only in Matthew do the 'Son of Man' sayings betray direct influence from the Book of Parables, but, due to a shared background in early Judaism, there are several characteristics common to the Enochic and synoptic manifestations of the messianic Son of Man, even apart from Matthew.[132] One of these is angelomorphism, which can be detected in two of the three Markan 'Son of Man' sayings that are unambiguously Danielic (the third saying, Mark 14.62, neither excludes nor suggests an interpretation in angelomorphic categories). In the first of these, the Son of Man 'will come in his Father's glory with the holy angels' (Mark 8.38), that is, as the commander-in-chief of the angelic host to perform the function traditionally reserved for Michael.[133] In the second passage this is even more explicit: 'Then they will see the Son of Man coming in clouds with great power (μετὰ δυνάμεως πολλῆς) and glory, and then he will send out the angels and gather his chosen ones from the four winds, from the limit of the earth to the limit of heaven' (13.26–7). Just as the expressions 'the Son of Man coming in clouds' and 'glory' quote Dan 7.13–14 only with slight alterations, the 'great power' has been thought to represent the 'authority' mentioned in Daniel.[134] But another interpretation is preferable. While neither the Old Greek nor Theodotion's Daniel employ 'power' (δύναμις) to render the Aramaic 'authority' (שׁלטן), they both frequently use the word to denote heavenly and earthly armies.[135] In view of the

---

[131] D. W. Suter, 'Enoch in Sheol: Updating the Dating of the Book of Parables', in G. Boccaccini (ed.), *Enoch and the Messiah Son of Man: Revisiting the Book of Parables* (Grand Rapids, MI: Eerdmans, 2007), pp. 415–43.

[132] L. W. Walck, 'The Son of Man in the Parables of Enoch and the Gospels', in Boccaccini (ed.), *Enoch and the Messiah Son of Man*, pp. 299–337.

[133] D. D. Hannah, *Michael and Christ: Michael Traditions and Angel Christology in Early Christianity*, WUNT 2:109 (Tübingen: Mohr Siebeck, 1999), pp. 38–40.

[134] Casey, *Son of Man*, p. 165.

[135] Dan 4.32; 8.10, 13; cf. 3.61 (all with reference to the heavenly host(s)); 6.24 LXX; 11.7; 11.10 Theod.; 11.13; 11.25–6*ter* Theod. (with reference to earthly armies).

immediately preceding reference to the 'powers (δυνάμεις) in heaven' (Mark 13.25), the 'great power' of 13.26 is probably to be construed as the 'numerous force' commanded by the archangel-like Son of Man (cf. 2 Thess 1.7). He then exercises his function as commander-in-chief by sending out the angels and supervising the gathering of the elect on behalf of the deity. This is the most obvious evidence for the angelomorphic character of some of the Son of Man sayings.

Let me bring this part of the argument to a conclusion. Mark 2.10 and 2.28 both belong to the Danielic type of 'Son of Man' sayings, which sometimes exhibit affinities with the angelomorphic portrayal of the Enochic Son of Man. They both associate the Son of Man with authority, a theme drawn ultimately from the Book of Daniel, but also a frequent notion in early Jewish angelology. In 2.10 further links to the angels can be seen in the qualification 'on earth' and in the forgiveness theme. Similarly, Jesus' authority over the Sabbath in 2.28 can be seen as a feature of his angelomorphic character, for *Jubilees*, which expresses the notion of angelic mediation of divine forgiveness (*Jub* 41.24), also portrays the Angel of the Presence as entrusted with the responsibility of mediating the Sabbath commandment and its *halakhah* to Israel (50.1–13). Thus, while each of the individual elements of 2.10 could be interpreted in other directions, their simultaneous presence serves to build up a cumulative argument for the characterization of this christology as angelomorphic. Jesus, the angel-like Messiah, has been authorized to forgive sins.

Implications for the historicity of Mark 2.10

As indicated earlier, the implications of this interpretation for the historicity of Mark 2.10 are thoroughly negative. This is not because it would be *a priori* impossible for a first-century Jew to harbour and to express a conviction of himself as angelomorphic or as angelic – albeit to my knowledge there is no evidence that such a claim was made by, or for, any living Jewish person of this period – but because the logic of the narrative is historically implausible. Additionally, as will be shown in Chapter 5, the claim is incoherent with the larger critical picture of the historical Jesus.

Mark 2.10 is so deeply embedded in its context that it cannot conceivably have originated and been transmitted as an isolated logion.[136] It is

---

[136] Lindars, *Jesus Son of Man*, p. 44; *pace* Gnilka, 'Das Elend', p. 205.

rather the climax of Jesus' argument throughout 2.8–10 and, as such, it must be viewed as a response to the charge of blasphemy in 2.7 which, as already shown, is prompted by the ambiguous forgiveness statement in 2.5. According to the logic of the narrative, then, Jesus counters an accusation of blasphemy with an unequivocal restatement of his right to do what the scribes considered blasphemous; the warrant for this claim is the healing of the paralytic. No further reaction of the scribes is reported. But this is a historically implausible scenario, for 2.8–10 in no way removes the opponents' grounds for thinking that Jesus has blasphemed; on the contrary, the argument affirms that the scribal interpretation of the statement in 2.5 was correct.[137] To this affirmation, 2.10 adds the further claim that Jesus is the angelomorphic Messiah, invested with an authority directly derived from God's own authority as expressed by Dan 4.14. If an accusation of blasphemy should be expected in the episode, its natural location would be after 2.10.

Conclusion

The search for early Jewish analogies to the forgiveness sayings in Mark 2.1–12 has enabled the following conclusions to be drawn.

First of all, the alleged analogies from early Jewish understandings of the (high) priesthood forwarded by some previous scholarship cannot explain the conflict narrated in 2.6–10. There is no compelling evidence that priests proclaimed the forgiveness of sins or that the high priest could claim an authority to forgive sins, nor is there the slightest indication in the Markan episode that questions concerning the temple and the priesthood are an issue.

Secondly, the scribal accusation of blasphemy in 2.6–7 is historically implausible, regardless of whether the implied agent of the passive formula in 2.5b is taken to be God or Jesus. In the light of analogous pronouncements of reconciliation ascribed to prophets in the literature (Isa 33.24; 40.2; *LAB* 30.7; Josephus, *Ant* III.24?; VII.153; VIII.257), and the passage(s) predicating forgiveness of a prophet (*Ant* VI.92; 4Q242 1–3 4?), the formula would have been heard as a claim to be a prophet more readily than as a blasphemous encroachment on the prerogatives of God.

Thirdly, modelled on Dan 4.14 and drawing on early Jewish angelology, the saying in 2.10 is strongly christological. It portrays Jesus as

---

[137] *Pace* D. Rhoads, J. Dewey and D. Michie, *Mark as Story: An Introduction to the Narrative of a Gospel*, 2nd edn (Minneapolis: Fortress, 1999), p. 88.

the angelomorphic Messiah Son of Man who has been granted authority by God to forgive sins. Early Judaism acknowledges angels as mediators of God's forgiveness (Isa 6.7; *Jub* 41.24; *TAbr* [A] 14.14) and may even predicate forgiveness of the Angel of the Lord (Exod 23.21; Zech 3.4?). It is implausible that the scribes, who purportedly heard Mark 2.5b as blasphemous, would not have reacted even more strongly to this amplification of the first saying.

5

FORGIVENESS IN THE MISSION
OF THE HISTORICAL JESUS

The preceding chapters have brought this investigation to a point where it seems reasonable to surmise that the forgiveness sayings in Mark 2.5b and Luke 7.47a come from the historical Jesus, while the controversy in Mark 2.6–10 probably does not. In the present chapter, the argument will be bolstered by an appeal to the criteria of coherence and incoherence. There are, as we shall see, distinctive traits in a plausible overall reconstruction of the career of the historical Jesus, with which the announcement of forgiveness in Mark 2.5b and Luke 7.47a, so to speak, fit particularly well; conversely, there is tension between Mark 2.6–10 and an overall picture of the historical Jesus. In addition to *authenticating* the historicity of the sayings, I will also make an attempt at *interpreting* them within the larger framework of Jesus' deeds and sayings.

I have singled out two prominent aspects of the mission of Jesus with which, as will be shown, Mark 2.5b and Luke 7.47a are positively coherent: his activity as a healer, and his identity (as expressed by himself and acknowledged by others) as a prophet. These two aspects are rarely questioned in historical Jesus research and have even been dubbed the two 'bedrock facts' about Jesus.[1] They are also suggested by the narrative contexts of the forgiveness sayings and, to some extent, by their parallels in early Jewish texts. Mark 2.1–12 portrays Jesus as announcing forgiveness as part of a miraculous healing, and Luke 7.36–47 endows him with prophetic characteristics. The phenomenon of prophetic forgiveness in early Judaism was dealt with at length in Chapter 4, where I also discussed the conjunction of healing and forgiveness in the *Prayer of Nabonidus*. A deepened study of the career of Jesus as a healer and prophet can, in this light, be expected to provide an appropriate context for the understanding of his forgiveness announcements.

---

[1] Davies, *Jesus the Healer*, pp. 43–4.

Forgiveness in Jesus' healing activity

The historical Jesus had a reputation as a successful healer.[2] There is no reason to assume that Mark 2.5b was ever transmitted without a surrounding narrative context, which related a miraculous healing. If Jesus announced forgiveness in this way, he most certainly (if not exclusively, as implied by Luke 7.36–47) did so in connection with healing. I will test the coherence of Mark 2.1–5, 11–12 with three different aspects of Jesus' healing activity. Firstly, the question will be raised as to whether the correlation between sin and illness implied by the Markan episode is consistent with the attitude of Jesus. Secondly, the possibility that Jesus acknowledged that healing and forgiveness were analogous, in the sense that faith was a requirement for both, will be considered. Thirdly and lastly, I will explore the Isaianic background of Jesus' own interpretation of his healing activity in eschatological terms as the framework that may have encouraged him to proclaim forgiveness when healing a paralytic.

Sin and illness

Fiedler has argued that Mark 2.5b is incoherent with the historical Jesus' denial of any correlation between sin and illness.[3] Early Jewish literature commonly regards illness as an outcome of, or punishment for, sin.[4] Repentance is regularly viewed as a prerequisite for healing, which is held to be concomitant with divine forgiveness.[5] To some extent at least, primitive Christianity perpetuates these notions.[6] Whether the historical Jesus espoused them is less clear, and attention will be given here to those Gospel passages which could express either an affirmation or a denial of the correlation between sin and illness. Drawing on the work of John Pilch, I will use the word 'illness' to denote a cultural construct

---

[2] B. L. Blackburn, 'The Miracles of Jesus', in Chilton and Evans (eds.), *Studying the Historical Jesus*, pp. 353–94 (pp. 354–63); Meier, *A Marginal Jew*, vol. II, pp. 617–45; Theissen and Merz, *Der historische Jesus*, pp. 269–75; Dunn, *Jesus Remembered*, pp. 677–83; E. Eve, *The Healer from Nazareth: Jesus' Miracles in Historical Context* (London: SPCK, 2009), pp. 118–44.

[3] Fiedler, *Jesus und die Sünder*, p. 108; Fiedler, 'Sünde und Sündenvergebung', p. 87.

[4] Ecclus 38.15; 3 Macc 2.21–2; *EpArist* 233; *Jub* 23.13–14; *TReub* 1.7–8; *TZeb* 5.2; *TGad* 5.9–11. On the theme in the OT, see M. L. Brown, *Israel's Divine Healer* (Grand Rapids, MI: Zondervan, 1995), pp. 101–5, 133–7, 239–42.

[5] Ecclus 3.28; 18.21; 28.3; *1 En* 95.4; *EpArist* 313–16 = Josephus, *Ant* XII.111–13; *bNed* 41a. On this topic in rabbinic literature, see K. Seybold and U. Müller, *Krankheit und Heilung* (Stuttgart: Kohlhammer, 1978), pp. 94–5.

[6] Acts 12.21–3; 1 Cor 11.27–32; Jas 5.14–16; *Herm Sim* 6.3.4.

which includes not only what would properly be termed disease, but also what might be called disability and demonic possession.[7]

Criticism of the correlation

Of the two passages sometimes put forward in order to demonstrate that the historical Jesus denied the correlation between sin and illness, Luke 13.1–5 has the stronger claim to authenticity, but concerns calamities other than illness as possible punishments for sin, while John 9.1–7 does indeed deal with illness, but its derivation from the historical Jesus is less certain.

Luke 13.1–5. Taken at face value, Jesus' rhetorical questions and answers concerning two disastrous incidents, in which people met a horrible death, could be seen as an explicit denial of the correlation between sin and misfortune.[8] Most questioning of the historicity of the passage has assumed that 13.1 is dependent on Josephus' account of Pilate's massacre of the Samaritans in the latter half of the 30s CE (*Ant* XVIII.87).[9] In reality, the points of resemblance between these reports are few and vague.[10] Since it is difficult to believe that Luke's very specific accounts should have been forged by primitive Christians, had they not been grounded in historical reminiscences, they seem to refer to events that are not recorded in other sources.[11] Nevertheless, the passage may have been composed by Luke.[12] The formula employed in 13.2, 4, 'Do you think that...? I tell you, no! But...', exactly replicates 12.51, which is drawn from Q; accordingly, if 13.1–5 should be viewed as substantially pre-Lukan, one must recognize that Luke has largely redressed the unit in his own language, just as 12.51 has been reformulated from its source. The best case that can be made for 13.1–5 as sayings of the historical Jesus is based on the coherence of this passage with Jesus' proclamation of the impending judgement.

It is of crucial importance that, despite the weight placed on this passage by Fiedler, it does not deny the relationship between sin and

---

[7] J. J. Pilch, *Healing in the New Testament: Insights from Medical and Mediterranean Anthropology* (Minneapolis: Fortress, 2000), p. 25.

[8] Jeremias, *Neutestamentliche Theologie*, p. 179.

[9] Bultmann, *Die Geschichte der synoptischen Tradition*, p. 57; Sanders, *Jesus and Judaism*, p. 110.

[10] A. Fitzmyer, *The Gospel according to Luke X–XXIV*, AB 28A (New York: Doubleday, 1985), pp. 1006–7.

[11] J. Becker, *Jesus von Nazaret* (Berlin: de Gruyter, 1996), pp. 16–19, 64.

[12] Goulder, *Luke*, p. 560.

calamity. On the contrary, it affirms it.[13] The point is not that the victims were innocent, but that they were no worse sinners than others, and that an equal punishment awaits all Israelites who fail to repent.[14] In other words, the passage is an admonition along the lines of other sayings of John the Baptist and Jesus that caution against self-deceptive trust in the face of the coming judgement (Q 3.9; 10.13–15).

John 9.1–7. In this healing episode, it is reasonable to regard at least 9.1, 6–7 as coming from a source or tradition that may well recollect a miracle performed by the historical Jesus.[15] According to the dialogue in 9.2–5, Jesus declares that 'neither has this one sinned nor his parents, but [he was born blind] in order that the works of God should be manifested through him' (9.3). Is the substance of this verdict pre-Johannine and, if so, can it be taken as evidence that the historical Jesus denied the correlation between sin and illness?

At least 9.5 is distinctly Johannine in both language and content, and the remainder of the dialogue also employs language characteristic of John.[16] Dodd nevertheless argued that 9.2–4 comes in substance, though not in language, from tradition. His reason for identifying the dictum in 9.3 as pre-Johannine was that, in raising the issue of theodicy, it is singular within the Gospel of John but in agreement with synoptic tradition as evidenced by Mark 2.1–12 and Luke 13.1–5.[17] However, neither of these passages actually questions the correlation between sin and temporal punishment, and John 9.2–3 may perhaps more conveniently be derived from the evangelist's own thinking.

Even if John 9.3 should be deemed traditional and historical, it is doubtful that it can be taken as an expression of a general principle about the issue of theodicy, for its scope is no more than the illness of a specific individual: '*this* one' (οὗτος) has not sinned, just as Jesus says of Lazarus' illness that '*this* (αὕτη) illness is not to death' (11.4).[18] Moreover, the construction 'not x but y' sometimes carries the sense 'not

---

[13]   Strauss, *Das Leben Jesu, kritisch bearbeitet*, vol. II, pp. 79–80; S. M. Bryan, *Jesus and Israel's Traditions of Judgement and Restoration*, SNTSMS 117 (Cambridge University Press, 2002), p. 75.

[14]   M. Reiser, *Die Gerichtspredigt Jesu: Eine Untersuchung zur eschatologischen Verkündigung Jesu und ihrem frühjüdischen Hintergrund*, NTA 23 (Münster: Aschendorff, 1990), p. 235.

[15]   Meier, *A Marginal Jew*, vol. II, p. 694–8; G. H. Twelftree, *Jesus the Miracle Worker: A Historical and Theological Study* (Downers Grove: InterVarsity Press, 1999), pp. 302–3.

[16]   Dodd, *Historical Tradition*, p. 185 n. 2.

[17]   *Ibid.*, pp. 186–8.

[18]   Lindars, *John*, p. 342.

primarily x but y', and this may be its force here also.[19] The emphasis in 9.3 is therefore placed not so much on the rejection of a correlation between sin and illness in general as on the divinely ordained purpose of this specific illness.

Affirmation of the correlation

Besides Mark 2.1–12 par., there are few passages in primitive Christian literature that depict Jesus as acknowledging the correlation between sin and illness. *Oxy840G* 2–7 attributes to Jesus the notion that evildoers are punished already during their lifetime, but does not mention illness. Only the injunction 'Sin no more' (μηκέτι ἁμάρτανε), delivered by Jesus after completed healings (John 5.14; *EgerG* 47; cf. John 8.11), can by inference be taken as an affirmation of the correlation.[20] Uncertainties abound concerning the import of this phrase in its three different contexts, the source-critical relationship between these attestations, and the ultimate origin of the phrase.

John 8.11. Strong text-critical and philological evidence has brought about the common opinion that John 7.53–8.11 did not originally belong to John's Gospel.[21] Evidently a short narrative which was basically identical to this episode circulated in early Christianity. According to Eusebius, already Papias had related 'a story about a woman who was accused of many sins before the Lord'. Eusebius stated that this story was also found in the *Gospel according to the Hebrews*, but he did not go into its details.[22] In the fourth century, Didymus the Blind quoted an episode which could well be the one that Eusebius had found in the apocryphal Gospel.[23] It ends by narrating that no one dared to strike the woman with a stone and by commenting: 'When they searched themselves and realized that they, too, were guilty of things, they dared not [strike] her [down].' Nothing is said of any concluding dialogue between

---

[19] J. D. M. Derrett, 'The True Meaning of Jn 9, 1–3', *FilNeot* 16 (2003), 103–6. See John 3.17; 12.47 (cf. 5.22, 30; 8.16, 26); and BDR, § 448₁.

[20] Strauss, *Das Leben Jesu, kritisch bearbeitet*, vol. II, pp. 76–9.

[21] U. Becker, *Jesus und die Ehebrecherin: Untersuchungen zur Text- und Überlieferungsgeschichte von Joh. 7,53–8,11*, BZNW 28 (Berlin: Töpelmann, 1963), pp. 8–91; D. B. Wallace, 'Reconsidering "The Story of Jesus and the Adulteress Reconsidered"', *NTS* 39 (1993), 290–6.

[22] Papias 2.17 = Eusebius, *Hist. Eccl.* 3.39.

[23] B. D. Ehrman, 'Jesus and the Adulteress', *NTS* 34 (1988), 24–44 (25–30); D. Lührmann, 'Die Geschichte von einer Sünderin und andere apokryphe Jesusüberlieferungen bei Didymos von Alexandrien', *NovT* 32 (1990), 289–316 (304–11).

Jesus and the woman.[24] A fuller retelling of what appears to be the same story is found in the third-century *Didascalia apostolorum*. Here Jesus concludes his dialogue with the woman by saying, 'Go, nor do I condemn you.'[25]

None of the witnesses to this episode in its pre-canonical form(s) mentions the injunction to stop sinning. To conclude that the phrase cannot have been part of the story because it is not explicitly mentioned is to argue from silence in an undue manner.[26] But the possibility that it was added at a late stage, and perhaps under influence from John 5.14, remains.

John 5.14. A more elaborate form of the injunction belongs to the episode about the healing at Bethesda: 'After this, Jesus found him at the temple and said to him, "Look, you have become well. Sin no more (μηκέτι ἁμάρτανε), lest something worse happens to you!"' (John 5.14). The passage presupposes a correlation between sin and illness. That Jesus' encounter with the healed man takes place in the temple precincts may indicate that the latter has gone there in order to have a sacrifice offered, along the lines of *EgerG* 44–7. To my knowledge, the affinities between John 5.14b and a passage from Ben Sira have not received due attention.

> My child, have you sinned (ἥμαρτες)? Do so no more (μὴ προσθῆς μηκέτι), and pray for what you previously committed. Flee from sin as from a serpent! For if you approach, it will bite you; the teeth of a lion are its teeth, destroying the souls of human beings. As a two-edged sword is all evil-doing; there is no healing for its blow.
>
> (Ecclus 21.1–3)

Ben Sira's words of wisdom spell out in full the notions that seem to be presupposed in John 5.14b. It is necessary to pray for sins committed, and such prayer may include the offering of sacrifices (Ecclus 38.9–11; cf. 17.25; 28.2; 39.5), but it is equally imperative to quit sinning (5.5–6; 17.25–6; 34.26). Since illness results from sin, healing and forgiveness are concomitant (18.19–21; 38.9–15). By warning that 'something

---

[24] *GosHeb* 3b = Didymus the Blind, *Eccl. T.* 223.6–13. See Lührmann, 'Die Geschichte von einer Sünderin', 296.

[25] *Didasc. ap.* 7 (p. 93, ll. 5–6). The longer Syriac reading 'Go, do not return to this work again' is secondary, since the expansion is absent from *Const. ap.* 2.24.6 = Latin *Didasc. ap.* 2.24.3.

[26] J. I. H. McDonald, 'The So-Called *Pericope de Adultera*', *NTS* 41 (1995), 415–27 (419).

worse' may happen to the healed man should he sin again, the Johannine Jesus gives voice to a concern similar to that of Ecclus 21.2–3. Whether the passage in John actually echoes Ben Sira or draws on common theology is difficult to say. As mentioned in Chapter 2 above, John 5.14b has sometimes been thought to echo Mark 2.1–12. In view of the observation that John 5.14b seems to reflect a more elaborate understanding of the relationship between sin and illness, I find it less likely that this passage can be derived from the more rudimentary allusion to this correlation in the Markan episode. Whether it once formed the ending of the miracle story in 5.2–7, or whether it is the evangelist's own creation – perhaps inspired by Ecclus 21.1–3 – cannot be settled here.

EgerG 47. The evidential value of the occurrence of the phrase in the *Egerton Gospel* is contingent on whether or not the fragmentary apocryphal Gospel is dependent on John. Its narration of the healing of a leprous man differs from the synoptic parallel episodes (Mark 1.40–4 par.) on a number of points, one of which is Jesus' concluding 'Sin no more' ([μ]ηκέτι ἁ[μά]ρτανε) just before the fragment of PKöln 255 breaks off.

As commonly restored, the *Egerton Gospel* portrays the leprous man as saying, 'when I walked together with lepers and ate together with them in the inn, I too was infected with leprosy' (36–9). This has been read as a confession of sin against the levitical law (Lev 13.45–6).[27] But both the restoration and this specific interpretation are far from self-evident.[28] More likely, the imperative not to sin again ought to be seen as part of *Egerton*'s allusion to the Mosaic stipulations about the cleansing of leprosy, which instruct the priest to offer both guilt- and sin-offerings for those to be purified, thereby 'atoning' for them (Lev 14.10–20). There is also strong evidence that leprosy was seen as a punishment for sin in early Judaism.[29] In the light of this, Jesus' exhortation to stop sinning comes as a natural conclusion to the episode.

If indeed the 'Johannine' elements of the *Egerton Gospel* are representative of an early stage, at which synoptic and Johannine traditions were still kept together,[30] the attestation of the expression here enhances

---

[27] J. B. Daniels, 'The Egerton Gospel: Its Place in Early Christianity', unpublished Ph.D. thesis, Claremont Graduate School (1990), pp. 143–4, 148.

[28] T. Kazen, *Jesus and Purity Halakhah: Was Jesus Indifferent to Impurity?*, CBNTS 38 (Stockholm: Almqvist & Wiksell 2002), pp. 124–6.

[29] *Ibid.*, pp. 116–17.

[30] K. Erlemann, 'Papyrus Egerton 2: "Missing Link" zwischen synoptischer und johanneischer Tradition', *NTS* 42 (1996), 12–34.

the likelihood that an exhortation to sin no more was issued by the historical Jesus in connection with some of his healings. If, on the other hand, the *Egerton Gospel* draws on John,[31] it is not difficult to imagine why the author preferred to insert the phrase here in preference to the rather puzzling synoptic conclusion. Since there is no consensus about the relationship between the *Egerton Gospel* and the canonical Gospels, the question can hardly be settled.

To sum up the discussion of the phrase 'Sin no more', it has not been possible to trace it to the historical Jesus with anything approaching certainty. The issue is too bound up with the as yet unresolved questions concerning the composition of John 5 and the relationship between the *Egerton Gospel* and the canonical Gospels.

Implications for the historicity of Mark 2.5b

It can be concluded that the few items of gospel tradition that deal with the correlation between sin and illness cannot, with the temporary exclusion of Mark 2.1–12 par., warrant a conclusion in either direction concerning Jesus' view of the matter.

On the one hand, Luke 13.1–5 and John 9.1–7 cannot be pressed to say that the historical Jesus denied the correlation in principle. Fiedler's thesis that the theodicean aspect of Mark 2.1–12 is incoherent with historical Jesus material does not hold.

On the other hand, whether John 5.14/*EgerG* 47 is a saying of the historical Jesus is uncertain. The strongest argument for its historicity is based on the criterion of coherence – in this case, coherence with Mark 2.5, 11, the authenticity of which is argued for in the present investigation. In other words, it is more feasible to argue for the historicity of the saying on the basis of its coherence with the Markan forgiveness episode than vice versa.

Faith and healing

In his study of synoptic miracle stories, Theissen pointed out that Mark 2.5b is not likely to be a secondary addition to the episode, since it constitutes a word of 'assurance' (*Zuspruch*) such as can frequently be found in episodes about the miracles of Jesus.[32] In the present section, I will

[31] J. W. Pryor, 'Papyrus Egerton 2 and the Fourth Gospel', *AusBR* 37 (1989), 1–13; Charlesworth and Evans, 'Jesus in the Agrapha and Apocryphal Gospels', pp. 514–25.

[32] G. Theissen, *Urchristliche Wundergeschichten: Ein Beitrag zur formgeschichtlichen Erforschung der synoptischen Evangelien*, SzNT 8 (Gütersloh: Mohn, 1974), p. 166. The

endeavour to take Theissen's observation one step further and argue that this insight can be used to support not only the traditionality of 2.5b but also, albeit with great caution, its historicity.

'Assurances' and faith formulae in healing episodes

The basic characteristic of the typical 'assurance' is, as commonly understood, its encouraging tenor; most of the examples collated by Theissen from non-Christian material contain the imperative 'Take heart!' (θάρρει).[33] Corresponding exhortations to take heart occur in the NT (Mark 10.49; Matt 9.2, 22), as do other formulae with the function of giving confidence to recipients of healings (Mark 5.36/Luke 8.50; Luke 7.13; Acts 20.10). However, Theissen also includes in the category of assurances a number of sayings which lack an explicit exhortation to confidence (Mark 2.5; 7.29; 9.23); furthermore, he lists, as variants, sayings which ask for faith (Matt 9.8) or which criticize the lack of faith (John 4.48) without any obvious purpose to encourage.[34] The absence of a manifest common trait in these sayings raises some doubt about the appropriateness of Theissen's classificatory model.

It appears to me that Theissen has actually grouped together, under the heading of 'assurance', two quite distinct elements, which do not necessarily entail each other, although they frequently occur together. On the one hand, statements about the relationship between faith and healing – such as 'Your faith has saved you' and 'Everything is possible to the one who believes' – repeatedly occur in the healing episodes and indeed seem to be without parallels outside the Gospels. They are formulae that stand in a subsidiary relationship to the effective word of healing, and they have the function of establishing a link between faith and healing. I refer to these formulae as 'faith formulae'. In fact, faith is explicitly mentioned in nearly all of the sayings which Theissen labels assurances, or in their immediate narrative contexts (while not mentioning faith explicitly, Mark 7.29 probably implies faith). On the other hand, a proper formula of encouragement, such as 'Take heart!' or 'Fear not!', is sometimes prefixed to the faith formula. Except in Luke 7.13, in which an encouraging word occurs apart from a faith formula, these formulae

---

translation of *Zuspruch* as 'assurance' has been adopted from the English translation: G. Theissen, *The Miracle Stories of the Early Christian Tradition*, transl. F. McDonagh (Edinburgh: T & T Clark, 1983).

[33] Lucian, *Philops.* 11; Philostratus, *V. A.* 3.38.3; 4.10.1; 7.38.2. Cf. Josephus, *Ant* VIII.326.

[34] Theissen, *Urchristliche Wundergeschichten*, p. 68.

of encouragement never stand on their own in the Gospels – Mark 10.49
is not spoken by Jesus and is thus a weak candidate for the category
(cf. 10.52), while Luke 13.12b is more readily seen as an effective word
of healing. If Matthew's reworking of Mark is reflective of a general
tendency, it is noteworthy that Matthew twice adds a word of encouragement to a faith formula (Matt 9.2, 22) and thus draws the utterances
closer to what one finds in standard Hellenistic healing stories, whereas
there are no examples of a faith formula having been added to an exhortation. Nor is the faith formula ever reduced to a mere motivation for the
word of encouragement. As a rule, then, the constitutive and primary
element is the faith formula, to which a word of encouragement may be
joined but will always remain subordinate. The faith formula is far more
than a therapeutic word intended to calm a troubled soul; it expresses the
conviction that healing is effected by the recipient's faith.

The historicity of the faith formulae

Several factors indicate that faith was an important theme in the preaching and healing activity of the historical Jesus. An important witness is
the saying about the unlimited power of faith, which occurs in two distinct forms:

> Amen, I tell you, whoever says to this mountain, 'Be removed
> and thrown into the sea!', and does not doubt it in his heart but
> believes that what he says comes to pass, for him it will happen.
>
> (Mark 11.23; cf. Matt 21.21)

> If you have faith like a grain of mustard, you would have said
> to this sycamore, 'Be uprooted and planted in the sea!' – and it
> would have obeyed you.
>
> (Luke 17.6; cf. Matt 17.20)

The saying is attested in both Mark and Q, with good reasons to identify
the Lukan variant as closest to Q.[35] While the variants in *Thomas* are
explainable as reformulations of Matt 17.20 in which the reference to
faith has been omitted in keeping with the general tendency (*GThom* 48;
106.2), Paul may also know of the saying in a shape close to that found in
Mark (1 Cor 13.2).[36] Thus, the criterion of multiple attestation is applied
here with a positive result. Moreover, there is discontinuity between the

---

[35] Davies and Allison, *Matthew*, vol. II, p. 726.
[36] J. D. G. Dunn, 'Jesus Tradition in Paul', in Chilton and Evans (eds.), *Studying the Historical Jesus*, pp. 155–78 (163).

saying and characteristic primitive Christian formulations, in as much as, here, 'faith' is not faith in Jesus Christ, but rather a strong trust placed in the efficacy of one's own commands.[37] Whereas the synoptic Gospels sometimes employ the verb 'believe' (πιστεύειν) to denote faith in Jesus, the noun 'faith' (πίστις) is remarkably void of christological emphasis and is also, with few exceptions (Mark 2.5 par.; Luke 17.5), found on Jesus' lips.[38] The historicity of Mark 11.23/Q 17.6 is, therefore, firmly established.[39]

Faith is regularly mentioned in a context of healing. If synoptic parallels are discounted, seven miracle episodes employ the noun. Three of these instances are likely to be redactional (Matt 9.29; 15.28; Luk 17.19).[40] Thus four occurrences of the noun remain (Mark 2.5; 5.34; 10.52; Q 7.9), to which is added the employment of the corresponding verb in two healing episodes (Mark 5.36; 9.23). As the topic of faith does not take on a comparable role in miracle stories outside the NT, it is improbable that its presence in the Gospel episodes has been prompted by literary conventions or by the freedom of storytelling.[41] Nor can it be reduced to a special Markan concern.[42] This theme is explicit also in the single episode of healing that is thought to have existed in Q, where Jesus claims that he has not found 'such faith' in Israel as the centurion expresses (Q 7.9).[43] In these synoptic episodes faith lacks christological dimensions. Thus, in addition to being multiply attested, the faith formulae in the healing episodes are, as an entity, coherent with the historical saying in Mark 11.23/Q 17.6 and discontinuous with the primitive Christian concept of faith as belief in Jesus himself.

A case can be made that the formula 'Your faith has saved you' (ἡ πίστις σου σέσωκέν σε, Mark 5.34 par.; Mark 10.52/Luke 18.42; Luke 7.50; 17.19) is a turn of phrase that was used by the historical Jesus.[44]

[37] Perrin, *Rediscovering the Teaching of Jesus*, pp. 137–8.
[38] Mark 4.40/Luke 8.25; Mark 5.34 par.; Mark 10.52/Luke 18.42; Mark 11.22/Matt 21.21; Matt 8.10/Luke 7.9; Matt 9.29; 15.28; Matt 17.20/Luke 17.6; Matt 23.23; Luke 7.50; 17.19; 18.8; 22.32.
[39] G. Ebeling, 'Jesus und Glaube', *ZTK* 55 (1958), 64–110 (90–9).
[40] R. Pesch, *Jesu ureigene Taten? Ein Beitrag zur Wunderfrage*, QD 52 (Freiburg/Basel/Vienna: Herder, 1970), p. 122; H. D. Betz, 'The Cleansing of the Ten Lepers', *JBL* 90 (1971), 314–28; Davies and Allison, *Matthew*, vol. II, pp. 133–4, 556.
[41] Ebeling, 'Jesus und Glaube', 93–4; Theissen, *Urchristliche Wundergeschichten*, pp. 133–6.
[42] *Pace* Funk, Hoover and the Jesus Seminar, *The Five Gospels*, p. 30.
[43] U. Wegner, *Der Hauptmann von Kafarnaum (Mt 7,28a; 8,5–10.13 par Lk 7,1–10): Ein Beitrag zur Q-Forschung*, WUNT 2:14 (Tübingen: Mohr Siebeck, 1985), pp. 420–2.
[44] H. K. Nielsen, *Heilung und Verkündigung: Das Verständnis der Heilung und ihres Verhältnisses zur Verkündigung bei Jesus und in der ältesten Kirche*, ATD 22 (Leiden/New

Unlike the two special Lukan occurrences, which seem to be redactional, the formula may well be traditional in the two healing episodes in Mark. It is also discontinuous with primitive Christianity, where faith and salvation are indeed closely related, but where both concepts tend to be charged with christological and soteriological contents (Rom 10.9; Acts 16.31). Moreover, faith is not commonly said to 'save', although salvation may come *through* faith (Eph 2.8). And while the Letter of James affirms that the faithful prayer of others may save people who suffer from illness in the sense of restoring them to health (Jas 5.15), it does not voice the synoptic concept that people are healed by their own faith.

In fact, apart from the formula 'Your faith has saved you', the only evidence that 'salvation' in the sense of healing is ascribed directly to the faith of an infirm person comes in a passage that has probably been influenced by the synoptic healing episodes. Luke narrates how Paul, on encountering a lame man in Lystra, 'fixed his gaze on him and, seeing that he had faith to be saved, said in a loud voice...' (Acts 14.9b–10a). It is unlikely, in view of the characteristically Lukan expression 'to fix one's gaze' (ἀτενίζειν),[45] that Luke here reproduces a traditional narrative without alterations. The mention of saving faith has probably been introduced to highlight the parallel between Paul's healing of the lame man and Jesus' healing of the paralytic in Capernaum, both of which occur in a context of teaching (Luke 5.17) or preaching (Acts 14.7, 9a): Paul's 'seeing that he had faith' (14.9b) echoes Jesus' 'seeing their faith' (Luke 5.20a). More plausibly than supposing that the formula 'Your faith has saved you' is a retrojection of primitive Christian belief into the life of the earthly Jesus, one may therefore conclude that Jesus' own manner of connecting faith with healing/salvation coloured Luke's portrayal of Paul's mission.

To sum up, the phrase 'Your faith has saved you' is substantially derivable from the historical Jesus by virtue of its discontinuity with primitive Christianity and its coherence with the saying about the unlimited power of faith (Mark 11.23/Q 17.6), the historicity of which is also supported by the criterion of multiple attestation.

Implications for the historicity of Mark 2.5b

Against Theissen's identification of Mark 2.5b as an 'assurance', Hofius argues that none of the parallels adduced by Theissen from the NT

York/Copenhagen/Cologne: Brill, 1987), pp. 71–4; M. W. Yeung, *Faith in Jesus and Paul: A Comparison with Special Reference to 'Faith that Can Remove Mountains' and 'Your Faith Has Healed/Saved You'*, WUNT 2:147 (Tübingen: Mohr Siebeck, 2002), pp. 53–63.

[45]   See Luke 4.20; 22.56; Acts 1.10; 3.4, 12; 6.15; 7.55; 10.4; 11.6; 13.9; 23.1.

and other Hellenistic literature makes any reference to forgiveness, as Joachim Gnilka pointed out earlier.[46] Secondly, Hofius points to the form of 2.5b: the vocative 'child' (τέκνον) should signal the introduction of a saying with performative force, just as such vocatives regularly do in the Gospels. Thus, Hofius concludes that 2.5b is itself an effective word, by which Jesus forgives the paralytic his sins.[47] Neither of these two arguments is, as far as I can see, decisive.

As far as the formal features are concerned, the vocative does indeed introduce an effective word of healing in the five passages listed by Hofius (Mark 5.41/Luke 8.54; Luke 7.14; 13.12; John 11.43). However, there are also instances in which a faith formula is prefixed with a vocative (Mark 5.34/Matt 9.22/Luke 8.48; Matt 15.28). The presence of the vocative 'child' in Mark 2.5b does not therefore militate against the view that this saying is analogous to the faith formulae, in which faith is explicitly mentioned. Moreover, there are indications that already the transmitters of gospel tradition and at least one of the evangelists recognized Mark 2.5b as belonging to the category of the faith formulae: the probably traditional comment on the faith of those who carried the paralytic (2.5a) serves to place the saying within the same conceptual framework as the faith formulae, and Matthew, who prefixes both 'Child, your sins are [being] forgiven' (Matt 9.2) and 'Daughter, your faith has saved you' (9.22) with 'Take heart!' (θάρσει), seems to regard the two sayings as parallel.

As regards the argument based on the contents, the absence of the forgiveness topic from the alleged Hellenistic parallels is no more salient than the corresponding absence of the faith topic itself. However, Gnilka's objection that 2.5b par. is 'completely singular' even within the Gospels deserves serious attention.[48] In no other healing episode does a saying concerning forgiveness occur. One ought to consider, though, the analogous relationship between, on the one hand, faith and healing and, on the other, faith and forgiveness. That Jesus experienced that he was only able to heal if people had faith in him – or, more precisely, if they had faith that healing would be possible through him – can be seen not only from the positive affirmations of this relationship in the faith formulae, but also from Mark's narratorial précis of Jesus' failed mission in Nazareth: 'He was not able to perform any mighty work there, except

[46] Gnilka, 'Das Elend', pp. 199–200.
[47] Hofius, 'Jesu Zuspruch der Sündenvergebung', pp. 132–3.
[48] J. Gnilka, *Das Evangelium nach Markus*, EKKNT 2, 2 vols. (Zürich/Einsiedeln/Cologne: Benziger, 1978–9), vol. I, p. 96 (my translation).

that he laid his hands on a few who were ill and healed them. And he mar-velled at their lack of faith' (Mark 6.5–6a). Lack of faith (ἀπιστία) here refers to the audience's failure to recognize that the force behind Jesus' teaching, wisdom and miracles is the Spirit of God. Faced with these spectacular words and deeds, the people of Nazareth 'are offended at' or 'reject' (σκανδαλίζεσθαι) Jesus (6.2–3); as a result, no healings can take place. Three features point to the historical core of this report. First of all, the blunt statement that Jesus 'was not able' to perform miracles was embarrassing: in Mark it is immediately modified to give the impres-sion that Jesus did, after all, heal some people (6.5b); Matthew, deleting the references to Jesus' incapability and marvelling, states that 'he did not perform many mighty works there, because of their lack of faith' (Matt 13.58); Luke has Jesus himself anticipate and dismiss a request for miracles to be performed in Nazareth (Luke 4.23).[49] Secondly, as Meier points out, the theme of Jesus 'marvelling' (θαυμάζειν) is attested in both Mark and Q, and in a strikingly consistent manner: in these two cases, what Jesus marvels at is faith (Q 7.19) or the lack of faith (Mark 6.6a).[50] Thirdly, the remark that Jesus' acquaintances were 'scandalized at him' because they could not accept the divine origin of his mission is coherent with Q 7.22–3 (on which see below in this chapter). Behind Mark 6.2–6a are the reminiscences of an occasion on which Jesus, con-trary to his expectation, failed to perform healings and attributed this to a distrustful attitude on the part of his audience.

This may now be compared to the traditional, and as it seems histor-ical, saying that the one who blasphemes against the Spirit will not be forgiven (Q 12.10; Mark 3.28–9). This saying, which is even more force-ful than Mark 6.2–6a, points out the dire consequences of rejecting God's Spirit, who is at work in the healing activity of Jesus (see Chapter 2). Mark 2.5 may be seen as a positive counterpart to Q 12.10/Mark 3.28–9: for those who display faith in Jesus' ability as a healer and recognize him as a vehicle of the Spirit, forgiveness is available (see Table 4). That this correlation between faith and forgiveness is only made explicit by the narrator's comment in Mark 2.5a cannot be turned into a weighty argument against its implicit presence in Jesus' saying in 2.5b. The trad-ition must have been capable of interpreting Jesus' deeds and sayings congenially and this seems to have been done in 2.5.

---

[49]   E. Gräßer, 'Jesus in Nazareth (Mc 6 1–6a): Bemerkungen zur Redaktion und Theologie des Markus', in W. Eltester (ed.), *Jesus in Nazareth*, BZNW 40 (Berlin/New York: de Gruyter, 1972), pp. 1–37 (pp. 25–7).

[50]   Meier, *A Marginal Jew*, vol. II, p. 771 n. 206.

Table 4 *The analogous relationship of healing and forgiveness to faith*

	Faith (positive)	Lack of faith (negative)
Healing	Mark 5.34; 10.52; Q 7.9	Mark 6.5–6a
Forgiveness	Mark 2.5	Mark 3.28–9/Q 12.10

To conclude this investigation of the relationship between Mark 2.5b
and the faith formulae, it should be emphasized that its results are beset
by numerous uncertainties and should only be used to confirm the conclusions drawn earlier in this study on the basis of the stronger criteria of
multiple attestation and discontinuity. Mark 2.5b is indeed coherent with
the distinct form and also with the contents of Jesus' 'faith formulae'.

Healing and the restoration of Israel

Within his paradigm of 'return from exile' as the appropriate category
for understanding the historical Jesus, Wright has argued that Jesus'
announcement of forgiveness is another expression of his message of
eschatological fulfilment, construed as the end of Israel's ongoing exile
and her restoration as foretold by the OT prophets.[51] It will be clear that
I think this is essentially correct, even if 'restoration' may be a more
adequate concept than 'end of exile'.[52] Wright's method of hypothesis
and verification sometimes imposes the paradigm on the Gospel material
without a detailed interpretation of the individual units, and Dunn criticizes Wright for doing this in asserting the equivalence of forgiveness
with return from an allegedly perceived exile.[53] While sharing Dunn's
apprehension about such a method, I suggest that, by the inductive and
criteriological approach employed in this study, it is in the present case
possible to arrive at a conclusion not far from Wright's.

The starting point for this section will be the insight that the forgiveness announcement in Mark 2.5b is delivered in connection with a healing, and that the historical Jesus' view of his healing activity is nowhere
more clearly expressed than in Q 7.18–23. An assessment of the historicity of the Q saying, and an exploration of its background in Isaiah
and in early Jewish interpretation of Isaiah's eschatology, will enable

---

[51] Wright, *Jesus and the Victory of God*, pp. 268–74.
[52] Bryan, *Jesus and Israel's Traditions*, pp. 12–20.
[53] Dunn, *Jesus Remembered*, p. 477 n. 445.

discussion of the possibility that Jesus' announcement of forgiveness was also prompted by reinterpreted Isaianic eschatology.

Jesus' reply to John the Baptist (Q 7.18–23)

In view of the prominent place occupied by healings in the synoptic narrative tradition, remarkably little material in the sayings tradition comments on Jesus' healing activity. Mention is made of his exorcisms alone (Q 11.20) and of exorcisms and other healings together (Luke 13.32–3), and two other sayings probably refer implicitly to miracles of healing (Q 10.13–15, 23–4), but the saying which sheds most light on the healing activity as a whole is certainly Jesus' response to John's question concerning his identity as the coming one (Matt 11.2–6/Luke 7.18–23).

Both Matthew and Luke present Jesus' saying as a reply to a question posed by the imprisoned John through his disciples. They also indicate that the events listed in the response refer to the healing and preaching activity of Jesus: Matthew speaks of John, who heard about 'the works of Christ', and he has arranged the preceding chapters 8–9 so as to exemplify each of the deeds mentioned in 11.5, while Luke inserts 7.20–1 into the Q material in order to have John's disciples see for themselves the miracles wrought by Jesus. Both the evangelists seem to take Jesus' veiled reply as an affirmation of his identity as the coming one.

Q can be reconstructed with relative ease in this case, since the divergences between Matthew and Luke are minor. Matthew's remark that John was 'in prison' was probably in Q.[54] On the other hand, his mention of 'the works of Christ' is universally acknowledged as redactional.[55] As already mentioned, Luke should be credited with 7.20–1. In Jesus' reply, the two Gospels agree nearly verbatim with only some slight polishing on Luke's part. Q will have contained the saying in this form: 'Go and proclaim to John what you hear and see: blind regain their sight and lame walk, lepers are cleansed and deaf hear, and dead are raised and poor people are evangelized. And blessed is the one who is not offended at me!' (Q 7.22–3). Bultmann pointed out that 7.22b cannot have been handed down without the macarism of 7.23, since this would render the saying pointless. By contrast, he held that the narrative framework, which introduces John the Baptist and his disciples (7.18–19, 22a), was a secondary addition to the originally isolated saying 7.22b–23.[56] But

---

[54] Meier, *A Marginal Jew*, vol. II, p. 198 n. 89.
[55] See, e.g., Catchpole, *The Quest for Q*, pp. 43–5.
[56] Bultmann, *Die Geschichte der synoptischen Tradition*, p. 22.

it is difficult to see how this introduction could have been created for a saying which did not in any way mention John or his disciples, and the purpose of the implied warning in 7.23 is incomprehensible without the introductory mention of John's deliberation.[57] These considerations indicate that 7.19, 22a belonged with 7.22b–23 already in the most primitive tradition.

The historicity of the saying has often been argued on the basis of its alleged discontinuity with primitive christology. Had 7.22b been crafted by primitive Christians, the argument goes, one would have expected a response less marked by ambiguity.[58] Rather than expressing the conviction that Jesus is the Messiah, the saying seems to point away from the question of Jesus' identity to focus instead on healings and preaching as signs of the kingdom or of the eschatological age.[59] And if 7.22b–23 does indeed say something about the identity of Jesus, it grants to him prophetic traits drawn from Isa 61.1–2 in a manner not characteristic of primitive Christianity.[60] However, there are reasons to question the applicability of the criterion of discontinuity in this case. Being framed by Q 7.19 and 7.23, the saying hardly loses its focus on the person of Jesus.[61] Moreover, prophetic christology is not absent from primitive Christianity, and the use of Isa 61.1–2 as a programmatic statement for Jesus' earthly career in Luke 4.16–30 is probably redactional.[62] Most importantly, the messianic interpretation of Isaiah's eschatological wonders in 4Q521, which has striking affinities with Q 7.18–23, suggests that an original audience may not have conceived of the saying as vague, but as making a quite clear messianic claim, albeit in an indirect way.

A more convincing argument for historicity seizes on the potential embarrassment involved in the episode's characterization of John the Baptist as one who is uncertain about Jesus' identity. It is not merely that John does not himself recognize Jesus as the coming one; the episode also ends without John having taken any clear stand towards Jesus, and

---

[57] W. G. Kümmel, *Jesu Antwort an Johannes den Täufer: Ein Beispiel zum Methodenproblem in der Jesusforschung*, Sitzungsberichte der wissenschaftlichen Gesellschaft an der Johann Wolfgang Goethe-Universität Frankfurt/Main 11:4 (Wiesbaden: Steiner, 1974), p. 31.

[58] M. Dibelius, *Die urchristliche Überlieferung von Johannes dem Täufer*, FRLANT 15 (Göttingen: Vandenhoeck & Ruprecht, 1911), p. 37.

[59] Bultmann, *Die Geschichte der synoptischen Tradition*, pp. 135–6; R. Latourelle, *Miracles de Jésus et théologie du miracle* (Paris: Cerf, 1986), p. 66.

[60] C. A. Evans, *Jesus and His Contemporaries: Comparative Studies* (Leiden: Brill, 1995), pp. 120–1.

[61] Nielsen, *Heilung und Verkündigung*, p. 62.

[62] R. C. Tannehill, 'The Mission of Jesus according to Luke IV 16–30', in Eltester (ed.), *Jesus in Nazareth*, pp. 51–75 (pp. 63–73).

the formulation of the macarism implies a warning directed specifically at the Baptist.[63] This is unlike all known primitive Christian reflection on John's role, which consistently depicts him as a witness to Jesus as the coming one.[64] Scholarly claims to the contrary tend to postulate hypothetical entities and are not persuasive. The suggestion originally made by Anton Fridrichsen that, in Q 7.18–23, John represents a community of disciples of the Baptist, is typical of early form-criticism, and it builds on a principle that induces flawed results (see Chapter 3 above).[65] Dunn's proposal that John is not portrayed as a witness to Jesus in Q, with which 7.18–23 is therefore consistent in its theological outlook, overlooks Q 7.27.[66] It is also methodologically unsound, since it assumes what it seeks to demonstrate: that the Baptist material in Q is an expression of Q theology and that it could not be discontinuous with the theology of whoever authored Q.[67] The lack of evidence for a strand of primitive Christianity, which was not convinced that John had testified to Jesus as the coming one, is illustrated by the assertion of another scholar that 'the picture of the Baptist as witness is presumably not the only one to have existed'.[68] But it is the only one that we know of, and 7.18–23 seems to create a problem for it, which is evident from the strained attempts in subsequent Christianity to explain away John's sending of his disciples by suggesting that it was for their sake that he did so. This favours the view that both the Baptist's question and Jesus' response are grounded in a historical exchange.

Jesus and the realization of Isaiah's eschatology

It is commonly recognized that Q 7.22b alludes to a variety of passages from the Book of Isaiah, which speak of marvellous events that belong to the future restoration of the nation 'on that day' (ביום ההוא), or which form part of the commissions of the Servant of the Lord and the Lord's

---

[63] Meier, *A Marginal Jew*, vol. II, pp. 135–6, 202 n. 104.

[64] Matt 3.14–15; John 1.6–8, 15, 29–36; 3.25–30; 10.41; Acts 13.23–5; 19.4; *GosEb* 3 = Epiphanius, *Panarion* 30.13.7–8.

[65] A. Fridrichsen, *Le problème du miracle dans le christianisme primitif*, EHPR 12 (Strasbourg/Paris: Istra, 1925), p. 66; Bultmann, *Die Geschichte der synoptischen Tradition*, p. 22; J. Ernst, *Johannes der Täufer: Interpretation – Geschichte – Wirkungsgeschichte*, BZNW 53 (Berlin/New York: de Gruyter, 1989), pp. 318–19.

[66] Dunn, *Jesus and the Spirit*, p. 56.

[67] S.-O. Back, *Han som kom: Till frågan om Jesu messianska anspråk*, Studier i exegetik och judaistik utgivna av Teologiska fakulteten vid Åbo Akademi 1 (Åbo Akademi, 2006), pp. 83–4 n. 94.

[68] Nielsen, *Heilung und Verkündigung*, p. 59 (my translation).

Anointed One respectively.[69] The clearest allusion to the Book of Isaiah is Jesus' assertion that 'poor are evangelized' (cf. Isa 61.1), but there is also an Isaianic background for 'blind regain their sight' (29.18; 35.5; 42.7, 18; 61.1 LXX), 'crippled walk' (35.6), 'deaf hear' (29.18; 35.5; 42.18) and 'dead are raised' (26.19). Only the reference to lepers who are being cleansed cannot be traced back convincingly to Isaiah, despite scholarly efforts to derive it from 35.8[70] or even 53.4.[71] In view of the strong links between Q 7.22b and Isaiah's eschatological expectation, it seems secure to conclude that Jesus believed that this eschatology was being realized, at least in part, during his own lifetime. However, as the explicit identification of the miracles with Jesus' healings is made only at the redactional level of the Gospels, Bultmann held that the saying as spoken by Jesus depicted the advent of the eschatological age in general terms, and that the saying draws on the Book of Isaiah without any intended reference to actual events in the activity of Jesus.[72] For a proper evaluation of Bultmann's proposal, early Jewish interpretations of the Isaianic prophecies must be taken into account.

With the exception of the prophecy about evangelizing, the Targum expresses a consistent non-literal interpretation of the prophecies. Blindness and deafness are conceived of as metaphors that denote Israel's inability to perceive and to observe the Torah; the interpreter sometimes makes this explicit by speaking of those who are '*like* deaf' or '*like* blind [to the Torah]' (*Tg*Isa 29.18; 42.7, 18). One quotation from the Targum suffices to elucidate its tendency: 'Then shall be opened the eyes of the house of Israel, the ones who are like blind to the Torah; and their ears, which are like deaf to receiving the words of the prophets, will hear' (35.5). The Aramaic interpreter does not envisage any literal miracles, but the final repentance of the people of Israel who will then turn to the observance of the Torah.

The so-called *Messianic Apocalypse* (4Q521) displays close formal and theological affinities with Q 7.22b.[73] Not only does the most complete fragment introduce the Lord's 'anointed one' (משיח, 2 ii 1), but it also contains a list of marvellous deeds, which will be wrought by the

[69] See, e.g., T. Hieke, 'Q 7,22 – A Compendium of Isaian Eschatology', *ETL* 82 (2006), 175–87 (178–84).

[70] J. Dupont, 'L'ambassade de Jean-Baptiste', *NRT* 83 (1961), 805–21, 943–59 (950); Pesch, *Jesu ureigene Taten?*, p. 42.

[71] M. F. Bird, *Are You the One Who Is to Come? The Historical Jesus and the Messianic Question* (Grand Rapids, MI: Baker, 2009), p. 101.

[72] Bultmann, *Die Geschichte der synoptischen Tradition*, p. 22.

[73] É. Puech, 'Une apocalypse messianique (4Q521)', *RevQ* 15 (1992), 475–522.

Lord: 'he will heal the mortally wounded, and the dead he will make live; the poor he will evangelize' (4Q521 2 ii 12). The awkwardness of having the Lord as the subject of 'evangelize' (בשר) has led Collins to make the plausible suggestion that God is described here as acting through an agent, probably through the anointed one mentioned at the beginning of the fragment.[74] Is this text evidence, then, for an early Jewish expectation that healings and resuscitations would be part of the mission of a prophetic Messiah? Kvalbein urges against such an understanding by pointing both to the prevalent early Jewish view of eschatological healing as metaphorical and to the apparent lack of distinction between the pious people and those who suffer from illness in 4Q521.[75] While Kvalbein's argument in favour of a metaphorical sense for the marvellous deeds in the Qumran text is not compelling,[76] his caution against assuming that they are meant to be literal deserves to be heeded. Whether the author imagined the eschatological healing as metaphorical, as did later the Targum, or as literal, as does Q, can hardly be decided.

On returning to Jesus and Q 7.22b, at least four circumstances contradict Bultmann's thesis that the saying has no referent in the activity of Jesus. First of all, if 7.22a belonged to the saying as spoken by the historical Jesus, 'what you hear and see' must refer to what is already taking place. Secondly, it is likely that the evangelizing of the poor in 4Q521 presupposes the involvement of a messianic agent. If not dependent on 4Q521, Q 7.22b appears to draw on a tradition that has also influenced the Qumran text and which thus plausibly involves the Messiah as an agent. Thirdly, the mention that lepers are cleansed, for which there is no precedent in Isaiah, indicates that the saying is modelled on Jesus' actual ministry.[77] Fourthly, the saying agrees terminologically with the narrative miracle traditions at least in its use of the verbs καθαρίζειν (cf. Mark 1.41) and ἐγείρειν (cf. Mark 5.41; Luke 7.14). If Jesus healed by word, which seems indisputable, and if he spoke of healing in so similar a language, those who heard him cannot have failed to understand the saying as a reference to his own activity of healing and preaching.

Jesus' reply to John, then, indicates that he saw his own activity as a healer as fulfilment – in a most literal way – of some of Isaiah's

---

[74] J. J. Collins, 'The Works of the Messiah', *DSD* 1 (1994), 98–112 (100).

[75] H. Kvalbein, 'Die Wunder der Endzeit: Beobachtungen zu 4Q521 und Matth 11,5p', *ZNW* 88 (1997), 111–25.

[76] J. Zimmermann, *Messianische Texte aus Qumran: Königliche, priesterliche und prophetische Messiasvorstellungen in den Schriftfunden von Qumran*, WUNT 2:104 (Tübingen: Mohr Siebeck, 1998), p. 364.

[77] H. Stettler, 'Die Bedeutung der Täuferanfrage in Matthäus 11,2–6 par Luk 7,18–23 für die Christologie', *Bib* 89 (2008), 173–200 (188–9).

prophecies concerning the eschatological age. With some justification, Sanders has chided A. E. Harvey for giving the impression that Jesus actively chose to perform the kind of miracles that would fulfil the prophecies.[78] It is more congruous with the narrative tradition that the historical Jesus healed those whom he had the occasion and the ability to heal.[79] But this should not obscure the implication of Q 7.18–23 that Jesus interpreted his success as a faith healer in the light of Isaiah's prophecies. His configuration of expressions drawn from different passages of the Book of Isaiah, while exhibiting close affinity with that of 4Q521, also contains distinctive elements. Jesus' saying and the Qumran text converge most strongly in their mention of the dead being raised (cf. Isa 26.19) and of the poor being evangelized (cf. 61.1). The differences in these cases seem to be prompted only by the preference for impersonal expressions in Q 7.22b over against the active verbs in 4Q521. Whereas 4Q521 2 ii 8 promises that the Lord will restore sight to the blind, this is evidently drawn from Ps 146.8, and there is no discernible influence from Isa 35.5 or 42.7; moreover, there is no mention of either the crippled or the deaf. That 'he will heal the mortally wounded' (ירפא חללים, 4Q521 2 ii 12) may rather, if it has at all been inspired by Isaiah, echo Isa 22.2; 30.26, and the formulation 'he will lead (ינהל) … and the hungry (רעבים) he will make rich' in 4Q521 2 ii 13 may be drawn from Isa 49.10 (cf. 40.11).

These considerations suggest that Jesus stood in the exegetical tradition evidenced by 4Q521 and offered his own selection of Isaiah's prophecies as an interpretation of his own healing and preaching activity. Again, the peculiar mention of the lepers who are cleansed indicates that Jesus made use of Isaiah in a distinctive and creative way and even – as it seems – ascribed to the book a piece of prophecy that is not actually found therein. And this now invites the question of whether his proclamation of forgiveness, which was closely connected with healing, may also have been motivated by, or interpreted in the light of, Isaiah's eschatological vision.

Implications for the historicity of Mark 2.5b

There is, as was pointed out in Chapter 4, a passage in Isaiah which juxtaposes forgiveness with eschatological healing, namely the conclusion of the prophetic vision of Israel's return to Zion at a time when

---

[78] A. E. Harvey, *Jesus and the Constraints of History: The Bampton Lectures, 1980* (London: Duckworth, 1982), pp. 115–18.
[79] Sanders, *Jesus and Judaism*, p. 163.

the foreigners are gone and the Lord rules as king (Isa 33.17–24). The MT says: 'Then will be divided the prey of a large spoil (עַד־שְׁלַל מרבה חֻלָּק); the lame will take booty. And no inhabitant will say, "I am ill"; the people who dwell in her [i.e. Zion], their iniquity is forgiven' (33.23b–24). The beginning of this passage is often emended to read 'Then will the blind divide a large spoil' (חֻלָּק עוּר שְׁלַל מרבה), which has some basis in the targumic mention of 'blind and lame' at this point; in this way, a better parallelism is attained in 33.23b.[80] If this was the original wording of the passage, it must nevertheless be noticed that both LXX and 1QIsa[a] support the reading of MT; the Greek translator erroneously renders the noun 'prey' (עַד) as the conjunction 'until' (עַד/ἕως οὗ). By the first century, therefore, the proto-masoretic form of the passage was well established.

Regardless of whether one finds in Isa 33.23b–24 a reference to the 'blind and lame' or merely to the 'lame', the affinities between this passage and 35.5–6 are patent. These two passages are the only ones within the Book of Isaiah that speak of the 'lame' or 'crippled' (פסח). Both of them depict the lame as doing what is normally outside their ability, which implies that they have been healed, and they do so in contexts that portray Israel's joyful return to Zion; moreover, 33.24 explicitly states that no inhabitant of restored Jerusalem will suffer from any illness of whatever kind, much as 35.5–6 enumerates four categories of illnesses that will be healed. Recollection of one of these passages may easily have brought the other one to mind.[81] If Jesus interpreted his successful faith healing of paralyzed or crippled individuals as the fulfilment of 35.6, which does indeed seem likely, it is plausible to assume that he would also have understood it as the fulfilment of 33.23b–24. The latter passage adds a notion that cannot be found in 35.5–6, namely that healing and forgiveness will be concomitant.

Mark 2.1–5, 11–12 can now be read as a narrative that reflects a healing performed by the historical Jesus, who understood himself as the instrument through whom Israel's Lord was fulfilling his promises granted through Isaiah. Viewed against the backdrop of Isa 33.23b–24, Jesus' announcement of forgiveness combined with his effective word of healing coheres with his overall understanding of his healing and preaching activity in the light of Isaiah's prophecies. Yet the echo of Isa 33.23b–24 is so subtle, and in the present text of Mark 2.1–12 so overlaid

---

[80] Cf. Lev 21.18; Deut 15.21; 2 Sam 5.6, 8*bis*; Job 29.15; Jer 31.8; Mal 1.8.
[81] See also Brown, *Israel's Divine Healer*, pp. 202–5, 242.

with subsequent reformulation and reinterpretation, that it can hardly be a product of a primitive Christian ambition to portray Jesus as the fulfiller of Isaiah. Where this tendency is present, it is normally much more forthrightly expressed (e.g., Mark 7.37). The concern of the Markan episode, as shown in Chapter 4 above, is to depict Jesus as the angelomorphic Messiah rather than as the one whose miracles realize Isaianic eschatology. But even if 2.6–10 is excised to leave us with an account of less elaborated christology in 2.1–5, 11–12, this more primitive narration does not seem to have been shaped in order to provide a conscious allusion to Isaiah. Rather than being designated as 'lame' (χωλός), the person healed in the episode is labelled a 'paralytic' (παραλυτικός); and rather than being said to 'leap' (Isa 35.6) or in some other way to express the joy implicit in 'dividing the prey' (33.23; cf. 9.2), he is portrayed quite laconically as rising, taking his pallet and leaving. In short, unlike Acts 3.1–10, where the use of the words χωλός and (ἐξ-)άλλεσθαι seems influenced by Isa 35.6, there is not much in the *narration* of Mark 2.1–5, 11–12 that is reminiscent of Isaiah's prophecies, and it is only by comparison with other material that comes from the historical Jesus that one can consider the possibility that the actual healing *event* was interpreted by the healer himself as a fulfilment of these prophecies.

Mark 2.1–5, 11–12 in the context of Jesus' healing activity

To conclude the part of this chapter devoted to the place of the announcement of forgiveness in the career of the historical Jesus as a healer, the following can be said: in the first section, in which I dealt with the correlation between sin and illness in the gospel tradition, I arrived at the conclusion that the few instances apart from Mark 2.5, 11, in which this topic emerges, are of little avail for the determination of Jesus' view of this correlation. The analysis in the second section led to a more positive conclusion: it was seen that Jesus spoke of forgiveness and healing as analogous to the extent that faith was a *sine qua non* for both, and that the statement about forgiveness in Mark 2.5b is analogous to the faith formulae attested in other healing episodes. Finally, in the third section, I suggested that the healing narrated in the Markan episode may have been the means by which Jesus enacted his quite literal understanding of Isaiah's prophecies about the restoration of Israel. If this is correct, the announcement of forgiveness is fully and distinctly coherent with Jesus' overall understanding of his healings.

Forgiveness and Jesus' prophetic identity

A large portion of Chapter 4 was devoted to the place of forgiveness in early Jewish interpretations of the OT prophets. Having concluded there that the utterance in Mark 2.5b could, in its first-century setting, have been heard as the pronouncement of a prophet, I now set out to explore the coherence of the synoptic forgiveness sayings with other traditional elements that assign a prophetic role to Jesus.

That Jesus was considered a prophet by his contemporaries, and that he also expressed his own identity in prophetic categories, is well attested in the sources.[82] The characterization of the historical Jesus as a prophet is, in fact, almost unanimously affirmed by scholarship. Yet what seems at first glance to be a rare instance of consensus among historical Jesus scholars may be a chimera: the label 'prophet' was employed with vagueness in antiquity, and critical scholars attach it to Jesus with equal flexibility.[83] To avoid emptying the label of its content, it is imperative not merely to state that Jesus was a prophet, but also to elucidate what kind of prophet he was.

I will seek to approach this question from two perspectives. First of all, I will take advantage of previous scholarly discussions about Jesus' location among other early Jewish prophets roughly contemporaneous with him, which will here be related to the topic of the present investigation. This assessment of Jesus' prophetic role within a taxonomy based on sociological categories will, secondly, be balanced by a brief study of the prophetic types and expectations that may have formed the framework of Jesus' own experience of his identity as a prophet. In this way, sociological and theological categories will not be contrasted, but employed alongside one another to function in a complementary manner.

Jesus among the early Jewish prophets

Scholarly efforts of recent decades have drawn attention to the persistence, indeed even the flourishing, of prophetic activity in early Judaism.[84]

---

[82] Mark 6.15/Luke 9.8; Mark 8.28 par.; Matt 21.11, 46; Luke 7.16; 24.19; John 4.19; 6.14; 7.40; 9.17; Acts 3.22–6; cf. Mark 6.4 par./John 4.44/*GThom* 31.1 = POxy 1 30–3; Mark 14.65 par.; Luke 13.33; John 7.52.

[83] M. Öhler, 'Jesus as Prophet: Remarks on Terminology', in M. Labahn and A. Schmidt (eds.), *Jesus, Mark and Q: The Teaching of Jesus and Its Earliest Records*, JSNTS 214 (Sheffield Academic Press, 2001), pp. 125–42; T. Kazen, 'The Christology of Early Christian Practice', *JBL* 127 (2008), 591–614 (594–8).

[84] Aune, *Prophecy in Early Christianity*, pp. 103–6; Gray, *Prophetic Figures*, pp. 7–34; A. P. Jassen, *Mediating the Divine: Prophecy and Revelation in the Dead Sea Scrolls and Second Temple Judaism*, STDJ 68 (Leiden: Brill, 2007), pp. 279–308.

It is now agreed that the cessation of prophecy was not a strict dogma in the first century, and that the numerous prophetic figures mentioned above all by Josephus provide material for the establishment of a differentiated typology of early Jewish prophecy, within which the understanding of Jesus as a prophet can reasonably be advanced.

Richard Horsley has drawn up a taxonomy of first-century prophets. He identifies three types of prophets: 'seers', who are found among the literary elite; 'oracular prophets', who belong to the peasantry, are either solitary or encircled by a limited group of disciples, and for whom prophecy is confined to the delivery of oracles; and 'action prophets', who also arise from among the populace, but are the leaders of mass movements and not only speak, but also act, prophetically.[85] Robert Webb, who builds on insights from Horsley and Aune, divides the 'seers' into the two groups of 'clerical prophets' and 'sapiential prophets' respectively, and launches the more appropriate labels of 'leadership popular prophets' and 'solitary popular prophets' for the two subtypes of Horsley's 'popular prophets'.[86] Webb's taxonomy will be followed here, except that clerical and sapiential prophets will be treated as subtypes of 'professional prophets' (identical to Horsley's 'seers').

In the following, I will consider Jesus' place within this typology and the possible analogies to his practice of announcing forgiveness, which can be drawn from these other early Jewish prophets. I will then devote a section to the various kinds of actions that were promised or performed by such prophets; this will involve reflection on the nature and function of the prophetic actions and/or 'signs' promised or performed by Jesus.

Professional prophets

The 'professional prophets' belong to the upper strata of society and they exercise their prophetic abilities in the context of the nation's political governance. These abilities are intrinsically linked with their 'profession'; either, as in the case of clerical prophets, with their high-priestly or priestly status, or, as with the sapiential prophets, with their recognized skill as learned experts in the scriptures. Their prophecies appear mostly, but not exclusively, to have consisted in foretelling the future. Dreams

---

[85] R. A. Horsley, '"Like One of the Prophets of Old": Two Types of Popular Prophets at the Time of Jesus', *CBQ* 47 (1985), pp. 435–63.

[86] Webb, *John the Baptizer*, pp. 307–48.

and scriptural interpretation frequently played a role in the method of prophecy employed by these individuals.[87]

It is fairly evident that Jesus was not a professional prophet. The Gospels contrast Jesus' style of teaching with that of the scribes (Mark 1.22/Matt 7.28–9) and report that his activities created amazement because he lacked formal education (Mark 6.2/Matt 13.54; John 7.15). Mark also describes how the learned elite questioned his authorization (Mark 11.27–33 par.). Meier suggests that Jesus received some elementary schooling in Nazareth, but he also remarks that the evidence points away from Jesus having pursued any studies at a higher level.[88] Only the *Testimonium Flavianum* seems to place Jesus in the category of sapiential prophets by labelling him 'a wise man' (σοφὸς ἀνήρ, *Ant* XVIII.63), an appellative elsewhere granted by Josephus to Solomon (VIII.53) and to Daniel, the clearest example of a sapiential prophet in the OT (X.237). This definitely unhistorical characterization of Jesus can be seen to parallel the insistence in the same passage that Jesus gained a large following among non-Jews, which, as Meier has argued, is probably based on the author's retrojection of the prevalent situation in his own time back into the activity of Jesus.[89] Likewise, the description of Jesus as a 'wise man' reflects knowledge of a developed christology and of the social location of primitive Roman Christianity, rather than accurate information about the historical Jesus.

Despite the fact that Jesus represented a type of prophecy that was different from that of the professional prophets, one passage in the *Antiquities* that seems to speak of sapiential prophets deserves some attention in the context of the present investigation, since it juxtaposes the mention of inspired speech with the sin–illness correlation. The passage has been briefly discussed by Webb.[90] In unsparing detail, Josephus describes the horrible ailments experienced by the dying Herod, which, according to the author, were a divine punishment for the king's transgressions (*Ant* XVII.168–9). This interpretation of Herod's illness was,

---

[87]   Clerical prophets as portrayed in the sources are Jaddua the high priest (336–323 BCE; Josephus, *Ant* XI.326–8); John Hyrcanus I (134–104 BCE; *Bell* I.68–9; *Ant* XIII.282–3, 299–300, 322); Joseph Caiaphas (18–36/7 CE; John 11.49–52); Flavius Josephus (37–*c.* 100 CE; *Bell* III.351–4, 400–2, 406–7, 622–9). Sapiential prophets are Judas the Essene (104–103 BCE; *Bell* I.78–80; *Ant* XIII.311–13); Samaias/Pollion the Pharisee (63–40 BCE; *Ant* XIV.172–6; XV.3–4, 370); Menahem the Essene (before 37 BCE; *Ant* XV.373–9); the Pharisees at Herod's court (20–5 BCE; *Ant* XVII.41–5); Simon the Essene (6 CE; *Bell* II.112–13).

[88]   Meier, *A Marginal Jew*, vol. I, pp. 276–8.

[89]   *Ibid.*, pp. 64–5.

[90]   Webb, *John the Baptizer*, p. 322 n. 41.

he claims, made already as the tyrant lay on his deathbed: 'It was told by those who were divinely inspired and who, by wisdom, had the ability to announce these things, that God was exacting this penalty from the king for his many impieties' (XVII.170). As Webb remarks, 'to be divinely inspired' (θειάζειν) denotes prophetic activity, regardless of whether the verb προαποφθέγγεσθαι should be translated 'to announce' or 'to predict'; these inspired persons' ability to identify the reason for the king's sufferings is said to come 'through wisdom' (σοφίᾳ). It is therefore reasonable to see in this passage a portrayal of sapiential prophets, who have insight into God's mind concerning sins committed by human beings, just as the prophets of old had. To some extent, this description is analogous to the synoptic episodes, in which Jesus exhibits a similar ability to proclaim God's attitude towards the past sins of an infirm individual.

Popular prophets

Prophets who arose from among the populace were either leadership popular prophets, who led mass movements that numbered hundreds or even thousands of adherents, or solitary popular prophets, who did not organize any such following for themselves. They seem to have made their appeals to the uneducated masses, either by announcing the nation's impending doom or – more frequently if Josephus' account represents historical reality – by promising divine intervention and salvation for those who heeded them. Unlike the solitary prophets, leadership popular prophets were in most cases impeded and executed by Roman forces. These prophets called the masses to action, and they normally promised some extraordinary event, which would be witnessed by those who joined their movements.[91]

From a socio-historical point of view, John the Baptist ought to be reckoned as a leadership popular prophet, as Webb argues convincingly. That John gained a following among the masses is evidenced by Josephus (*Ant* XVIII.118) and by primitive Christian sources (Mark 1.5; Matt 21.32/Luke 7.29 (Q?)) alike. Those who heeded John's call 'to

---

[91] Leadership popular prophets are the Samaritan (in 36 CE; Josephus, *Ant* XVIII.85–7); Theudas (44–6 CE; *Ant* XX.97–9; Acts 5.36); the group of prophets during Felix (52–60 CE; *Bell* II.258–60; *Ant* XX.167–8); the Egyptian (52–60 CE; *Bell* II.261–3; *Ant* XX.169–72; Acts 21.38); a prophet during Festus (60–2 CE; *Ant* XX.188); a Jerusalemite prophet (70 CE; *Bell* VI.283–5); possibly also Jonathan the Sicarius (73 CE; *Vita* 424; *Bell* VII.437–8). Solitary popular prophets are the ecstatic Jerusalemites during Herod's siege (37 BCE; *Bell* I.347); the various prophets who appeared shortly before the destruction of Jerusalem (70 CE; *Bell* VI.286–8); Jesus son of Ananias (62–70 CE; *Bell* VI.300–9).

come together in a baptism' formed a movement of people who 'seemed to be going to do everything at his advice', which was perceived as so acute a threat to political stability that Herod Antipas had the Baptist executed (*Ant* XVIII.116–19). Moreover, in the same way as Theudas, the Egyptian, and the unnamed prophets under Felix and Festus later in the first century, John also summoned his movement to make a journey through the wilderness.[92] To those who repented and who submitted to his baptism, John also promised salvation, as some other leadership prophets did later on, although they may have envisaged salvation from the current hardships rather than at the impending judgement.

As was pointed out above, Jesus himself must be categorized as a popular prophet. That he attracted a large following, to the point of being considered a political threat and executed as an insurrectionist, merits his inclusion among the leadership popular prophets.[93] Like John, who also had a narrower group of disciples, so Jesus also summoned some individuals to be his disciples, and he appointed the Twelve as the inner circle of his movement. Similar differentiations within the movements can be discerned in Josephus' descriptions of the leadership prophets in the following decades: the Samaritan's movement had several leaders, presumably second in rank to the prophetic figure himself, and the Egyptian prophet planned to set up a bodyguard of those who would break into Jerusalem with him (*Ant* XX.87; *Bell* II.262). As the prophetic leader of a sizable movement, Jesus therefore belongs to the category of leadership popular prophets.

As far as the sources tell, John and Jesus were the only popular prophets to offer, in some way or another, the forgiveness of sins. Whereas Josephus seems to contradict Mark's claim that John proclaimed 'a baptism of repentance for the forgiveness of sins' (Mark 1.4), by alleging that John's baptism could not be used 'for asking forgiveness for some sins' (*Ant* XVIII.117), the fact that he brings up the topic of sin and forgiveness indicates that John's prophetic message must somehow have involved this theme. Those who joined his popular movement by being baptized and by heeding his call to righteousness were being forgiven by God. John can therefore be seen as a mediator of forgiveness, just like some of the OT prophets. Viewing John's baptism as an expression of protest against the Jerusalemite temple establishment, Webb

---

[92] Webb, *John the Baptizer*, pp. 350–5, 361–4.

[93] R. A. Horsley, 'Popular Prophetic Movements at the Time of Jesus: Their Principal Features and Social Origins', *JSNT* 26 (1986), 3–27 (21–2); Meier, *A Marginal Jew*, vol. III, pp. 21–7.

even speculates that 'John, the mediator of forgiveness, might have pronounced the person forgiven, just as a priest pronounced a person forgiven after offering a sacrifice in the temple.'[94] Although it is unlikely that first-century priests pronounced forgiveness in connection with sacrifices (see Chapter 4), Webb's suggestion remains intriguing, in view of the forgiveness announcements made by Jesus of Nazareth, who was himself a member of the Baptist movement.[95]

Prophetic actions

The identification of Jesus as a leadership popular prophet, based on sociological categories, invites further consideration of the typically prophetic traits in Jesus' acting and speaking (see Luke 24.19). All types of first-century Jewish prophets, whether professional or popular, prophesied to some extent by word: even the leadership prophets must have appealed to oracles so as to gather the masses successfully around themselves.[96] That the historical Jesus spoke as a prophet in manifold ways – announcing the immediacy of salvation, predicting alleged future events and delivering oracles of judgement – is certain.[97] His prophetic *actions* are more complicated to classify and to interpret, in view of the differences in nature and function between the various kinds of 'signs' and wondrous deeds performed by, or expected from, first-century prophets. There is a danger of neglecting the elasticity of the term 'sign', both as it is used in the ancient sources and as it is employed by current scholarship. Actually, three distinct types of prophetic actions have been designated 'signs', and it is necessary to consider each of these categories individually.

Symbolic acts. While infrequently labelled 'signs' in the sources (Isa 8.18; 20.3; Ezek 4.3), prophetic symbolic acts are sometimes designated as such by critical scholars. Hooker aptly describes this phenomenon as 'the dramatic equivalent of the spoken oracle'.[98] As described in the OT, prophetic symbolic acts typically consist of God's command to the prophet, the performance of the act itself (normally in public) and an

---

[94] Webb, *John the Baptizer*, p. 193. See also Hengel and Schwemer, *Jesus und das Judentum*, pp. 313–16.

[95] See also G. R. Shafer, 'John the Baptist, Jesus, and Forgiveness of Sins', *PEGLMBS* 26 (2006), 51–67.

[96] Webb, *John the Baptizer*, p. 315.

[97] Aune, *Prophecy in Early Christianity*, pp. 171–88.

[98] M. D. Hooker, *The Signs of a Prophet: The Prophetic Actions of Jesus* (London: SCM, 1997), p. 38 (original emphasis removed).

accompanying oracle that establishes a point of comparison between the symbolic act and the event prophesied. In itself, the act may appear odd or even absurd, but there is nothing astonishing or miraculous about it; it frequently involves an object of everyday life, such as Ahijah's garment (1 Kgs 11.29–31), Jeremiah's girdle and jar (Jer 13.1–7; 19.10) and the yoke carried by Jeremiah but smashed by Hananiah (28.10). The interpretative oracle usually makes the analogy between symbol and prophesied event explicit.[99]

Of the several actions attributed to Jesus in the Gospels that have been identified as prophetic symbolic acts, only two actually constitute prophetic actions of the type laid out above. Firstly, Jesus' action in the temple (Mark 11.15–16 par./John 2.14–15) can be seen as a dramatic prophecy about its destruction, especially if coupled with the sayings to that effect (Mark 13.2 par.; Mark 14.58/15.29/Matt 26.61/27.40/John 2.19/GThom 71; cf. Acts 6.14).[100] Secondly, the breaking of the bread and sharing of the cup at the last supper (1 Cor 11.23–5/Luke 22.17–23; Mark 14.22–5/Matt 26.26–9) is open to such symbolic interpretation. A quite ordinary act, which involves common food and beverage, here seems to symbolize something else, perhaps Jesus' impending death.[101] The interpretation of these two events is very uncertain, but they conform remarkably well to the pattern of prophetic symbolic acts.

The one instance of symbolic action in this sense reported about an early Jewish prophet other than Jesus of Nazareth presupposes the sin–illness correlation and may have some bearing on the present investigation. Menahem the Essene, who had hailed the young boy Herod as king of the Jews, continued by prophesying Herod's rise and fall: 'With a gentle smile, Menahem slapped him on the backside and said, "And you will become a king. In the beginning you will do well, for you have been found worthy by God. And remember Menahem's slaps, so that this may be for you a symbol of your changing fortune"' (Josephus *Ant* XV.374). The prophet then goes on to relate how Herod will forget piety and justice, for which he will be punished at the end of his life. Menahem's symbolic spanking of Herod has been correctly identified as a prophetic act.[102] His

---

[99] 1 Kgs 11.31; Isa 20.3–4; Jer 13.9; 19.11; 27.8, 11–12; 28.2, 4, 11; Ezek 4.13.

[100] Trautmann, *Zeichenhafte Handlungen Jesu*, pp. 129–31; Sanders, *Jesus and Judaism*, pp. 61–76.

[101] Hahn, *Christologische Hoheitstitel*, p. 381 n. 2; Theissen and Merz, *Der historische Jesus*, pp. 382–3; D. Stacey, 'Appendix: The Lord's Supper as Prophetic Drama', in Hooker, *The Signs of a Prophet*, pp. 80–95.

[102] R. Meyer, 'προφήτης κτλ: C. Prophetentum und Propheten im Judentum der hellenistisch-römischen Zeit', in *TWNT*, vol. VI, pp. 813–28 (pp. 823–4).

oracle interprets it as an announcement of the punishment to be meted out for the king's sins. The possible implications of this passage for the interpretation of Mark 2.5b will be dealt with below.

Authenticating signs. If symbolic acts characteristically engage commonplace actions and objects, authenticating signs by nature involve a miraculous aspect. Some of the 'signs' (σημεῖα/אתות) performed by OT prophets are works normally beyond the capability of human beings (Exod 4.1–9; 2 Kgs 20.5–11); in other cases the prophet's foreknowledge of otherwise unexceptional events constitutes the miraculous feature (1 Sam 10.1–9; Isa 7.10–17). In an article that deals with miracles in the writings of Josephus, Betz points to some traits that generally distinguish signs from other miraculous events, which are labelled epiphanies: unlike epiphanies, which are divine acts of liberation, signs function to authenticate the prophet's claim to be a messenger of God. The epiphany has an overwhelming impact on all who experience it and leads them to praise God; the sign can be disbelieved, and it aims at creating faith and hope.[103] While Betz's observations pertain primarily to Josephus, the tendency to distinguish authenticating signs from epiphanies is found already in the OT.

How sharp a line can be drawn between 'epiphanies', on the one hand, and authenticating 'signs', on the other, is a question that has figured most prominently in the discussion of early Jewish prophets whom Josephus describes as having promised 'signs'.[104] While Rebecca Gray argues strongly for an understanding of all these 'signs' as authenticating signs, Eric Eve points out that Josephus' use of the terminology seems to go beyond the technical sense of authenticating signs.[105] Moreover, even if it is agreed that Josephus uses the terminology with reference to authenticating miracles, it is doubtful that he was so well acquainted with the popular prophets, or so interested in their message, that he was able, or indeed willing, to lay out their claim with detailed accuracy. That the notion of signs to validate the claims of a messenger of God was current in the first century is nevertheless certain, not only from Josephus' tendency in *Antiquities* to elaborate on the signs performed by the biblical prophets, but also from the presence of the topic in the Gospels.

---

[103] O. Betz, 'Miracles in the Writings of Flavius Josephus', in L. H. Feldman and G. Hata (eds.), *Josephus, Judaism, and Christianity* (Leiden: Brill, 1987), pp. 212–35 (pp. 222–5).

[104] Josephus, *Bell* II.259; VI.285; VII.438; *Ant* XX.168.

[105] Gray, *Prophetic Figures*, pp. 125–33; E. Eve, *The Jewish Context of Jesus' Miracles*, JSNTS 231 (London/New York: Sheffield Academic Press, 2002), pp. 30–2, 308, 319–20.

The historical Jesus' attitude towards authenticating signs seems to be accurately preserved in Mark 8.11–12; Q 11.16, 29. The historicity of the tradition concerning Jesus' refusal to comply with the demand to produce such a miracle is likely, not only in view of its multiple attestation, but also because of its discontinuity with the primitive Christian notion of Jesus as one who performed 'signs'[106] and with the constituent role played by 'signs' in primitive Christianity.[107] Moreover, if it is acknowledged that his denial of the request was caused, not so much by a determined strategy, as by the circumstance that his miracle-working capability was dependent on the recipients' faith, it coheres with the pre-Markan reminiscence of Jesus' limitations as a faith healer (Mark 6.5–6a). The tradition is significant for the present investigation in two major ways. On the one hand, Jesus would not, or could not, perform an authenticating sign, and his miracles were obviously not regarded as 'signs' in this sense, either by Jesus himself or by his potential adherents.[108] On the other hand, that Jesus was requested to offer a sign indicates that at least some of his contemporaries expected his mission to conform to a pattern evinced during the following decades by the Palestinian prophets of Josephus' chronicle.[109] This confirms the categorization of Jesus as a leadership popular prophet.

We have no evidence that any 'sign' was offered to authenticate a prophet's claim to mediate forgiveness. According to Josephus, the popular prophets who were active during the procuratorship of Felix claimed that 'signs of liberty' (*Bell* II.259; cf. *Ant* XX.168) would take place in the wilderness, and the false prophet at the temple promised 'the signs of salvation' (*Bell* VI.285) to his desperate followers. Whereas it is possible to see forgiveness as an aspect of 'liberty' as well as of 'salvation', what these prophets anticipated was probably liberation and rescue in a more concrete sense. As mentioned already, it is uncertain whether their 'signs' really had an authenticating function. In the latter case it is even unlikely.

Wondrous deeds. Miracles which are not authenticating signs are more sparsely attributed to OT prophets, with Elijah, Elisha and to some extent Moses being notable exceptions to this rule. While the OT itself lacks a terminology for categorizing miraculous events, Josephus

---

[106] Acts 2.22; cf. 4.30, and the Johannine tendency to portray Jesus as a sign-worker (John 2.11, 23; 3.2; 4.48, 53–4; 6.2, 14, 26, 30; 7.31; 9.16; 11.47; 12.18, 37).

[107] Acts 2.43; 4.16, 22; 5.12; 6.8; 8.6, 13; 14.3; 15.12; Rom 15.19; 2 Cor 12.12; Heb 2.4.

[108] Evans, *Jesus and His Contemporaries*, p. 79.

[109] Dunn, *Jesus Remembered*, p. 660.

characteristically employs the term 'wondrous' (παράδοξος) to denote miracles with a focus on their unexpected and surprising character.[110] He frequently uses the word for the large-scale saving miracles worked by God, which Betz identifies as epiphanies, but also for miraculous events of smaller dimensions.[111] In two cases, the working of 'wondrous deeds' is closely associated with intermediaries. First of all, when Moses turned his rod into a snake and changed the water into blood, he performed a 'wondrous thing' (παράδοξον, *Ant* II.285, 295). Secondly, and more prominently, Josephus highlights Elisha's miracle-working as the most important aspect, indeed the decisive proof, of his prophetic status: 'Shortly after this, the prophet finally died, a man famous for his righteousness and clearly favoured by God, for he displayed marvellous and wondrous deeds through his being a prophet (θαυμαστὰ γὰρ καὶ παράδοξα διὰ τῆς προφητείας ἐπεδείξατο ἔργα), and was reckoned worthy of a bright remembrance among the Hebrews' (*Ant* IX.182). Earlier in the narrative, Josephus offers one explicit example of what these wondrous deeds were. His rewriting of the biblical episode about Elisha's escape from the king of Aram (2 Kgs 6.8–23) emphasizes the miraculous nature of the Syrian soldiers who were blinded and who then regained their eyesight at the prophet's prayer. Josephus calls this 'a divine and wondrous event' (θεῖον καὶ παράδοξον πρᾶγμα, *Ant* IX.58). He also adds a brief scene, in which the Syrian king acknowledges the miraculous power of Elisha: 'Ader marvelled at the wondrous thing (τὸ παράδοξον), at the epiphany (ἐπιφάνειαν) and power of the Israelites' God, and at the prophet, with whom the Deity was so manifestly present; and so he decided no longer to attack the king of the Israelites in secret' (IX.60). Several important features of Josephus' view of Elisha's 'wondrous deeds' can be inferred from these passages. First of all, their basic characteristic is the amazement they cause because they were unexpected and commonly held to be outside the realm of ordinary human capabilities. Although the miracle referred to above is the only one to be singled out as 'wondrous', it is likely that Josephus also meant to include the rest of Elisha's extraordinary accomplishments in this designation. Secondly, they are wondrous *deeds* (ἔργα, IX.182), that is, in some sense worked by Elisha himself. Thirdly, this does not distract from the point that the ultimate source of the miracles is God himself. It is through prayer that Elisha moves God to make the Syrians blind and

---

[110] Eve, *The Jewish Context*, p. 28–9. Cf. Jdt 13.13; Wisd 5.2; 3 Macc 6.33; 4 Macc 4.14.

[111] See, e.g., Josephus, *Ant* II.223, 267; X.28.

seeing (IX.56–7), and the miracle is recognized as an 'epiphany' (IX.60). Fourthly, because of the fact that the miracles are ultimately worked by God, they serve to verify Elisha as a true prophet. Ader concludes from the miracle that God is 'manifestly present' with Elisha (IX.60), and in his eulogy Josephus takes the prophet's wondrous deeds as evidence that he was 'clearly favoured by God' (IX.182).[112] One of Elijah's miracles functions similarly (VIII.327). It is important to notice that this verifying effect of some miracles does not turn them into authenticating signs. The wondrous deeds are not worked for the purpose of self-authentication; nevertheless, they testify to the identity of the human being who performs them.

Apart from Jesus of Nazareth, none of the early Jewish prophets reported by Josephus is explicitly said to have worked 'wondrous deeds'. Many of the popular prophets promised that some miraculous event was about to occur. It is quite possible that, had they really come to pass (or had Josephus thought they had), most of these miracles would have merited recognition as 'wondrous deeds'. While they would certainly have been seen as 'epiphanies', at least two of them were also expected to happen through the active agency of the respective prophet (*Ant* XX.97, 170).[113] But these prophets appear to have expected a single, grandiose miracle to occur. They did not, as far as Josephus tells, aim at a career of repeatedly performing 'wondrous deeds'.

Jesus, for what can be known from the sources, promised one large-scale miracle that, like those announced by Theudas and the Egyptian prophet, failed to be realized before he was executed: the destruction of the current temple and the subsequent erection of a new one.[114] To what degree Jesus expected to take an active role in this event is very difficult to say, but it is noticeable that those versions of the saying that include a reference to the building of a new temple attribute this to Jesus.[115] His miracles of healing, on the other hand, ought to be regarded as 'wondrous deeds' of the kind associated with Elijah and Elisha. This is so, not only because Josephus appears to have described Jesus as a 'doer

---

[112] C. Begg, *Josephus' Story of the Later Monarchy (AJ 9,1–10,185)*, BETL 145 (Leuven University Press/Peeters, 2000), p. 218 n. 52.

[113] See Gray, *Prophetic Figures*, pp. 116–18; Eve, *The Jewish Context*, pp. 301–2, on the relative historical reliability of *Ant* XX.170 over against *Bell* II.262.

[114] Theissen and Merz, *Der historische Jesus*, p. 279.

[115] Mark 14.58/15.29/Matt 26.61/27.40; John 2.19; cf. *GThom* 71; Acts 6.14; Mark 13.2 par. See J. Ådna, *Jesu Stellung zum Tempel: Die Tempelaktion und das Tempelwort als Ausdruck seiner messianischen Sendung*, WUNT 2:119 (Tübingen: Mohr Siebeck, 2000), pp. 142–53.

of wondrous deeds' (παραδόξων ἔργων ποιητής, *Ant* XVIII.63), but also because the healings, as narrated in the gospel tradition, display the four features discerned above in Josephus' description of Elisha's wondrous deeds. First of all, while it is only Luke's version of the healing of the paralytic that characterizes Jesus' miracles as 'wondrous things' (παράδοξα, Luke 5.26), several of his healings create marvel and astonishment (Mark 1.27; 2.12; 5.20, 42; 7.37). Secondly, the healings are clearly 'deeds' of Jesus. Apart from the evangelists' explicit interpretation of Jesus' activity in these terms (Matt 11.2; Luke 24.19), it is significant that numerous episodes record gestures by which Jesus performs healings (Mark 1.31, 41; 5.41; 7.33; 8.23, 25; Luke 7.14; 13.13) and that Jesus is depicted as an active subject with the power to heal at his own will (Mark 1.27, 40–1; 5.13, 20; 7.37). Thirdly, as epiphanies the miracles generate praise of God, a theme emphasized in Luke (7.16; 13.13; 17.15) but present already in Mark (2.12). Fourthly, while not authenticating signs in the technical sense, they serve to verify who Jesus is. In Mark, to be sure, the messianic secret precludes the observers of Jesus' miracles from inferring too much about his identity from them (see Mark 1.27), but, in his reply to John the Baptist, Jesus expects John to take his healings as evidence that he is 'the coming one' (Q 7.18–23). Thus, even though the Lukan tendency to depict the miracles as deeds that both depend on and reveal Jesus' prophetic identity (Luke 7.16; 24.19) may have been prompted by an ambition to portray Jesus as a prophet like Elijah and Elisha, this portrayal is not without foundation in the career of the historical Jesus.

Implications for the historicity of Mark 2.5b, 10; Luke 7.47

Categorizing the historical Jesus as a leadership popular prophet is not tantamount to saying that his prophetic mission was in all respects similar to the careers of those later prophets. If they promised to offer 'signs' to authenticate their status as true prophets – which, I have argued, we cannot know for certain – Jesus did not. He seems to have performed at least two symbolic acts, thus availing himself of a distinctly prophetic form of action, for which there is no evidence from other early Jewish popular prophets, but rather from the sapiential prophet Menahem the Essene. His activity as a 'doer of wondrous deeds' in accordance with first-century perceptions of Elijah and Elisha is without parallel among the early Jewish prophets.

Whether other early Jewish prophets purported to forgive sins is unknown. It is quite possible that Jesus of Nazareth was not the only one to do so. As demonstrated in Chapter 4, the literature of the period displays an increased tendency to portray OT prophets as commissioned to 'forgive sins', in the sense of announcing God's forgiveness. This could reflect contemporaneous prophetic claims. Josephus' report about the sapiential prophets at Herod the Great's court shortly before his death indicates that those recognized as prophets were held to be able, like the prophets of old, to know what sins were causing God's punishment of any particular human being. John the Baptist, the leadership popular prophet from whose circle Jesus originated, functioned in some sense as a mediator of divine forgiveness. It is important to bear in mind, however, that no actual evidence indicates that John announced forgiveness verbally in the way that Jesus seems to have done. Thus, it is also possible that the announcement of forgiveness by word was one of the distinctive traits of Jesus' mission, especially if it was inspired by his interpretation of Isaiah's eschatological prophecies, as I have suggested above.

Mark 2.5b; Luke 7.47. The announcement of God's forgiveness, being a speech form characteristic of OT prophets as interpreted by early Judaism (and possibly also of actual early Jewish prophets), is positively coherent with Jesus' identity as a prophet. In my judgement, this lends some further support to the claim that Mark 2.5b can be traced back to the historical Jesus. Hooker suggests that Jesus' healing of the paralytic should be viewed 'as a sign that in the ministry of Jesus, men and women are experiencing the forgiveness of their sins', that is, as a prophetic symbolic act.[116] If this is appropriate, an inverted relationship would seem to exist between the symbolic acts of Menahem and those of Jesus respectively: whereas the former foretold Herod's sins and symbolically mediated the divine punishment for them, the latter recognized that the paralyzed man needed forgiveness for his past sins and mediated forgiveness in an equally symbolic manner. However, unlike the OT prophetic symbolic acts, and unlike Menahem's use of this form of action, Jesus' healing of the paralyzed man is a miracle, a 'wondrous deed'. It is thus preferable to regard Jesus' conjunction of the pronouncement of forgiveness with a miracle of healing as an expression of his 'contextual distinctiveness' (see Chapter 1).

In Luke 7.36–47, the portrayal of Jesus as a prophet is consistent with Luke's redactional tendency and therefore more difficult to evaluate. But the strong indications that 7.36–47 is substantially pre-Lukan (see Chapter 2), together with the insight that Luke's prophetic christology is the development of a feature of the historical Jesus' self-understanding,

---

[116] Hooker, *The Signs of a Prophet*, p. 40.

favour the conclusion that this is another instance where Luke may have made explicit a theme already extant in the episode he took from his source or tradition.

Mark 2.10. In Chapter 4, I employed the criterion of implausibility to argue that Mark 2.6–10 is unhistorical; this verdict can now be corroborated by use of the criterion of incoherence.

Although the historical Jesus certainly owed much of his success to his reputation as a healer, and although he also viewed his miracles as expressions of his identity (Q 7.18–23), he refused to perform 'signs' as the means of self-authentication (Mark 8.11–12; Q 11.16, 29). By contrast, Mark 2.10–11 portrays Jesus as doing precisely this, since, by virtue of this passage, the miracle of healing functions to authenticate his authority as the messianic Son of Man.[117] The absence of the word 'sign' is hardly decisive, for the Markan episode is related through other means to narratives about authenticating miracles performed by OT prophets. Its crucial statement of purpose, 'But so that you may know that...' (ἵνα δὲ εἰδῆτε ὅτι, Mark 2.10), parallels Elijah's prayer in the episode about his contest with the prophets of Baal:

> Lord, God of Abraham, Isaac, and Israel! Hear me, Lord, hear my [prayer and answer it] through fire, and may all this people realize that (καὶ γνώτωσαν πᾶς ὁ λαὸς οὗτος ὅτι) you are the Lord, the God of Israel, and I am your servant and have done these works on your behalf. Hear me, Lord, hear my [prayer and answer it] through fire, and may this people realize that (καὶ γνώτω ὁ λαὸς οὗτος ὅτι) you are the Lord God, and you have turned their hearts back.
>
> (1 Kgs 18.36–7)

The episode in 1 Kgs 18.30–40 does not employ the term 'sign' either but, in view of the purpose expressed, it cannot be doubted that Elijah performs an authenticating miracle. Another OT episode, which introduces the authenticating signs of Moses (Exod 4.1–9), contains a striking syntactic parallel to Mark 2.10: ' "So that they may believe you that (ἵνα πιστεύσωσίν σοι ὅτι) the Lord has appeared to you, the God of their fathers, the God of Abraham and the God of Isaac and the God of Jacob" – and the Lord said to him (εἶπεν δὲ αὐτῷ κύριος) again...' (Exod 4.5–6). In accordance with the structure of Exod 4.5–6, Mark 2.10 consists of a final clause without an apodosis and is

---

[117] J. Lierman, *The New Testament Moses: Christian Perceptions of Moses and Israel in the Setting of Jewish Religion*, WUNT 2:173 (Tübingen: Mohr Siebeck, 2004), p. 59.

immediately followed by the narrator's voice: 'he says to the paralytic'. Interesting as this structural agreement is, the more important point here is that 2.10 clearly places the Markan episode in the tradition of narrated authenticating signs. Furthermore, as Jeffrey Gibson points out, Jesus' question 'Which is easier…' and his comparison of two extraordinary pronouncements in 2.9 echo the dialogue between Isaiah and Hezekiah in 2 Kgs 20.8–10, where the king demands a 'sign' and then declares one of two alternatives offered by the prophets to be 'easy'.[118] Although the two episodes are not fully parallel, since Jesus does not leave it to his interlocutors to decide his course of action, Gibson is right to conclude that the Markan episode narrates an authenticating miracle.

A final point to be noted is Jesus' refusal according to Mark 11.27–33 to discuss the origin of his authority, a dialogue which arguably reflects a controversy in the career of the historical Jesus.[119] The saying in 2.10, which makes clear that Jesus is authorized by God and which invokes a miracle of healing in support of this claim to authority, is incoherent with the historical material.

Jesus as the prophetic Messiah

If, in retrospect, Jesus is appropriately placed among the first-century leadership popular prophets, to what category would he have been assigned by his contemporaries? According to Mark, Jesus was held to be either John the Baptist, or Elijah, or 'one of the prophets', and only the closest circle of followers recognized him as the Messiah (Mark 6.14–15; 8.28–9). The Gospel of John has the Baptist ward off similar proposals concerning his own identity (John 1.20–1, 25). The Gospels thus presume that there were in Jesus' lifetime certain expectations that one or several prophetic figures would come, who would be either revivified prophets of the past or new prophets, with or without a typological relationship to a particular OT prophet. Early Jewish literature confirms this picture to some extent, and it is appropriate to consider to what degree Jesus' mission may have been shaped to conform to such expectations, and what this implies for the authentication and interpretation of the synoptic forgiveness sayings.

---

[118] J. Gibson, 'Jesus' Refusal to Produce a "Sign" (Mk 8.11–13)', *JSNT* 38 (1990), 37–66 (58 n. 13).

[119] Meier, *A Marginal Jew*, vol. II, pp. 163–7.

Expectations for a coming prophet

It has been argued that expectations for a coming eschatological prophet are sparsely attested in early Jewish literature.[120] That the Qumranites entertained such speculation is nevertheless clear, however, and, besides the NT, there is sufficient evidence to prevent this expectation from being limited to only a sectarian concern. To compile from the various sources a coherent picture of the prophet to come is impossible, not only because the sources are generally vague in their descriptions, but also because they seem to conceive of the expected prophet in various ways. Some references merely indicate that a prophet will appear (1 Macc 4.46; 14.41; 1QS ix 11); others attribute to the coming prophet characteristics drawn from OT prophetic figures. The latter category can be divided into three basic types: those that speak of the prophet like Moses, the returning Elijah and the Prophet-Messiah (or 'the anointed prophet') respectively. It must be kept in mind that, while based on tendencies in the literature, this threefold division is a theoretical construction and no governing law.[121] An endless variety of speculations probably existed, in which, for example, Elijah could be identified as the prophet like Moses, and the image of the Prophet-Messiah could subsume traits of Moses, Elijah and other prophets.

The prophet like Moses. Secure early Jewish evidence for the notion of a coming prophet like Moses is found only in Qumran. Deut 18.18–19 is quoted in the *Testimonia* (4Q175 5–8) as a prophecy about a coming prophet. The juxtaposition of this passage with Num 24.15–17 and Deut 33.8–11 seems to suggest that the expectation was either that a single figure, who would be a prophet, a ruler and a priest, would come, or that there would be three distinctive figures coming (cf. 1QS ix 11).[122]

In some quarters of early Judaism, Moses himself was expected to return at the end of time.[123] Scholars have also argued that the first-century leadership popular prophets deliberately took up the role of the prophet like Moses.[124] This is possible, but not certain. The motives of 'wilderness', of 'passing through water', of 'signs and wonders' in the careers of these prophets all appear to recall the Exodus, but in a more

---

[120] Horsley, '"Like One of the Prophets of Old"', 437–43.

[121] Dunn, *Jesus Remembered*, pp. 656–7.

[122] Zimmermann, *Messianische Texte*, pp. 434–6.

[123] D. C. Allison, *The New Moses: A Matthean Typology* (Minneapolis: Fortress, 1993), p. 75 n. 172.

[124] Betz, 'Miracles', pp. 226–31; Allison, *The New Moses*, pp. 78–82; P. Bilde, *Den historiske Jesus* (Copenhagen: Anis, 2008), pp. 75, 78–9.

general manner and not necessarily with the focus on Moses. John the Baptist, one of the leadership popular prophets whose activity played on Exodus typology, did not claim to be a prophet like Moses, and as far as we can tell he was never identified as such by others.

A variety of primitive Christian literature associates Jesus with Moses. Most overtly, Acts 3.17–26 identifies Jesus as the prophet like Moses who is also the Messiah (cf. 7.37), and, when the Johannine Jesus is recognized as 'the prophet' (John 6.14; 7.40), this probably refers to the same concept.[125] Further points of contact between Moses and Jesus as they are depicted in the NT have been noted.[126] Wolfgang Kraus proposes that this identification is rooted in the mission of the historical Jesus, who claimed an authority vis-à-vis the Torah that could only be exercised by a prophet like Moses. This christology survived until the end of the first century, Kraus argues, but it was then replaced by other categories, partly due to the tendency of non-Jewish Christianity to distance itself from Judaism.[127] However, the purported allusions to Jesus' function as a prophet like Moses in the gospel tradition are vague, and whereas Jesus, as mentioned earlier, may have been identified by the masses as Elijah or as 'one of the prophets', the suggestion is never that he is Moses or a prophet like Moses. Moreover, the thesis of a gradual disappearance of the prophet-like-Moses christology is problematic: Mosaic typology is more prominent in later sources (Matthew and John) than in earlier ones (Mark), and the outright identification of Jesus as 'the prophet' is made in the Gospel of John, which more clearly than any other first-century writing distinguishes the disciples of Jesus from the disciples of Moses, that is, from 'the Jews' (John 9.28). It may be more adequate to understand the portrayal of Jesus in terms of the prophet like Moses as an intermediate step between, on the one hand, the most primitive prophetic christology (which was not specifically Mosaic) and, on the other, the triumph of a christology so high that prophetic categories as a whole were deemed insufficient and inappropriate.

The returning Elijah. The foundation for the belief that Elijah himself would return at the end of time is the prophecy of Mal 3.23–4, which, by the second century BCE, had become part of early Jewish eschatological expectations (cf. Ecclus 48.10).[128] It also appears to be attested in Qumran

[125] W. A. Meeks, *The Prophet-King: Moses Traditions and the Johannine Christology*, NovTSup 14 (Leiden: Brill, 1967), pp. 45–6, 87–99.

[126] Lierman, *The New Testament Moses*, pp. 271–86.

[127] W. Kraus, 'Die Bedeutung von Dtn 18,15–18 für das Verständnis Jesu als Prophet', *ZNW* 90 (1999), 153–76.

[128] Horsley, '"Like One of the Prophets of Old"', 440.

(4Q558 1 ii 4; cf. 4Q521 2 iii 2). With the possible exception of 4Q521, to which I will come back later, none of the texts that express a hope for the return of Elijah integrates in it the characteristics of the prophet's earthly mission as a doer of wondrous deeds. It remains obscure what first-century Jews thought that Elijah would do at his return, except for the general expectation that he would be a restorer of some kind. That he would forgive sins is not part of the documented expectations.[129]

Apart from Jesus, the only first-century prophet to be identified explicitly as Elijah in the sources is John the Baptist. But the identification is far from unanimous even within the NT, where Matthew alone has Jesus state explicitly that John is Elijah (Matt 11.14; 17.10–13; cf. Mark 9.11–13; Luke 1.17). In the Gospel of John, the Baptist denies that he is Elijah (John 1.21), and Josephus' notice about the Baptist does not portray him in Elijah-like terms (*Ant* XVIII.117). In spite of this, Markus Öhler points to several features that may indicate that John was identified as Elijah during his lifetime. The application of Mal 3.1 to John is doubly attested (Q 7.27; Mark 1.2) and thus very early, and the description of his Elijah-like clothing is most probably historically accurate (Mark 1.6; cf. Q 7.25; 2 Kgs 1.8). Öhler finds further evidence for John's identity as the returning Elijah in the dependence of his preaching on the Book of Malachi, in his concern with the marital status of Herod Antipas, and in his activity beyond the Jordan, where Elijah had been taken up to heaven.[130] None of this is entirely compelling, and the difficulty that pertains to the question of whether the historical John the Baptist played the role of Elijah is well illustrated by the lack of anything approaching scholarly consensus.[131]

The simplest and most convincing explanation for Mark's reports that Jesus was variously recognized as John the Baptist, Elijah or – somewhat strangely – 'a prophet like one of the prophets' (Mark 6.14–15; 8.28–9) is that such suggestions were made during his lifetime.[132] It must be noted, first of all, that Elijah *redivivus* was only one among several proposals that were offered concerning Jesus' identity. Suggestions were made that he was actually identical with the recently killed Baptist, or that he was a new prophet of the classic type. Matthew adds Jeremiah to

---

[129] *Pace* Kellermann, 'Wer kann Sünden vergeben außer Elia?', pp. 171–3.

[130] M. Öhler, *Elia im Neuen Testament: Untersuchungen zur Bedeutung des alttestamentlichen Propheten im frühen Christentum*, BZNW 88 (Berlin/New York: de Gruyter, 1997), pp. 103–5.

[131] *Ibid.*, p. 105 n. 403.

[132] N. T. Wright, *Christian Origins and the Question of God*, vol. III: *The Resurrection of the Son of God* (London: SPCK, 2003), p. 412; Dunn, *Jesus Remembered*, p. 657.

the list of options (Matt 16.14), and Luke claims that some held that one of the prophets of old had arisen (Luke 9.8, 19). Secondly, as has often been pointed out, the identification of Jesus as Elijah seems to have little to do with the expectations for an eschatological return of this prophet as reviewed above. Öhler perceptively remarks that Jesus' avowal to bring division through families and between generations (Q 12.51–3/*GThom* 16; cf. Q 14.26/*GThom* 55; 101; Mark 13.12 par.) is in outright opposition to the reconciliatory work expected of the eschatological Elijah.[133] Instead, what primarily prompted the recognition that Jesus was Elijah were probably certain aspects of his mission, which brought to mind the career of the *earthly* Elijah, first and foremost his ability to perform miracles. I have already consented to the view that Jesus' 'wondrous deeds' place him in a prophetic category, of which above all Elisha, but also Elijah and in some respects Moses, stand as representatives.[134] Meier draws attention to some other features evocative of Elijah in the mission of the historical Jesus: the itinerant character of his ministry and its concentration to Galilee, his calling of disciples in a manner analogous to Elijah's calling of Elisha, and his appointment of the Twelve as a step towards the re-establishment of the tribes of Israel. From this configuration of 'carefully chosen, programmatic actions', Meier concludes that it was 'the intention of Jesus to present himself to his fellow Jews as the Elijah-like prophet of the end time'.[135] However, with the exception of the last feature, all these components reflect the image of the earthly Elijah rather than the eschatological restorer.[136] Moreover, it is questionable whether all of these features were really deliberate strategies employed by Jesus to act out the role of Elijah.[137] The evidence does not seem to allow for the conclusion that Jesus himself programmatically strove to present himself as a 'prophet like Elijah' or even as Elijah *redivivus*.

The prophetic Messiah. The expectation that a prophetic Messiah would appear, based primarily on the Book of Isaiah, seems to have been current in more than one quarter of early Judaism. *Targum Jonathan* provides evidence for a messianic hope that combines royal, priestly and prophetic traits in the figure of the Servant. It is now widely held that

---

[133] Öhler, *Elia im Neuen Testament*, p. 249 n. 676.

[134] Meier, *A Marginal Jew*, vol. II, pp. 1044–5; Öhler, *Elia im Neuen Testament*, pp. 135–9, 199–202, 247–8; R. L. Webb, 'Jesus Heals a Leper: Mark 1.40–45 and *Egerton Gospel* 35–47', *JSHJ* 4 (2006), 177–202 (185, 201–2).

[135] Meier, *A Marginal Jew*, vol. III, pp. 623–4.

[136] See also Öhler, *Elia im Neuen Testament*, pp. 248–9.

[137] T. Hägerland, 'A Prophet like Elijah or according to Isaiah? Rethinking the Identity of Jesus' (in press).

*Tg*Isa 52.13–53.12 originated in the period 70–132 CE independently of primitive Christian interpretations of Isaiah 53.[138] That the targumic Servant-Messiah is a ruler is evident, but Koch has argued that in 52.13–53.12 the Messiah transcends his previous role as a Davidic king by appropriating priestly traits.[139] In addition, Jostein Ådna makes the plausible suggestion that the Servant-Messiah is also a prophet here.[140] In Qumran, the notion of the prophetic Messiah, or the Anointed Prophet, is developed on the primary basis of Isa 61.1–2.[141] The *Melchizedek* text quotes Isa 52.7 and identifies its 'messenger' (מבשר) as the 'anointed one of the spirit' ([ח]משיח הרו], 11Q13 ii 18), which is one of several echoes of Isa 61.1–2 in this text.[142] Similarly, the *Messianic Apocalypse* speaks of the Lord's 'anointed one' (משיח, 4Q521 2 ii 1) through whom, it seems, the Lord will perform wondrous deeds, such as belong to the mission of the spirit-filled prophet in Isa 61.1 (4Q521 2 ii 11–13). Collins proposes that the messianic agent in this text is in fact Elijah or a 'prophet like Elijah'.[143] It may, however, be more appropriate to speak of an image of the eschatological prophetic Messiah, into which have been subsumed certain features associated with the earthly Elijah, such as the obedience of the sky.

Both *Targum Jonathan* and the *Melchizedek* fragment mention the elimination of sins in connection with the Messiah, and these two texts have been suggested as antecedents for Mark 2.1–12.[144] Koch's claim that the Targum presents a Messiah who forgives sins has been convincingly refuted.[145] The Qumran text remains interesting as a possible background

[138] B. D. Chilton, *The Glory of Israel: The Theology and Provenience of the Isaiah Targum*, JSOTS 23 (Sheffield: JSOT Press, 1982), pp. 91–6; R. Syrén, 'Targum Isaiah 52:13–53:12 and Christian Interpretation', *JJS* 40 (1989), 201–12 (208–10).

[139] K. Koch, 'Messias und Sündenvergebung in Jesaja 53-Targum: Ein Beitrag zu der Praxis der aramäischen Bibelübersetzung', *JSJ* 3 (1972), 117–48 (134–5, 144).

[140] J. Ådna, 'Herrens tjener i Jesaja 53 skildret som triumferende Messias: Profettargumens gjengivelse og tolkning av Jes 52,13–53,12', *TTK* 63 (1992), 81–94 (89–90); J. Ådna, 'Der Gottesknecht als triumphierender und interzessorischer Messias. Die Rezeption von Jes 53 im Targum Jonathan untersucht mit besonderer Berücksichtigung des Messiasbildes', in Janowski and Stuhlmacher (eds.), *Der leidende Gottesknecht*, pp. 129–58 (pp. 156–7).

[141] J. J. Collins, *The Scepter and the Star: The Messiahs of the Dead Sea Scrolls and Other Ancient Literature*, ABRL (New York: Doubleday, 1995), pp. 116–23.

[142] M. P. Miller, 'The Function of Isa 61:1–2 in 11Q Melchizedek', *JBL* 88 (1969), 467–9.

[143] Collins, 'The Works of the Messiah', 102.

[144] Koch, 'Messias und Sündenvergebung', 136 (*Targum Jonathan*); C. A. Evans, 'The New Quest for Jesus and the New Research on the Dead Sea Scrolls', in Labahn and Schmidt (eds.), *Jesus, Mark and Q*, p. 173 (*Melchizedek*).

[145] Koch, 'Messias und Sündenvergebung', 136, 148; cf. Fiedler, *Jesus und die Sünder*, p. 95; Ådna, 'Der Gottesknecht als triumphierender Messias', pp. 153–4; Hofius, 'Kennt der Targum zu Jes 53 einen sündenvergebenden Messias?', pp. 94–8.

to Jesus' announcement of forgiveness. In the Book of Isaiah, the prophet professes that the Lord has sent him 'to announce liberty to captives … to announce a year of grace of the Lord' (Isa 61.1–2). 11Q13 instead speaks of 'the year of grace of Melchizedek' (ii 9) and explicates the contents of the preaching as a 'cancellation' of the 'debt' of sin: '[Melchize]dek [?], who will let them return to them and will announce liberty to them to cancel for them [the debt] of all their sins (עוונותיהמה לעזוב להמה [משא] כול)' (11Q13 ii 5–6). The interpretation is uncertain at a number of points, not least due to the fragmentary character of the column. Towards the end of line 5, דק is commonly restored to מלכי צדק, thus identifying the preacher of liberty as Melchizedek. Johannes Zimmermann remarks that if this conjecture is not presupposed, the 'anointed one of the spirit' (ii 18), rather than Melchizedek, could be taken as the grammatical subject of 'will announce' (ויקרא). This understanding is more convincing in the light of Isa 61.1.[146] Another possibility is to regard Melchizedek and the anointed one as identical throughout the text.[147]

Sven-Olav Back's recent study argues convincingly that the historical Jesus viewed himself as the prophetic Messiah of Isa 61.1–2. Jesus' response to the Baptist's question about his identity in Q 7.22–3 embodies an exegetical tradition also represented by 4Q521, which interprets the Book of Isaiah in prophetic-messianic categories. As the Qumran text expects a Messiah who will be a prophet, who will preach good news to the poor and who will heal, so Jesus claimed that his preaching and successful healings indicated that he was indeed the prophetic Messiah.[148] Two aspects of Jesus' preaching confirm this thesis. First of all, his 'gospel' of the kingdom of God (Mark 1.15) has clear affinities with the targumic interpretation of Isaiah.[149] The kingdom also plays a role in 4Q521 2 ii 7 and, most significantly, in the proclamation of the 'anointed one of the Spirit' according to 11Q13 ii 16 ('Your God [is king]', cf. Isa 52.7).[150] Secondly, some of the beatitudes, especially the macarism on the poor (Q 6.20b), seem to draw on Isaiah 61.[151] A

---

[146] Zimmermann, *Messianische Texte*, p. 397.

[147] R. Van de Water, 'Michael or Yhwh? Toward Identifying Melchizedek in 11Q13', *JSP* 16 (2006), 75–86 (81). For criticism of such an identification, see J. J. Collins, 'A Herald of Good Tidings: Isaiah 61:1–3 and Its Actualization in the Dead Sea Scrolls', in C. A. Evans and S. Talmon (eds.), *The Quest for Context and Meaning: Studies in Biblical Intertextuality*, FS J. A. Sanders, BIS 28 (Leiden/New York/Cologne: Brill, 1997), pp. 225–40 (p. 230).

[148] Back, *Han som kom*, pp. 123–31.

[149] B. D. Chilton, *God in Strength: Jesus' Announcement of the Kingdom*, SNTU B 1 (Freistadt: Plöchl, 1979), pp. 70–95.

[150] Back, *Han som kom*, pp. 108–15.

number of scholars have concluded that the opening verses of Isaiah 61 shaped Jesus' itinerant mission and were the matrix through which he interpreted it.[152] In view of 11Q13 and 4Q521, it is reasonable to think that this would imply a claim on Jesus' part to being the prophetic Messiah. And if Peter identified Jesus as the Messiah (Mark 8.29), he may have had in mind the 'anointed one of the Spirit' just as well as the royal-Davidic messianic concept traditionally assumed to be expressed.

Implications for the historicity of Mark 2.5b; Luke 7.47

Whereas some features of the mission of the historical Jesus evoked the early Jewish image of the earthly Elijah, the only designation of which Jesus himself seems to have approved – albeit in a subtle and restrained manner – was that of the 'anointed one of the spirit'. The question poses itself: can Jesus' practice of announcing forgiveness be viewed as a facet of his self-understanding as the prophetic Messiah?

The possibility that 11Q13 says that the prophetic Messiah will forgive sins is intriguing, but, as pointed out earlier, the interpretation of this passage is too uncertain to allow for any far-reaching conclusions. First of all, what it means 'to cancel (עזב) the debt of sins' is not clear. This may be a reference to forgiveness; but it may also be a reference to cultic atonement, for example. Secondly, whether Melchizedek and the Messiah are one and the same person or two different figures is not obvious; the grammatical subject in 11Q13 ii 5–6 is also in doubt. Thirdly, in contrast to 4Q521, the *Melchizedek* text is distinctly sectarian.[153] Notions found only in this document may have been peculiar to the Qumran community and should not be ascribed to early Judaism in general. Thus, it would be incorrect to suggest that the forgiveness of sins formed part of a concept of the prophetic Messiah current at the time of Jesus.

It is nonetheless possible that Jesus' distinctive version of the prophetic-messianic image included the announcement of forgiveness. The inclusion of this feature may have been prompted by either or both of two impulses. The first is the already noted capability of the prophetic-messianic concept of subsuming activities and characteristics that are not Isaianic but imported from notable 'prophets of old'. This phenomenon is at work in 4Q521, where the obedience of the heavens towards the

---

[151] Dunn, *Jesus Remembered*, p. 516.

[152] Evans, *Jesus and His Contemporaries*, pp. 120–1; Dunn, *Jesus Remembered*, p. 662; Hengel and Schwemer, *Jesus und das Judentum*, p. 467; Bird, *Are You the One Who Is to Come?*, pp. 98–104.

[153] Collins, 'A Herald of Good Tidings', p. 238.

Messiah appears to draw on Elijah's command of the sky.[154] It is also discernible in Q 7.22, where Jesus' mention of lepers being cleansed has no antecedent in Isaiah, but recalls the wondrous deeds of Moses and Elisha.[155] Accordingly, it cannot be ruled out that Jesus thought it appropriate for the prophetic Messiah to emulate OT prophets also by announcing God's forgiveness. A second impulse may have been the Isaianic prophecy about the eschatological healing and forgiveness of Israel (Isa 33.23b–24). If, as I suggested above, this passage inspired Jesus to announce forgiveness in conjunction with healing, a corollary seems to be that he viewed this announcement as a function of his identity as the prophetic Messiah. Like 4Q521, Jesus held that the eschatological wonders prophesied in the Book of Isaiah would be performed by the Messiah as an agent of God. He went beyond the Qumran document by claiming that these wonders were already happening, but his selection of messianic deeds also differed from that of 4Q521 and plausibly included the announcement of forgiveness.

Mark 2.1–5, 11–12; Luke 7.36–47 as expressions of Jesus' prophetic identity

Whether observed from a phenomenological point of view or through the lens of his contemporaries, the historical Jesus is firmly placed within the prophetic category, and his practice of announcing God's forgiveness is coherent with his identity as a prophet. The prophets of old had done so according to early Jewish interpretations of the scriptures. While there is no hard evidence that other first-century individuals exercised this function, the sources indicate in a few cases that prophets continued to bring attention to sin and forgiveness: Menahem the Essene is said to have foretold and acted out symbolically the divine punishment for the injustice wrought by Herod the Great; the professional prophets at Herod's deathbed identified the king's impiety as the source of his sufferings; and the popular prophet John the Baptist promised forgiveness to those Israelites who submitted to his baptismal ritual and turned to righteousness. Jesus' way of announcing forgiveness by word has no parallel among contemporary historical persons, but fits well within this general direction of early Jewish prophecy. It is also a possibility worthy of consideration that Jesus' understanding of Isaiah's eschatological prophecies motivated his declarations of forgiveness for individuals. As

---

[154] Collins, 'The Works of the Messiah', 102.
[155] Webb, 'Jesus Heals a Leper', 185.

the prophetic Messiah foretold by Isaiah, Jesus may have viewed this practice as an essential aspect of his mission, in addition to his performance of healings and his preaching of the gospel to the poor.

Conclusion

Some conclusions can now be drawn concerning the coherence of Mark 2.1–5, 11–12 and Luke 7.36–47 with the historical Jesus' career as a healer and prophet.

First of all, the supposed incoherence of Mark 2.1–5, 11–12 with Jesus' alleged denial of the correlation between sin and illness cannot be held against the historicity of the pre-Markan unit, since the evidence (apart from this very unit) is too meagre and ambiguous for Jesus' view on this matter to be established with certainty.

Secondly, in Jesus' preaching, forgiveness is analogous to healing in the sense that both are dependent on faith. His announcement of forgiveness in conjunction with healing (Mark 2.5b) is coherent with this attitude.

Thirdly, since he interpreted his success as a faith healer in the light of Isaiah's prophecies about the time of restoration, which include the promise of eschatological forgiveness, Jesus' announcement of forgiveness coheres with his understanding of his healings as eschatological – indeed as messianic – events.

Fourthly, the practice of announcing forgiveness is coherent with Jesus' identity as a prophet. This holds true independently of whether his inspiration in this regard came from early Jewish readings of narratives about the OT prophets, from contemporary prophets, from existing expectations for a prophetic Messiah, or from Jesus' own creative interpretation of the Book of Isaiah.

Fifthly, in Mark 2.10–11, Jesus employs a miracle of healing to prove to his critics that God has granted him messianic authority, which is incoherent with Mark 8.11–12/Q 11.16, 19; Mark 11.27–33. This seals the verdict on 2.6–10 as fictitious.

6

FORGIVENESS FROM JESUS TO THE GOSPELS

Recent historical Jesus scholarship has once again raised the demand that the application of negative criteria for historicity should be supplemented with a credible explanation of the origin of unhistorical material (see Chapter 1 above). To meet this rightful expectation, I will here sketch a tentative history of the development of the tradition behind Mark 2.1–12 from the earliest eyewitness account of a historical event, via oral transmission, up to its final integration into the Gospel of Mark.

To appreciate the present chapter correctly, it is necessary to note that its function is radically different from that of Chapters 2–5, all of which have assessed, by the use of conventional criteria, the historicity of the forgiveness episodes. The present chapter presupposes that this assessment is valid, and does not in and of itself provide an argument either for or against the historicity of the various elements of the episodes. Its purpose is to provide the 'missing links' that, granted the validity of my argument above, are needed to explain how and why the secondary material in Mark 2.6–10 was added to the episode.

The reconstructed – and, of course, entirely hypothetical – tradition- and redaction-history of the episode will be schematized into three phases. First of all, attention will be given to the historical event itself and also to the shape of the eyewitness account that must have existed. Secondly, I will turn to the form in which the story was transmitted orally, to the rhetorical elaboration which I suggest gave rise to 2.6–10, and to its *Sitz im Leben*. Thirdly, I will discuss briefly the impact of the inclusion of this episode within the larger narrative units: first within a written collection of controversy episodes, and then within the Gospel of Mark.

First phase: the historical event and its earliest recollection

A healing performed by the historical Jesus

The historical core of Mark 2.1–12 par. is Jesus' successful healing of a man who suffered from paralysis. Its venue cannot be settled with certainty, but it is entirely plausible that the setting was indeed a house in Capernaum, as Mark alleges. While geographical names are not frequent enough to be categorized a stock item of miracle episodes in the Gospels, Gerhardsson's comparison with rabbinic material demonstrates that they often fulfil a mnemonic function in oral transmission.[1] Thus, it is not impossible that the reference to Capernaum in Mark 2.1 derives from an oral form of the episode. Moreover, as Theissen has pointed out, the passing mention of a toll-booth in the subsequent episode (2.14) is congruent with a setting in Capernaum and presupposes the political state of affairs prior to the death of Herod Antipas in 39 CE.[2] If the oral stories behind 2.1–12 and 2.13–14 were transmitted together, the healing would also have been depicted as taking place in Capernaum. Thirdly, as mentioned in Chapter 2 above, Mark's narration – unlike the parallel in Luke – of how the roof was dug through in order to bring the paralyzed man to Jesus is consonant with first-century rural Galilean architectural realities. Whereas the description of the space in front of the door being crowded with people (2.2) is under suspicion as redactional (cf. 1.33), it is nevertheless remarkable how well both this detail and the implied reference to a thatched roof fit with the 'house of Peter' excavated in the late 1960s – although that precisely this was indeed the venue of the event cannot, of course, be proven.[3] None of these circumstances constitutes positive evidence that Mark's location of the event in Capernaum is historically accurate, but they indicate that there is nothing inherently implausible about this setting.

For the healing itself, stronger indicators of historicity can be identified. First of all, Jesus' practice of healing people who suffered from paralysis is multiply attested across sources and forms by virtue of Q 7.22; put differently, Mark 2.3–5, 11–12 is coherent with this saying of the historical Jesus in Q.[4] Secondly, and more importantly, in the present study I have argued that Jesus' announcement of forgiveness in 2.5b should be acknowledged as authentic according to the criteria of

[1] Gerhardsson, *Memory and Manuscript*, p. 145.

[2] G. Theissen, *Lokalkolorit und Zeitgeschichte in den Evangelien: Ein Beitrag zur Geschichte der synoptischen Tradition*, 2nd edn (Göttingen: Vandenhoeck & Ruprecht, 1992), pp. 127–8.

[3] V. Corbo, *The House of Saint Peter at Capharnaum: A Preliminary Report of the First Two Campaigns of Excavations, April 16–June 19, Sept. 12–Nov. 26, 1968*, transl. S. Saller, SBF Collectio minor 5 (Jerusalem: Franciscan Printing Press, 1969), pp. 35–41, 48. See also J. H. Charlesworth, *Jesus within Judaism: New Light from Exciting Archaeological Discoveries* (London: SPCK, 1989), pp. 109–15; J. D. Crossan and J. L. Reed, *Excavating Jesus: Beneath the Stones, Behind the Texts* (New York: HarperCollins, 2002), pp. 92–7.

[4] Meier, *A Marginal Jew*, vol. II, pp. 685–7.

multiple attestation, discontinuity and coherence. Jesus' announcement is so deeply embedded in its narrative context that it can hardly have been transmitted independent thereof. Accordingly, the historicity of 2.5b implies the historicity of some rudimentary form of the episode about the healing of the paralytic. The following elements seem indispensable to the narration and probably formed part of the historical event: the diagnosis of the illness as paralysis; the bringing of the paralyzed man to Jesus; Jesus' announcement of forgiveness and his command to the paralytic to rise and walk; and the successful outcome of the healing.

If this much can be labelled a historical event with a reasonable degree of certainty, all attempts to determine what significance Jesus himself attributed to the healing will necessarily be far more speculative. In Chapter 5, I nevertheless ventured to suggest how this event may have been interpreted within the wider context of Jesus' mission as a healer and prophet, and I will summarize my proposal in the following.

Reflecting on his extraordinary capability to heal those individuals who trustfully acknowledged the Spirit of God at work in him, Jesus came to think of these healings as the fulfilment of Isaiah's prophecies about the restoration of Israel – prophecies which were known to him from public readings of the scriptures, and which he, perhaps unlike more learned hearers and readers, interpreted in a literal sense. His success as a healer, probably coupled with charismatic experiences of the Spirit, further led him to think (or at least to ponder the possibility) that he was in fact the 'anointed one of the Spirit', the prophetic Messiah speaking in the Book of Isaiah. He was the agent through whom God was establishing his rule over a restored Israel. This rule – the kingdom of God – meant not only the restoration of health for those who suffered from bodily ailments, but also a reversal of the misfortunes for the poor and the forgiveness of sins, in accordance with Jesus' understanding of Isaiah (cf. Isa 61.1; 33.24).

The paralyzed man was brought to Jesus in an atmosphere of expectation that Jesus would be able to heal this person. It is under such circumstances that Jesus, as a faith healer, succeeded in healing people; when the attitude was critical, he could not produce any miracles (Mark 6.5a; cf. Q 11.16, 29/Mark 8.11–12), nor would he mediate God's forgiveness (Q 12.10/Mark 3.28–9). In the case under consideration, Jesus apparently sensed enough recognition of himself as the agent of God to enable him to heal the paralyzed man. Announcing God's forgiveness, he acted like the prophets of old, but he also manifested his understanding of the expected healing as a realization of Isaiah's prophecies about an eschatological age in which 'the lame' would 'leap like a deer' and 'take booty', and no one would be ill, since the people's 'iniquity' would be 'forgiven' (Isa 33.23b–24; 35.6).

The earliest recollection of the event

If a historical event underlies the Markan episode, it follows that the ultimate source of the narrative must be one or several eyewitnesses who, having been present at the event, recalled and retold it. As a matter of fact, if the unhistorical portion 2.6–10 is excised from the episode, we are left with a brief story which contains no inherently unrealistic details, and which as a whole conforms to what could be expected of a first-hand report of such an event.

The identity of the eyewitness(es), in the present case, remains unknown. The lack of personal names other than that of Jesus is significant in view of Richard Bauckham's recent proposal that the naming of some minor characters in the Gospel of Mark implies their status as eyewitnesses; for example, according to Bauckham, the ultimate source of the passage about how Levi son of Alphaeus became a disciple (Mark 2.14) may be Levi himself.[5] In some other Markan episodes, the individuals healed by Jesus may have been the primary eyewitnesses of the miraculous events.[6] The paralyzed man in Mark 2.1–12 not only remains unnamed, but lacks any specific characteristics; once he has been healed, the narrator loses all interest in him. He is such a colourless and anonymous figure in the narrative that it is highly unlikely that he has functioned as the source of this event. Furthermore, unlike some other episodes, which indeed contain indications of having been derived from Peter's testimony (see especially 1.29),[7] nothing in this episode or indeed throughout 2.1–3.6 suggests a specifically Petrine perspective, although it is possible that the incident occurred in the house of Peter's family. Peter is not mentioned, and the proposal that the reference to Jesus' being 'at home' (2.1) presupposes Peter as the narrator is not compelling.[8] The eyewitness behind the narrative in its earliest form is, therefore, anonymous. It may have been Peter, a member of his household, another disciple, or a group of

---

[5] R. Bauckham, 'The Eyewitnesses and the Gospel Traditions', *JSHJ* 1 (2003), 28–60 (44–7); R. Bauckham, *Jesus and the Eyewitnesses: The Gospels as Eyewitness Testimony* (Grand Rapids, MI: Eerdmans, 2006), pp. 39–66.

[6] Bauckham, *Jesus and the Eyewitnesses*, pp. 52–4.

[7] *Ibid.*, pp. 158–9; Byrskog, 'The Early Church', 218.

[8] Cf. J. Weiss, *Das älteste Evangelium: Ein Beitrag zum Verständnis des Markus-Evangeliums und der ältesten evangelischen Überlieferung* (Göttingen: Vandenhoeck & Ruprecht, 1903), p. 155.

people present on the occasion; we cannot know, but for the event to have been remembered and narrated at all, the presence of one or more eyewitnesses must be assumed. The earliest recollection of the event quite probably included details that are now irrecoverably lost. It lies in the nature of traditio-historical investigation that, whereas additions can frequently be identified in a given unit, abbreviations and loss of detail are normally impossible to reconstruct. The dramatic and seemingly irrelevant details of how the paralyzed man was 'carried by four' and brought to Jesus through the roof could have been included in the earliest recollection.[9] On the other hand, in keeping with the general tendency, such details may equally well have been added at a later stage of the tradition.[10] Moreover, two interpretative elements in the episode may either go back to eyewitness memory or derive from a secondary expansion. Firstly, the assertion that it was on 'seeing their faith' (2.5) that Jesus announced forgiveness is an interpretation of the chain of events, which could have been made by an observer who had witnessed other healings at which Jesus acknowledged the 'faith' of those who sought to be healed by him. Secondly, the final remark about the amazement of the crowd could reflect the emotional reaction of those present to what they perceived to be a miraculous event. Both features may, however, equally well have been added to the story during subsequent retelling.

Second phase: the oral tradition and its rhetorical elaboration

In Chapter 1, I mentioned the affinities between individual units of the gospel tradition on the one hand and the ancient rhetorical categories of chreia and apomnemoneuma on the other. This part of the present chapter will be devoted to reconstructing, first of all, the shape of the traditional unit behind Mark 2.1–12 in its earliest oral form, and, secondly, the process of rhetorical elaboration that may explain the inclusion of secondary and unhistorical elements into the episode.

Chreiai and apomnemoneumata are not distinctly oral forms of narration. On the contrary, chreiai were read and copied in writing at the primary stage of Hellenistic education, with the purpose of acquiring

---

[9] Taylor, *Mark*, p. 192; Meier, *A Marginal Jew*, vol. II, p. 680.
[10] E. P. Sanders, *The Tendencies of the Synoptic Tradition* (Cambridge University Press, 1969), pp. 144–6.

and improving the skills of reading and writing well.[11] However, the dividing line between oral and literary modes of expression is hardly absolute, and students were also expected to memorize and recite chreiai.[12] Moreover, some evidence that gospel tradition was transmitted orally in forms influenced by these literary rhetorical categories comes from Paul's rehearsal in writing of a tradition that he had earlier transmitted orally to the church at Corinth:

> The Lord Jesus, on the night when he was about to be handed over, took bread and, having given thanks, broke it and said, 'This is my body, which is for you. Do this in remembrance of me'; likewise also the cup, after having dined, saying, 'This cup is the new covenant through my blood. Do this, as often as you drink, in remembrance of me'.
>
> (1 Cor 11.23b–25)

The structure of this traditional formulation comes very close to that of the 'chreia proper', that is, the chreia in its most concise form. Michel Patillon suggests that the formal composition of a 'single syntactic system', in effect one main clause which may be qualified through participial clauses, is an integral characteristic of the chreia. If the chreia is expanded through the further addition of main clauses, it ceases to be a chreia in the narrow sense.[13] In 1 Cor 11.23b–25, the two instances of parataxis ('and ... broke it and said') preclude the formal classification of the unit as a perfect example of an unexpanded chreia according to the textbooks. The shape of the passage nevertheless indicates that some items of gospel tradition were transmitted in chreia-like oral form.

A brief apomnemoneuma

On the premise that the oral tradition underlying Mark 2.1–12 also conformed to progymnastic patterns, three main possibilities exist. First of all, the earliest tradition may have circulated in the form of a chreia proper, only to be expanded at a secondary (oral or literary) stage into the present apomnemoneuma. Secondly, a relatively brief apomnemoneuma comprising the content of the earliest recollection, as I tentatively

---

[11] R. F. Hock and E. N. O'Neil, *The Chreia and Ancient Rhetoric: Classroom Exercises: Translated and Edited*, SBLWGRW 2 (Atlanta: Society of Biblical Literature, 2002), pp. 1–49.

[12] Byrskog, 'The Early Church', 213–14.

[13] M. Patillon (ed.), *Aelius Théon: Progymnasmata: Texte établi et traduit* (Paris: Les Belles Lettres, 1997), pp. lviii–lix.

reconstructed it above, may have been elaborated further through the insertion of secondary elements into a longer apomnemoneuma. Thirdly, it is conceivable that the entire episode, or at least 2.3–12, reproduces the earliest attainable tradition without substantial alterations. The third alternative would mean that the story was told from the beginning with the inclusion of fictional elements. Some considerations, however, make this last alternative less likely. As scholars have noticed ever since Wrede, the Markan episode leaves an impression of being composite in character, not least through its sudden introduction of the scribes in 2.6. Had the apomnemoneuma been transmitted originally as a conflict story, it would have been appropriate to introduce Jesus' adversaries at its opening, as is the case in Luke's rewritten version (Luke 5.17; see Chapter 2 above). Indeed, as I will argue below, the controversy dialogue in 2.6–10 makes good sense as an instance of rhetorical expansion of 2.3–5, 11–12. Here I will therefore confine myself to the first and second options.

A chreia proper in Mark 2.5, 11

At first glance, the hypothesis of a chreia proper as the core around which the rest of the episode has been subsequently built may appear attractive. Such a chreia can be isolated within the episode, once the secondary expansion 2.6–10 has been expurgated: 'Jesus, seeing their faith, said to the paralytic, "Child, your sins are [being] forgiven. I tell you, Rise, take your pallet, and go to your home!"' (Mark 2.5, 11). This passage meets the criteria for a chreia established in the *Progymnasmata*: it is a concise pronouncement attributed to a specific person.[14] Moreover, it is fully congruent with Patillon's formal criterion that these features should be contained within a single syntactic system. The chreia proper begins with a conjunct participle phrase, 'Jesus, seeing (ἰδών) their faith', which is a frequent characteristic of unexpanded chreiai. Since Jesus has not been named earlier in the Markan episode, the mention of his name in the participial phrase draws attention to the pronouncement to come. Then follows a brief, and somewhat surprising, statement, 'Child, your sins are being forgiven', in direct speech introduced with 'he said' (λέγει).[15] The chreia thus reconstructed can be compared to Theon's example of a 'concise chreia' (σύντομος χρεία): 'Epameinondas, dying childless, said to his friends: "I have left two daughters, the victory at Leuctra and the one

---

[14] Theon, *Prog.* 201.16–18; 202.2–5, 13–15; Hermogenes, *Prog.* 6.3–5; 7.4–6; Aphthonius, *Prog.* 3.21–2; Nicolaus, *Prog.* 19.7–9; PSI 1.85 1–4.
[15] Cf. Hermogenes, *Prog.* 7.16–17.

at Mantineia'" (Theon, *Prog.* 213.16–17). According to the ancient text-books, a chreia like this should be classified as a verbal chreia (χρεία λογική), since it is made up exclusively of words and does not involve any action on the part of the principal character.[16] Theon's comprehensive classificatory system makes a more precise categorization of Mark 2.5, 11 possible. There exist, according to Theon, two forms of the verbal chreia: the declarative (ἀποφαντικόν) and the responsive (ἀποκριτικόν).[17] Since the latter subcategory comprises verbal chreiai pronounced in response to some verbal activity by a speaker other than the principal character, and no one but Jesus has spoken in the Markan episode up to this point, the chreia should be classified as declarative. Among the declarative verbal chreiai, Theon further distinguishes between those pronounced 'voluntarily' (καθ' ἑκούσιον) on the one hand and those that are prompted by some circumstances (κατὰ περίστασιν) on the other. In the former type the chreia is given without mention of any preceding event or specific situation. The chreia recorded by Theon to exemplify the latter type comes close to the expression in Mark 2.5: '"Diogenes the cynic philosopher, on seeing (ἰδών) a wealthy ill-mannered young man, said, This is silver-plated filth." For Diogenes did not state it spontane-ously, but from what he saw' (*Prog.* 203.6–9). In Theon's classification system, therefore, Mark 2.5, 11 can be identified as a declarative verbal chreia prompted by special circumstances.

The reference to 'their faith' (Mark 2.5) is meaningful only in the light of some preceding relating of the circumstances. Thus, if the chreia proper was ever transmitted independently of the narration in 2.3–4, it must have been reworked in order to fit its present context. That this should have happened in the expansion process is not unthinkable. A student was to some extent at liberty to adapt and to improve the word-ing of a chreia prescribed by the teacher.[18] As Theon says, to present the chreia would mean to 'express [it] with utter clarity, in the same words, if possible, or even in other words' (210.7–9). In later *Progymnasmata* such rewording becomes compulsory, so that the reproduction of a chreia is labelled 'paraphrastic'.[19] It is also natural for a chreia to be adapted

---

[16] Theon, *Prog.* 202.18–21; Hermogenes, *Prog.* 6.6–14; Aphthonius, *Prog.* 4.2–5. The translation 'verbal chreia' has been imported from G. A. Kennedy (transl.), *Progymnasmata: Greek Textbooks of Prose Composition and Rhetoric: Translated with Introductions and Notes*, SBLWGRW 10 (Atlanta: Society of Biblical Literature, 2003), p. 16.

[17] Theon, *Prog.* 203.2–205.19. See Hock and O'Neil, *The Chreia*, pp. 27–32.

[18] Hock and O'Neil, *The Chreia*, pp. 37–9; Patillon, *Aelius Théon*, p. 24, n. 145.

[19] Aphthonius, *Prog.* 4.13–14.

to the narrative context when included in a biographical work.[20] If the chreia in Mark 2.5, 11 has been manipulated in this way, it is conceivable that its 'circumstance' was differently phrased in an earlier version of the chreia, for example, 'Jesus, seeing a paralytic, said to him...' Before this hypothesis can be evaluated, another option has to be considered.

A brief apomnemoneuma in Mark 2.3–5, 11–12

I turn now to the possibility that Mark 2.3–5, 11–12 was already in its most primitive shape an apomnemoneuma, in which an *exordium* narrating the background events (2.3–4) was followed by the chreia proper (2.5, 11) and a brief *conclusio* (2.12). This structure would roughly correspond to that of an expanded chreia as illustrated by the chreia chapter in Theon's *Progymnasmata*.

An *exordium* (προοίμιον), according to Theon, should 'not be such as to suit other chreiai, but peculiar to the one being prescribed' (216.10–12). This applies to the exercise that later theorists call elaboration (ἐργασία), which should not be confused with the exercise of expansion (ἐπεκτείνειν), but Theon's illustrative example of chreia expansion makes clear that a kind of exordium is appropriate to the latter exercise as well. Theon expands the short description of Epameinondas as 'dying childless' into a eulogy of Epameinondas' good character and a more detailed description of the circumstances that led up to the pronouncement. Besides being encomiastic, the *exordium* thus provides the *narratio* of events that form a backdrop to the chreia: 'As a Boeotarch at Leuctra, he conquered the enemy, and as he was fighting during a campaign for his country, he died at Mantineia. Now when he had been wounded and was dying, while his friends were lamenting among other things that he was going to die childless, he said, smiling...' (213.21–6). Since Mark 2.1–2 exhibits some traces of Markan redaction (see Chapter 2 above), it is likely that the *exordium* of the traditional apomnemoneuma encompassed 2.3–4 (and possibly also included the mention of Capernaum now found in 2.1). From a rhetorical point of view, at least two reasons for the vivid depiction of events in 2.3–4 can be discerned. First of all, it is in keeping with Theon's general instruction that an *exordium* should be specific and unique to the individual chreia; stock introductions should be avoided. Secondly, it is a common characteristic of the *exordium* to build up tension and, as it were, compel

---

[20] Hezser, 'Die Verwendung der hellenistischen Gattung Chrie', 392–3.

the speaker to deliver the chreia proper.[21] In this case, the determined and almost insolent effort being made by the companions of the paralyzed man presents Jesus with a challenge that cannot be evaded. When Theon comes to the 'point' of his expanded chreia, that is, to the saying attributed to Epameinondas, he paraphrases it in accordance with the progymnastic ideal of attaining clarity. Whereas the brief chreia has Epameinondas say 'I have left behind two daughters: the victory at Leuctra, and the one at Mantinea' (213.16–17), in Theon's expansion he is verbose, even over-explicit: '"Stop crying, friends", he said, "for I have left to you two immortal daughters, two victories of our native country against the Lacedaemonians: the one at Leuctra as the older one, and as the younger the one I now have gained at Mantinea"' (213.26–214.4). The pre-Markan apomnemoneuma shows no signs of such expansion of Jesus' words in 2.5, 11.

Theon's example of an expanded chreia does not involve a *conclusio*, but that such an element should be included is not unexpected in view of the fact that later textbooks specify it for the exercise of elaboration. Hermogenes advises the student to round off his elaboration with an exhortation (παράκλησις) that brings trustworthiness to the principal actor or speaker of the chreia.[22] Correspondingly, Aphthonius lists a brief *conclusio* (ἐπίλογος) as the final part of the elaborated chreia, to follow on the various arguments (*Prog.* 4.15). The latter author provides us with such a conclusion at the end of his model chreia elaboration: 'On seeing this, one must marvel at how splendidly Isocrates philosophized about education' (6.18–19). Mark 2.12 forms a narrative *conclusio* to the apomnemoneuma. The description of how the paralytic rises, takes up his pallet and departs serves to confirm the efficiency of the command in 2.11, with the effect that Jesus' trustworthy character is underlined, and the multitude's reaction is phrased in πάθος-vocabulary akin to that of Aphthonius above.

In my opinion, it is plausible that the earliest attainable shape of the tradition behind the Markan episode was made up mainly of historical reminiscences, with some details derived from the interpretative memory of the eyewitness(es), and that it corresponded roughly to what is now Mark 2.3–5, 11–12. In view of the fact that traditions were not necessarily transmitted in the 'pure' form of chreiai proper, this is the simplest and therefore preferable solution: Mark 2.5, 11 was not handed down as an independent chreia, but formed part of a longer unit, that is, an

[21] Mack and Robbins, *Patterns of Persuasion*, pp. 75–6, 91.
[22] Hermogenes, *Prog.* 8.12–13; cf. Nicolaus, *Prog.* 24.12–13.

apomnemoneuma including the narrative elements of 2.3–4. This piece of gospel tradition was therefore transmitted in accordance with the pro-gymnastic rhetorical form of apomnemoneuma.

To be sure, there is an important difference between this tradition and the apomnemoneuma as exemplified by Theon: the pre-Markan trad-itional unit is more thoroughly narrativized. Thus, whereas in Theon the *exordium* uses the voice of the 'narrator' to praise the principal character by the overt telling of his virtues, in the pre-Markan apomnemoneuma words of praise and astonishment are placed on the lips of the crowd in the *conclusio*. A corresponding exploitation of characters within the nar-rative at the expense of the narrator's voice occurs in the secondary parts of the elaborated apomnemoneuma, as will be shown shortly below. This difference from the standard shape of the rhetorical units may be due to the fact that, as individual units, the chreiai and apomnemoneumata about Jesus from early on formed part of a larger narrative, which even-tually resulted in the composition of written Gospels in the biographical genre. This obvious and recurring point of difference between the pro-gymnastic units and the gospel tradition must not be allowed to obscure the striking points of agreement.

The elaboration of the apomnemoneuma

I have argued in Chapters 4 and 5 above that Mark 2.6–10 is fictitious in the sense that this dialogue does not represent an exchange between the historical Jesus and his critics. It is now time to see how the passage can be explained as the result of rhetorical elaboration of the original brief apom-nemoneuma into a longer unit. We cannot know whether this process of elaboration occurred in the oral tradition or as part of literary activity. For reasons to be given in the next part of this chapter, 2.6–10 was probably already included in the episode when Mark integrated it into his Gospel, but it is entirely possible that the passage had no existence prior to the composition of a written source, which was later utilized by Mark. Equally possible, however, is the hypothesis that the elaboration took place orally, and I will discuss the elaboration in the present part of the chapter without presuming to have demonstrated that it belongs to the oral phase.

A quaestio *and second chreia proper including* argumentatio *in Mark 2.6–10*

The introduction in 2.6–7 of the scribal questioning of Jesus' state-ment in 2.5 does not conform strictly to what the rhetorical textbooks recommend. From the *Progymnasmata*, one would expect an elaboration of the chreia to consist of different kinds of arguments to substantiate it, offered by the elaborator himself and placed immediately after the chreia proper. But from the perspective of rhetorical criticism, 2.6–7 seems more closely tied to what follows it, that is, a second chreia proper in 2.8–11, than to what precedes it. Moreover, the argumentation is not given in the voice of the narrator but is placed on the lips of Jesus himself. The scribal protest prepares for the next chreia proper by providing a *quaestio* (στάσις) to which Jesus may then respond in 2.8–11. While the introduction of *quaestio* is not part of the elaboration exercise as presented by the ancient textbooks, it occurs rather frequently in the Gospel episodes that have been identified as elaborated chreiai, which often effectively turns them into judicial rhetoric.²³ This is also how the *quaestio* of 2.6–7 functions: it presents the case against Jesus through an enthymemic statement, in which the scribes state their major premise (that God alone can forgive sins) and the logical conclusion (that Jesus blasphemes), leaving out the minor premise (that Jesus has claimed to forgive sins) which is by no means obvious, since the agent of forgiveness is unspecified in 2.5.

Formally, Jesus' response, which begins in 2.8, corresponds to the statement of 2.5: a participial phrase, 'Immediately Jesus, discerning in his spirit that they were thinking like this within themselves', is followed by direct speech, again introduced with 'he said (λέγει) to them'. Here too Jesus is mentioned by name, which signals that the saying is a second chreia proper, in fact, another 'declarative verbal chreia prompted by special circumstances'. Moreover, and also just as 2.5, the second chreia proper cannot stand independently of what precedes it: the statement that 'they were thinking like this within themselves' requires the scribal *quaestio* in order to be meaningful. This could indicate that the introduction of the chreia proper has been reworked in order to fit the present context or, far more plausibly, that it never had a separate existence apart from 2.6–7.

As compared to the succinct chreia proper at 2.5, Jesus' statement, which begins in 2.8, is remarkably elaborate and sets forth a rather complex chain of argumentation. As mentioned already, this distinguishes 2.8–11 from the pattern of chreia elaboration proposed by the ancient textbooks, according to which the student should make a clear distinction between the paraphrased chreia proper and the *argumenta*, the latter

---

²³ J. H. Neyrey, 'Questions, *Chreiai*, and Challenges to Honor: The Interface of Rhetoric and Culture in Mark's Gospel', *CBQ* 60 (1998), 657–81.

of which should be presented in the elaborator's voice rather than being placed on the lips of the principal character of the chreia. However, within the Gospel narratives, it is usually Jesus himself, and not the narrator, who substantiates his claims with logical argumentation and authoritative proofs. Mark 2.8–11 forms a splendid example of this phenomenon.

Jesus opens his speech of defence in 2.8 by countering the scribes' initial rhetorical question ('Why does he speak like this?') through a structurally corresponding rhetorical question that efficiently demonstrates his superiority ('Why do you think this in your hearts?'). Jesus' counter-argumentation does not target the seemingly weakest link in the scribal argument, that is, the premise that Jesus actually claims to have forgiven the paralytic's sins. Rather, he appears to argue that the scribes' major premise, that God alone may forgive sins, is false. Formally, the argument can be arranged in a syllogistic scheme:

(A)   Major premise: The one who can say 'Rise, take up your pallet, and walk' can also say 'Your sins are forgiven' (2.9).

(B)   Minor premise: Jesus can say 'Rise, take up your pallet, and go home' (2.11).

(C)   Conclusion: The Son of Man has authority to forgive sins (2.10).

The argument is rather complex in that it involves both minor arguments and enthymemes.

(A) The major premise is itself established through an argument *a maiore ad minus*, put in the form of a rhetorical question. While interpreters of 2.9 have at times found this question difficult, or impossible, to answer, the overall argument presupposes that to say 'Your sins are forgiven' is the easier part. To *say* that someone's sins are forgiven is 'easier' than to *say* 'Rise and walk' to a paralytic, since the former is beyond empirical verification and does not risk putting the speaker's honour in doubt – which a failed attempt at healing would certainly do.

(B) By commanding the paralytic to rise and go home, Jesus demonstrates that he can indeed do the more difficult thing. The enduring focus on *saying* is marked through the introduction of Jesus' command by 'he said to the paralytic' (2.10) and his opening words 'to you I say' (2.11).

(C) 2.10 is the logical conclusion to be drawn from the two premises. Michael Wolter has made an important observation concerning the structure of this verse. The employment of a final clause (ἵνα δὲ εἰδῆτε…) without an apodosis is neither an expression of grammatical clumsiness nor an indication of redactional stitch sewing, but a means of introducing evidence in judicial rhetoric. Wolter presents six textual specimens from classical Greek texts which consist, like Mark 2.10, of a subordinate clause 'in order that you should know… (ἵνα (δὲ) εἰδῆτε)', an ὅτι-clause specifying the point to be proven (in five of the specimens), and a seemingly abrupt change of addressees through a second-person singular imperative form. The imperative expresses a command to bring in or read aloud some testimony or a law.[24] In a similar manner, the Markan Jesus commands the paralytic to rise and go home in order to provide evidence for the *propositio* of his case, that is, that the Son of Man has authority to forgive sins.

Finally, it should be noticed that the logical conclusion presupposes two moves that are not overtly stated and that can be labelled enthymemes. Firstly, Jesus apparently agrees with the scribal opinion voiced in 2.7 that to say 'Your sins are forgiven' is tantamount to forgiving sins. This, as we have seen, was the enthymemic minor premise of the scribes' argument; it is accepted by Jesus, who puts their major premise into question. Secondly, the conclusion is valid only if the Son of Man is Jesus.

The Sitz im Leben *of the elaborated apomnemoneuma*

The elaboration results in a change of emphases within the episode. Whereas Jesus' prophetic and messianic identity was at most implied in the brief apomnemoneuma, christology is the focus of interest in the elaborated version. With the inclusion of 2.6–10, the episode expresses an angelomorphic christology, according to which Jesus, as the Son of Man who is God's representative on earth, has been authorized to forgive sins (see Chapter 4). Wrede's claim, that Mark 2.1–12 is a secondarily 'christologized' version of a more primitive narration that lacked this emphasis, seems to be vindicated. However, in view of the considerations in the present study, two frequently voiced notions concerning the origin of 2.6–10 need to be challenged. Both have to do with the *Sitz im Leben* of this passage.

First of all, seeing that the episode narrates a controversy between Jesus and the scribes, proponents of classic form-criticism have inferred that the passage originated in a setting of conflict, be it a clash between Christians and non-Christian Jews or a controversy within the primitive Church (see Chapter 3 above). Christopher Tuckett aptly criticizes this approach:

---

[24] M. Wolter, '"Ihr sollt aber wissen…": Das Anakoluth nach ἵνα δὲ εἰδῆτε in Mk 2,10–11 parr.', *ZNW* 95 (2004), 269–75.

In the work of Bultmann, the attempt was often made to deduce the *Sitz im Leben* of a tradition from the tradition itself. Thus controversy stories involving Jesus and opponents reflected (all but identical) early church controversies with (very similar) opponents. Yet at times the 'evidence' for the existence of such controversies in early Christianity arises solely from the Gospel evidence itself. The possibility that the presence of such stories in the tradition might represent more of an 'archaic feature' is ruled out by Bultmann almost a priori. The circularity inherent in the form-critical argument here might thus become a rather dangerous hermeneutical circle, and the claim about the *Sitz im Leben* may in part be determined in advance by the methodological approach adopted. [25]

A rhetorical analysis of the episode reveals that the presence of 'some of the scribes' and their accusation in 2.6–7 are prompted by the aim to prepare the ground for Jesus' logical argument in 2.8–10, which in itself can be recognized as an elaboration meant to bring out more forcefully and convincingly what the elaborator held to be the fuller implication of 2.5. If so, the scribes figure in the episode for purely rhetorical purposes, and attempts at deciphering them as representatives of a group of historical people are inherently misguided. The elaborated apomnemoneuma does not aim to convince outsiders but to corroborate and deepen the faith of those who are already believers. Maisch's identification of the episode as a *Lehrstück* is therefore quite to the point, in so far as the elaboration appears to have served a didactic purpose.[26]

Secondly, the fact that 2.10 conveys a christology that postdates the historical Jesus' lifetime has led scholars to suggest that its origin lies with primitive Christian faith in Jesus as the risen Son of God. In Chapter 3, we saw some examples of this line of reasoning, the most developed of which is Michl's proposal that the saying is a retrojection of one of the divine characteristics of the exalted Lord into the life of the earthly Jesus. In the same chapter, however, I also demonstrated that the basis for this hypothesis is not firm enough. Primitive Christian texts contain few traces of a christology by which the heavenly Jesus is expected to forgive sins. Such a christology can therefore hardly have been the driving force behind Mark 2.10. Instead, the impetus seems to have been the memory

---

[25] C. Tuckett, 'Form Criticism', in Kelber and Byrskog (eds.), *Jesus in Memory*, pp. 21–38 (pp. 34–5).

[26] Maisch, *Die Heilung des Gelähmten*, pp. 84–5, 104.

of an expression employed by the historical Jesus, namely, Mark 2.5b, which was reinterpreted and generalized by the use of angelomorphic categories. The insight that the apomnemoneuma in its elaborated shape actually mediates the elaborator's 'memories' of the past, rather than being a sheer retrojection of the present interests of the 'community', is congruent with, and may illustrate, Byrskog's recent highlighting of the mnemonic character of the *Sitz im Leben* of the gospel tradition:

> Most form critical thinking of the last century focused on different present activities in the Churches. The notion of memory was largely ignored. Leading form-critical scholars neglected that the *Sitz im Leben* deals in the present with material from the past and about the past and that this negotiation between the two temporal horizons is central to what it is.[27]

As should be clear from this quotation, Byrskog's emphasis on the importance of the past for the transmitters and elaborators of gospel tradition by no means denies the influence of their present situation on how the tradition was handled. Likewise, the present investigation lends support to the conclusion that primitive christology was of crucial importance for the shaping of Mark 2.6–10. Much scholarship has taken an inadvisable route, however, by suggesting that the topic of forgiveness in the Markan episode derives *solely* from primitive Christian concerns. In reality, it is rooted in these primitive Christians' memory of the earthly Jesus, and ultimately in the activity of the historical Jesus himself.

Third phase: the written source and its integration within a Gospel

An item in the pre-Markan collection of controversies about authorization

The existence and the extent of a written source behind Mark 2.1–3.6

Originally forwarded by Martin Albertz in 1921, the suggestion that either the whole or part of Mark 2.1–3.6 was taken over from a collection of controversy episodes has been accepted and modified in various

---

[27] S. Byrskog, 'A Century with the *Sitz im Leben*: From Form-Critical Setting to Gospel Community and Beyond', *ZNW* 98 (2007), 1–27 (21–2).

directions by other scholars.[28] Different arguments have been employed in favour of this hypothesis; here I will focus on those that seem to be most decisive.

It is evident that 2.1–3.6 is a remarkably coherent and unified section of the Gospel of Mark: each of the five units (2.1–12, 13–17, 18–22, 23–28; 3.1–6) is an apomnemoneuma marked by controversy between Jesus and members of the Pharisaic group, and each unit involves a christological claim. Joanna Dewey's study in particular demonstrates how the arrangement of the five units exhibits a sophisticated literary structure, which is both concentric and linear, culminating in the decision to kill Jesus (3.6).[29] The concept of 'authority' or 'rightfulness' recurs throughout the section under a variety of Greek expressions, all of which overlap semantically: like the personal expressions 'to have authority' (ἐξουσίαν ἔχειν, 2.10) and 'to be lord' (κύριον εἶναι, 2.28), the impersonal 'it is lawful' (ἔξεστιν, 2.24, 26; 3.4) corresponds to the Aramaic שׁלִיט (cf. Ezra 7.24). This is not necessarily an indication that the section ever existed in Aramaic since, as was pointed out in Chapter 4, early Jewish and Christian literature composed in Greek also treat 'to have authority' and 'to be lord' as interchangeable expressions. *Prima facie*, this focus on authority could be taken as an indication that the section was compiled by the evangelist, who introduces the theme already in 1.22, 27.[30] However, there is also some tension between 2.1–3.6 and the rest of the Gospel, which makes it more likely that Mark took over the section from an extant source.

The strongest indication of the section's pre-Markan origin is the two occurrences of the 'Son of Man' expression, which seem to come 'too early' in the narrative. Apart from 2.10, 28, Jesus does not speak of himself as the Son of Man until 8.31, where his use of the expression is directly prompted by Peter's groundbreaking recognition of Jesus as the Messiah (8.29). It is unlikely that Mark, had he not been handling older material, should have composed the Son of Man sayings in 2.10, 28 and placed them at a point in the narrative which militates against the structure of the Gospel.[31] Against this reasoning, Jarmo Kiilunen has argued

---

[28] M. Albertz, *Die synoptischen Streitgespräche: Ein Beitrag zur Formengeschichte des Urchristentums* (Berlin: Trowitzsch & Sohn, 1921), pp. 5–16; Kuhn, *Ältere Sammlungen*, pp. 53–98; J. D. G. Dunn, 'Mark 2.1–3.6: A Bridge between Jesus and Paul on the Question of the Law', in *Jesus, Paul, and the Law: Studies in Mark and Galatians* (Louisville, KY: Westminster/John Knox, 1990), pp. 10–36.

[29] Dewey, *Markan Public Debate*, pp. 65–130.

[30] Kiilunen, *Die Vollmacht im Widerstreit*, p. 26.

[31] Albertz, *Die synoptischen Streitgespräche*, p. 5; H. E. Tödt, *Der Menschensohn in der synoptischen Überlieferung*, 4th edn (Gütersloh: Mohn, 1978), p. 123; Kuhn, *Ältere Sammlungen*, pp. 75, 87.

that the 'Son of Man' expression fits well with the references to Jesus' impending suffering and death within the complex (2.20; 3.6), since the Markan Son of Man is the suffering Son of Man (8.31; 9.12, 31; 10.33–4, 45; 14.21, 41). Mark could thus have crafted the two sayings in 2.10, 28.[32] But this misses an important point, that is, the public and unveiled character of these sayings. Until his climactic confession before the high priest (14.61–2), Jesus refrains from speaking of himself as the Son of Man to interlocutors other than his disciples. The disciples are even told not to reveal Jesus' identity as the Messiah (8.30). Only the sayings in 2.10, 28 deviate from this pattern – here Jesus uses the expression 'Son of Man' in a way that makes it clear to all bystanders, including his antagonists, that he claims this identity for himself. Acknowledging a redactional origin of the christological claims in 2.10, 28 and of the command to silence in 8.30 alike seems to presuppose that the evangelist contradicted himself.[33] In my opinion, the otherwise carefully structured development of the messianic theme within the narrative makes it more probable that the Son of Man sayings in Mark 2 antedate the evangelist's redactional work.

Different views about the extent of this pre-Markan collection have been forwarded. Kuhn holds that the bulk of Mark 2 belonged to it, but that the evangelist reformulated 2.1–2 and added 2.13–14, 25–6, perhaps also 2.21–2. The item in 3.1–6 is Markan in its entirety, according to Kuhn.[34] According to Maisch and Dunn, the pre-Markan source begins only at 2.15, while 2.3–12 was added at an intermediary stage between the compilation of the source on the one hand, and the redaction of the Gospel on the other.[35] The latter scenario, which implies that the apomnemoneuma concerning forgiveness came to Mark from tradition, but that it did not originally belong to his major source behind 2.15–3.6, is unconvincing. First of all, the exclusion of the apomnemoneuma depends too heavily on form-critical considerations. Maisch points to the mixed *Gattung* (controversy and healing) of 2.1–12 that sets it apart from the subsequent episodes, which are 'pure' controversy episodes.[36] Dunn argues that, while the episodes throughout 2.15–3.6 had their *Sitz im Leben* in halakhic disputes, 2.1–12 does not concern the interpretation

[32] Kiilunen, *Die Vollmacht im Widerstreit*, pp. 42–4, 118–19, 198.
[33] See H. Räisänen, *The 'Messianic Secret' in Mark's Gospel* (Edinburgh: T & T Clark, 1990), pp. 224–8.
[34] Kuhn, *Ältere Sammlungen*, pp. 88–9.
[35] Maisch, *Die Heilung des Gelähmten*, pp. 112–17; Dunn, 'Mark 2.1–3.6', pp. 25–6.
[36] Maisch, *Die Heilung des Gelähmten*, pp. 112–13.

of the Law.[37] It is, however, a questionable assumption that a pre-Markan source could only have contained items with the same form and function. Secondly, the wording of the second 'Son of Man' saying, 'the Son of Man is lord *also* of the Sabbath' (2.28), presupposes the first one (2.10). Even if one might suggest that 'also' (καί) was secondarily added to 2.28, it remains significant that the two sayings in 2.10 and 2.28 are structurally parallel,[38] that they both evince a christology of the same angelomorphic type (see Chapter 4) and that 2.28, like 2.10, can reasonably be seen as the product of rhetorical elaboration of more primitive material.[39] In view of these similarities, it is more natural to assume that 2.10 and 2.28 come from the same pre-Markan hand than to hypothesize that it was Mark who brought them together from two different sources or traditions. The outcome of this is that most of Mark 2, and quite probably also 3.1–6, belonged to a single source.[40]

Two final questions concerning the pre-Markan collection need to be addressed. What ground is there for identifying it as a written source, as opposed to a sequence of oral traditions? And in what language did it come to Mark? Kuhn points out that the evidently composite character of 2.1–12 and 2.15–17 indicates a written rather than an oral collection. One would expect oral transmission to have cast these items in a more unified shape without the literary seams that are still visible within them.[41] Concerning the language of the collection, Casey proposes that 2.23–3.6 'is a literal translation of an Aramaic source', a source which presumably also included 2.10.[42] To demonstrate this, Casey offers a retranslation of 2.23–3.6 into Aramaic, where some of the oddities in the Greek text are resolved; most significantly, Casey identifies ὁδὸν ποιεῖν (2.23) and ἀρχιερέως (2.26) as mistranslations of Aramaic expressions.[43] However, these are not compelling, and 2.1–3.6 contains numerous features that pose obvious difficulties for Casey, pointing towards the conclusion that the language of the collection was Greek.[44] If the formal identification of

[37] Dunn, 'Mark 2.1–3.6', pp. 26–7.

[38] Kiilunen, *Die Vollmacht im Widerstreit*, pp. 42–4.

[39] Mack and Robbins, *Patterns of Persuasion*, pp. 107–41; Parrott, 'Conflict and Rhetoric', 139–70.

[40] Dunn, 'Mark 2.1–3.6', pp. 14–15.

[41] Kuhn, *Ältere Sammlungen*, p. 97.

[42] M. Casey, *Aramaic Sources of Mark's Gospel*, SNTSMS 102 (Cambridge University Press, 1998), pp. 163, 172, 191. Cf. Casey, *The Solution to the 'Son of Man' Problem*, pp. 144–67.

[43] Casey, *Aramaic Sources*, pp. 138, 140, 151–2.

[44] ὥστε + infinitive (Mark 2.2, 28; Casey, *Aramaic Sources*, pp. 164–5; *The Solution to the 'Son of Man' Problem*, p. 145), ἀποστεγάζειν and ἐξορύσσειν (2.4; *ibid.*, pp. 150–1), εὐκοπώτερον (2.9; *ibid.*, p. 158) and οὐδέποτε (2.12, 25; *Aramaic Sources*, p. 151).

the units within the collection as apomnemoneumata is correct, the close relationship between this form and the Hellenistic school may also suggest Greek as the language of Mark's source.

Mark 2.3–12 within the collection

As the elaboration of the apomnemoneuma in Mark 2.3–5, 11–12 into a longer unit relocated the focus of the narrative, its placement within a collection of several apomnemoneumata results in a shift in the nuances of meaning. Two of these slight modifications that result from the pre-Markan context of the episode are especially noteworthy, since they have sometimes guided scholarly interpretations and evaluations of 2.1–12.

First of all, the pre-Markan context creates the impression that the controversy in 2.6–10 concerns a halakhic question. As has been mentioned already, the unifying theme of the collection is the concept of 'authority', 'authorization' or 'rightfulness'. Taken on its own, the 'authority' of the Son of Man in 2.10 is an angelomorphic extension of God's authority (see Chapter 4 above). Dunn correctly points out that '[i]t is not possible to uncover a form of [2.1–12] where the issue is a point of *halakah*'.[45] However, read in the context of a debate concerning what is or is not 'rightful' (ἔξεστιν, 2.24, 26; 3.4) the 'authority' (ἐξουσία) to forgive sins takes on a legal shade. The scribal query about who can forgive sins (2.7) now becomes a halakhic question on a par with those concerning the appropriateness of eating with sinners and toll-collectors (2.16), the practice of regular fasting (2.18), and Sabbath observance (2.24; 3.4). In view of the secondary nature of the association of 2.1–12 with discussions pertaining to legal interpretation, the tendency to approach historical questions about Jesus and forgiveness within the framework of his stance towards the Law and its interpretation seems inadvisable.[46] The legal aspect of the episode derives from its location within the collection and is absent from the apomnemoneuma as such, and – *a fortiori* – from the historical event that ultimately brought it into being.

Secondly, the scribes' silent accusation of blasphemy (2.7) is, within the collection, the first in a series of more or less inimical encounters between Jesus and his antagonists, which culminates in the decision of the Pharisees and Herodians to eliminate Jesus (3.6). In the independent apomnemoneuma, the scribes' rhetorical questions and their charge of

---

[45] Dunn, 'Mark 2.1–3.6', pp. 26–7.
[46] Cf. Broer, 'Jesus und das Gesetz'; Loader, *Jesus' Attitude towards the Law*, pp. 47–9.

blasphemy provide the occasion for Jesus to develop his argument in
2.8–10; after this, their critical attitude disappears from the scene, and
one may even suppose that the scribes belong to 'all' those who react
to the successful healing with awe and praise (2.12). By contrast, the
pre-Markan context of the episode includes Jesus' explicit claim to the
authority to forgive sins among the offensive actions that merit his execution. Thus, Jesus' authenticating miracle in 2.10–12 does not convince
his opponents about his authority; on the contrary, it corroborates their
charge of blasphemy. Again it is striking to notice how some studies
that purport to study 2.1–12 in its own right, with an aim of extracting
historical information therefrom, read into the episode the irreparable
conflict depicted by the collection as a whole, and thus associate it with
Jesus' execution.[47] As a matter of fact, the link between Jesus' claim to
the authority to forgive sins and his death is established only through the
inclusion of the apomnemoneuma within the pre-Markan collection.

An episode in Mark's Life of Jesus

It is not possible, within the limitations of this study, to explore fully how
the understanding of Mark 2.1–12 is affected by the episode's placement
within the Gospel as a whole, but some brief consideration of this topic
seems to be appropriate.

Far from being mutually exclusive concepts, biography and apomnemoneuma are closely aligned entities in antiquity and the latter is frequently contained within the former. A work consisting of literary units
categorized as apomnemoneumata also qualifies for the generic designation apomnemoneumata, as in the case of Xenophon's *Memorabilia*.[48]
This genre, in turn, overlaps with the biographical genre. A mere collection of anecdotes does not qualify as biography, however, unless it is
placed within some chronological framework. Xenophon's *Memorabilia*
is not usually regarded as biography, despite its biographical tendencies. By contrast, while Lucian's *Life of Demonax* consists mainly of
unconnected anecdotes, it also contains a brief narration of the main
character's birth, education, later years and death, which assigns it to
the genre of ancient biography, as its title implies.[49] Some of the literary units that make up the major part of *Demonax* can be recognized as

---

[47] Bock, 'Jesus as Blasphemer', pp. 82–3.
[48] See Nicolaus, *Prog.* 26.1–8.
[49] A. Momigliano, *The Development of Greek Biography* (Cambridge, MA: Harvard
University Press, 1971), pp. 52–4, 73.

apomnemoneumata (e.g., 13, 50), and the work as a whole has also been generically categorized by this name.[50] The Gospel of Mark, which to a large part is made up of apomnemoneumata, can similarly be designated a Life of Jesus.

As has been remarked, the pre-Markan collection seems to have been integrated within the Gospel very carefully and deliberately: the preceding section (1.21–45) prepares for 2.1–3.6 and affects the manner in which it is appreciated.[51] Markan additions to the collection also alter some of its nuances. The vocabulary of 2.1–2 indicates that this introduction was composed by Mark, possibly to replace an original introduction that may already have contained the reference to Capernaum (see Chapter 2 and above in the present chapter). Traces of such redaction can be found in several places throughout the rest of the section. In the following, I will draw attention to three aspects, in which the construal of Jesus' authority to forgive sins is influenced by the placement of the episode within the Gospel of Mark.

First of all, in the Gospel Jesus' authority to forgive sins is subsumed into his more general authority as a teacher. Whereas neither the independent apomnemoneuma nor the pre-Markan collection explicitly depicted Jesus as teaching, Mark suggests that this is the primary activity within which the controversies in 2.1–3.6 take place. The theme of Jesus' authority is introduced in the summarizing notice of 1.21–2, where people react to Jesus' teaching with astonishment, since 'he was teaching them as with authority' (1.22); his teaching is then acclaimed as 'a new teaching with authority' (1.27). The mention of 'authority' in 2.10 is then naturally interpreted in the light of these references to Jesus' teaching authority. Moreover, Mark has framed the episode as it came to him (2.3–12), with descriptions of how Jesus taught the crowd: 'he was speaking the word to them' (2.2) and 'he taught them' (2.13) are both redactional phrases which result in an emphasis on the teaching capacity of Jesus.

Secondly, this emphasis on Jesus' authoritative teaching modifies his relationship to the Pharisees and scribes. The people in the synagogue

---

[50] O. Overwien, 'Das Gnomologium, das Gnomologium Vaticanum und die Tradition', *GFA* 4 (2001), 99–131 (104). See also H. Cancik, 'Bios und Logos: Formengeschichtliche Untersuchungen zu Lukians "Demonax"', in H. Cancik (ed.), *Markus-Philologie: Historische, literargeschichtliche und stilistische Untersuchungen zum zweiten Evangelium*, WUNT 33 (Tübingen: Mohr Siebeck, 1984), pp. 115–30; M. C. Moeser, *The Anecdote in Mark, the Classical World and the Rabbis*, JSNTS 227 (Sheffield Academic Press, 2002), pp. 87–105.
[51] Thissen, *Erzählung der Befreiung*, pp. 261–95.

in Capernaum recognize him as a competitor with the scribes in the field of teaching; Jesus' authority is set in contrast to the scribes' lack of authority (1.22).[52] Narrative critics acknowledge that Mark's Gospel is essentially a story about conflict over authority.[53] In the isolated apomnemoneuma and in the pre-Markan collection, Jesus' claim to authority (2.10) was derived from God's own authority and carried no polemical connotation. In the Markan context, however, since Jesus competes with the scribes for authority, the assertion that Jesus has authority to forgive sins also implies that the scribes lack such authority.

Thirdly, as is generally recognized, Mark has created an *inclusio* by inserting the collection this early in the Gospel. Being part of the first confrontation between Jesus and the religious establishment, the scribes' accusation 'He blasphemes!' (2.7) sets the tone for the subsequent narrative. It is then picked up towards the end of the Gospel in the high priest's decisive 'You have heard the blasphemy' (14.64). The Gospel of Mark depicts Jesus' controversial career as framed by charges of blasphemy. It has been suggested that this goes back to historical circumstances: perhaps Jesus' allegedly blasphemous bestowal of forgiveness was one of the charges brought against him before the Sanhedrin?[54] In view of the results yielded by the present investigation, it appears more likely that the connection between Jesus' claim to forgive sins and his execution belongs to the literary level. While the connection was made already in the pre-Markan collection, Mark's arrangement of his material results in an enhancement of this theme.

Conclusion

The reconstruction in this chapter of how an eyewitness account of the event that underlies Mark 2.1–12 may have resulted in the episode as we have it in Mark's Gospel will now be summarized in a few points. It goes without saying that this summary cannot lay any stronger claim to certitude than the hypothetical reasoning in the body of the chapter. Considering the previous discussion, what is offered here is nevertheless a plausible history of development.

---

[52] J. C. Iwe, *Jesus in the Synagogue of Capernaum: The Pericope and Its Programmatic Character for the Gospel of Mark: An Exegetico-Theological Study of Mk 1:21–28*, Tesi Gregoriana Serie Teologia 57 (Rome: Editrice Pontificia Università Gregoriana, 1999), pp. 59–63.

[53] J. D. Kingsbury, *Conflict in Mark: Jesus, Authorities, Disciples* (Minneapolis: Fortress, 1989), p. 67; S. H. Smith, *A Lion with Wings: A Narrative-Critical Approach to Mark's Gospel* (Sheffield Academic Press, 1996), pp. 93–4, 98.

[54] Dodd, *The Founder of Christianity*, pp. 158–9.

First of all, it is likely that the eyewitness account of the event included the recollection of how Jesus healed a man from paralysis by announcing that his sins were forgiven and by commanding him to rise and walk; the eyewitness(es), whose identity is irrecoverable, may have interpreted Jesus' course of actions as a response to the faith of the paralyzed man and of those who brought him to Jesus.

Secondly, the story may have been transmitted orally in the form of a brief apomnemoneuma which comprised Mark 2.3–5, 11–12 and which accordingly corresponded more or less to the earliest recollection of the event.

Thirdly, elaboration inspired by the progymnastic exercises is a plausible explanation for the insertion of 2.6–10 into the apomnemoneuma. In this elaboration, the rhetorically motivated introduction of the opponents allows Jesus to develop a judicial argument for his authority to forgive sins. Hereby the focal point of the apomnemoneuma becomes christological.

Fourthly, when Mark 2.3–12 is integrated into a pre-Markan collection of apomnemoneumata, the controversy at its centre is juxtaposed to a number of halakhic questions. This creates the impression that the debate about forgiveness is somehow related to conflicting interpretations of the Law. Moreover, the collection establishes a link between Jesus' claim to forgive sins and his execution.

Fifthly, the evangelist placed the pre-Markan source after his introduction of the theme of 'teaching with authority' (1.21–8), and reformulated the opening of the forgiveness episode (2.1–2) and its sequel (2.13). Due to these moves, the Markan Jesus' authority to forgive sins is an extension of his teaching authority. As such it is contrasted with the teaching of the scribes, who lack any real authority: the scribes can neither work miracles nor forgive sins. Moreover, the two charges of blasphemy against the Markan Jesus (2.7; 14.64) serve to strengthen the connection between the claim to such authority and Jesus' death at the initiative of the religious establishment.

7

CONCLUSION

Results of the study

The study now coming to its conclusion has been a project of authentication and interpretation. As a microcosm of the Gospels as a whole, the primary text, Mark 2.1–12, has been found to contain a mixture of historical data and fictitious elements. By using the criteria of multiple attestation, discontinuity and coherence I have judged the announcements of forgiveness in Mark 2.5b and Luke 7.47a to be derived ultimately from the historical Jesus. When evaluated by the criteria of implausibility and incoherence, Mark 2.10 has been deemed an inauthentic saying. It is explicable as the product of rhetorical elaboration of Mark 2.5b.

In Chapter 6, I outlined, in the fullest possible detail, the historical event that arguably underlies Mark 2.1–12. There is no reason to duplicate this reconstruction. Before I turn to some implications of this study in a wider perspective, suffice it to address the preliminary questions posed at its very beginning. These can now be answered with some confidence.

First of all, it is indeed plausible that the historical Jesus used the phrase 'Your sins are [being] forgiven.' In the context of early Judaism, 'to forgive sins' could be used with reference to this speech act. The question of whether Jesus forgave sins must therefore be answered affirmatively.

Secondly, it is likely that Jesus acknowledged that God was the ultimate source of forgiveness and that his own role was that of an agent. Accordingly, he 'forgave sins' in the sense of mediating God's forgiveness. In the case of the paralyzed man, Jesus appears not to have conceived of forgiveness primarily as a remission of debt or as an acquittal of guilt, but as doing away with the consequence of sin (that is, bodily illness). To forgive was also to heal.

Thirdly, Jesus' announcement of forgiveness is appropriately seen as an expression of his identity as the Anointed One of the Spirit, the prophetic

Messiah who was thought to have been prefigured in the prophecies of the Book of Isaiah. Through Jesus, God was allegedly healing those who suffered from illness, communicating good news to the poor, and forgiving those who had sinned, thereby restoring the people of Israel.

Implications for historical Jesus research

The development of tradition

Paradoxically, reflection on the character of the gospel tradition and its development has not occupied a prominent place in historical Jesus research. More often than not, the early form-critical view of the processes of tradition has been imported, consciously or unconsciously, by those scholars whose primary aim has been to study the historical Jesus, despite the internal methodological contradictions created by this approach. A conflict inevitably emerges as the attempt is made to combine, on the one hand, the form-critical insistence that traditions tend to be shaped according to the concerns of primitive Christianity and, on the other hand, the conviction that some of these traditions are dissimilar to these concerns and may therefore be traced back to the historical Jesus. The present study has identified the traditions that attribute to the earthly Jesus the activity of announcing God's forgiveness as such dissimilar traditions, which have not been adapted to full conformity with primitive Christian belief. On this point, the early form-critical conception of the transmission process must accordingly be questioned.

This questioning obviously does not imply that there was no substantial development and alteration of the tradition. On the contrary, in this study I have argued that the part which now forms the focal point of Mark 2.1–12 – the controversy between Jesus and the scribes, which culminates in the 'Son of Man' saying in 2.10 – is indeed a secondary addition to a more archaic tradition. But it is crucial to note how this secondary element seems to have originated. In contrast to traditional form-critical explanations, it is not likely that it was prompted either by a concern of the community to defend its practices or by a prophetic revelation of a christological tenet. It seems rather to have evolved out of the extant tradition, that is, out of the primitive Christian 'memory' of how the earthly Jesus 'forgave sins' in the sense of announcing God's forgiveness. Certainly, the secondary development draws on christology and brings it to expression, but christology is here exploited to reinterpret a received tradition rather than to associate Jesus with a theme which has no roots in 'memory'. To allow the complex notion of memory to be seriously reconsidered as an appropriate category for understanding the gospel tradition is a promising way forward for historical Jesus research. Decisive steps have already been taken along this route, and the present study can only underline the importance of continuing this project.

In order to identify in greater detail the mechanics of this development, I have explored the possibility that the handling of tradition was inspired by progymnastic rhetoric, and I have proposed that this is an apposite model for understanding the tradition-history of the Markan episode. Future research may involve the test of the applicability of this model to other units of the gospel tradition.

Methodology

The above considerations about gospel tradition have corollaries for a discussion of method in historical Jesus research. My investigation relies on the conviction that the criteria-oriented approach for authenticating gospel tradition is still viable and that it can lead to real progress within this field of study. This, I argue, is even more so if the approach is broadened to include a reconstruction of the tradition-history of any individual unit under scrutiny, for the purpose of accounting for the addition of secondary and unhistorical elements to it, *subsequently* to the application of the criteria. However, in view of the completed investigation, I suggest that one of the criteria needs to be slightly modified in relationship to its formulation at the outset of the study, namely, the criterion of discontinuity.

This suggestion is occasioned by the 'disturbing' observation that there appears to be a clash between, on the one hand, the criterion of discontinuity and, on the other hand, the criteria of implausibility and incoherence. Having applied the criterion of discontinuity to Mark 2.1–12, I concluded that the association of the earthly Jesus with forgiveness cannot be derived from primitive Christian theology; at this stage, the historicity of the episode in its entirety seems to be established, including the pivotal saying in 2.10. By contrast, when the criteria of implausibility and incoherence are applied to the episode, 2.6–10 stand out as unhistorical. The criteria obviously seem to contradict each other. Is this an indication that the method is flawed, or can the tension be resolved?

I propose that the contradiction arises from a deficit in the formulation of the criterion of discontinuity. The conventional understanding of the criterion, which I have adopted in the introduction, and which maintains that 'items that cannot be derived from primitive Christianity … are likely to be derived from Jesus himself', presupposes two possible origins of any given item. According to this understanding, an item can be traced back either to the historical Jesus or to the theological tendencies of primitive Christianity – *tertium non datur*. What the model neglects is precisely that, as I have underlined above, some material in the gospel tradition appears to belong to a third category. Such items are neither faithfully preserved historical traditions nor outright retrojections of primitive Christian belief, but reinterpretations and developments of extant traditions, which can ultimately be derived from the historical Jesus. In its conventional formulation, the criterion of discontinuity will – erroneously – identify items of this third category as authentic deeds and sayings of Jesus. My suggestion for correcting this shortcoming is the following reformulation of the criterion: 'Items that cannot be derived from primitive Christianity *and that cannot conveniently be explained as having developed out of another extant item* are likely to be derived from Jesus.'

Jesus' prophetic identity

Finally and most importantly, the present study offers a tiny yet relevant piece of information for our understanding of how Jesus construed his own mission as a prophet, or even as *the* prophet, that is, as the 'Anointed One of the Spirit'. Jesus' practice of announcing forgiveness seems to be an expression of his identity as the prophet through whom God was fulfilling Isaiah's prophecies about the eschatological restoration of Israel. The study thus lends support to the current in historical Jesus research that interprets him within this eschatological paradigm. I have suggested tentatively that the Isaianic prophecies, employed by Jesus as an interpretative framework for his success as a faith healer, inspired him to act out the prophecies also through his announcement of forgiveness. Further research may perhaps detect other aspects of the historical Jesus' mission that can be explained as similarly motivated by his knowledge and interpretation of the Book of Isaiah.

The outcome of my investigation confirms that Jesus' place within early Judaism is marked by both 'contextual appropriateness' and 'contextual distinctiveness', to borrow the terminology of Theissen and Winter. Expressions of the former that have surfaced in this study are Jesus' acceptance of the correlation between sin and illness (and thus of healing and forgiveness), his espousal of eschatological expectations, based primarily on the Book of Isaiah, and his adoption of the announcement of forgiveness as a prophetic form of speech. To the distinctive accents set by Jesus to these traditional notions belong his literal interpretation of the Isaianic prophecies (which probably resulted from his experience as a successful healer), and his integration of the prophetic announcement of forgiveness into the picture of the prophetic Messiah.

Jesus' relationship to primitive Christianity is, as far as concerns the topic of forgiveness, one of discontinuity within continuity. There is, on the one hand, a discontinuous element in Christianity's relocation of forgiveness from Jesus' mission as a prophet and healer to his death and resurrection. On the other hand, primitive Christianity inherits and develops the notion of forgiveness as an eschatological event which is being fulfilled. The correlation between Jesus' announcement of forgiveness and prophetic announcements of forgiveness in the primitive Church could be another point of continuity, but the nature of this relationship can hardly be determined without further study.

BIBLIOGRAPHY

Primary sources

Aelius Théon: Progymnasmata: Texte établi et traduit, ed. M. Patillon (Paris: Les Belles Lettres, 1997).

Aphthonii Progymnasmata, ed. H. Rabe, Rhetores Graeci 10 (Leipzig: Teubner, 1926).

Apocalypsis Baruchi Graece, ed. J.-C. Picard, PVTG 2 (Leiden: Brill, 1967).

Apocalypsis Henochi Graece, ed. M. Black, PVTG 3 (Leiden: Brill, 1970).

The Apostolic Fathers: Greek Texts and English Translations, ed. M. W. Holmes, 3rd edn (Grand Rapids, MI: Baker, 2007).

Die Apostolischen Väter: Griechisch-deutsche Parallelausgabe, ed. A. Lindemann and H. Paulsen (Tübingen: Mohr Siebeck, 1992).

The Aramaic Bible: The Targums, vol. III: *Targum Neofiti, 1: Leviticus; Targum Pseudo-Jonathan: Leviticus*, transl. M. McNamara and M. Maher (Wilmington, DE: Glazier, 1994).

The Aramaic Levi Document: Edition, Translation, Commentary, ed. J. C. Greenfield, M. E. Stone and E. Eshel, SVTP 19 (Leiden/Boston: Brill, 2004).

Aristide: Apologie: Introduction, textes critiques, traductions et commentaire, ed. B. Pouderon, M.-J. Pierre, B. Outtier and M. Guiorgadzé, SC 470 (Paris: Cerf, 2003).

The Assumption of Moses: A Critical Edition with Commentary, ed. J. Tromp, SVTP 10 (Leiden: Brill, 1993).

The Bible in Aramaic: Based on Old Manuscripts and Printed Texts, ed. A. Sperber, 3 vols. 2nd imprint (Leiden: Brill, 1992).

Biblia Hebraica Stuttgartensia, ed. K. Elliger and W. Rudolph, 4th edn (Stuttgart: Deutsche Bibelgesellschaft, 1990).

Biblia Sacra iuxta Vulgatam versionem, ed. R. Weber and R. Gryson, 4th edn (Stuttgart: Deutsche Bibelgesellschaft, 1994).

The Book of Jubilees, ed. J. C. VanderKam, 2 vols., CSCO 510–11/CSCO Scriptores Aethiopici 87–8 (Leuven: Peeters, 1989).

'The Chreia Discussion of *The Vatican Grammarian*', in R. F. Hock and E. N. O'Neil, *The Chreia in Ancient Rhetoric*, vol. I: *The* Progymnasmata, SBLTT 27 (Atlanta: Scholars, 1986), pp. 271–93.

Clément d'Alexandrie: Les Stromates: Stromate IV, ed. A. van den Hoek, SC 463 (Paris: Cerf, 2001).

Clément d'Alexandrie: Les Stromates: Stromate VI, ed. P. Descourtieux, SC 446 (Paris: Cerf, 1999).

The Complete Works of Josephus, transl. W. Whiston (Grand Rapids, MI: Kregel Publications, 1960 (1st edn 1737)).

Les Constitutions apostoliques, ed. M. Metzger, 3 vols., SC 320, 329, 336 (Paris: Cerf, 1985–7).

The Coptic Gnostic Library: A Complete Edition of the Nag Hammadi Codices, ed. J. M. Robinson, 5 vols. (Leiden: Brill, 2000).

The Dead Sea Scrolls Study Edition, ed. F. García Martínez and E. J. C. Tigchelaar, 2 vols., paperback edn (Leiden: Brill, 2000).

The Didascalia Apostolorum in Syriac, ed. A. Vööbus, 4 vols., CSCOSS 175–6, 179–80 (Leuven: Secrétariat du CorpusSCO, 1979).

Didascalia et Constitutiones apostolorum, ed. F. X. Funk, 2 vols. (Paderborn: Schoeningh, 1905).

Didymos der Blinde: Kommentar zum Ecclesiastes (Tura-Papyrus), vol. IV: *Kommentar zu Eccl. Kap. 7–8,8*, ed. J. Kramer and B. Krebber, Papyrologische Texte und Abhandlungen 16 (Bonn: Habelt, 1972).

Epiphanius, vol. II: *Panarion haer. 34–64*, ed. J. Dummer and K. Holl, GCS, 2nd edn (Berlin: Akademie-Verlag, 1980).

The Ethiopic Book of Enoch: A New Edition in the Light of the Aramaic Dead Sea Fragments, ed. M. A. Knibb, 2 vols. (Oxford: Clarendon, 1978).

Eusèbe de Césarée: Histoire ecclésiastique, vol. II: *Livres 5–7*, ed. G. Bardy, SC 41 (Paris: Cerf, 1955).

Los Evangelios Apócrifos: Colección de textos griegos y latinos, versión crítica, estudios introductorios y comentarios, ed. A. de Santos Otero, BAC 148, 10th edn (Madrid: Biblioteca de Autores Cristianos, 2002).

Flavius Josephus: Translation and Commentary, vol. IV: *Flavius Josephus Judean Antiquities 5–7*, transl. C. T. Begg (Leiden: Brill, 2005).

Flavius Josephus: Translation and Commentary, vol. V: *Flavius Josephus Judean Antiquities 8–10*, transl. C. T. Begg and P. Spilsbury (Leiden/Boston: Brill, 2005).

Fragmenta pseudepigraphorum quae supersunt Graeca: Una cum historicum et auctorum Judaeorum Hellenistarum fragmentis, ed. A. M. Denis, PVTG 3 (Leiden: Brill, 1970).

Fragmente apokryph gewordener Evangelien in griechischer und lateinischer Sprache, ed. D. Lührmann, MTS 59 (Marburg: Elwert, 2000).

The Gospel of the Savior: An Analysis of P.Oxy 840 and Its Place in the Gospel Traditions of Early Christianity, ed. M. J. Kruger, TENT 1 (Leiden/Boston: Brill, 2005).

Hebrew–English Edition of the Babylonian Talmud, ed. I. Epstein, 30 vols. (London: Soncino, 1983–90).

Hermogenis opera, ed. H. Rabe, Rhetores Graeci 6 (Leipzig: Teubner, 1913).

Hippolytus: Refutatio omnium haeresium, ed. M. Marcovich, Patristische Texte und Studien 25 (Berlin/New York: de Gruyter, 1986).

Joseph und Aseneth, ed. C. Burchard, PVTG 5 (Leiden: Brill, 2003).

Josephus, transl. and ed. H. St J. Thackeray, R. Marcus and L. Feldman, LCL, 10 vols. (Cambridge, MA: Harvard University Press, 1926–65).

'Latin Text', in H. Jacobson, *A Commentary on Pseudo-Philo's* Liber Antiquitatum Biblicarum: *With Latin Text and English Translation*, AGJU 31, 2 vols. (Leiden/New York/Cologne: Brill, 1996), pp. 1–87.

Lettre d'Aristée à Philocrate: Introduction, texte critique, traduction et notes, index complet des mots grecs, ed. A. Pelletier, SC 89 (Paris: Cerf, 1962).

The Life of Adam and Eve in Greek: A Critical Edition, ed. J. Tromp, PVTG 6 (Leiden/Boston: Brill, 2005).

Luciani opera, ed. M. D. MacLeod, SCBO, 4 vols. (Oxford: Clarendon, 1972–84).

Mishnayoth, ed. P. Blackman, 7 vols. (New York: Judaica, 1990).

Neophyti I: Targum Palestinense, ms de la Bibliotheca Vaticana, ed. A. Díez Macho, 6 vols. (Madrid: Consejo Superior de Investigaciones Científicas, 1968–79).

Nicolai Progymnasmata, ed. J. Felten, Rhetores Graeci 11 (Leipzig: Teubner, 1913).

Novum Testamentum Domini nostri et Servatoris Jesu Christi Æthiopice, ed. T. P. Platt (London: Watts, 1830).

Novum Testamentum Graece, ed. Eb. Nestle, Er. Nestle, B. Aland, K. Aland, J. Karavidopoulos, C. M. Martini and B. M. Metzger, 27th edn (Stuttgart: Deutsche Bibelgesellschaft, 1993).

Die Oracula Sibyllina, ed. J. Geffcken, GCS 8 (Leipzig: Hinrich, 1902).

Paraleipomena Jeremiou, ed. R. A. Kraft and A.-E. Purintun, SBLTT 1, Pseudepigrapha Series 1 (Missoula, MT: Society of Biblical Literature, 1972).

Das Petrusevangelium und die Petrusapokalypse: Die griechischen Fragmente mit deutscher und englischer Übersetzung, ed. T. J. Kraus and T. Nicklas, GCS NF 11, Neutestamentliche Apokryphen 1 (Berlin/New York: de Gruyter, 2004).

Philo, ed. F. H. Colson and G. H. Whitaker, LCL, 12 vols. (London: Heinemann, 1929–53).

Philostratus: Apollonius of Tyana, ed. C. P. Jones, LCL, 3 vols. (Cambridge, MA.: Harvard University Press, 2005–6).

Progymnasmata: Greek Textbooks of Prose Composition and Rhetoric: Translated with Introductions and Notes, transl. G. A. Kennedy, SBLWGRW 10 (Atlanta: Society of Biblical Literature, 2003).

Prophetarum vitae fabulosae, indices apostolorum discipulorumque Domini Dorotheo, Epiphanio, Hippolyto aliisque vindicata, ed. T. Schermann (Leipzig: Teubner, 1907).

Quintilian, ed. H. Butler, LCL 124–7, 4 vols. (London: Heinemann, 1920–2).

Qumran Cave 4, vol. I: *4Q158–4Q186*, ed. J. M. Allegro, DJD 5 (Oxford: Clarendon, 1968).

Qumran Cave 4, vol. XII: *1–2 Samuel*, ed. F. M. Cross, D. W. Parry, R. J. Saley and E. Ulrich, DJD 17 (Oxford: Clarendon, 2005).

Qumran Cave 4, vol. XVII: *Parabiblical Texts, Part 3*, ed. G. Brooke, DJD 22 (Oxford: Clarendon, 1996).

Qumran Cave 4, vol. XXI: *Parabiblical Texts, Part 4: Pseudo-Prophetic Texts*, ed. D. Dimant, DJD 30 (Oxford: Clarendon, 2001).

Qumran Cave 11, vol. II: *11Q2–18, 11Q20–31*, ed. F. García Martínez, E. J. C. Tigchelaar and A. S. van der Woude, DJD 23 (Oxford: Clarendon, 1998).

Sancti Cypriani episcopi epistularium, ed. G. F. Diercks, CC Series Latina 3, 3 vols. (Turnholt: Brepols, 1996).

Septuaginta: Id est Vetus Testamentum graece iuxta lxx interpretes, ed. A. Rahlfs (Stuttgart: Deutsche Bibelgesellschaft, 1979).

'2 (Slavonic Apocalypse of) Enoch', transl. F. I. Andersen, in *The Old Testament Pseudepigrapha*, ed. J. H. Charlesworth, 2 vols. (New York: Doubleday, 1983–5), vol. I, pp. 91–221.

Targum Pseudo-Jonathan of the Pentateuch: Text and Concordance, ed. E. G. Clarke (Hoboken: Ktav, 1984).

Testamenta XII patriarcharum, ed. M. de Jonge, PVTG 1 (Leiden: Brill, 1964).

Le Testament grec d'Abraham: Introduction, édition critique des deux recensions grecques, traduction, ed. F. Schmidt, TSAJ 11 (Tübingen: Mohr Siebeck, 1986).

Testamentum Iobi, ed. S. Brock, PVTG 2 (Leiden: Brill, 1967).

'Text 18. PSI 1.85', in R. F. Hock and E. N. O'Neil, *The Chreia and Ancient Rhetoric: Classroom Exercises: Translated and Edited*, SBLWGRW 2 (Atlanta: Society of Biblical Literature, 2002), pp. 94–7.

'Text of the Egerton Gospel Fragments', in J. B. Daniels, 'The Egerton Gospel: Its Place in Early Christianity', unpublished Ph.D. thesis, Claremont Graduate School (1990), pp. 12–21.

'Θέωνος Προγυμνάσματα', in *Rhetores Graeci: Ex codicibus Florentinis Mediolanensibus Monacensibus Neapolitanis Parisiensibus Romanis Venetis Taurinensibus et Vindobonensibus*, ed. C. Walz, vol. I (Stuttgart/ Tübingen: J. G. Cottae, 1832), pp. 145–257.

Secondary literature

Ådna, J., 'Der Gottesknecht als triumphierender und interzessorischer Messias. Die Rezeption von Jes 53 im Targum Jonathan untersucht mit besonderer Berücksichtigung des Messiasbildes', in B. Janowski and P. Stuhlmacher (eds.), *Der leidende Gottesknecht: Jesaja 53 und seine Wirkungsgeschichte*, FzAT 14 (Tübingen: Mohr Siebeck, 1996), pp. 129–58.

'Herrens tjener i Jesaja 53 skildret som triumferende Messias: Profettargumens gjengivelse og tolkning av Jes 52,13–53,12', *TTK* 63 (1992), 81–94.

Jesu Stellung zum Tempel: Die Tempelaktion und das Tempelwort als Ausdruck seiner messianischen Sendung, WUNT 2:119 (Tübingen: Mohr Siebeck, 2000).

Albertz, M., *Die synoptischen Streitgespräche: Ein Beitrag zur Formengeschichte des Urchristentums* (Berlin: Trowitzsch & Sohn, 1921).

Albertz, R., *Der Gott des Daniel: Untersuchungen zu Daniel 4–6 in der Septuagintafassung sowie zu Komposition und Theologie des aramäischen Danielbuches*, SBS 131 (Stuttgart: Katholisches Bibelwerk, 1988).

Alexander, L., 'Memory and Tradition in the Hellenistic Schools', in W. H. Kelber and S. Byrskog (eds.), *Jesus in Memory: Traditions in Oral and Scribal Perspectives* (Waco, TX: Baylor University Press, 2009), pp. 113–53.

Allison, D. C., *Jesus of Nazareth: Millenarian Prophet* (Minneapolis: Fortress, 1998).

The New Moses: A Matthean Typology (Minneapolis: Fortress, 1993).

Review of Theissen and Winter, *The Quest for the Plausible Jesus*, *Int* 58 (2004), 88.

Anderson, P. N., *The Fourth Gospel and the Quest for Jesus: Modern Foundations Reconsidered*, LNTS 321 (New York: T & T Clark, 2006).

Aune, D. E., *Prophecy in Early Christianity and the Ancient Mediterranean World* (Grand Rapids, MI: Eerdmans, 1983).

Revelation 1–5, WBC 52A (Dallas: Word Books, 1997).

Aurelius, E., *Der Fürbitter Israels: Eine Studie zum Mosebild im Alten Testament*, CBOTS 27 (Stockholm: Almqvist & Wiksell, 1988).

Ausloos, H., 'The "Angel of YHWH" in Exod. xxiii 20–33 and Judg. ii 1–5: A Clue to the "Deuteronom(ist)ic Puzzle?"', *VT* 58 (2008), 1–12.

Auvinen, V., *Jesus' Teaching on Prayer* (Åbo Akademi University, 2003).

Back, S.-O., *Han som kom: Till frågan om Jesu messianska anspråk*, Studier i exegetik och judaistik utgivna av Teologiska fakulteten vid Åbo Akademi 1 (Åbo Akademi, 2006).

Jesus of Nazareth and the Sabbath Commandment (Åbo Akademi University Press, 1995).

Bailey, J. A., *The Traditions Common to the Gospels of Luke and John* (Leiden: Brill, 1963).

Balentine, S. E., 'The Prophet as Intercessor: A Reassessment', *JBL* 103 (1984), 161–73.

Bauckham, R., 'The Eyewitnesses and the Gospel Traditions', *JSHJ* 1 (2003), 28–60.

James: Wisdom of James, Disciple of Jesus the Sage (London/New York: Routledge, 1999).

Jesus and the Eyewitnesses: The Gospels as Eyewitness Testimony (Grand Rapids, MI: Eerdmans, 2006).

Bauer, B., *Kritik der evangelischen Geschichte*, 2nd edn (Leipzig: Wigand, 1846).

Bauer, H., and Leander, P., *Grammatik des Biblisch-Aramäischen* (Halle: Max Niemeyer, 1927).

Beasley-Murray, G. R., *Baptism in the New Testament* (Grand Rapids, MI: Eerdmans, 1962).

Becker, J., *Jesus von Nazaret* (Berlin: de Gruyter, 1996).

Becker, U., *Jesus und die Ehebrecherin: Untersuchungen zur Text- und Überlieferungsgeschichte von Joh. 7,53–8,11*, BZNW 28 (Berlin: Töpelmann, 1963).

Begg, C. (T.), *Flavius Josephus: Translation and Commentary*, vol. IV: *Flavius Josephus Judean Antiquities 5–7* (Leiden: Brill, 2005).

Josephus' Story of the Later Monarchy (AJ 9,1–10,185), BETL 145 (Leuven University Press/Peeters, 2000).

'Samuel's Farewell Discourse according to Josephus', *SJOT* 11 (1997), 56–77.

Begg, C. T., and Spilsbury, P., *Flavius Josephus: Translation and Commentary*, vol. V: *Flavius Josephus Judean Antiquities 8–10* (Leiden/Boston: Brill, 2005).

Berding, K., *Polycarp and Paul: An Analysis of Their Literary and Theological Relationship in Light of Polycarp's Use of Biblical and Extra-Biblical Literature*, VCSup 62 (Leiden: Brill, 2002).

Berger, K., 'Almosen für Israel: Zum historischen Kontext der paulinischen Kollekte', *NTS* 23 (1977), 180–204.

Formen und Gattungen im Neuen Testament, UTB 2532 (Tübingen: Francke, 2005).

'Materialien zu Form und Überlieferungsgeschichte neutestamentlicher Gleichnisse', *NovT* 15 (1973), 1–37.

Betz, H. D., 'The Cleansing of the Ten Lepers', *JBL* 90 (1971), 314–28.

Betz, O., 'Jesu Lieblingspsalm: Die Bedeutung von Psalm 103 für das Werk Jesu', *TBei* 15 (1984), 253–69.

'Miracles in the Writings of Flavius Josephus', in L. H. Feldman and G. Hata (eds.), *Josephus, Judaism, and Christianity* (Leiden: Brill, 1987), pp. 212–35.

Bilde, P., *Den historiske Jesus* (Copenhagen: Anis, 2008).

Bird, M. F., *Are You the One Who Is to Come? The Historical Jesus and the Messianic Question* (Grand Rapids, MI: Baker, 2009).

Blackburn, B. L., 'The Miracles of Jesus', in B. Chilton and C. A. Evans (eds.), *Studying the Historical Jesus: Evaluations of the State of Current Research*, NTTS 19 (Leiden: Brill, 1994), pp. 353–94.

Blass, F., Debrunner, A., and Rehkopf, F., *Grammatik des neutestamentlichen Griechisch*, 18th edn (Göttingen: Vandenhoeck & Ruprecht, 2001).

Bock, D. L., 'Jesus as Blasphemer', in S. McKnight and J. B. Modica (eds.), *Who Do My Opponents Say that I Am? An Investigation of the Accusations against Jesus*, LNTS 327 (London: T & T Clark, 2008), pp. 76–94.

Proclamation from Prophecy and Pattern: Lucan Old Testament Christology, JSNTS 12 (Sheffield: JSOT Press, 1987).

'The Son of Man in Luke 5:24', *BBR* 1 (1991), 109–21.

Borgen, P., 'John and the Synoptics', in D. L. Dungan (ed.), *The Interrelations of the Gospels: A Symposium Led by M.-É. Boismard – W. R. Farmer – F. Neirynck: Jerusalem 1984*, BETL 95 (Leuven University Press, 1990), pp. 408–58.

Boring, M. E., *The Continuing Voice of Jesus: Christian Prophecy and the Gospel Tradition* (Louisville, KY: Westminster/John Knox, 1991).

'The Historical-Critical Method's "Criteria of Authenticity": The Beatitudes in Q and Thomas as a Test Case', *Semeia* 44 (1988), 9–44.

Sayings of the Risen Jesus: Christian Prophecy in the Synoptic Tradition (Cambridge University Press, 1982).

'The Unforgivable Sin Logion Mark III 28–29/Matt XII 31–32/Luke XII 10: Formal Analysis and History of the Tradition', *NovT* 18 (1976), 258–79.

Böttrich, C., 'The Melchizedek Story of 2 *(Slavonic) Enoch*: A Reaction to A. Orlov', *JSJ* 32 (2001), 445–70.

Bousset, W., *Jesu Predigt in ihrem Gegensatz zum Judentum: Ein religionsgeschichtlicher Vergleich* (Göttingen: Vandenhoeck & Ruprecht, 1892).

Kyrios Christos: Geschichte des Christusglaubens von den Anfängen des Christentums bis Irenaeus, 2nd edn (Göttingen: Vandenhoeck & Ruprecht, 1921).

Breytenbach, C., *Versöhnung: Eine Studie zur paulinischen Theologie*, WMANT 60 (Neukirchen-Vluyn: Neukirchener, 1989).

Broer, I., 'Jesus und das Gesetz – Anmerkungen zur Geschichte des Problems und zur Frage der Sündenvergebung durch den historischen Jesus', in I. Broer (ed.), *Jesus und das jüdische Gesetz* (Stuttgart: Kohlhammer, 1992), pp. 61–104.

Brown, C. A., *No Longer Be Silent: First Century Jewish Portraits of Biblical Women: Studies in Pseudo-Philo's* Biblical Antiquities *and Josephus's* Jewish Antiquities (Louisville, KY: Westminster/John Knox, 1992).

Brown, M. L., *Israel's Divine Healer* (Grand Rapids, MI: Zondervan, 1995).
Brown, R. E., *The Epistles of John: A New Translation with Introduction and Commentary*, AB 30 (New York: Doubleday, 1982).
The Gospel according to John I–XII: A New Translation with Introduction and Commentary, AB 29 (Garden City, NY: Doubleday, 1966).
The Gospel according to John XIII–XXI: A New Translation with Introduction and Commentary, AB 29A (Garden City, NY: Doubleday, 1970).
Brown, S. K., 'Jewish and Gnostic Elements in the Second Apocalypse of James (CG V, *4*)', *NovT* 17 (1975), 225–37.
Bryan, S. M., *Jesus and Israel's Traditions of Judgement and Restoration*, SNTSMS 117 (Cambridge University Press, 2002).
Bultmann, R., *Das Evangelium des Johannes*, KEK (Göttingen: Vandenhoeck & Ruprecht, 1941).
Die Geschichte der synoptischen Tradition (Göttingen: Vandenhoeck & Ruprecht, 1921 (1st edn); 1931 (2nd edn); 1995 (10th edn)).
Jesus, 3rd edn (Tübingen: Mohr Siebeck, 1964).
Theologie des Neuen Testaments, 7th edn (Tübingen: Mohr Siebeck, 1977).
Burchard, C., 'Zu einigen christologischen Stellen des Jakobusbriefes', in C. Breytenbach and H. Paulsen (eds.), *Anfänge der Christologie*, FS F. Hahn (Göttingen: Vandenhoeck & Ruprecht, 1991), pp. 353–68.
Burkett, D., *Rethinking the Gospel Sources,* vol. I: *From Proto-Mark to Mark* (New York/London: T & T Clark, 2004).
Rethinking the Gospel Sources, vol. II: *The Unity and Plurality of Q*, SBLECL 1 (Atlanta: Society of Biblical Literature, 2009).
Burkitt, F. C., *The Gospel History and Its Transmission*, 3rd edn (Edinburgh: T & T Clark, 1911).
Burridge, R. A., *What Are the Gospels? A Comparison with Graeco-Roman Biography*, 2nd edn (Grand Rapids, MI: Eerdmans, 2004).
Byrskog, S., 'A Century with the *Sitz im Leben*: From Form-Critical Setting to Gospel Community and Beyond', *ZNW* 98 (2007), 1–27.
'The Early Church as a Narrative Fellowship: An Exploratory Study of the Performance of the *Chreia*', *TTK* 78 (2007), 207–26.
'From Memory to Memoirs: Tracing the Background of a Literary Genre', in M. Zetterholm and S. Byrskog (eds.), *The Making of Christianity: Conflicts, Contacts and Constructions*, CBNTS (Winona Lake, IN: Eisenbrauns, in press 2011).
Jesus the Only Teacher: Didactic Authority and Transmission in Ancient Israel, Ancient Judaism and the Matthean Community, CBNTS 24 (Stockholm: Almqvist & Wiksell, 1994).
'A New Perspective on the Jesus Tradition: Reflections on James D. G. Dunn's *Jesus Remembered*', *JSNT* 26 (2004), 459–71.
Story as History – History as Story: The Gospel Tradition in the Context of Ancient Oral History, WUNT 123 (Tübingen: Mohr Siebeck, 2000).
'The Transmission of the Jesus Tradition', in T. Holmén and S. E. Porter (eds.), *Handbook for the Study of the Historical Jesus*, 4 vols. (Leiden: Brill, 2011), vol. II, pp. 1465–94.
'The Transmission of the Jesus Tradition: Old and New Insights', *EC* 1 (2010), 1–28.
Cadbury, H. J., *The Beginnings of Christianity, Part I: The Acts of the Apostles*, vol. IV: *English Translation and Commentary*, ed. F. J. Foakes Jackson

and K. Lake, paperback edn (Grand Rapids, MI: Baker, 1979 (1st edn 1933)).

Cancik, H., 'Bios und Logos: Formengeschichtliche Untersuchungen zu Lukians "Demonax"', in H. Cancik (ed.), *Markus-Philologie: Historische, literargeschichtliche und stilistische Untersuchungen zum zweiten Evangelium*, WUNT 33 (Tübingen: Mohr Siebeck, 1984), pp. 115–30.

Capps, D., *Jesus the Village Psychiatrist* (Louisville, KY: Westminster John Knox, 2008).

Carlston, C. E., 'Reminiscence and Redaction in Luke 15:11–32', *JBL* 94 (1975), 368–90.

Carson, D. A., *The Gospel according to John*, The Pillar New Testament Commentary (Grand Rapids, MI: Eerdmans, 1991).

Casey, M., *Aramaic Sources of Mark's Gospel*, SNTSMS 102 (Cambridge University Press, 1998).

The Solution to the 'Son of Man' Problem, LNTS 343 (London: T & T Clark, 2007).

Son of Man: The Interpretation and Influence of Daniel 7 (London: SPCK, 1979).

Catchpole, D. R., *The Quest for Q* (Edinburgh: T & T Clark, 1993).

Ceroke, C. P., 'Is Mk 2,10 a Saying of Jesus?', *CBQ* 22 (1960), 369–90.

Charlesworth, J. H., *Jesus within Judaism: New Light from Exciting Archaeological Discoveries* (London: SPCK, 1989).

Charlesworth, J. H., and Evans, C. A., 'Jesus in the Agrapha and Apocryphal Gospels', in B. Chilton and C. A. Evans (eds.), *Studying the Historical Jesus: Evaluations of the State of Current Research*, NTTS 19 (Leiden: Brill, 1994), pp. 479–533.

Chilton, B. (D.), *A Galilean Rabbi and His Bible: Jesus' Own Interpretation of Isaiah* (London: SPCK, 1984).

The Glory of Israel: The Theology and Provenience of the Isaiah Targum, JSOTS 23 (Sheffield: JSOT Press, 1982).

God in Strength: Jesus' Announcement of the Kingdom, SNTU B 1 (Freistadt: Plöchl, 1979).

Review of Sung, *Vergebung der Sünden*, *RBL* 26 June 2000 (www. bookreviews.org/pdf/2562_1799.pdf).

Chilton, B., and Evans, C. A., 'Jesus and Israel's Scriptures', in B. Chilton and C. A. Evans (eds.), *Studying the Historical Jesus: Evaluations of the State of Current Research*, NTTS 19 (Leiden: Brill, 1994), pp. 281–335.

Collins, A. Y., *Mark: A Commentary* (Minneapolis: Fortress, 2007).

Collins, J. (J.), '4QPrayer of Nabonidus ar', in G. Brooke (ed.), *Qumran Cave 4*, vol. XVII: *Parabiblical Texts, Part 3*, DJD 22 (Oxford: Clarendon, 1996), pp. 83–93.

'A Herald of Good Tidings: Isaiah 61:1–3 and Its Actualization in the Dead Sea Scrolls', in C. A. Evans and S. Talmon (eds.), *The Quest for Context and Meaning: Studies in Biblical Intertextuality*, FS J. A. Sanders, BIS 28 (Leiden/New York/Cologne: Brill, 1997), pp. 225–40.

The Scepter and the Star: The Messiahs of the Dead Sea Scrolls and Other Ancient Literature, ABRL (New York: Doubleday, 1995).

'The Son of Man and the Saints of the Most High in the Book of Daniel', *JBL* 93 (1974), 50–66.

'The Works of the Messiah', *DSD* 1 (1994), 98–112.

Colpe, C., 'ὁ υἱὸς τοῦ ἀνθρώπου', in G. Kittel and G. Friedrich (eds.), *Theologisches Wörterbuch zum Neuen Testament*, 10 vols. (Stuttgart: Kohlhammer, 1933–79), vol. VIII, pp. 403–81.

Corbo, V., *The House of Saint Peter at Capharnaum: A Preliminary Report of the First Two Campaigns of Excavations, April 16–June 19, Sept. 12–Nov. 26, 1968*, transl. S. Saller, SBF Collectio minor 5 (Jerusalem: Franciscan Printing Press, 1969).

Corley, K. E., 'The Anointing of Jesus in the Synoptic Tradition: An Argument for Authenticity', *JSHJ* 1 (2003), 61–72.

Private Women, Public Meals: Social Conflict in the Synoptic Tradition (Peabody, MA: Hendrickson, 1993).

Cosgrove, C. H., 'A Woman's Unbound Hair in the Greco-Roman World, with Special Reference to the Story of the "Sinful Woman" in Luke 7:36–50', *JBL* 124 (2005), 675–92.

Costin, T., *Il perdono di Dio nel vangelo di Matteo: Uno studio esegetico-te- ologico*, Tesi Gregoriana Serie Teologia 133 (Rome: Editrice Pontificia Università Gregoriana, 2006).

Cousland, J. R. C., *The Crowds in the Gospel of Matthew*, NovTSup 102 (Leiden/ Boston/Cologne: Brill, 2002).

Cranfield, C. E. B., *A Critical and Exegetical Commentary on the Epistle to the Romans*, ICC, 2 vols. (Edinburgh: T & T Clark, 1975–9).

Cross, F. M., 'Fragments of the Prayer of Nabonidus', *IEJ* 34 (1984), 260–4.

Crossan, J. D., *The Historical Jesus: The Life of a Mediterranean Jewish Peasant* (HarperSanFrancisco, 1991).

Crossan, J. D., and Reed, J. L., *Excavating Jesus: Beneath the Stones, Behind the Texts* (New York: HarperCollins, 2002).

Daniels, J. B., 'The Egerton Gospel: Its Place in Early Christianity', unpublished Ph.D. thesis, Claremont Graduate School (1990).

Danker, F. W., Bauer, W., Arndt, F. W., Gingrich, F. W., Aland, K. and Aland, B., with Reichmann, V., *A Greek–English Lexicon of the New Testament and Other Early Christian Literature*, 3rd edn (University of Chicago Press, 2000).

Dauer, A., *Johannes und Lukas: Untersuchungen zu den johanneisch-lukanischen Parallelperikopen Joh 4,46–54/Lk 7,1–10 – Joh 12,1–8/Lk 7,36–50; 10,38– 42 – Joh 20,19–29/Lk 24,36–49*, FzB 50 (Würzburg: Echter, 1984).

Davies, S. L., *Jesus the Healer: Possession, Trance, and the Origins of Christianity* (London: SCM, 1995).

Davies, W. D., and Allison, D. C., *A Critical and Exegetical Commentary on the Gospel according to Saint Matthew*, ICC, 3 vols. (Edinburgh: T & T Clark, 1988–97).

De Boer, M. C., 'Ten Thousand Talents? Matthew's Interpretation and Redaction of the Parable of the Unforgiving Servant', *CBQ* 50 (1988), 214–32.

Delobel, J., 'Lk 7,47 in Its Context: An Old Crux Revisited', in F. Van Segbroeck, C. M. Tuckett, G. Van Belle and J. Verheyden (eds.), *The Four Gospels 1992*, FS F. Neirynck (Leuven University Press, 1992), pp. 1581–90.

Derrett, J. D. M., 'Binding and Loosing (Matt 16:19; 18:18; John 29:23 [sic])', *JBL* 102 (1983), 112–17.

'The True Meaning of Jn 9, 1–3', *FilNeot* 16 (2003), 103–6.

Dewey, J., *Markan Public Debate: Literary Technique, Concentric Structure and Theology in Mark 2:1 to 3:6*, SBLDS 48 (Chico, CA: Scholars, 1980).

Dibelius, M., *Die Formgeschichte des Evangeliums* (Tübingen: Mohr Siebeck, 1919 (1st edn); 1933 (2nd edn)).

Die urchristliche Überlieferung von Johannes dem Täufer, FRLANT 15 (Göttingen: Vandenhoeck & Ruprecht, 1911).

Dibelius, M., and Greeven, H., *James: A Commentary on the Epistle of James* (Philadelphia: Fortress, 1975).

Dodd, C. H., *The Founder of Christianity* (New York: Collier, 1970).

Historical Tradition in the Fourth Gospel (Cambridge University Press, 1963).

History and the Gospel (London: Nisbeth, 1938).

Doughty, D. J., 'The Authority of the Son of Man (Mk 2,1–3,6)', *ZNW* 74 (1983), 161–81.

Downing, F. G., 'The Ambiguity of "The Pharisee and the Toll-Collector" (Luke 18:9–14) in the Graeco-Roman World of Late Antiquity', *CBQ* 54 (1992), 80–99.

Draper, J. A., 'The Jesus Tradition in the Didache', in J. A. Draper (ed.), *The Didache in Modern Research*, AGJU 37 (Leiden: Brill, 1996), pp. 72–91.

Dunn, J. D. G., 'Altering the Default Setting: Re-Envisaging the Early Transmission of the Jesus Tradition', *NTS* 49 (2003), 139–75.

The Epistles to the Colossians and to Philemon: A Commentary on the Greek Text (Grand Rapids, MI: Eerdmans, 1996).

Jesus and the Spirit: A Study of the Religious and Charismatic Experience of Jesus and the First Christians as Reflected in the New Testament (London: SCM, 1975).

Jesus Remembered, Christianity in the Making 1 (Grand Rapids, MI: Eerdmans, 2003).

'Jesus Tradition in Paul', in B. Chilton and C. A. Evans (eds.), *Studying the Historical Jesus: Evaluations of the State of Current Research*, NTTS 19 (Leiden: Brill, 1994), pp. 155–78.

'John and the Oral Gospel Tradition', in H. Wansbrough (ed.), *Jesus and the Oral Gospel Tradition*, JSNTS 64 (Sheffield: JSOT Press, 1991), pp. 351–79.

'Mark 2.1–3.6: A Bridge between Jesus and Paul on the Question of the Law', in *Jesus, Paul, and the Law: Studies in Mark and Galatians* (Louisville, KY: Westminster/John Knox, 1990), pp. 10–36. (Revised version of an article published in *NTS* 30 (1984), 395–415.)

The Partings of the Ways: Between Christianity and Judaism and Their Significance for the Character of Christianity, 2nd edn (London: SCM, 2006).

Romans 1–8, WBC 38A (Dallas: Word Books, 1988).

The Theology of Paul the Apostle (Grand Rapids, MI: Eerdmans, 1998).

Dupont, J., 'L'ambassade de Jean-Baptiste', *NRT* 83 (1961), 805–21, 943–59.

Dupont-Sommer, A., *Les écrits esséniens découverts près de la mer Morte* (Paris: Payot, 1959).

'Exorcismes et guérisons dans les écrits de Qoumrân', in *Congress Volume: Oxford 1959*, VTSup 7 (Leiden: Brill, 1960), pp. 246–61.

Ebeling, G., 'Jesus und Glaube', *ZTK* 55 (1958), 64–110.

Ehrman, B. D., 'Jesus and the Adulteress', *NTS* 34 (1988), 24–44.

Emerton, J. A., 'Binding and Loosing – Forgiving and Retaining', *JTS* 13 (1962), 325–31.

Erlemann, K., 'Papyrus Egerton 2: "Missing Link" zwischen synoptischer und johanneischer Tradition', *NTS* 42 (1996), 12–34.

Ernst, J., *Johannes der Täufer: Interpretation – Geschichte – Wirkungsgeschichte*, BZNW 53 (Berlin/New York: de Gruyter, 1989).

Evans, C. A., *Jesus and His Contemporaries: Comparative Studies* (Leiden: Brill, 1995).

'The New Quest for Jesus and the New Research on the Dead Sea Scrolls', in M. Labahn and A. Schmidt (eds.), *Jesus, Mark and Q: The Teaching of Jesus and Its Earliest Records*, JSNTS 214 (Sheffield Academic Press, 2001), pp. 163–83.

Review of Theissen and Winter, *Die Kriterienfrage in der Jesusforschung*, *JBL* 118 (1999), 551–3.

To See and Not Perceive: Isaiah 6.9–10 in Early Jewish and Christian Interpretation, JSOTS 64 (Sheffield: JSOT Press, 1989).

Eve, E., *The Healer from Nazareth: Jesus' Miracles in Historical Context* (London: SPCK, 2009).

The Jewish Context of Jesus' Miracles, JSNTS 231 (London/New York: Sheffield Academic Press, 2002).

'Meier, Miracle and Multiple Attestation', *JSHJ* 3 (2005), 23–45.

Feldman, L. H., *Josephus's Interpretation of the Bible* (Berkeley/Los Angeles/London: University of California Press, 1998).

'On Professor Mark Roncace's Portraits of Deborah and Gideon in Josephus', *JSJ* 32 (2001), 193–220.

'Prophets and Prophecy in Josephus', *JTS* 41 (1990), 386–422.

Studies in Josephus' Rewritten Bible, JSJSup 58 (Leiden/Boston/Cologne: Brill, 1998).

Feuillet, A., 'L'*exousia* du Fils de l'homme', *RSR* 42 (1954), 161–92.

Fiedler, P., 'Gottes Vergebungsbereitschaft und Heilswille', in L. Schenke, I. Broer, R. Hoppe, P. Fiedler, D. Zeller, J. Nützel, L. Oberlinner, H. Gollinger and H. Y. Zimmermann (eds.), *Jesus von Nazaret – Spuren und Konturen* (Stuttgart: Kohlhammer, 2004), pp. 164–92.

Jesus und die Sünder, BET 3 (Frankfurt: Peter Lang, 1976).

Review of Sung, *Vergebung der Sünden*, *ThRev* 91 (1995), 386–8.

'Sünde und Sündenvergebung in der Jesustradition', in H. Frankemölle (ed.), *Sünde und Erlösung im Neuen Testament*, QD 161 (Freiburg: Herder, 1996), pp. 76–91.

Fitzmyer, J. A., *The Gospel according to Luke I–IX*, AB 28 (New York: Doubleday, 1970).

The Gospel according to Luke X–XXIV, AB 28A (New York: Doubleday, 1985).

The One Who Is to Come (Grand Rapids, MI: Eerdmans, 2007).

Romans: A New Translation with Introduction and Commentary, AB 33 (London: Geoffrey Chapman, 1993).

Fletcher-Louis, C. H. T., 'Jesus as the High Priestly Messiah: Part 2', *JSHJ* 5 (2007), 57–79.

Luke-Acts: Angels, Christology and Soteriology, WUNT 2:94 (Tübingen: Mohr Siebeck, 1997).

Flint, P. W., 'The Daniel Tradition at Qumran', in J. J. Collins and P. W. Flint (eds.), *The Book of Daniel: Composition and Reception*, VTSup 83, 2 vols. (Leiden: Brill, 2001), vol. II, pp. 329–67.

Forbes, C., *Prophecy and Inspired Speech in Early Christianity and Its Hellenistic Environment*, WUNT 2:75 (Tübingen: Mohr Siebeck, 1995).

Forkman, G., *The Limits of the Religious Community: Expulsion from the Religious Community within the Qumran Sect, within Rabbinic Judaism, and within Primitive Christianity*, CBNTS 5 (Lund: Gleerup, 1972).

Fossum, J. E., *The Name of God and the Angel of the Lord: Samaritan and Jewish Concepts of Intermediation and the Origin of Gnosticism*, WUNT 36 (Tübingen: Mohr Siebeck, 1985).

Frickenschmidt, D., *Evangelium als Biographie: Die vier Evangelien im Rahmen antiker Erzählkunst*, TANZ 22 (Tübingen: Francke, 1997).

Fridrichsen, A., *Le problème du miracle dans le christianisme primitif*, EHPR 12 (Strasbourg/Paris: Istra, 1925).

Fuller, R. H., *The Foundations of New Testament Christology* (New York: Scribner, 1965).

Funk, R. W., Hoover, R. W., and the Jesus Seminar, *The Five Gospels: The Search for the Authentic Words of Jesus* (New York: Polebridge, 1993).

Furlani, G., 'Aram. *Gāzrīn* = Scongiuratori', *Atti della Accademia nazionale dei Lincei: Rendiconti: Classe di Scienze morali, storiche e filologiche: Serie 8* 3 (1948), 177–96.

García Martínez, F., *Qumran and Apocalyptic: Studies on the Aramaic Texts from Qumran*, STDJ 9 (Leiden: Brill, 1992).

Gerhardsson, B., *The Gospel Tradition*, CBNTS 15 (Lund: Gleerup, 1986).

Memory and Manuscript: Oral Tradition and Written Transmission in Rabbinic Judaism and Early Christianity, ASNU 22 (Uppsala: Almqvist & Wiksell, 1961).

The Mighty Acts of Jesus according to Matthew, Scripta minora Regiae Societatis humaniorum litterarum Lundensis 1978–9:5 (Lund: Gleerup, 1979).

Gibson, J., 'Jesus' Refusal to Produce a "Sign" (Mk 8.11–13)', *JSNT* 38 (1990), 37–66.

Gieschen, C. A., *Angelomorphic Christology: Antecedents and Early Evidence*, AGJU 42 (Leiden: Brill, 1998).

Gnilka, J., 'Das Elend vor dem Menschensohn (Mk 2,1–12)', in R. Pesch and R. Schnackenburg (eds.), *Jesus und der Menschensohn*, FS A. Vögtle (Freiburg: Herder, 1975), pp. 196–209.

Das Evangelium nach Markus, EKKNT 2, 2 vols. (Zürich/Einsiedeln/Cologne: Benziger, 1978–9).

Jesus von Nazaret (Freiburg: Herder, 1992).

Goodacre, M., *The Case against Q: Studies in Markan Priority and the Synoptic Problem* (Harrisburg, PA: Trinity, 2002).

Goulder, M. D., *Luke: A New Paradigm*, JSNTS 20 (Sheffield Academic Press, 1989).

'Those Outside (Mk. 4:10–12)', *NovT* 33 (1991), 289–302.

Gräßer, E., 'Jesus in Nazareth (Mc 6 1–6a): Bemerkungen zur Redaktion und Theologie des Markus', in W. Eltester (ed.), *Jesus in Nazareth*, BZNW 40 (Berlin/New York: de Gruyter, 1972), pp. 1–37.

Gray, R., *Prophetic Figures in Late Second Temple Jewish Palestine: The Evidence from Josephus* (Oxford University Press, 1993).

Green, J. B., *The Gospel of Luke*, NICNT (Grand Rapids, MI: Eerdmans, 1997).

Gregg, B. H., *The Historical Jesus and the Final Judgment Sayings in Q*, WUNT 2:207 (Tübingen: Mohr Siebeck, 2006).

Gregory, A. F., '*1 Clement* and the Writings that Later Formed the New Testament', in A. Gregory and C. Tuckett (eds.), *The New Testament and the Apostolic Fathers*, vol. I: *The Reception of the New Testament in the Apostolic Fathers* (Oxford University Press, 2005), pp. 129–57.

Gundry, R. H., *Matthew: A Commentary on His Handbook for a Mixed Church under Persecution*, 2nd edn (Grand Rapids, MI: Eerdmans, 1994).

Haenchen, E., 'Johanneische Probleme', *ZTK* 56 (1959), 19–54.

Hägerland, T., '"Ge inte giltighet åt denna deras synd!" Stefanos förbön och den tidiga kristologin', in G. Samuelsson and T. Hägerland (eds.), *Så som det har berättats för oss: Om bibel, gudstjänst och tro: En hyllning till Lennart Thörn på hans 65-årsdag* (Örebro: Libris, 2007), pp. 91–105.

'Jesus and the Rites of Repentance', *NTS* 52 (2006), 166–87.

'The Power of Prophecy: A Septuagintal Echo in John 20:19–23', *CBQ* 71 (2009), 84–103.

'A Prophet like Elijah or according to Isaiah? Rethinking the Identity of Jesus' (in press).

'Rituals of (Ex-)Communication and Identity: 1 Cor 5 and 4Q266 11; 4Q270 7', in B. Holmberg and M. Winninge (eds.), *Identity Formation in the New Testament*, WUNT 227 (Tübingen: Mohr Siebeck, 2008), pp. 43–60.

Hahn, F., *Christologische Hoheitstitel: Ihre Geschichte im frühen Christentum*, 5th edn (Göttingen: Vandenhoeck & Ruprecht, 1995).

Hampel, V., *Menschensohn und historischer Jesus: Ein Rätselwort als Schlüssel zum messianischen Selbstverständnis Jesu* (Neukirchen-Vluyn: Neukirchener, 1990).

Hannah, D. D., *Michael and Christ: Michael Traditions and Angel Christology in Early Christianity*, WUNT 2:109 (Tübingen: Mohr Siebeck, 1999).

Hansen, S. E., 'Forgiving and Retaining Sin: A Study of the Text and Context of John 20:23', *HBT* 19 (1997), 24–32.

Hardon, J. A., 'The Miracle Narratives in the Acts of the Apostles', *CBQ* 16 (1954), 303–18.

Harrison, P. N., *Polycarp's Two Epistles to the Philippians* (Cambridge University Press, 1936).

Hartin, P. J., *James and the Q Sayings of Jesus*, JSNTS 47 (Sheffield: JSOT Press, 1991).

Hartman, L., 'Baptism "Into the Name of Jesus" and Early Christology: Some Tentative Considerations', *ST* 28 (1974), 21–48.

'*Into the Name of the Lord Jesus': Baptism in the Early Church* (Edinburgh: T & T Clark, 1997).

Hartman, L. F., and Di Lella, A. A., *The Book of Daniel: A New Translation with Introduction and Commentary*, AB 23 (Garden City, NY: Doubleday, 1978).

Hartog, P., *Polycarp and the New Testament: The Occasion, Rhetoric, Theme, and Unity of the Epistle to the Philippians and Its Allusions to New Testament Literature*, WUNT 2:134 (Tübingen: Mohr Siebeck, 2002).

Harvey, A. E., *Jesus and the Constraints of History: The Bampton Lectures, 1980* (London: Duckworth, 1982).

Hatch, E., and Redpath, H. A., *A Concordance to the Septuagint and the Other Greek Versions of the Old Testament (Including the Apocryphal Books)*, 2 vols. (Oxford: Clarendon, 1897).

Head, P. M., *Christology and the Synoptic Problem: An Argument for Markan Priority*, SNTSMS 94 (Cambridge University Press, 1997).

Held, H. J., 'Matthäus als Interpret der Wundergeschichten', in G. Bornkamm, G. Barth and H. J. Held (eds.), *Überlieferung und Auslegung im Matthäusevangelium*, WMANT 1 (Neukirchen: Neukirchener, 1960), pp. 155–287.

Hengel, M., 'Probleme des Markusevangeliums', in P. Stuhlmacher (ed.), *Das Evangelium und die Evangelien: Vorträge vom Tübinger Symposium 1982*, WUNT 28 (Tübingen: Mohr Siebeck, 1983), pp. 221–65.

Hengel, M., and Schwemer, A. M., *Jesus und das Judentum*. Geschichte des frühen Christentums 1 (Tübingen: Mohr Siebeck, 2007).

Henze, M., *The Madness of King Nebuchadnezzar: The Ancient Near Eastern Origins and Early History of Interpretation of Daniel 4*, JSJSup 61 (Leiden/ Boston/Cologne: Brill, 1999).

Hezser, C., 'Die Verwendung der hellenistischen Gattung Chrie im frühen Christentum und Judentum', *JSJ* 27 (1996), 371–439.

Hieke, T., 'Q 7,22 – A Compendium of Isaian Eschatology', *ETL* 82 (2006), 175–87.

Hock, R. F., and O'Neil, E. N., *The Chreia in Ancient Rhetoric*, vol. i: *The Progymnasmata*, SBLTT 27 (Atlanta: Scholars, 1986).

The Chreia and Ancient Rhetoric: Classroom Exercises: Translated and Edited, SBLWGRW 2 (Atlanta: Society of Biblical Literature, 2002).

Hofius, O., 'Fußwaschung als Erweis der Liebe: Sprachliche und sachliche Anmerkungen zu Lk 7,44b', *ZNW* 81 (1990), 171–7.

'Jesu Zuspruch der Sündenvergebung: Exegetische Erwägungen zu Mk 2,5b', in I. Baldermann, E. Dassmann, O. Fuchs, B. Hamm, O. Hofius, B. Janowski, N. Lohfink, H. Merklein, N. H. Schmidt, G. Stemberger, P. Stuhlmacher, M.-T. Nacker, M. Welker and R. Weth (eds.), *Sünde und Gericht*, JBT 9 (Neukirchen-Vluyn: Neukirchener, 1994), pp. 125–43.

'Kennt der Targum zu Jes 53 einen sündenvergebenden Messias?', in O. Hofius, *Neutestamentliche Studien*, WUNT 132 (Tübingen: Mohr Siebeck, 2000), pp. 70–107.

'Vergebungszuspruch und Vollmachtsfrage: Mk 2,1–12 und das Problem priesterlicher Absolution im antiken Judentum', in H.-G. Geyer, J. M. Schmidt, W. Schneider and M. Weinrich (eds.), *'Wenn nicht jetzt, wann dann?'*, FS H.-J. Kraus (Neukirchen-Vluyn: Neukirchener, 1983), pp. 115–27.

'Das vierte Gottesknechtslied in den Briefen des Neuen Testamentes', in B. Janowski and P. Stuhlmacher (eds.), *Der leidende Gottesknecht: Jesaja 53 und seine Wirkungsgeschichte*, FzAT 14 (Tübingen: Mohr Siebeck, 1996), pp. 107–28.

Holmberg, B., 'Karisma som sociologisk förklaringsmodell i tolkningen av Jesus', *SEÅ* 67 (2002), 61–77.

Paul and Power: The Structure of Authority in the Primitive Church as Reflected in the Pauline Epistles, CBNTS 11 (Lund: Gleerup, 1978).

Holmén, T., 'Authenticity Criteria', in C. A. Evans (ed.), *Encyclopedia of the Historical Jesus* (London: Routledge, 2008), pp. 43–54.

'Doubts about Double Dissimilarity: Restructuring the Main Criterion of Jesus-of-History Research', in B. Chilton and C. A. Evans (eds.), *Authenticating the Words of Jesus*, NTTS 28:1 (Leiden: Brill, 1999), pp. 47–80.

Jesus and Jewish Covenant Thinking, BIS 55 (Leiden: Brill, 2001).

'Jesus and Magic: Theodicean Perspectives to the Issue', in M. Labahn and B. J. Lietaert Peerbolte (eds.), *A Kind of Magic: Understanding Magic in the New Testament and Its Religious Environment*, LNTS 306 (London: T & T Clark, 2007), pp. 43–56.

'Knowing about Q and Knowing about Jesus: Mutually Exclusive Undertakings?', in A. Lindemann (ed.), *The Sayings Source Q and the Historical Jesus*, BETL 158 (Leuven: Peeters, 2001), pp. 497–514.

Review of Theissen and Winter, *The Quest for the Plausible Jesus, JTS* 55 (2004), 216–28.

Holst, R., 'The One Anointing of Jesus: Another Application of the Form-Critical Method', *JBL* 95 (1976), 435–46.

Hooker, M. D., 'Christology and Methodology', *NTS* 17 (1970–1), 480–8.

The Signs of a Prophet: The Prophetic Actions of Jesus (London: SCM, 1997).

Horbury, W., 'Extirpation and Excommunication', *VT* 35 (1985), 13–38.

Horsley, R. A., *Jesus and the Spiral of Violence: Popular Jewish Resistance in Roman Palestine* (Minneapolis: Fortress, 1993).

'"Like One of the Prophets of Old": Two Types of Popular Prophets at the Time of Jesus', *CBQ* 47 (1985), 435–63.

'Popular Prophetic Movements at the Time of Jesus: Their Principal Features and Social Origins', *JSNT* 26 (1986), 3–27.

Hurtado, L. W., *Lord Jesus Christ: Devotion to Jesus in Earliest Christianity* (Grand Rapids, MI: Eerdmans, 2003).

Iwe, J. C., *Jesus in the Synagogue of Capernaum: The Pericope and Its Programmatic Character for the Gospel of Mark: An Exegetico-Theological Study of Mk 1:21–28*, Tesi Gregoriana Serie Teologia 57 (Rome: Editrice Pontificia Università Gregoriana, 1999).

Janowski, B., 'Sündenvergebung "um Hiobs willen": Fürbitte und Vergebung in 11QtgJob 38 2f. und Hi 42 9f. LXX', *ZNW* 73 (1982), 251–80.

Japhet, S., *I & II Chronicles: A Commentary*, Old Testament Library (London: SCM, 1993).

Jassen, A. P., *Mediating the Divine: Prophecy and Revelation in the Dead Sea Scrolls and Second Temple Judaism*, STDJ 68 (Leiden: Brill, 2007).

Jastrow, M., *A Dictionary of the Targumim, the Talmud Babli and Yerushalmi, and the Midrashic Literature* (New York: Judaica, 1992).

Jeremias, J., *Die Gleichnisse Jesu*, 7th edn (Göttingen: Vandenhoeck & Ruprecht, 1965).

Neutestamentliche Theologie: Erster Teil: Die Verkündigung Jesu (Gütersloh: Mohn, 1971).

'Tradition und Redaktion in Lukas 15', *ZNW* 62 (1971), 172–89.

Johnson, L. T., *Brother of Jesus, Friend of God: Studies in the Letter of James* (Grand Rapids, MI: Eerdmans, 2004).

The Gospel of Luke, Sacra Pagina (Collegeville, MN: Liturgical, 1991).

The Letter of James: A New Translation with Introduction and Commentary, AB 37A (New York: Doubleday, 1995).

Jongeling, B., Labuschagne, C. J., and van der Woude, A. S., *Aramaic Texts from Qumran: With Translations and Annotations*, SSS 4 (Leiden: Brill, 1976).

Käsemann, E., 'Das Problem des historischen Jesus', *ZTK* 51 (1954), 125–53.

'Sätze heiligen Rechtes im Neuen Testament', *NTS* 1 (1955), 248–60.

Kazen, T., 'The Christology of Early Christian Practice', *JBL* 127 (2008), 591–614.

Jesus and Purity Halakhah: Was Jesus Indifferent to Impurity?, CBNTS 38 (Stockholm: Almqvist & Wiksell, 2002).

Keim, T., *Geschichte Jesu von Nazara: In ihrer Verkettung mit dem Gesammtleben seines Volkes: Frei untersucht und ausführlich erzählt*, 3 vols. (Zürich: Orell, Füssli und Comp, 1867–72).

Kellermann, U., 'Wer kann Sünden vergeben außer Elia?', in P. Mommer, W. H. Schmidt and H. Strauss (eds.), *Gottes Recht als Lebensraum*, FS H. J. Boecker (Neukirchen-Vluyn: Neukirchener, 1993), pp. 165–77.

Kennedy, G. A. (trans.), *Progymnasmata: Greek Textbooks of Prose Composition and Rhetoric: Translated with Introductin and Notes*, SBLGRW 10 (Atlanta: Society of Biblical Literature, 2003).

Keown, G. L., 'Prophecy in 1 and 2 Samuel', *RevExp* 99 (2002), 175–84.

Kertelge, K., 'Die Vollmacht des Menschensohnes zur Sündenvergebung (Mk 2,10)', in P. Hoffmann (ed.), *Orientierung an Jesus: Zur Theologie der Synoptiker*, FS J. Schmid (Freiburg: Herder, 1973), pp. 205–13.

Kiilunen, J., *Die Vollmacht im Widerstreit: Untersuchungen zum Werdegang von Mk 2,1–3,6*, AASFDHL 40 (Helsinki: Suomalainen Tiedeakatemia, 1985).

Kilgallen, J. J., 'Forgiveness of Sins (Luke 7:36–50)', *NovT* 40 (1998), 105–16.

'John the Baptist, the Sinful Woman, and the Pharisee', *JBL* 104 (1985), 675–9.

'What Does It Mean to Say that there Are Additions in Luke 7,36–50?', *Bib* 86 (2005), 529–35.

Kingsbury, J. D., *Conflict in Mark: Jesus, Authorities, Disciples* (Minneapolis: Fortress, 1989).

'The Developing Conflict between Jesus and the Jewish Leaders in Matthew's Gospel: A Literary-Critical Study', *CBQ* 49 (1987), 57–73.

Matthew: Structure, Christology, Kingdom, paperback edn (Minneapolis: Fortress, 1989).

Kirchschläger, W., 'Exorzismus in Qumran?', *Kairos* 18 (1976), 135–53.

Klauck, H.-J., 'Die Frage der Sündenvergebung in der Perikope von der Heilung des Gelähmten (Mk 2,1–12 parr)', *BZ* NS 25 (1981), 223–48.

'Heil ohne Heilung? Zu Metaphorik und Hermeneutik der Rede von Sünde und Vergebung im Neuen Testament', in H. Frankemölle (ed.), *Sünde und Erlösung im Neuen Testament*, QD 161 (Freiburg: Herder, 1996), pp. 18–52.

Koch, K., 'Is Daniel Also among the Prophets?', *Int* 39 (1985), 117–30.

'Messias und Sündenvergebung in Jesaja 53-Targum: Ein Beitrag zu der Praxis der aramäischen Bibelübersetzung', *JSJ* 3 (1972), 117–48.

'Sühne und Sündenvergebung um die Wende von der exilischen zur nachex-ilischen Zeit', *EvT* 26 (1966), 217–39.

Kraus, W., 'Die Bedeutung von Dtn 18,15–18 für das Verständnis Jesu als Prophet', *ZNW* 90 (1999), 153–76.

Kuhn, H.-W., *Ältere Sammlungen im Markusevangelium*, SUNT 8 (Göttingen: Vandenhoeck & Ruprecht, 1971).

Kümmel, W. G., *Jesu Antwort an Johannes den Täufer: Ein Beispiel zum Methodenproblem in der Jesusforschung*, Sitzungsberichte der wissen-schaftlichen Gesellschaft an der Johann Wolfgang Goethe-Universität Frankfurt/Main 11:4 (Wiesbaden: Steiner, 1974).

Kvalbein, H., 'The Authorization of Peter in Matthew 16:17–19: A Reconsideration of the Power to Bind and Loose', in J. Ådna (ed.), *The Formation of the Early Church*, WUNT 183 (Tübingen: Mohr Siebeck, 2005), pp. 145–74.

'Die Wunder der Endzeit: Beobachtungen zu 4Q521 und Matth 11,5p', *ZNW* 88 (1997), 111–25.

Lambrecht, J., 'A Note on John 20,23b', *ETL* 83 (2007), 165–8.

Lane, W. L., *The Gospel of Mark* (Grand Rapids, MI: Eerdmans, 1974).

Latourelle, R., *Miracles de Jésus et théologie du miracle* (Paris: Cerf, 1986).

Le Déaut, R., 'Aspects de l'intercession dans le judaïsme ancien', *JSJ* 1 (1970), 35–57.

Legault, A., 'An Application of the Form-Critique Method to the Anointings in Galilee (Lk 7, 36–50) and Bethany (Mt 26, 6–13; Mk 14, 3–9; Jn 12, 1–8)', *CBQ* 16 (1954), 131–45.

Leroy, H., *Zur Vergebung der Sünden: Die Botschaft der Evangelien*, SBS 73 (Stuttgart: Katholisches Bibelwerk, 1974).

Levine, B. A., *Numbers 1–20: A New Translation with Introduction and Commentary*, AB 4A (New York: Doubleday, 1993).

Liddell, H. G., Scott, R., and Jones, H. S., *A Greek–English Lexicon*, 9th edn with supplement (Oxford: Clarendon, 1968).

Lierman, J., *The New Testament Moses: Christian Perceptions of Moses and Israel in the Setting of Jewish Religion*, WUNT 2:173 (Tübingen: Mohr Siebeck, 2004).

Lietzmann, H., *Der Menschensohn: Ein Beitrag zur neutestamentlichen Theologie* (Freiburg/Leipzig: Mohr Siebeck, 1896).

Lindars, B., *The Gospel of John*, NCB (London: Oliphants, 1972).

Jesus Son of Man: A Fresh Examination of the Son of Man Sayings in the Gospels in the Light of Recent Research (London: SPCK, 1983).

Linnemann, E., *Gleichnisse Jesu: Einführung und Auslegung*, 6th edn (Göttingen: Vandenhoeck & Ruprecht, 1975).

Loader, W. R. G., *Jesus' Attitude towards the Law: A Study of the Gospels*, WUNT 2:97 (Tübingen: Mohr Siebeck, 1997).

Löhr, H., *Studien zum frühchristlichen und frühjüdischen Gebet: Untersuchungen zu 1 Clem 59 bis 61 in seinem literarischen, historischen und theologischen Kontext* (Tübingen: Mohr Siebeck, 2003).

Löhr, W. A., *Basilides und seine Schule: Eine Studie zur Theologie- und Kirchengeschichte des zweiten Jahrhunderts*, WUNT 83 (Tübingen: Mohr Siebeck, 1996).

Lohse, E., 'Jesu Worte über den Sabbath', in W. Eltester (ed.), *Judentum, Urchristentum, Kirche*, FS J. Jeremias, BZNW 26 (Berlin: Töpelmann, 1960), pp. 79–89.

Loisy, A., *L'Évangile selon Marc* (Paris: Nourry, 1912).

Les évangiles synoptiques, 2 vols. (Montier-en-Der: Ceffonds, 1907–8).

Lona, H. E., *An Diognet: Übersetzt und erklärt*, KfA 8 (Freiburg: Herder, 2001).

Lövestam, E., *Spiritus blasphemia: Eine Studie zu Mk 3,28f par Mt 12,31f, Lk 12,10*, Scripta minora Regiae Societatis humaniorum litterarum Lundensis 1966–7:1 (Lund: Gleerup, 1968).

Lüdemann, G., *Jesus after 2000 Years: What He Really Said and Did*, transl. J. Bowden (London: SCM, 2000).

Lührmann, D., 'Die Geschichte von einer Sünderin und andere apokryphe Jesusüberlieferungen bei Didymos von Alexandrien', *NovT* 32 (1990), 289–316.

Luttikhuizen, G. P., *The Revelation of Elchasai: Investigations into the Evidence for a Mesopotamian Jewish Apocalypse of the Second Century and Its Reception by Judeo-Christian Propagandists* (Tübingen: Mohr Siebeck, 1985).

Luz, U., 'Das Primatwort Matthäus 16:17–19 aus Wirkungsgeschichtlicher Sicht', *NTS* 37 (1991), 415–33.

Mack, B. L., and Robbins, V. K., *Patterns of Persuasion in the Gospels* (Sonoma, CA: Polebridge, 1989).

Maisch, I., *Die Heilung des Gelähmten*, SBS 52 (Stuttgart: KBW, 1971).

Manson, T. W., *The Teaching of Jesus: Studies of Its Form and Content* (Cambridge University Press, 1931).

Manson, W., *Jesus the Messiah: The Synoptic Tradition of the Revelation of God in Christ, with Special Reference to Form-Criticism* (London: Hodder and Stoughton, 1943).

Mantey, J. R., 'Distorted Translations in John 20:23; Matthew 16:18–19 and 18:18', *RevExp* 78 (1981), 409–16.

Marcus, J., 'Son of Man as Son of Adam', *RB* 110 (2003), 38–61.

'Son of Man as Son of Adam: Part II: Exegesis', *RB* 110 (2003), 370–86.

Massaux, E., *The Influence of the Gospel of Saint Matthew on Christian Literature before Saint Irenaeus*, vol. III: *The Apologists and the Didache*, NGSt 5:3 (Leuven: Peeters, 1993).

McCarter, P. K., *II Samuel: A New Translation with Introduction and Commentary*, AB 9 (New York: Doubleday, 1984).

McCown, C. C., 'Luke's Translation of Semitic into Hellenistic Custom', *JBL* 58 (1939), 213–20.

McDonald, J. I. H., 'The So-Called *Pericope de Adultera*', *NTS* 41 (1995), 415–27.

McKnight, S., *Jesus and His Death: Historiography, the Historical Jesus, and Atonement Theory* (Waco, TX: Baylor University Press, 2005).

Meeks, W. A., *The Prophet-King: Moses Traditions and the Johannine Christology*. NovTSup 14 (Leiden: Brill, 1967).

Meier, J. P., *A Marginal Jew: Rethinking the Historical Jesus*, A[Y]BRL, 4 vols. (New York: Doubleday, 1991–2001; New Haven/London: Yale University Press, 2009).

Merklein, H., 'Paulus und die Sünde', in H. Frankemölle (ed.), *Sünde und Erlösung im Neuen Testament*, QD 161 (Freiburg: Herder, 1996), pp. 123–63.

Meyer, A., *Jesu Muttersprache: Das galiläische Aramäisch in seiner Bedeutung für die Erklärung der Reden Jesu und der Evangelien überhaupt* (Freiburg/ Leipzig: Mohr Siebeck, 1896).
Meyer, B. F., *The Aims of Jesus* (London: SCM, 1979).
Meyer, R., *Das Gebet des Nabonid: Eine in den Qumran-Handschriften wiederentdeckte Weisheitserzählung* (Berlin: Akademie-Verlag, 1962).
'προφήτης κτλ: C. Prophetentum und Propheten im Judentum der hellenistisch-römischen Zeit', in G. Kittel and G. Friedrich (eds.), *Theologisches Wörterbuch zum Neuen Testament*, 10 vols. (Stuttgart: Kohlhammer, 1933–79), vol. VI, pp. 813–28.
Michaelis, W., *Die Gleichnisse Jesu: Eine Einführung*, 3rd edn (Hamburg: Furche, 1956).
Michl, J., 'Sündenbekenntnis und Sündenvergebung in der Kirche des Neuen Testaments', *MThZ* 24 (1973), 189–207.
'Sündenvergebung in Christus nach dem Glaube der frühen Kirche', *MThZ* 24 (1973), 25–35.
Milavec, A., 'The Purifying Confession of Failings Required by the Didache's Eucharistic Sacrifice', *BTB* 33 (2003), 64–76.
Milgrom, J., *Leviticus 1–16: A New Translation with Introduction and Commentary*, AB 3 (New York: Doubleday, 1991).
Studies in Levitical Terminology, vol. I: *The Encroacher and the Levite: The Term 'Aboda'* (Berkeley: University of California Press, 1970).
Milik, J. T., '"Prière de Nabonide" et autres écrits d'un cycle de Daniel: Fragments araméens de Qumrân 4', *RB* 63 (1956), 407–15.
Miller, M. P., 'The Function of Isa 61:1–2 in 11Q Melchizedek', *JBL* 88 (1969), 467–9.
Moeser, M. C., *The Anecdote in Mark, the Classical World and the Rabbis*, JSNTS 227 (Sheffield Academic Press, 2002).
Momigliano, A., *The Development of Greek Biography* (Cambridge, MA: Harvard University Press, 1971).
Murphy-O'Connor, J., 'Péché et communauté dans le Nouveau Testament', *RB* 74 (1967), 161–93.
Mussner, F., *Der Jakobusbrief*, HTKNT 13, 5th edn (Freiburg: Herder, 1987).
Myllykoski, M., 'The Sinful Woman in the *Gospel of Peter*: Reconstructing the Other Side of P.Oxy. 4009', *NTS* 55 (2009), 104–15.
Nave, G. D., *The Role and Function of Repentance in Luke-Acts*, Academia Biblica 4 (Atlanta: SBL, 2002).
Neirynck, F., 'John and the Synoptics: Response to P. Borgen', in D. L. Dungan (ed.), *The Interrelations of the Gospels: A Symposium Led by M.-É. Boismard – W. R. Farmer – F. Neirynck: Jerusalem 1984*, BETL 95 (Leuven University Press, 1990), pp. 438–50.
Neyrey, J. H., 'Questions, *Chreiai*, and Challenges to Honor: The Interface of Rhetoric and Culture in Mark's Gospel', *CBQ* 60 (1998), 657–81.
Niederwimmer, K., 'Der Didachist und seine Quellen', in C. N. Jefford (ed.), *The Didache in Context: Essays on Its Text, History and Transmission*, NovTSup 77 (Leiden: Brill, 1995), pp. 15–36.
Nielsen, H. K., *Heilung und Verkündigung: Das Verständnis der Heilung und ihres Verhältnisses zur Verkündigung bei Jesus und in der ältesten Kirche*, ATD 22 (Leiden/New York/Copenhagen/Cologne: Brill, 1987).

'Kriterien zur Bestimmung authentischer Jesusworte', *SNTU* 4 (1979), 5–26.

Öhler, M., *Elia im Neuen Testament: Untersuchungen zur Bedeutung des alttestamentlichen Propheten im frühen Christentum*, BZNW 88 (Berlin/New York: de Gruyter, 1997).

'Jesus as Prophet: Remarks on Terminology', in M. Labahn and A. Schmidt (eds.), *Jesus, Mark and Q: The Teaching of Jesus and Its Earliest Records*, JSNTS 214 (Sheffield Academic Press, 2001), pp. 125–42.

Ollilainen, V., 'Jesus and the Parable of the Prodigal Son', unpublished Ph.D. thesis, Åbo Akademi (2008).

Orlov, A., *The Enoch-Metatron Tradition*, TSAJ 107 (Tübingen: Mohr Siebeck, 2005).

Osiek, C., *The Shepherd of Hermas: A Commentary* (Minneapolis: Fortress, 1999).

Otto, R., *Reich Gottes und Menschensohn: Ein religionsgeschichtlicher Versuch* (Munich: C. H. Beck, 1934).

Overwien, O., 'Das Gnomologium, das Gnomologium Vaticanum und die Tradition', *GFA* 4 (2001), 99–131.

Paffenroth, K., *The Story of Jesus according to L*, JSNTS 147 (Sheffield Academic Press, 1997).

Park, J., 'Sündenvergebung: Ihre religiöse und soziale Dimension im Matthäusevangelium', unpublished Ph.D. thesis, University of Heidelberg (2001).

Parrott, R., 'Conflict and Rhetoric in Mark 2:23–28', *Semeia* 64 (1994), 139–70.

Patillon, M. (ed.), *Aelius Théon: Progymnasmata: Texte établi et traduit* (Paris: Les Belles Lettres, 1997).

Patterson, S. J., *The Gospel of Thomas and Jesus* (Sonoma, CA: Polebridge, 1993).

Patton, C. S., 'Did Jesus Call Himself the Son of Man?', *JR* 2 (1922), 501–11.

Perrin, N., *Rediscovering the Teaching of Jesus* (London: SCM, 1967).

Pesch, R., *Jesu ureigene Taten? Ein Beitrag zur Wunderfrage*, QD 52 (Freiburg/Basel/Vienna: Herder, 1970).

Pilch, J. J., *Healing in the New Testament: Insights from Medical and Mediterranean Anthropology* (Minneapolis: Fortress, 2000).

Polkow, D., 'Method and Criteria for Historical Jesus Research', *SBLSP* 26 (1987), 336–56.

Porter, S. E., *The Criteria for Authenticity in Historical-Jesus Research: Previous Discussion and New Proposals*, JSNTS 191 (Sheffield Academic Press, 2000).

'The Criterion of Greek Language and Its Context: A Further Response', *JSHJ* 4 (2006), 69–74.

'Luke 17.11–19 and the Criteria for Authenticity Revisited', *JSHJ* 1 (2003), 201–24.

Poschmann, B., *Paenitentia secunda: Die kirchliche Buße im ältesten Christentum bis Cyprian und Origenes: Eine dogmengeschichtliche Untersuchung*, Theophaneia 1 (Bonn: Hanstein, 1940).

Pouderon, B., 'Introduction', in B. Pouderon, M.-J. Pierre, B. Outtier and M. Guiorgadzé (eds.), *Aristide: Apologie: Introduction, textes critiques, traductions et commentaire*, SC 470 (Paris: Cerf, 2003), pp. 21–180.

Pryor, J. W., 'Papyrus Egerton 2 and the Fourth Gospel', *AusBR* 37 (1989), 1–13.

Puech, É., 'Une apocalypse messianique (4Q521)', *RevQ* 15 (1992), 475–522.

'La prière de Nabonide (4Q242)', in K. J. Cathcart and M. Maher (eds.), *Targumic and Cognate Studies*, FS M. McNamara, JSOTS 230 (Sheffield Academic Press, 1996), pp. 208–27.

Räisänen, H., *The 'Messianic Secret' in Mark's Gospel* (Edinburgh: T & T Clark, 1990).

Rasmussen, E., *Jesus: En sammenlignende Studie* (Copenhagen: Nordiske Forfatteres Forlag, 1905).

Rau, E., *Jesus – Freund von Zöllnern und Sündern: Eine methodenkritische Untersuchung* (Stuttgart: Kohlhammer, 2000).

Reiser, M., *Die Gerichtspredigt Jesu: Eine Untersuchung zur eschatologischen Verkündigung Jesu und ihrem frühjüdischen Hintergrund*, NTA 23 (Münster: Aschendorff, 1990).

'Die Stellung der Evangelien in der antiken Literaturgeschichte', *ZNW* 90 (1999), 1–27.

Renan, E., *Histoire des origines du Christianisme*, vol. I: *Vie de Jésus* (Berlin: Springer, 1863).

Rhoads, D., Dewey, J., and Michie, D., *Mark as Story: An Introduction to the Narrative of a Gospel*, 2nd edn (Minneapolis: Fortress, 1999).

Riesner, R., 'Back to the Historical Jesus through Paul and His School (The Ransom Logion—Mark 10.45; Matt 20.28)', *JSHJ* 1 (2003), 171–99.

Jesus als Lehrer: Eine Untersuchung zum Ursprung der Evangelien-Überlieferung, WUNT 2:7, 3rd edn (Tübingen: Mohr Siebeck, 1988).

Roncace, M., 'Josephus' (Real) Portraits of Deborah and Gideon: A Reading of *Antiquities* 5.198–232', *JSJ* 31 (2000), 247–74.

Rordorf, W., 'La rémission des péchés selon la Didachè', *Irénikon* 46 (1973), 283–97.

Ross, J. M., 'Further Unnoticed Points in the Text of the New Testament', *NovT* 45 (2003), 209–21.

Rowland, C., 'A Man Clothed in Linen: Daniel 10.6ff. and Jewish Angelology', *JSNT* 24 (1985), 99–110.

The Open Heaven: A Study of Apocalyptic in Judaism and Early Christianity (London: SPCK, 1982).

Sahlin, H., 'Wie wurde ursprünglich die Benennung "Der Menschensohn" verstanden?', *ST* 37 (1983), 147–79.

Sanders, E. P., *The Historical Figure of Jesus* (London: Allen Lane, 1993).

Jesus and Judaism (London: SCM, 1985).

Jewish Law from Jesus to the Mishnah: Five Studies (London: SCM/ Philadelphia: Trinity, 1990).

Judaism: Practice and Belief 63 BCE–66 CE (London: SCM, 1992).

Paul and Palestinian Judaism: A Comparison of Patterns of Religion (London: SCM, 1977).

The Tendencies of the Synoptic Tradition (Cambridge University Press, 1969).

Sanders, J. T., 'The Criterion of Coherence and the Randomness of Charisma: Poring through Some Aporias in the Jesus Tradition', *NTS* 44 (1998), 1–25.

Satran, D., *Biblical Prophets in Byzantine Palestine: Reassessing the* Lives of the Prophets, SVTP 11 (Leiden/New York/Cologne: Brill, 1995).

Schaller, B., *Fundamenta Judaica: Studien zum antiken Judentum und zum Neuen Testament*, SUNT 25 (Göttingen: Vandenhoeck & Ruprecht, 2001).

Schenk, W., '"Den Menschen" Mt 9,8', *ZNW* 54 (1963), 272–5.

Schenkel, D., *Das Charakterbild Jesu: Ein biblischer Versuch*, 3rd edn (Wiesbaden: C. W. Kreidel, 1864).

Schmidt, N., 'The Son of Man in the Book of Daniel', *JBL* 19 (1900), 22–8.

Schmiedel, O., *Die Hauptprobleme der Leben-Jesu-Forschung*, 2nd edn (Tübingen: Mohr Siebeck, 1906).

Schneiders, S. M., 'The Raising of the New Temple: John 20.19–23 and Johannine Ecclesiology', *NTS* 52 (2006), 337–55.

Schoedel, W. R., *Ignatius of Antioch: A Commentary on the Letters of Ignatius of Antioch* (Philadelphia: Fortress, 1995).

Schottroff, L., 'Das Gleichnis vom verlorenen Sohn', *ZTK* 68 (1971), 27–52.

Schottroff, L., and Stegemann, W., *Jesus von Nazareth – Hoffnung der Armen*, 3rd edn (Stuttgart: Kohlhammer, 1990).

Schrage, W., *Das Verhältnis des Thomas-Evangeliums zur synoptischen Tradition und zu den koptischen Evangelienübersetzungen: Zugleich ein Beitrag zur gnostischen Synoptikerdeutung*, BZNW 29 (Berlin: Töpelmann, 1964).

Schramm, T., *Der Markus-Stoff bei Lukas: Eine literarkritische und redaktionsgeschichtliche Untersuchung*, SNTSMS 14 (Cambridge University Press, 1971).

Schürmann, H., 'Kritische Jesuserkenntnis. Zur kritischen Handhabung des "Unähnlichkeitskriteriums"', in H. Schürmann, *Jesus: Gestalt und Geheimnis*, ed. K. Scholtissek (Paderborn: Bonifatius, 1994), pp. 420–34.

Traditionsgeschichtliche Untersuchungen zu den synoptischen Evangelien: Beiträge (Düsseldorf: Patmos, 1968).

Schüssler Fiorenza, E., *The Book of Revelation: Justice and Judgment* (Philadelphia: Fortress, 1985).

Schweitzer, A., *Geschichte der Leben-Jesu-Forschung*, 9th edn (Tübingen: Mohr Siebeck, 1984).

Schwemer, A. M., *Studien zu den frühchristlichen Prophetenlegenden* Vitae Prophetarum, vol. I: *Die Viten der großen Propheten Jesaja, Jeremia, Ezechiel und Daniel: Einleitung, Übersetzung und Kommentar*, TSAJ 49 (Tübingen: Mohr Siebeck, 1995).

Segal, A. F., *Two Powers in Heaven: Early Rabbinic Reports about Christianity and Gnosticism* (Leiden: Brill, 1977).

Seybold, K., and Müller, U., *Krankheit und Heilung* (Stuttgart: Kohlhammer, 1978).

Shafer, G. R., 'John the Baptist, Jesus, and Forgiveness of Sins', *PEGLMBS* 26 (2006), 51–67.

Shin, H. W., *Textual Criticism and the Synoptic Problem in Historical Jesus Research: The Search for Valid Criteria*, CBET 36 (Leuven: Peeters, 2004).

Smith, S. H., *A Lion with Wings: A Narrative-Critical Approach to Mark's Gospel* (Sheffield Academic Press, 1996).

Snodgrass, K. R., *Stories with Intent: A Comprehensive Guide to the Parables of Jesus* (Grand Rapids, MI: Eerdmans, 2008).

Stacey, D., 'Appendix: The Lord's Supper as Prophetic Drama', in M. D. Hooker, *The Signs of a Prophet: The Prophetic Actions of Jesus* (London: SCM, 1997), pp. 80–95.

Stanton, G., 'Matthew as a Creative Interpreter of the Sayings of Jesus', in P. Stuhlmacher (ed.), *Das Evangelium und die Evangelien: Vorträge vom Tübinger Symposium 1982*, WUNT 28 (Tübingen: Mohr Siebeck, 1983), pp. 273–87.

Stein, R. H., 'The "Criteria" for Authenticity', in R. T. France and D. Wenham (eds.), *Gospel Perspectives: Studies of History and Tradition in the Four Gospels*, vol. I (Sheffield: JSOT Press, 1980), pp. 225–63.

Steinmann, A., 'The Chicken and the Egg: A New Proposal for the Relationship between the *Prayer of Nabonidus* and the *Book of Daniel*', *RevQ* 20 (2002), 557–70.

Stendahl, K., 'Prayer and Forgiveness', *SEÅ* 22–3 (1957–8), 75–86.

Stettler, H., 'Die Bedeutung der Täuferanfrage in Matthäus 11,2–6 par Luk 7,18–23 für die Christologie', *Bib* 89 (2008), 173–200.

Strack, H. L., and Billerbeck, P., *Kommentar zum Neuen Testament aus Talmud und Midrasch*, vol. I, 9th edn (Munich: Beck, 1986).

Strauss, D. F., *Das Leben Jesu für das deutsche Volk bearbeitet*, 18th edn (Stuttgart: Alfred Kröner, n.d. (1st edn 1864)).

Das Leben Jesu, kritisch bearbeitet, 4th edn, 2 vols. (Tübingen: Ossiander, 1840).

Strecker, G., *Die Bergpredigt: Ein exegetischer Kommentar* (Göttingen: Vandenhoeck & Ruprecht, 1984).

Strobel, A., *Erkenntnis und Bekenntnis der Sünde in neutestamentlicher Zeit*, AzT 1 37 (Stuttgart: Calwer, 1968).

Stuhlmacher, P., *Biblische Theologie des Neuen Testaments*, 2nd edn, 2 vols. (Göttingen: Vandenhoeck & Ruprecht, 1997).

Sullivan, K. P., *Wrestling with Angels: A Study of the Relationship between Angels and Humans in Ancient Jewish Literature and the New Testament*, AGJU 55 (Leiden: Brill, 2004).

Sung, C.-H., *Vergebung der Sünden: Jesu Praxis der Sündenvergebung nach den Synoptikern und ihre Voraussetzungen im Alten Testament und frühen Judentum*, WUNT 2:57 (Tübingen: Mohr Siebeck, 1993).

Suter, D. W., 'Enoch in Sheol: Updating the Dating of the Book of Parables', in G. Boccaccini (ed.), *Enoch and the Messiah Son of Man: Revisiting the Book of Parables* (Grand Rapids, MI: Eerdmans, 2007), pp. 415–43.

Syrén, R., 'Targum Isaiah 52:13–53:12 and Christian Interpretation', *JJS* 40 (1989), 201–12.

Tannehill, R. C., 'The Mission of Jesus according to Luke IV 16–30', in W. Eltester (ed.), *Jesus in Nazareth*, BZNW 40 (Berlin/New York: de Gruyter, 1972), pp. 51–75.

Taylor, J. E., *The Immerser: John the Baptist within Second Temple Judaism* (Grand Rapids, MI/Cambridge: Eerdmans, 1997).

Taylor, V., *Forgiveness and Reconciliation: A Study in New Testament Theology* (London: Macmillan, 1946).

The Gospel according to St. Mark (London: Macmillan, 1953).

Theissen, G., *Lokalkolorit und Zeitgeschichte in den Evangelien: Ein Beitrag zur Geschichte der synoptischen Tradition*, 2nd edn (Göttingen: Vandenhoeck & Ruprecht, 1992).

Urchristliche Wundergeschichten: Ein Beitrag zur formgeschichtlichen Erforschung der synoptischen Evangelien, SzNT 8 (Gütersloh: Mohn, 1974); English translation: *The Miracle Stories of the Early Christian Tradition*, transl. F. McDonagh (Edinburgh: T & T Clark, 1983).

'Wanderradikalismus: Literatursoziologische Aspekte der Überlieferung von Worten Jesu im Urchristentum', *ZTK* 70 (1973), 245–71.

Theissen, G., and Merz, A., *Der historische Jesus: Ein Lehrbuch*, 3rd edn (Göttingen: Vandenhoeck & Ruprecht, 2001).

Theissen, G., and Winter, D., *Die Kriterienfrage in der Jesusforschung: Vom Differenzkriterium zum Plausibilitätskriterium*, NTOA 34 (Göttingen: Vandenhoeck & Ruprecht, 1997); English translation: *The Quest for the Plausible Jesus: The Question of Criteria*, transl. M. E. Boring (London: Westminster John Knox, 2002).

Theobald, M., *Herrenworte im Johannesevangelium*, HBS 34 (Freiburg: Herder, 2002).

Thiselton, A. C., *The First Epistle to the Corinthians: A Commentary on the Greek Text*, NIGTC (Grand Rapids, MI: Eerdmans, 2000).

Thissen, W., *Erzählung der Befreiung: Eine exegetische Untersuchung zu Mk 2,1–3,6*, FzB 21 (Würzburg: Echter, 1976).

Thompson, M. M., 'Intercession in the Johannine Community: 1 John 5.16 in the Context of the Gospel and Epistles of John', in M. J. Wilkins and T. Paige (eds.), *Worship, Theology and Ministry in the Early Church*, FS R. P. Martin (Sheffield Academic Press, 1992), pp. 225–45.

Thompson, W. G., *Matthew's Advice to a Divided Community: Mt. 17,22 – 18,35*, AnBib 44 (Rome: Biblical Institute Press, 1970).

Thyen, H., 'Βάπτισμα μετανοίας εἰς ἄφεσιν ἁμαρτιῶν', in E. Dinkler (ed.), *Zeit und Geschichte*, FS R. Bultmann (Tübingen: Mohr Siebeck, 1964), pp. 97–125.

Studien zur Sündenvergebung: Im Neuen Testament und seinen alttestamentlichen und jüdischen Voraussetzungen, FRLANT 96 (Göttingen: Vandenhoeck & Ruprecht, 1970).

Tödt, H. E., *Der Menschensohn in der synoptischen Überlieferung*, 4th edn (Gütersloh: Mohn, 1978).

Trautmann, M., *Zeichenhafte Handlungen Jesu: Ein Beitrag zur Frage nach dem geschichtlichen Jesus*, FzB 37 (Würzburg: Echter, 1980).

Tuckett, C. (M.), 'Form Criticism', in W. H. Kelber and S. Byrskog (eds.), *Jesus in Memory: Traditions in Oral and Scribal Perspectives* (Waco, TX: Baylor University Press, 2009), pp. 21–38.

'Synoptic Tradition in the Didache', in J. A. Draper (ed.), *The Didache in Modern Research*, AGJU 37 (Leiden: Brill, 1996), pp. 92–128.

'Thomas and the Synoptics', *NovT* 30 (1988), 132–57.

Twelftree, G. H., *Jesus the Miracle Worker: A Historical and Theological Study* (Downers Grove: InterVarsity Press, 1999).

Ulrich, E., 'Josephus' Biblical Text for the Books of Samuel', in L. H. Feldman and G. Hata (eds.), *Josephus, the Bible, and History* (Detroit: Wayne State University Press, 1989), pp. 81–96.

Valantasis, R., *The Gospel of Thomas* (London/New York: Routledge, 1997).

Van de Water, R., 'Michael or Yhwh? Toward Identifying Melchizedek in 11Q13', *JSP* 16 (2006), 75–86.

Venturini, K. H. G., *Natürliche Geschichte des grossen Propheten von Nazareth*, 2nd edn (Bethlehem, 1806).

Vermes, G., 'Appendix E: The Use of נש בר/נשא בר in Jewish Aramaic', in M. Black (ed.), *An Aramaic Approach to the Gospels and Acts*, 3rd edn (Oxford: Clarendon, 1967), pp. 310–30.

The Authentic Gospel of Jesus (London: Allen Lane, 2003).

The Changing Faces of Jesus (London: Allen Lane, 2000).

Jesus the Jew: A Historian's Reading of the Gospels, 2nd edn (London: SCM, 1983).

The Religion of Jesus the Jew (Minneapolis: Fortress, 1993).

Vogt, E., 'Precatio regis Nabonid in pia narratione iudaica (4Q)', *Bib* 37 (1956), 532–4.

von Heijne, C., *The Messenger of the Lord in Early Jewish Interpretations of Genesis* (Uppsala universitet, 2008).

von Rad, G., *Theologie des Alten Testaments*, vol. I: *Die Theologie der geschichtlichen Überlieferungen Israels*, 6th edn (Munich: Kaiser, 1969).

Theologie des Alten Testaments, vol. II: *Die Theologie der prophetischen Überlieferungen Israels* 10th edn (Gütersloh: Kaiser, 1993).

Wachob, W. H., and Johnson, L. T., 'The Sayings of Jesus in the Letter of James', in B. Chilton and C. A. Evans (eds.), *Authenticating the Words of Jesus*, NTTS 28:1 (Leiden: Brill, 1999), pp. 431–50.

Walck, L. W., 'The Son of Man in the Parables of Enoch and the Gospels', in G. Boccaccini (ed.), *Enoch and the Messiah Son of Man: Revisiting the Book of Parables* (Grand Rapids, MI: Eerdmans, 2007), pp. 299–337.

Wallace, D. B., 'Reconsidering "The Story of Jesus and the Adulteress Reconsidered"', *NTS* 39 (1993), 290–6.

Watts, R. E., 'Jesus' Death, Isaiah 53, and Mark 10:45: A Crux Revisited', in W. H. Bellinger, Jr. and W. R. Farmer (eds.), *Jesus and the Suffering Servant: Isaiah 53 and Christian Origins* (Harrisburg, PA: Trinity, 1998), pp. 125–51.

Webb, R. L., 'Jesus Heals a Leper: Mark 1.40–45 and *Egerton Gospel* 35–47', *JSHJ* 4 (2006), 177–202.

John the Baptizer and Prophet: A Socio-Historical Study, JSNTS 62 (Sheffield: JSOT Press, 1991).

Wegner, U., *Der Hauptmann von Kafarnaum (Mt 7,28a; 8,5–10.13 par Lk 7,1–10): Ein Beitrag zur Q-Forschung*, WUNT 2:14 (Tübingen: Mohr Siebeck, 1985).

Weinel, H., *Biblische Theologie des Neuen Testaments: Die Religion Jesu und des Urchristentums*, 2nd edn (Tübingen: Mohr Siebeck, 1913).

Weiss, J., *Das älteste Evangelium: Ein Beitrag zum Verständnis des Markus-Evangeliums und der ältesten evangelischen Überlieferung* (Göttingen: Vandenhoeck & Ruprecht, 1903).

Die Predigt Jesu vom Reiche Gottes, 2nd edn (Göttingen: Vandenhoeck & Ruprecht, 1900).

Weiss, W., '*Eine neue Lehre in Vollmacht': Die Streit- und Schulgespräche des Markus-Evangeliums*, BZNW 52 (Berlin/New York: de Gruyter, 1989).

Werline, R. A., *Penitential Prayer in Second Temple Judaism: The Development of a Religious Institution*, SBLEJL 13 (Atlanta: Scholars, 1998).

Wernle, P., *Jesus*, 2nd edn (Tübingen: Mohr Siebeck, 1916).

Westermann, C., *Das Buch Jesaja: Kapitel 40–66*, ATD 19, 3rd edn (Göttingen: Vandenhoeck & Ruprecht, 1976).

Wevers, J. W., *Notes on the Greek Text of Exodus*, SBLSCS 30 (Atlanta: Scholars, 1990).

Wilckens, U., 'Vergebung für die Sünderin', in P. Hoffmann (ed.), *Orientierung an Jesus: Zur Theologie der Synoptiker*, FS J. Schmid (Freiburg: Herder, 1973), pp. 394–424.

Witkamp, L. Th., 'The Use of Traditions in John 5.1–18', *JSNT* 25 (1985), 19–47.

Wolter, M., '"Ihr sollt aber wissen…" : Das Anakoluth nach ἵνα δὲ εἰδῆτε in Mk 2,10–11 parr.', *ZNW* 95 (2004), 269–75.

Wrede, (D.) W., *Das Messiasgeheimnis in den Evangelien: Zugleich ein Beitrag zum Verständnis des Markusevangelium* (Göttingen: Vandenhoeck & Ruprecht, 1901).

'Zur Heilung des Gelähmten (Mc 2,1ff.)', *ZNW* 5 (1904), 354–8.

Wright, N. T., *Christian Origins and the Question of God*, vol. i: *The New Testament and the People of God* (London: SPCK, 1992).

Christian Origins and the Question of God, vol. ii: *Jesus and the Victory of God* (London: SPCK, 1997).

Christian Origins and the Question of God, vol. iii: *The Resurrection of the Son of God* (London: SPCK, 2003).

Yates, R., 'Colossians 2,14: Metaphor of Forgiveness', *Bib* 71 (1990), 248–59.

Yeung, M. W., *Faith in Jesus and Paul: A Comparison with Special Reference to 'Faith that Can Remove Mountains' and 'Your Faith Has Healed/Saved You'*, WUNT 2:147 (Tübingen: Mohr Siebeck, 2002).

Ziegler, J., *Untersuchungen zur Septuaginta des Buches Isaias* (Münster: Aschendorffsche Verlagsbuchhandlung, 1934).

Zimmermann, J., *Messianische Texte aus Qumran: Königliche, priesterliche und prophetische Messiasvorstellungen in den Schriftfunden von Qumran*, WUNT 2:104 (Tübingen: Mohr Siebeck, 1998).

INDEX OF PASSAGES

Early Christian literature

INDEX OF MODERN AUTHORS

INDEX OF TOPICS